JULIAN
APOSTATE

Flavius Claudius Julianus (361-363)
Known to History as "Julian the Apostate"
Ancient Statue in the Louvre at Paris

JULIAN THE APOSTATE

By

Abbot Giuseppe Ricciotti

Translated By

M. Joseph Costelloe, S.J.

TAN BOOKS AND PUBLISHERS, INC.
Rockford, Illinois 61105

Nihil Obstat: John F. Murphy, S.T.D.
               Censor Librorum

Imprimatur: ✠ William E. Cousins
             Archbishop of Milwaukee
             December 2, 1959

ISBN 0-89555-632-4

Library of Congress Catalog Card No.: 98-61403

Printed and bound in the United States of America.

TAN BOOKS AND PUBLISHERS, INC.
P.O. Box 424
Rockford, Illinois 61105
1999

"The slaughter of his relatives must have been a severe shock to Julian as a child, but its full consequences appeared only later when, having passed through adolescence into the full consciousness of maturity, he tried to discover the motives behind this horrible crime and to identify those responsible for it. As we have seen, when he was able to speak freely, Julian attributed the responsibility for the murders to Constantius himself. Since this was his conviction, it was natural that his rancor should be concentrated on the emperor, but this only aggravated him the more and increased his desire for revenge.

"This hatred for the all-powerful Constantius was bound to extend to every facet of his being, beginning with his adherence to Christianity. Julian was driven to hate this religion, not by any philosophical or abstract reasons, but by the fact that his murderous cousin was a Christian."

—Chapter III, Page 42

PUBLISHER'S PREFACE

Why should a person read a whole book about Julian the Apostate? He was, historically speaking, a fairly minor figure among the Roman emperors. He ruled only some 20 months. He became emperor mainly because he was the nephew of Constantine the Great (307-337). His achievements are not all that notable. He left no posterity. He swam against the current of history, and as matters developed, history washed away his influence. Therefore, why study his life? Hopefully, a reading of Abbot Giuseppe Ricciotti's *Julian the Apostate* will give that answer, but as a preparation for the reader, a few salient reasons might be mentioned.

In actuality, this historical biography is a continuation of or a sequel to the author's book *The Age of Martyrs*. And as a panorama of the 4th-century Roman world, the book is truly far more than simply a biography. For example, the life of Julian shows some of the problems attendant upon succession as the Roman Emperor: Julius Caesar, when he finally came to power in 44 B.C., forgave his political enemies in an act of magnanimity, but *they* did not forgive *him*. They assassinated him. This led to five bloody civil wars over the next 17 years or so, wars that saw tens of thousands of Roman citizens killed. When Caesar's nephew Octavian (Augustus) assumed total power in 27 B.C., he executed a handful of his potential enemies and had peace. Ever after, Roman emperors by and large followed suit. Even Constantine, cognizant of the danger of usurpation, had his own son, Crispus, put to death. Julian himself was sent to Gaul (France) when just a military neophyte, with the thought that he would be killed in battle. But to his credit, Julian quickly learned the military craft and soon became an able and successful general.

What makes *Julian the Apostate* an interesting and authoritative book is that the author quotes original sources. And because the historian Ammianus Marcellinus was a friend of Julian, travelled with him and recorded events as he saw and experienced them, we have in his extant writings a first-hand account of many of the happenings in Julian's public life, a fact which is generally not true for other emperors. We can see firsthand, therefore, the problems the Emperors faced in governing such a vast empire. Also, we can see the problems the Empire faced from barbarian incursions. We have a graphic description of the Battle of Strasbourg (357) that will fascinate even the student of military science. We see the infighting and intrigue among the Roman courtiers, despite the Empire's facing serious challenges from the barbarians without. We see finally how Julian's own army declared him "Augustus," even while Constantius II (337-361), Julian's cousin, was still on the throne. We see Julian lose perspective about the extent of his forces and therefore his chances for success when he rashly marched against his cousin, the Emperor. We see him early in life lose his Catholic faith through the reading of philosophy, and we are reminded of St. Paul's warning: "Beware lest any man cheat you by philosophy and vain deceit." (*Col.* 2:8). In Julian we have a prime example of a young person who delved into the mystery religions of the ancient world—following, among others, the teachings of the Theurgist Iamblichus—with the result that he became immersed in the occult and returned to the worship of the ancient gods. We are reminded of David's saying, "All the gods of the Gentiles are devils." (*Ps.* 95:5). In effect, Julian had become a New-Ager in the 4th century. His apostasy would ultimately become his undoing, as he lost the special blessings and disregarded the guidance of Almighty God.

We can see from this biography that Constantine had not outlawed the ancient pagan religion of Rome, but had let it co-exist with Christianity, and how it was dying out until Julian tried to revive it. Also, we see that Julian tried to reform the pagan priesthood on the model of the Catholic priesthood, which the former could never sustain. We see him even attempt to rebuild the Jewish Temple, but how "natural disasters" thwarted that effort.

And finally, we see Julian's rashness lead him into the disastrous campaign against the Persians in lower Mesopotamia, where weather, distance, logistics, unfamiliarity with the region and failure to await the arrival of his allies and ancillary army led to ultimate defeat—this despite numerous warnings, signs and portents against his undertaking this war (making one think that God had perhaps not entirely abandoned him—or if He had, that He still allowed these warnings for the good of the Empire).

Abbot Giuseppe Ricciotti has painted a picture of Julian that is remarkably balanced and favorable, showing his nobility, idealism, fairness and love of the Empire . . . but alongside this portrayal, the author also shows his rashness, impetuosity and willingness to depart from the truth and have commerce with the occult. In the balance, *Julian the Apostate* is a remarkably accurate snapshot of an era of Roman history that alone makes it well worth reading. But it is also a fascinating study in contrasts within the character of a man who possessed the elements of greatness in combination with flaws that destroy. Ultimately, care for the truth saves, but error and rashness destroy. Apostasy from the True Faith always has dire consequences because one loses the special blessings and guidance of Almighty God. With Julian the errors and the flaws destroyed, but the reader will ever after be wondering, "What if . . . ?" Yes, "What if all the energy and talent, nobility and idealism possessed by Julian had been channeled differently? What if he had *not* lost the True Faith? How would history then have read?"

Thomas A. Nelson
Publisher
February 9, 1999

AUTHOR'S PREFACE

This book is a continuation of the general theme of *The Age of Martyrs: Christianity from Diocletian to Constantine* (Milwaukee: The Bruce Publishing Company, 1959), which ends with the death of the latter emperor.

Among Constantine's successors, his sons Constantine II and Constantius are of no particular significance, while the two who are here discussed, his son Constantius II and his nephew Julian the Apostate, are highly important historical figures. As a consequence, the continuity between this book and its predecessor is practically uninterrupted.

To no other person in history is the norm laid down by Tacitus of writing without wrath or partiality (*"sine ira et studio"* — *Annales*, 1. 1) so applicable as to Julian. But even here he has been unfortunate: where in antiquity he was habitually sinned against through *ira*, today the error is rather that of *studium*. Pagan and Christian writers, ancient orators and modern politicians have too often gazed upon him in the light of their own particular polemic, and while some berate him as the author of countless ills, others exalt him as an incomparable genius.

In order to avoid such partisanship, a contemporary historian should make use of all the reliable sources still extant and strive to display in equal light his many laudable qualities and his numerous defects.

I have sought to do this in the present work. My hope is that the reader will pay close attention to the sources which are cited. From them he may draw his own conclusions.

As in *The Age of Martyrs*, an expository style has been employed. The book is thus not a simple collection of data but a critical "narration" in the tradition of the ancient masters of historiography.

The frequent references to sections in other parts of the book should assist the reader to correlate persons and events mentioned in other contexts.

The general index at the end of the book should be useful for a rapid orientation.

LIST OF ABBREVIATIONS

BT — *Bibliotheca Scriptorum Graecorum et Romanorum Teubneriana.*

Budé — *Collection des Universités de France publiée sous le patronage de l'Association Guillaume Budé.*

LCL — *Loeb Classical Library.*

PG — J.-P., Migne, *Patrologiae Cursus Completus. Series Graeca.*

PL — J.-P., Migne, *Patrologiae Cursus Completus. Series Latina.*

Ricciotti, Martyrs — Giuseppe Ricciotti, *The Age of Martyrs: Christianity from Diocletian to Constantine,* translated by the Rev. Anthony Bull, C.R.L. (Milwaukee: The Bruce Publishing Company, 1959).

METHOD OF CITATION

Julian's works are cited wherever possible according to the standard pagination of Spanheim's edition (Leipzig, 1696).

A series of three numbers without further identification indicates a citation from Ammianus Marcellinus.

Ancient and modern authors are cited merely by name with appropriate numbers for orations, books, chapters, pages, or paragraphs, except where there is a possibility that some ambiguity might arise. For complete references see the bibliography at the end of the volume.

CONTENTS

Preface xi

I. The First Years 3

II. Julian's Moral World 29

III. Troubled Years 42

IV. From Athens to Gaul 61

V. In Gaul 77

VI. The Battle of Strasbourg 94

VII. In the North of Gaul 108

VIII. Julian as Governor of Gaul 116

IX. The Revolt 128

X. From Peace to War 145

XI. Julian as Emperor 173

XII. Against the Christians 194

XIII. Reforms and Writings 204

XIV. Reconstruction of the Temple at Jerusalem and the Laws
on Funerals 223

XV. The Persian Campaign 229

Bibliography 261

Index 265

MAPS

1. The Roman Empire at the Time of Diocletian's Tetrarchy, p. 9.
2. Gaul and the Rhine, p. 78.
3. The Battle of Strasbourg, p. 98.
4. Julian's Persian Campaign, p. 239.

JULIAN THE APOSTATE

CONSTANTINE'S FAMILY TREE

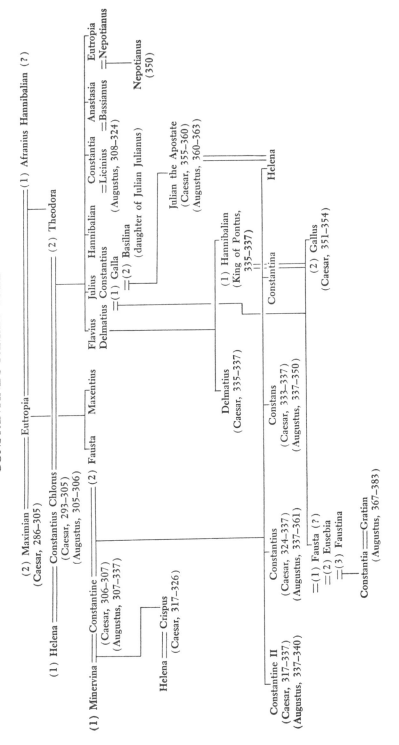

I. THE FIRST YEARS

§§ 1–3. *Julian's Family.*   §§ 4–7. *His Birth and the Slaughter of His Relatives.*   §§ 8–10. *First Teachers; Mardonius.* §§ 11–14. *Banishment to Macellum.*   §§ 15–19. *Christian Influences.*   §§ 20–23. *Gallus "Caesar." Julian at Constantinople.*   §§ 24–25. *Julian in Nicomedia. Libanius.*

1. Flavius Claudius Julianus, surnamed "the Apostate," was the son of a half brother of Constantine the Great; but even though they were related, it would be difficult to find in history two rulers so different in their make-up as this uncle and his nephew.

Julian's father was Julius Constantius, who like Constantine was a son of Constantius Chlorus, but of different mothers. Theodora, stepdaughter of Maximian and legitimate wife of Constantine Chlorus, was the mother of Julius Constantius. Constantine's mother, on the other hand, was Helena, a woman of low birth who had lived with Constantius Chlorus before his election as Caesar, but who was dismissed after this election. Constantine's extraordinary success redounded upon his mother, to whom he was greatly attached. Her rival, his stepmother Theodora, and her legitimate sons, among whom was Julius Constantius, were left in the shade. The jealousy that arose between the two women was naturally transmitted to their respective descendants, but at the beginning its effects were moderate enough.

When Helena became the most influential person in the court of her son Constantine, Theodora's sons, Julius Constantius, Delmatius, and Hannibalian, abandoned it, realizing that the atmosphere there was no longer favorable to them. The three brothers spent some time at Toulouse (Tolosa), where they lived as wealthy but private citizens entirely cut off from politics and the problems of succession. This was, of course, the best way to allay the suspicions of the all-powerful Constantine and Helena. Later, after A.D. 324, when the two rulers had nothing more to fear from their ousted relatives, the tension of the earlier years slackened. The three brothers, who were now being

3

treated with less reserve, traveled about the empire making an appearance in one place and then another. This was particularly true of Delmatius, who received various commissions from Constantine. Still this was a superficial reconciliation due only to Constantine's overwhelming superiority. The flame of the rivalry was, as a matter of fact, always alive under the ashes, and as soon as Constantine passed from the scene, it burst forth and enveloped those who until then had escaped it.

2. Julius Constantius was married to the noble Galla, whose brothers Rufinus and Cerealis had received the high honors of consul and prefect. The third child born to this marriage was Gallus, half brother of Julian the Apostate. Gallus, who was to be closely associated with the trials of Julian's youth, first saw the light of day in 325 or 326 among the Etruscans at Massa Veternensis, the modern Tuscan Maremma. Later his father left Italy and, in 330, after a stay at Corinth, took up his residence in Constantinople. This was the new capital which his half brother, the emperor, had finished building and inaugurated in this same year. Since, in the meantime, Julius' wife Galla had died at Constantinople in 331, he took as his second wife Basilina, the future mother of Julian the Apostate.

Basilina's father was Julius Julianus. He had held high offices under Emperor Licinius. Her mother had possessions in Bithynia and Ionia. Her religion, as is indicated in one way or another by our ancient sources, was almost certainly Christian, though it is quite probable that she was not orthodox in her beliefs but Arian. This may be argued not only from the continued diffusion of Arianism even after the Council of Nicaea in 325, but also from the fact that one of Julian's parents — and it is more likely that it was his mother than his father — was distantly related to Eusebius of Nicomedia (22. 9. 4).

This Eusebius, who is to be distinguished from the great Church historian Eusebius of Caesarea, was an ardent patron of Arius and Arianism. Ambitious and highly efficient, he had first been bishop of Berytus (modern Beirut) in Phoenicia, but about the year 318 he succeeded in becoming bishop of Nicomedia, a see more advantageous to his aspirations since it was then the residence of the imperial court. Finally, for the same reason, after the death of Constantine he obtained the see of the new capital, Constantinople. Although he was not endowed with a very speculative mind, Eusebius declared himself in favor of Arius' doctrines from their very first appearance, and he defended them with remarkable courage even after their condemnation at Nicaea. He incurred as a consequence the displeasure of Constantine, always the jealous guardian of Nicaea, who without further ado sent him into exile. But Eusebius soon gave proof of his consummate tact. By clever maneuvering he managed to have himself recalled as early as A.D. 328. Subsequently introduced to the court through the good graces of Constantia, widow of Licinius and half sister of Constantine, he gained the ever increasing confidence of the fickle monarch.

3. Constantia had considerable influence in the imperial court, particularly in religious matters. It was probably through her intercession that Constantine had so soon called Eusebius back from exile. Certainly it was through her intervention that in 334, toward the end of his life, the emperor established direct contact with Arius himself, intending to effect a reconciliation with all the Arians. Just as Constantine favored the orthodox, so Constantia favored the Arians, and she was able to make the weight of her opinions felt in the decisions respecting religious matters of her imperial half brother. In business of this kind the princess naturally had as her trusty consultant Eusebius of Nicomedia, who, if he enjoyed such good credit at court, must have had as a relative even greater authority within Julian's family itself. It is reasonable then to suppose that the Christianity of the family was the same as Eusebius', that is, a more or less diluted form of Arianism.

Under the tutelage of a learned slave, the eunuch Mardonius, Basilina received an excellent literary education. He later fulfilled the same office for her son Julian. In Julian's own words, "He was my mother's guide through the poems of Homer and Hesiod" (*Misopogon*, 352b), that is, through the writings which served as the foundation of Greek culture.

4. It was into such an environment that Julian was born in Constantinople toward the end of the year 331. Very soon he had the misfortune of losing his mother, of whose death he has given the following description: "After bearing me, her first and only child, she died within a few months, carried off, while still a young girl, from many calamities by the motherless maiden" (*ibid.*). This "motherless maiden" was the goddess Athena, and the "calamities" were the murders which a few years later bloodied Constantine's descendants. Other references to his mother indicate that Julian cherished the thought of her even though he had really never known her. Later he even named a town

founded near Nicaea Basilinopolis in her honor. On the other hand, there is no such remembrance of his father in any of his writings. It may easily be imagined that as an infant he was first entrusted to nurses and then later to the women of the palace. Since these had their own separate quarters, he would have had only fleeting contacts with his father. At this time his immediate relatives were murdered. He seems never to have fully recovered from this tragic shock which influenced many of his decisions in later life.

In A.D. 335, in the thirtieth year of his reign, Constantine set about devising a plan of succession. This was no easy task since there was bound to be a conflict between the demands of the immense empire with its heterogenous population and the aspirations of his numerous sons and relatives. A somewhat similar situation had confronted Diocletian more than forty years before when he set about restoring and stabilizing the empire by the creation of the tetrarchy. To solve his own problem, Constantine decided to follow his predecessor's example in dividing up the empire.

5. The eldest of the three sons born to Constantine by his second wife Fausta was named Constantine after his father. He was assigned Gaul, Spain, and Britain, which Constantine the Great had received from his own father, Constantius Chlorus. The second son, Constantius, obtained Asia, Syria, and Egypt. The third son, Constans, received Illyricum, Italy, and Africa. But others besides Constantine's own sons profited in the distribution of the empire. These were the sons of his half brother Delmatius, one of whom was named Delmatius after his father, and the other Hannibalian after an uncle (§ 1). Departing from the norm of direct descent, perhaps with the intention of strengthening the position of his future successors, Constantine gave Thrace, Macedonia, and Achaia to Delmatius. To Hannibalian he gave Armenia Minor, Pontus, and Cappadocia, with the title of King of Kings.

Marriages were arranged between the various descendants of Constantine to solidify the new division of the empire. A half sister of Julian the Apostate (probably, though not certainly, named Fausta), who had been born to Julius Constantius by his first wife (§ 2), was married to Constantius; and Hannibalian in his turn married Constantine's daughter, Constantina.*

---

* This is the name given to this daughter of Constantine by Ammianus Marcellinus, though in other ancient historians she is at times called Constantia. For practical purposes it is best to retain the name employed by Ammianus to avoid confusing her with Constantia, the half sister of Constantine and wife of Licinius.

This infiltration of collateral relatives into the line of Constantine's direct descendants, instead of strengthening the succession, caused the crumbling and eventual collapse of the whole structure erected by the aged monarch. As long as he lived his personal authority was sufficient to check the ambitions of his destined successors, but when he died on May 22, 337, the reaction set in.

When Constantius, who had been on the eastern frontier keeping watch over the threatening Persians, learned of the death of his father, he returned as quickly as possible to Constantinople to take part in the solemn obsequies. The uncertainty about the dynastic succession caused for a time a kind of interregnun, and it even seems that in this period laws were still being issued in the name of the deceased emperor. But on September 9, his three sons, the direct heirs, proclaimed themselves Augusti and assumed control of the empire. Violence unexpectedly broke out in favor of the new rulers. For no apparent reason the army slew a number of high magistrates, including Ablabius, prefect of the praetorium, as well as various relatives of the new Augusti. A list of the victims from his own immediate family was later drawn up by Julian when he charged Emperor Constantius with the crime: "It is obvious that in the paternal line both Constantius and I are descended from the same stock. Our fathers were brothers, sons of the same father. And what this most beneficent emperor did for us who were so closely related to him! Six of our common cousins, his uncle, my father, and another uncle on our father's side, and my eldest brother, he put to death without a trial. My other brother and I, whom he had intended to kill, were eventually sent into exile" (*To the Athenians*, 270cd).*

6. An historian confronted with these slaughters naturally looks for the motive and the man behind them. Our ancient sources either have little to say or give different versions about the matter, and some are more or less tendentious. Our best informed source is Eusebius of Caesarea (*De vita Constantini*, 4. 68–69), but he was to a certain extent the mouthpiece of the court. According to him the slaughters had their origin in a spontaneous decision of the soldiers throughout the empire, who recognized only the three sons of the deceased as

---

* Of these victims, the following have already been mentioned: "my father," Julius Constantius; "another uncle," Delmatius, brother of Julius Constantius; of the "six cousins" only two are known, Delmatius and Hannibalian, sons of the elder Delmatius; nothing is known of "my eldest brother"; "my other brother" has reference to Gallus, who will be discussed later.

their rulers and wanted them to assume the title of "Augusti." To corroborate this, he adds that the Roman senate also "acclaimed as emperors and Augusti only his sons, and no others." This insistence of the servile historian upon the exclusion of aspirants who were not Constantine's sons is eloquent. Gregory Nazianzen (4. 21) also attributes full responsibility for the murders to the soldiers. Socrates (2. 25), on the other hand, includes Constantius on the scene: though he gave no actual command to the soldiers, he did not attempt to check them. Eutropius (10. 9) attributes an equal share in the crime to the soldiers and to Constantius. Philostorgius (2. 16) recounts a popular rumor according to which the slaughter was ordered by Constantine himself before his death. Other writers, however, attribute the responsibility directly to Constantius. Among these are to be numbered not only St. Jerome, St. Athanasius, and Zosimus, but also Ammianus Marcellinus, a pagan and friend of Julian: "At the very beginning of his reign he uprooted and destroyed all those who were related to him by blood and race" (inter imperandi exordia, cunctos sanguine et genere se contingentes, stirpitus interemit — 21. 16. 8).

In speaking of the murders, Julian himself adopted two different attitudes. We have already seen that he openly attributed them to Constantius when he drew up a list of the victims — but this was after he had broken completely with the emperor. Earlier, when he was still subject to Constantius, he had referred to the crime in these words: "Due to the force of circumstances, despite your own desires, you were unable to check the evil deeds of others" (I Constantius, 17a). The difference in tone is to be explained by the different position in which the speaker found himself. It is even possible to recognize a certain measure of courage on Julian's part, though veiled, in this allusion. One of a more fawning disposition would have kept silent about the matter.

7. Since some conclusion must be drawn from this conflicting evidence, a question commonly asked in penal investigations may be posed: Cui bono? — "Who profited by the crime?" Actually, of course, all three brothers profited by it; but since Constantine II and Constans were far away and Constantius was the only one at hand, upon him rests a well-founded, but not absolutely certain, suspicion of ultimate responsibility. Further confirmation of this may be found in a passage from Julian referring to the period of his life which he spent with his brother Gallus at Macellum. There the two boys were regaled by their

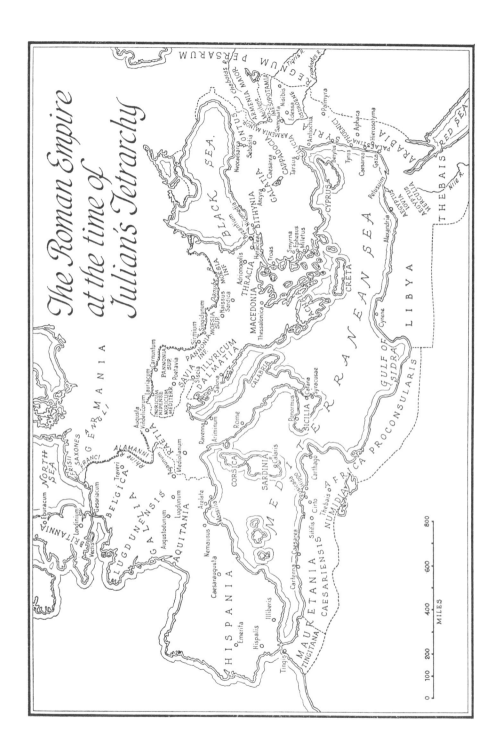

The Roman Empire at the time of Julian's Tetrarchy

guardians with an account of the slaughter bearing the stamp of the court's approval: Constantius had acted as he did partly because he had been deceived, and partly because he had been compelled to do so by the rioting soldiers; deeply regretting what he had done, he was now being punished with childlessness and the unfortunate war with the Persians (*To the Athenians*, 270d–271b). Devices of this sort have been found in every court.

When the soldiers had dispatched their adult victims, they turned to the two young sons of Julius Constantius. They found the twelve-year-old Gallus seriously ill, and spared his life since they probably thought it useless to send to the next world one who would go there by himself within a few days. The six-year-old Julian seems to have escaped death because of his tender years. It was later said that the child had been hidden in a Christian church, and that one of those who had saved him was none other than the Marcus of Arethusa who met his own death at the hands of the pagans during Julian's reign (Gregory Nazianzen, 4. 91; Theodoret, 3. 3; Sozomen, 5. 10; cf. § 159).
8. Besides his relatives, Julian also lost his property. What he was to have inherited from his father passed under the complete control of Constantius: "Nothing of my father's estate came to me. I acquired nothing of the great wealth which had naturally belonged to my father, not the smallest clod, not a slave, not a house. For the noble Constantius had inherited in my place my father's entire substance, and he left me, as I have said, not even the least trifle of it. Further, though he gave my brother a few things that had belonged to our father, he deprived him entirely of his mother's estate" (*To the Athenians*, 273b). Later, however, Julian's maternal grandmother came to his assistance; and still later he recovered the goods which had been confiscated (*Eusebia*, 118a; cf. *To a Priest*, 290cd).

Constantius had already taken some interest in the two orphans, partly for appearance' sake and partly to keep them under surveillance. In the first place he had separated them: Gallus, the elder, had been sent to Asia where he was able to attend school at Ephesus; Julian was sent to Nicomedia, a city which only a few years before had yielded its rank of capital to Constantinople. But it was imperative that Julian, who was just seven years old, should be entrusted to someone who could supervise his education. Possibly through a practical agreement between Constantius and the child's maternal grandmother, Eusebius, the bishop of Nicomedia (§ 2), was chosen for the task. With an eye to his own interests Eusebius accepted the offer, and in his new position gained further favor with Constantius. In 338, through the emperor's benevolence, he obtained the highly important see of Constantinople, where he died in 342.

Eusebius' commission had little practical effect on Julian's education. It is certain, despite the contrary opinion of some modern historians, that he did not follow Eusebius to Constantinople; and when in 337–338 the two were living in Nicomedia, the ambitious prelate was too busy with his own affairs to be seriously concerned about the orphan entrusted to his care. We find, in fact, no record of Eusebius in Julian's writings, and the figure of the negligent tutor must have passed almost like a shadow before the eyes of the frightened child.

9. Julian's real teacher was the pedagog who had been assigned to him. It was the same Mardonius who had earlier been the teacher of his mother Basilina (§ 3). As a mature man Julian seems to grow almost tender when recalling him, as if he were recalling the fondest remembrance of his childhood. Among so many memories of blood and outrage only that of Mardonius came to the emperor's mind like a beam of light shining in the darkness, and he spoke of him with the affection which he might have employed in speaking of his mother. Julian describes him as his *pedagog*, that is, one who within the home gave the first formal lessons to a child and accompanied him when he went to teachers outside the house. It is a term used by St. Paul (Gal. 3:24; 1 Cor. 4:15). That Mardonius accompanied Julian to school is known from Julian's own account (*Misopogon*, 351a; cf. Socrates, 3. 1), but it was particularly in the field of literature that Mardonius left an indelible trace on the mind of his pupil.

As he had already done for his mother, the pedagog led the boy step by step along the paths of ancient Greek literature, and especially that of Homer. But Mardonius did not rest at the bare text. He would from time to time draw practical conclusions from it by adapting it to his pupil's needs. The boys of Julian's time, for example, were wild about the theater, races, and similar public attractions. Mardonius therefore offered the following advice: "Never let the crowd of your playmates flocking to the theaters lead you astray so that you crave such spectacles. Do you long for horse races? There is one very cleverly described in Homer (*Iliad*, 23. 362–513). Take up the book and study it! Do you hear them talking about dancers in pantomime? Let them be! The lads among the Phaecians dance in a more manly fashion (*Odyssey*, 8. 250–265). And you have Phemius for a citharode and Demodocus for a singer. Moreover, in Homer there are many plants more pleasant to hear about than those we see: 'Even so near the altar of Apollo on Delos did I once see the young shoot of a date palm burgeoning' (Odysseus to Nausicaa — *Odyssey*, 6. 162–163). And there is the wooded isle of Calypso, and the caves of Circe, and the garden of Alcinous. Know well that you will see nothing more delightful than these" (*Misopogon*, 351c–352a).

But, coming down to a more practical level, Julian's conscientious tutor also furnished him with rules for his daily conduct: "My pedagog taught me to keep my eyes on the ground as I went to school. And I never saw a theater until I had more hair on my chin than I did on my head, and even at that age I never went of my own accord or will; but three or four times, know it well, my kinsman and near relative the emperor, 'doing a favor to Patroclus,' ordered me to attend. And this happened when I was still a private citizen" (*Misopogon*, 351ab).

10. This raises the question of whether or not Mardonius was a Christian, and also whether Julian was one at this period.

Although the first question has been widely discussed, no definite conclusion has been reached. There is simply no explicit evidence with regard to it. The implicit arguments which are used to support one side or the other are always open to an opposite interpretation. A pedagog like Mardonius had to give his pupil a literary education which was based primarily upon Homer and Hesiod, but this could be done by a Christian as well as by a pagan. The example of Bishop Synesius of Cyrene a half century later shows how deeply attached even sincere Christians could be to their Hellenic literary patrimony. Nor, on the other hand, does the fact, that Mardonius gave sound moral guidance to his pupil prove that he was a Christian, since pagan pedagogs of an upright life and teaching were not unknown. Whatever he was, Mardonius exercised his office as instructor neutrally so far as religion was concerned. But such evidence is of a greater theoretical than practical import: Mardonius' influence over Julian's activities at a later date, during and after his stay at Macellum (§ 12), favors the opinion that he was an honest pagan.

As to the second question — whether Julian was by this time a Christian — we are confronted with absolute silence on his part. When in his writings he has occasion to speak of his past life and comes to the threshold of his Christian period, he brusquely breaks off and withdraws terrified like a child seeing a snake. At such times Julian employs brief phrases of summary condemnation, such as, "Let that darkness be forgotten" (*Helios*, 131a), "When I wandered as it were in darkness" (*Mother of the Gods*, 174c), etc. But despite this silence everything leads us to believe that Julian received some instruction in Christian doctrine along with Mardonius' teaching from this time on, although he was not baptized until a little later during his banishment at Macellum. The well-informed historian Sozomen asserts that Julian was initiated into Sacred Scripture and Christian worship from his infancy, that he was educated by bishops and ecclesiastics, and that during his stay at Macellum he continued to receive instruction in literature and religion (5. 2; cf. Socrates, 3. 1).

11. Mardonius, however, was not his only teacher of profane subjects. In Constantinople, Julian studied grammar under Nicocles and rhetoric under Hecebolius. According to Socrates (3. 1), their schools were like those attended by Gallus at Ephesus. If this is to be understood in the sense that Julian and Gallus were both studying the same subjects at the same time, then it must be admitted that about the year 342, on the death of Eusebius of Nicomedia, the Emperor Constantius appointed another guardian for Julian, who took him from Nicomedia to Constantinople. But other historians have solid reasons for maintaining that Julian attended the schools of Nicocles and Hecebolius only later, after his stay at Macellum (§ 22).

At various times when he was still in Nicomedia, Julian went for a vacation to an estate assigned to him by his maternal grandmother. This was situated near the Propontis, some twenty stadia (less than two and one third miles) from the shore and not far from Constantinople. At this beautiful spot Julian spent many delightful days working in the gardens or playing on the beach. In later years he was to recall it in idyllic terms (*To Evagrius*, 426d–428a).

If at this period Julian attended schools in Constantinople, it certainly could not have been for very long. About the year 344, a more precise date cannot be determined, Julian was transferred to Macellum, where he remained for six years (*To the Athenians*, 271c). This shift was ordered by Constantius, whose suspicions had been aroused either by events in the empire or by rumors at court. His relations with his brother Constans had been marred by hidden jealousies, especially after Constans, upon the death of their brother Constantine II, had become the Augustus of the entire West. In the East the Persian threat was constantly becoming more serious. The dynastic question was dormant for the moment, but it could be awakened at any time, perhaps even by the mere presence of his two cousins, Gallus and Julian. It seemed best to remove them from the public eye. This could be done by keeping them under guard in some secluded spot. The place chosen was Macellum.

12. The name Macellum is of Latin origin, though it was later taken over and used by the Greeks as well. It indicated any large market where edibles of all sorts — fish, meat, fruits, and vegetables — were to be found. In such a sense the word was used by St. Paul (1 Cor. 10:25). Perhaps the place to which the two brothers were banished received its name from a market of this type in the vicinity. It was a piece of imperial property in Cappadocia not far from the capital Caesarea in eastern Asia Minor. The region was dominated by the lofty peak of Mt. Argaeus and was surrounded by dense woods infested with wild beasts, which only emphasized its barbaric character. The palace within this preserve, however, was spacious and the emperor stayed there on his hunting expeditions, as happened once while Julian was at Macellum (*To the Athenians*, 274a). It was, moreover, well stocked with slaves, although of a crude and uncultivated type. In later years Julian was to compare the palace with one of the fortresses in which the Persians guarded their hostages and important prisoners (*To the Athenians*, 271c).

At Macellum, Julian found himself, after some years of separation, in the company of his brother Gallus (§ 8), who was now about twenty years old. But there was no spiritual affinity between the brothers since they were of such opposite temperaments. Ammianus Marcellinus (14. 11. 28), an expert judge of character, compares them to Titus and Domitian, both sons of Vespasian, though so different from each other. Gallus was later honored with the office of Caesar; but yielding to his natural violence, he played the tyrant and was put to death by Constantius (§ 49).

Although he recognized his brother's defects, Julian speaks of him with a certain compassion. He attributes these defects to the poor education which Gallus had received and to his lack of "philosophy," which had been his own salvation. Julian's description of their sojourn at Macellum is worth quoting: "No strangers came near us, nor could any of our old friends visit us. We passed the time shut off from every liberal study and from all free intercourse, being reared in the midst of a brilliant servitude, and sharing in the activities of our slaves as though they were our equals. For no one of our own age came near us, nor were they allowed to do so. From that place with luck and the help of the gods I barely escaped. But my brother was detained at court and his lot was more wretched than any other who has ever lived.* If there was anything rude or harsh in his disposition it was aggravated by his having been educated among those mountains. Consequently, the emperor is to blame for this also, since he provided such a bringing-up for us against our wills. The gods, by means of philosophy, preserved me untouched and unharmed by it, but no one conferred this favor on him" (cf. *To the Athenians*, 271c–272a).

13. In recalling the periods of his cultural formation, Julian has left us two important autobiographical details. In one, speaking ironically to the Antiochians, he mentions Mardonius, but without specific reference: " 'Very well,' you say, 'but what are your qualifications for trying to hear and decide cases of contracts? Certainly your pedagog did not also teach you this since he did not even know if you would reign.' But that terrible old man did persuade me to do so, and you also do well in helping me abuse him since he is the most responsible of all for my way of life. And it should be known that he, too, was deceived by others. Since they have frequently been ridiculed on the comic stage, their names are well known to you: Plato, Socrates, Aristotle, and Theophrastus. They convinced this old man, in his folly, and later, when he found me, since I was young and a lover of literature, he convinced me in turn that if I should strive to imitate these men in every respect, I would become better, perhaps not than other men, for the contest was not with them, but better than my former self. And since I had nothing else that I could do, I obeyed him and am no longer able to change my ways" (*Misopogon*, 353bc). It is clear that the pedagog of whom Julian is here speaking is Mardonius. He was therefore not only his guide to the poetry of Homer and Hesiod (§ 9), but also into the philosophy of Plato, Socrates, Aristotle, and Theophrastus.

The other autobiographical passage is contained in his polemic *Against the Cynic Heraclius*. It was written about the same time as the preceding, that is, in 362. In his remarks to Heraclius, Julian ob-

---

* This refers to Gallus' election as Caesar in 351, the occasion of his ultimate ruin (§ 21).

serves: "For you were not well educated, nor did you have the good fortune to be led as I was through the poets by the philosopher here present. And later on I came to the threshold of philosophy to be initiated into it by a man who in my opinion surpasses all those of my time. He taught me to practice virtue in preference to everything else and to look upon the gods as the guides to all that is good and noble. If his labors have had any practical effect, he himself must know, and even more than he the gods who are our rulers. But he at least freed me of such madness and boldness as is yours, and he tried to make me more prudent than I was by nature. And though, as you know, I was winged with great external advantages, I nonetheless submitted to my guide, to his friends and contemporaries, and to those who were associated with him; and I eagerly listened to all those who were praised by him, and I read all the books he recommended. Thus then by those guides was I initiated, by a philosopher who instructed me in the preparatory subjects, and by a consummate philosopher who received me at the threshold of philosophy" (235ac).

14. In this passage reference is made to "the philosopher here present" who guided Julian in his poetical studies and conducted him "to the threshold of philosophy." But precisely on that threshold, at the entrance to the temple of philosophy, Julian was met by another whom he believed to be superior to all those of his own time and who was moreover "a consummate philosopher." The allegory employed throughout the passage is remarkable. It reflects the pageantry of the pagan mystery rites, especially in the double reference to "being initiated" (τελεῖσθαι), a technical term used in the mystery religions. As for the persons to whom Julian alludes, Mardonius immediately comes to mind as the one who conducted him to the threshold of the sacred temple of philosophy, and Maximus of Ephesus as the one who led him across that threshold. And, as a matter of fact, Maximus actually "initiated" Julian into theurgy (§ 39). Nevertheless, other identifications have been suggested. According to some, the two unnamed individuals would be Maximus of Ephesus for the first and Iamblichus for the second. Others have thought of Nicocles (§§ 11, 22). If the first of the two instructors is actually Mardonius, he must have given something more than a purely literary training to the future emperor. Besides teaching him the poetry of Homer and Hesiod, he must have imparted to him at least the rudiments of philosophy. This would explain why he is here called a philosopher.

Taken together with the special gratitude which Julian always showed him, this would confirm the hypothesis that Mardonius was a pagan, as we have already inferred (§ 10).

Consequently, if Mardonius was with Julian at Macellum, the latter's statement that the two brothers lived there "shut off from every liberal study and all free intercourse" (§ 12) must be taken as a polemical exaggeration, since at this very time his faithful pedagog was furnishing him with high moral principles (§ 9) and introducing him to Plato, Socrates, Aristotle, and Theophrastus (§ 13; cf. *Misopogon*, 359c). But besides Mardonius, he must have had other teachers at Macellum, and these were certainly Christians. True to his principle of silence about his earlier Christianity, Julian never mentions them, though their presence is attested by others (§ 10). In fact it would have been difficult for the boys, who were wards of the Arian Constantius and under the tutelage of the Arian bishop, Eusebius, to have had their religious education completely neglected. The catechizers of the two brothers could have come from time to time to Macellum, perhaps from Caesarea, but of this we know nothing.

15. But there is one salient fact to be considered. A Christian ecclesiastic, George of Cappadocia, who later became the Arian bishop of Alexandria, where he was murdered by the infuriated populace (§ 158), was living at the time not far from Macellum. He owned a fairly good library which Julian examined while there on a visit. In a letter of the year 362 to the prefect of Egypt, Julian states that when he was exiled in Cappadocia he was spurred on by his passion for books to borrow some for copying, and among them were "many dealing with philosophy, with rhetoric, and with the teachings of the impious Galileans [the Christians], which I would like to see entirely destroyed" (*To Ecdicius*, 378ac). In another letter, Julian reveals that the same library contained "philosophers of every school and many historians and, not least of all, numerous books of every kind by the Galileans" (*To Porphyry*, 411cd). Julian therefore ordered Ecdicius to recover what he could of George's library dispersed in the uprising. This evidence coming from Julian himself shows that his status at Macellum was not exactly that of a lion in a cage, as it might seem to have been, and that his love of books and literary research was to a certain extent gratified.

Moreover, if this period of his life was not a complete loss for his secular training, it certainly contributed a great deal to his knowledge of that Christianity against which he was later to direct all his political and cultural activities. We have just seen a text in which Julian expresses his desire to see the books of the Christians "entirely destroyed," but he well knew that the best way to destroy a book is to refute it by pointing out its intrinsic errors. That is why in the last months of his life he set himself to the task of composing an extensive refutation of Christianity by writing his work *Against the Galileans*. For the present it is not necessary to determine whether or not in this work he shows himself thoroughly acquainted with the true spirit of Christianity. Certain it is, however, that he manifests a good material knowledge of the sacred books containing this doctrine. Starting with the Book of Genesis, he moves gradually through the whole of the Bible, quoting from many books of both the Old and New Testaments.

In what period of his life could he have acquired such a knowledge of these texts? It could not have been right after his departure from Macellum when he was totally engrossed in Neoplatonism and theurgy, since to waste his time investigating the foolish Christian doctrines would have seemed to him a kind of sacrilege; nor could he have made such a study as governor of Gaul when under the strict surveillance of the Christian Constantius he was preoccupied with grave political and military problems. Later, however, when he had been carried away by his hatred of Christianity, he recalled what he had read and refreshed his memory by rereading the texts he proposed to refute. It must then have been at Macellum that he stored up the arsenal of weapons he was later to turn against Christianity.

16. But, interestingly enough, Julian was at this time not only a student but also a propagator of Christian doctrines. We have already conjectured (§ 10) that Julian was baptized during his stay at Macellum rather than at some earlier period, but in the absence of precise information on the matter it is useless to insist upon it. But here we come upon a wholly unexpected bit of information: Julian and his brother were enrolled among the Christian clergy and read the Scriptures to the people in their assemblies (Gregory Nazianzen, 4. 23, 97; cf. Sozomen, 5. 2; Theodoret, 3. 1). This office of reading the sacred books to the people was proper to the lowest rank of the clergy, the "lectors." At about thirteen, boys were admitted to this office if they showed some talent for it and were deemed to have the requisite piety. Each church had, as a rule, a fair number of these readers, who

stirred up the congregations with their high-pitched voices. Julian must have been attached to the church at Caesarea in Cappadocia, and we may well imagine that Dianaeus, the bishop, who like Constantius favored Arianism, received the two boys into the clergy all the more readily because of their illustrious connection with the emperor.

What spirit animated Julian and his brother in the performance of their office? They probably carried out their duties with that exterior promptness natural to boys of their age, who eagerly volunteer for tasks that will put them into the limelight and allow them to show their skill. About the brothers' internal appreciation of their office we can say nothing. Nevertheless, even then a difference was noted between the two. They practiced debating between themselves, but it was noted that while Gallus defended the Christians, Julian almost always preferred to defend the Hellenes, that is, the pagans, alleging that theirs was the weaker and more difficult side to uphold. And he did this with so much ardor and enthusiasm that his hearers began to suspect that he spoke more out of conviction than for the sake of rhetorical exercise (Gregory Nazianzen, 4. 30). This trifle would probably never have been recorded if the subsequent events of Julian's life had not suggested that it be interpreted as a serious omen.

17. Mention was also made of another portent. Some twenty years earlier Constantine and his mother Helena had erected large buildings over the sites venerated by the Christians in Palestine, such as Golgotha and the Holy Sepulcher in Jerusalem, the Mount of Olives, Bethlehem, and Mambre. A similar honor was occasionally given to places made sacred by the Christian martyrs. In the neighborhood of Macellum was a little chapel in honor of the martyr Mama, or Mamans, who had been put to death in the time of Aurelian. His cult, which was fairly widespread in Cappadocia, was later propagated in the West. The two princes visited his shrine near Macellum and came to the conclusion that it was too shabby. They decided to replace it with a more elaborate structure, each assuming a part of the work. It turned out, however, that while the part constructed by Gallus rose rapidly and solidly, the part built by Julian progressed for a short while and then collapsed completely as if the earth refused to accept the labors of the future apostate.

This episode is narrated by Sozomen (5. 2); and, without specific reference to the martyr Mama, it is found in Theodoret (3. 1) and Gregory Nazianzen (4. 24–26). Gregory even calls to witness residents of the area, as he was himself. This supplies us with sufficient evidence for maintaining that there is a nucleus of truth in the story — the erection of a new shrine by the two brothers. But the epilog of the narration has all the appearances of a legend which grew up after Julian's death as a kind of tragic symbol of his whole life.

When, as emperor, Julian issued his edicts against the honors paid to the dead by the Christians, he must have had in mind his earlier visits to the tomb of Mama and other shrines. Such recollections as these furnished him with more material for his attack upon Christianity.

But if these experiences gave impetus to his reaction, there was a great deal in Christianity to be imitated; and historically and psychologically this is of considerably greater import for evaluating Julian's achievements. When he set out to instill a new life into dying paganism, he outlined a radical reform that would introduce new elements into pagan religious institutions. An almost random selection of some of these innovations gives an indication of the extent of this reform.

18. A pagan priest ought to be exemplary in his conduct "exercising above all philanthropy" (*To a Priest*, 289a). — "I would say, even though it is a paradox, that it would be an act of piety to share our food and clothing with our enemies" (πολεμίοις, or perhaps "with the wicked" — πονηροῖς — according to Hertlein's emendation of the mss. — 290d). — "And the priests must keep themselves pure not only from unclean and shameful acts, but also from speaking or hearing words of such a character. Accordingly we must banish all offensive jests and all scurrilous intercourse. And in order that you may know what I mean by this, let no priest read Archilochus or Hipponax or anyone else who writes in their manner. And let him avoid everything of the sort in Old Comedy, for it is better that he should; and on every count philosophy alone becomes us who are priests" (300cd). This matter of reading was especially important for a pagan priest, and Julian returns to it with keen insistence: "We must avoid all the fictitious narratives of the past such as love stories, and, in general, everything of the kind. For just as not every road is suitable for priests, but these must be assigned them, so not every type of reading becomes a priest. For words beget a certain disposition in the soul, which little by little stirs up desires, and then suddenly bursts out into a fierce flame, against which I believe one ought to be armed in advance. Nor should any admittance be given to the works of Epicurus or

Pyrrho" (301bc). Further, the outward comportment of a pagan priest should be nourished by a continual internal asceticism and pious meditations: "Let each one of us, setting out from moral virtues and pursuits such as reverence for the gods, kindness toward men, purity of body, abound in acts of piety, always trying to think piously of the gods, and by looking on their temples and statues with due honor and veneration, worship them as if we saw them present" (292d–293a). As for public entertainments, "I conjure the priests to refrain from, and to leave to the common people the licentiousness of the theater" (304c). Actually, Julian had thought of expurgating the theaters "in order to restore them purified to Dionysus," but since he was convinced that at the time the attempt would prove to be futile, he simply gave orders that "no priest should enter a theater" (304b). A pagan priest should occupy himself with hymns and sacred canticles instead of with the stage: "We ought to learn by heart the many beautiful hymns to the gods which have been composed by men of old and in more recent times, though we ought also to know those which are being sung in the temples" (301d). — Not even the social question, from the pagan point of view, escaped him: "It is my opinion that when the poor came to be overlooked and neglected by the priests, the impious Galileans noticed it and devoted themselves to this kind of philanthropy. And they have made their worst deeds prevail through the good repute they have won by such practices. For just as those who deceive children throw a cake to them two or three times and lure them on, and then, when they are far from their homes put them on board a ship and sell them, and what for a little time seemed sweet has become bitter for the rest of their lives, in the same manner the Galileans also, beginning with what they call their 'love-feast,' or 'hospitality,' or 'waiting-on-tables' (for the name is as diverse as their way of carrying it out) have led very many into atheism" (350bd). With this, the *Letter to a Priest* abruptly ends. Its conclusion was possibly suppressed by some ancient Christian scribe as blasphemous.

19. Confronted with this evidence a modern historian is in about the same position as the blind Isaac was when Jacob came before him disguised as Esau. The old man hearing his son's voice and touching the hairy covering of his hands exclaimed perplexedly: "The voice indeed is the voice of Jacob, but the hands are the hands of Esau" (Gen. 27:22). The speaker is undoubtedly Julian, but what he has

to say is not his own. In his enthusiasm for paganism he unconsciously proffers contraband wares, representing as consequent to the worship of the gods a genuine product of Christianity.

It would surely be superfluous to prove that paganism (with the exception of some late trends in the mystery religions, and even these under only a few aspects) was never concerned with the prescriptions here imposed by Julian. Paganism was not particularly interested in what Julian calls philanthropy, the term he used to avoid the Christian word "charity"; it never prescribed the help of one's enemies; it never compiled an index of forbidden books for its priests on the basis of their lascivious, Epicurean, or Sceptic content; it never asked these priests to make pious meditations, to avoid the theater, and the like. Whence, then, did Julian draw his inspiration when he laid down these norms? Where were these plants produced which he attempted to transplant into the climate of paganism? His reference to the "philanthropy" of "the impious Galileans" clearly indicates that his inspiration was Christianity; if only as a reaction.

When Basil, Julian's fellow student at Athens, became bishop of Caesarea in Cappadocia, he provided for the social welfare of his people by the erection of orphanages, leprosaria, trade schools, and similar institutions. These were so numerous that they seemed almost to constitute a separate city. This charitable foundation was adjacent to Caesarea, and consequently near Macellum, where Julian had spent his adolescent years. It is true that these institutions were established shortly after Julian's death, but the same kind of social work must have been common among the Christians of Caesarea at a much earlier date. This is confirmed by the fact that at Edessa in Syria, Ephraem, a contemporary of Basil, was engaged in caring for the temporal needs of his people. The Syrian biographers of this illustrious figure stated that the last months of his life were wholly dedicated to relieving the untold harm caused by the invasion of the Huns and the subsequent general want.*

In conclusion, the instructions given by Julian to the pagan priests are of Christian provenience; and, in the light of his subsequent career (§ 15), they must have come originally from the Christian environment of Macellum. These norms had penetrated his soul and had been partially assimilated. He later believed that the gods

---

* Cf. G. Ricciotti, *Sant'Efrem Siro*, Turin, 1925, pp. 85–86.

had inspired him with them and they were consequently his own. He then set about introducing them into paganism like one attempting to transplant the palms of the fiery Sahara to the frozen wastes of the Arctic.

20. During the final period of the princes' residence at Macellum, important events were taking place in the Roman Empire. On the eastern frontier the Persians were increasing their pressure. Three times they besieged Nisibis (in 338, 346, and 350). Constantius engaged them in many new battles, some of which ended in defeat, and none proved to be a decisive victory. Even in the battle of Singara (348), where the Romans at first overwhelmed the enemy, they later lost their advantage (Ammianus, 18. 5. 7; Libanius, 59. 99 ff., 119 ff.; cf. I Constantius, 27a–28d). In the interior of the empire conditions were in a turmoil, and the dynasty was threatened from various quarters.

A general of barbarian origin in the service of Constantius, Flavius Magnus Magnentius proclaimed himself Augustus at Autun (Augustodunum) with the aid of Marcellinus, the state treasurer (comes sacrarum largitionum), in January, 350. Constans fled, but was pursued and killed at Elna near the Pyrenees. Thereupon all the West except Illyricum passed to Magnentius. He remained in power until 353, but had his own rivals. First of all, Vetranio, a general of the Danubian troops, revolted. In March, 350, he had himself proclaimed Caesar at Sirmium. He was an old man and completely illiterate, but courageous, loved by his soldiers, and, above all, a favorite of Constantine's daughter, the clever and intriguing Constantina (Constantia), widow of Hannibalian (§ 5). A short time later, on June 3, 350, a nephew of Constantine, Nepotianus, proclaimed himself Augustus at Rome. After reigning for only twenty-eight days, he was conquered and slain by Marcellinus, a supporter of Magnentius. Through the mediation of Constantina, Vetranio was able to come to terms with Constantius at Naissus in 350. He gave up his command and withdrew to Prusa in Bithynia where he spent the rest of his life as a private citizen.

Only Magnentius remained as a rival to Constantius, but he was much more formidable than the other two candidates since he had under his control the entire West with strong and courageous troops. Constantius, making an all-out attack on him, defeated him first at Mursa (modern Osijek) in 351. He then followed him across the Alps and confined him to Gaul where, at Lyons, on August 1, 353, Magnentius committed suicide. Thereupon Constantius stood alone at the summit of the whole empire.

21. Constantius was sorely troubled by these internal and external dangers from the year 350. Confronted with the same problems that had induced Diocletian and Constantine to divide the imperial authority (§ 5), he was more than ever concerned about the permanence of the dynasty after the revolt of Nepotianus. Something had to be done. He should no longer remain isolated while retaining supreme authority in the empire; he should seek the assistance of individuals who were related to him and who were the recipients of his favors. In this way he could parry the kind of blow that had been attempted by Nepotianus.

Looking about, however, he saw no one near at hand who would do. He had had as his first wife the half sister of Julian the Apostate (§ 5), but she appears almost as a shadow in his life, having died before 350 without offspring. Then Constantius thought of the two brothers banished to Macellum, his cousins, and, at the same time, his brothers-in-law. Even though they were at a distance, he was well informed about their conduct, and he found nothing in the reports to deter him from his project. He decided to begin the experiment with Gallus, the elder, now twenty-five years of age. In March, 351, he appointed him Caesar and entrusted the East to him.

After his election, Gallus left Macellum for Constantinople. It is certain that on this occasion Julian also left Macellum to further his studies (Gregory Nazianzen, 4. 31). He was later accused of having left his place of banishment without authorization, but he succeeded in clearing himself by showing that he had not acted without permission (Ammianus, 15. 2. 7–8). Eunapius gives a sound psychological reason for this permission. He states that Constantius released Julian "since he was anxious that he should be free to amuse himself with books rather than that he should brood over his family and place in the empire" (473). Such a motive, besides being consistent with Constantius' character, is also indicative of the career for which he had destined Julian: no military training and no experience in government, but only literature and philosophy.

22. The uncertain sequence of events following Julian's departure from Macellum is bound up with the uncertainty of his first stay at Constantinople (§ 11). According to Sozomen (5. 2), Julian went directly to the capital. There, according to Ammianus Marcellinus (15. 2. 7), he would have met Gallus as he was heading for the East. Socrates (3. 1), on the other hand, maintains that Gallus went to meet Julian in Nicomedia. Libanius (18. 17) also mentions an encounter in Bithynia, the province in which Nicomedia was located.

As has already been observed (§ 11), there are good, but not compelling, reasons, because of the gaps and contradictions in our sources, for believing that Julian satisfied his thirst for study after moving to Constantinople by attendance at the schools of Nicocles and Hecebolius. The former, a pagan, had a good reputation as a grammarian, and Julian retained his affection for him even as emperor. The latter, a professor of rhetoric, was a cheap opportunist who was Christian or pagan according to circumstances. A zealous Christian under Constantius, he was an equally zealous pagan under Julian, and after the Apostate's death he begged to be received again into the Church, prostrating himself before its gate and asking to be trampled upon like salt that has lost its savor (Socrates, 3. 1, 13). In the older editions of Julian's works are to be found two letters addressed to Hecebolius (387ad, 424c–425a). More recent editions, however, as a rule place one of these among spurious writings attributed to Julian and assign the other to a different addressee.

Because of his family connections, Julian at once became an object of curiosity to the students at Constantinople. But there were others also, not of the scholastic but of the political world, who took an interest in him. For forty years Constantine the Great and his successors had favored Christianity to the detriment of paganism. It was well known, however, that many of the emperor's subjects had bowed their heads reluctantly. In their hearts there still lived a vague hope, an undefined suspicion, that the last word had not yet been spoken. The glorious patrimony of the Greeks could not suffer a gradual eclipse that would end in darkness. The gods of old, the marvelous temples, the solemn cults, the literary monuments narrating the various activities of these same gods high on Mt. Olympus and here on earth, the wise men who had flourished for centuries in Ionia, in Attica, in Egypt, in southern Italy, all this was something eternal, irreplaceable. And what was the substitute proposed by the wretched Galileans? One of the most authoritative of them all, Paul of Tarsus, had openly proclaimed it. He had recognized that "the Greeks seek after wisdom," but he had rejected this ideal in stating that the Galileans preached "Christ crucified . . . unto the Gentiles foolishness" (1 Cor. 1:22–23). Could anything be more absurd and presumptuous? Unfortunately that dolt of a Constantine, "leading the life of a pastrycook and hairdresser" (*Caesars*, 335b), had been infatuated with the contemptible breed and had protected it in every way. This explained its ephemeral triumph. But very soon the wisdom of the Greeks would triumph over the folly of Constantine and his wards. If Constantine and his house had fallen so low, there was no reason why one of his relatives or successors should not come to his senses and rise up as the restorer of Hellenism. 23. To a greater or less extent such thoughts as these were occupying the minds of many in Constantinople when Julian began to walk through the streets of the city on his way to class. Accompanied by his faithful Mardonius (§ 9), whose precepts he still followed, his outward appearance was no different from that of his fellow students. Plainly dressed and modest in deportment, there was nothing about him to attract the attention of the passers-by if it had not been for the invisible hopes placed in him. With his school companions he was affable and courteous, to his teachers respectful and obedient, asking for no favors for himself (Libanius, 18. 11, 13).

One of the few poetical fragments which have come down to us from Julian's pen consists of eight verses on the playing of an organ (Wright, 3:304–306). A scholium on the manuscript containing this epigram (*Parisinus*, 690) notes that Julian composed these verses as he was leaving the Church of the Holy Apostles in a procession. This, the most sumptuous church in Constantinople, had been built by Constantine near the Gate of Charisius as his place of burial. If this scholium is accepted, and there is no reason for rejecting it, Julian must have taken part in the Christian services during his stay at Constantinople. Indirect confirmation of this is to be found in the tradition that during his later residence in Nicomedia he not only worshiped with the Christians but even continued to exercise his office of lector (Socrates, 3. 1; cf. Sozemen, 5. 2).

Nevertheless, through informers Constantius still kept his eyes upon the student at Constantinople. What must have increased the emperor's suspicion was Julian's popularity with the lower classes, his indifference to distinction, in such marked contrast with Constantius' own solemn austerity whenever he appeared in public. What did Julian expect to gain with these wiles? Was he attempting to reveal a facet of his character that distinguished him from his uncle the emperor? It would not have been the first time that such a device had been employed to lay the grounds for the overthrow of a monarch: Constantius might have learned from Sacred Scripture that Absalom had followed the same plan in rebelling against his father David (2 Kings 15:2-7). Reports of the popularity of the young prince in the pagan circles of the city coming upon such reflections prompted Constantius to remove the fuel from the flame. He ordered Julian to return to Nicomedia, enjoining him at the same time to refrain from attending the lectures of Libanius. So ended the year 351.

24. This transfer marks the beginning of Libanius' influence over Julian, an influence which was to increase continually until the Apostate's death. In his *Misopogon* (345c), addressed to the Antiochians, Julian refers to Libanius as "your fellow-citizen, a man dear to Hermes and to me, an excellent fashioner of speeches." Without necessarily intending it, Julian here gives a summary but precise description of Libanius. He was heartily opposed to Christianity and thoroughly imbued with pagan Hellenism ("dear to Hermes"), a rhetorician ("an excellent fashioner of speeches"), but without depth of thought; in other words, a brilliant literary peacock. A very profuse writer, he left a vast legacy of orations, declamations ($\mu\epsilon\lambda\epsilon\tau\alpha\iota$), rhetorical exercises, and more than fifteen hundred letters on a variety of themes. Born in 314, he had studied in Athens in the company of SS. Basil and Gregory Nazianzen, and later had been the teacher of St. John Chrysostom. He opened a school in Constantinople in 340, but the envy of his colleagues forced him to move first to Nicaea and later to Nicomedia. During the five years he was in the latter place his fame became widespread. He then returned to Constantinople. After other changes of residence he retired to Antioch where he died about 393.

According to Christian historians, Constantius had forbidden Julian's attendance at Libanius' lectures to safeguard the faith of his young nephew. According to Libanius, another person (§ 22) would also have had a part in it. Hecebolius, who at this time still claimed to be a Christian, out of jealousy made Julian swear that he would not attend the lectures of his pagan rival. But these restrictions had only a material effect on Julian's conduct. Finding himself on the threshold of a new spiritual world and enjoying a certain amount of liberty, he felt that the light he was seeking was to be found precisely there where he was forbidden to go, and he began to approach it, though he shunned the highly perilous course of openly disobeying Constantius by attending Libanius' lectures. Instead, he followed them in secret, paying students to bring him synopses of each of the master's discourses. He also secured his writings and with diligent study so thoroughly mastered them that he gained the reputation of being a closer follower of Libanius' teaching than any of those who actually heard him speak.

25. It is well, however, to point out that Julian later showed little sympathy for rhetoricians. The following diatribe directed against the Cynic Heraclius and his colleagues reveals his contempt for these word mongers whose hackneyed orations were more notable for their expression than their thought: "You criticize everybody, but do nothing yourself deserving praise. Your eulogies are worse than those of the most ignorant rhetoricians. Since they have nothing to say and cannot find anything to discuss in current happenings, they are always dragging in Delos and Leto and her children, and 'the shrill song of swans and the trees that echo them,' and 'dewy meadows lined with deep soft grass,' and 'the fragrance of flowers,' and 'spring in person,' and similar figures. Where did Isocrates do this in his panegyrics? And when did any of those men of old who were genuinely dedicated* to the Muses, and not like men today, carry on in such a fashion?" (*Heraclius*, 236ab.) But, as often happened in Julian's life, this outburst of his was more theoretical than practical. Harsh realities forced him to attenuate and even to abandon his distrust of the rhetoricians. After he had obtained the highest authority in the state, he often treated them as friends and even employed them for various errands. Further, he occasionally imitated their style of writing, though only in jest (*To Hermogenes*, 389d).

While taking delight in the flowery rhetoric of Libanius, Julian was at the same time absorbing something more substantial, the philosophical lees from which this fragrance rose — Neoplatonism in its decline.

---

* Julian here employs the expression "initiated" (ἐτελοῦντο) derived from the mystery religions (cf. § 14).

II. JULIAN'S MORAL WORLD

§§ 26–28. Neoplatonism. Plotinus. §§ 29–31. Porphyry. Iamblicus. The Theurgists. §§ 32–34. Julian as a Man. §§ 35–39. At the School of the Theurgists.

26. At the close of the third century the Roman world was in possession of a rich and varied philosophical inheritance: a great mixture of Pythagorean, Platonic, Aristotelian, and Stoic elements that had been accumulated and handed down by different schools during the course of the centuries. Though this Hellenic legacy was held in high esteem, it needed to be integrated into a compact philosophical system which, while retaining whatever was substantial, would reject everything that was of only incidental worth. Further, this systematization needed to be more practical than theoretical so that a soul searching for the truth might enter the calm haven of peace. Philosophy ought not to be a telescopic view of truth banished to the highest heavens but a molding of one's conscience and an indoctrination of the inner man.

The soul in its noble ascent (*itinerarium mentis*) should employ as its initial guide the rational principles of Greek philosophy, but when it came close to its goal it should be able to dispense with this help and, as if by an infallible instinct, hurl itself toward the possession of the Supreme Good. The Egyptian Plotinus (A.D. 205–270), who traced this *itinerarium* in a grandiose systematization of the earlier Greek philosophies, is credited with the founding of Neoplatonism. The real founder of Neoplatonism, however, was Plotinus' teacher, the Alexandrian Ammonius Saccas; but since he left nothing in writing and little about him has been handed down by our ancient sources, no reconstruction can be made of his personal teaching. In Ammonius, Plotinus found what he had vainly sought in the other philosophers of Alexandria: a teacher who was at the same time a spiritual father, one who taught with his words and confirmed his teaching with the example of his own life. When he was forty years old, Plotinus moved to Rome where, following the practice of his master, he conducted a school which was both speculative and practical, giving spiritual direction to his pupils, encouraging and admonishing them. In this way the doctrines of Plato were brought down to earth and put to the test. The procedure gained great authority for Plotinus with the nobility and even with Emperor Gallienus — so much so, in fact, that, enlarging his program, he conceived the idea of actually founding a city of philosophers to be governed according to the *Laws* of Plato. The city, which was to have been established in Campania (perhaps on the site of ancient Pompeii or Herculaneum), was to be named "Platonopolis." This *coenobium*, or community, of choice souls was never actually founded since it lost the imperial favor, but Plotinus continued to assist orphans and the indigent, to admonish those who had gone astray, and to take part in the common readings and discussions of his disciples. Only when he was some fifty years old did he yield to the entreaties of his friends and write down the fruit of these seminars. His essays were edited by his disciple Porphyry in six books, each of which is divided into nine treatises. These are the famous *Enneads* ('Εννεάδες — "groups of nine"), without doubt the most elaborate systematization of ancient thought.

27. At the summit of everything according to Plotinus stands the supreme fount of being, the One (τὸ ἕν). The One transcends all intelligible determination and is to be identified with the Supreme Good. From it emanates an effusion (πρόοδος) into all that is, and toward it evolves a reconversion (ἐπιστροφή) of all that is. The Intellect (νοῦς), which is the divine substance thinking, and which is to be identified with the Platonic Demiurge, emanates from the One by generation; and from the Intellect contemplating itself emanates the Soul (ψυχή), to be identified with the Platonic World-Soul. These three hypostases constitute the Divine or Intelligible World which, through a hierarchically graded outpouring into material beings, gives rise to the Sensible World.

From man, a composite of matter and spirit, begins the intellectual and volitional act of "reconversion" toward the One. This salutary journey which conducts man back to his natural goal, or fatherland (πατρίς), is achieved through different grades or steps. These are first represented by the "political" or social virtues (prudence, fortitude, temperance, and justice, which taken together comprise wisdom), then by the cathartic or purifying virtues, somewhat similar to the preceding but on a higher level, and finally by the "paradigmatic" or exemplary virtues, which are the prerequisites for divine contemplation and ecstasy. The ultimate goal of this ethical asceticism is, as a matter of fact, the "assimilation to God" (ὁμοίωσις θεῷ), attainable only by one who has stripped himself of everything, that is, by the completely unencumbered soul that has arrived at the supreme ecstasy.

The motto of the Christian ascetic, "Forsake all and thou shalt find all" (Dimitte omnia, et invenies omnia — Thomas à Kempis, Imitation of Christ, 3. 32), had already been enunciated, though in a different sense, by Plotinus: "Remove everything" (ἄφελε πάντα — Enn., 5. 3. 17). The soul, after running through the whole course of its "reconversion" will have transcended everything less than, and derived from, the One and will have arrived at that One which is also the supreme unity of itself. It is the flight which the soul alone completes toward the "Alone" (Enn., 6. 9. 11). This concept of "the lover to his beloved" also agrees with the teaching of the Christian ascetic who sets up as the supreme goal for his reader "that thou alone mayest . . . be united to Him alone" (ut . . . solus cum solo uniaris — A Kempis, 2. 8). 28. Even from this very summary exposition, the ethicoreligious character of the system should be clear despite the fact that in many details it may seem to be defective and unreal. Plotinus' purpose had been to follow the authentic teaching of Plato, casting aside all the apocrypha attributed to the great master then in circulation; but by a twist of fate, shortly after his death, there arose the custom of introducing into the Platonico-Plotinian system elements from other sources.

This change was due to external circumstances of a practical nature. Plotinus' system was so elevated that it was inaccessible to the masses and appealed only to a chosen few. Its religious aspect was so inward and abstract that it rejected on principle anything so material as temples and formal worship, the very things which were the chief foundations of the ordinary pagan religion. On one occasion when Plotinus was asked to take part in a religious ceremony, he refused, saying: "It is for those beings to come to me, not for me to go to them" (Porphyry, Life of Plotinus, 10). Obviously, such an attitude did not favor the spread of Plotinus' doctrines among the unsophisticated.

Furthermore, there was a dangerous competitor, Christianity, which was spreading its doctrines without much difficulty among the learned and the unlearned, among nobles and plebeians. The road leading to it had, therefore, to be blocked, and the common people removed from it and reorientated toward the ancient Hellenic cults. But since there was a need of rites, ceremonies, symbols, and whatever else serves to kindle the imagination to impress the masses, such props had to be introduced into the austere religion taught by Plotinus. In the very name of him who had pointed out the goal of the soul's ascent toward God completely above the sensible world had to be taught a descent toward the material.

29. Porphyry, the editor of Plotinus' works, the author of the *Life of Plotinus*, and a prolific writer in his own right, was Plotinus' most distinguished disciple. He was born in 232 or 233, and entered the school of Plotinus when he was about thirty years old. It seems that Porphyry, as is evidenced by his writings (*On the Philosophy Derived From the Oracles; On Statues*), was at this time dabbling in magic and theurgy; but when he became a follower of Plotinus, he rejected every form of occultism in order to adhere solely to reason and Plato, though this did not prevent an occasional dissent from Plotinus.

The two threats to Plotinus' system, the decline of Greek religion and the growth of Christianity, provoked a vigorous reaction in Porphyry. In a hortatory letter to his wife Marcella, he described the sublimity of "the salvation of one's soul" (ἡ τῆς ψυχῆς σωτηρία), the ultimate goal of philosophy, and his own desire to achieve it. In a letter to Anebo he made a radical attack on magical practices. His fifteen books *Against the Christians*, which has survived only in fragments, was certainly more substantial than Celsus' *True Discourse* published a century before. Throughout the Middle Ages, Porphyry's fame remained attached to his *Isagoge* ("*Introduction*") *to the Categories of Aristotle*, which was translated into Latin and several Oriental languages.

At the beginning of the fourth century the center of Neoplatonism shifted to the East where the Syrian school with its various ramifications flourished. Its most renowned representative was Iamblicus, who had been born about the year 250 at Chalcis in Coelesyria and who died before 330. He was the author of many works, the most important of which was a semipopular encyclopedia of Pythagoreanism in ten books, parts of which are still extant. He was most likely also the author of another work attributed to him, *On the Mysteries of Egypt*. Its original title was *A Reply of Abammon to Porphyry's "Letter to Anebo"* (the letter already mentioned above). His lost *Perfect Chaldean Theology*, which seems to have been connected with the earlier

Chaldaic Oracles of uncertain origin, must have been particularly important for theurgy.

30. Characteristic of Iamblicus, and more or less of his followers, is the tendency to augment the intermediaries between the One of Plotinus and the Sensible World. Not only are the links of the chain connecting the two extremes increased, but even above Plotinus' One is placed a First One, an absolutely ineffable principle (ἡ πάντη ἄρρητος ἀρχή) which is at the same time distinct from the Good. The Intellect (νοῦς) of Plotinus is split into the Intelligible (νοητός) World and the Intellectual (νοερός) World. The former is the world of the ideas, the latter of the intelligences; but each of these two worlds, through descending gradations, is subdivided first into a trinity (Father, Power, Intellect) and then into triads until finally the Sensible World is reached. The Sensible World is likewise broken up into the Upper World, which is the home of the gods, angels, demons, and heroes, and the Lower World, which is only material. Man is the intermediary between these two worlds, but he has a natural aspiration for the Supreme Good and at the same time an intuition of the gods.

On the practical level, Iamblicus withdrew further and further from Plotinus and abandoned himself to an impulsive and enthusiastic mysticism which drew its support from every possible source. If the principle is granted that the divine element is echeloned and scattered throughout the whole range of being, fragments or reflections of that divine element may be found at every step on the scale of being — in the material phenomena of nature, in dreams, in the analysis of numbers, and finally in the inner movements of the soul. A calf born with two heads can be a "revealer" equally as well as a divine inspiration received in the most secret recesses of one's conscience. All this material which had been cast contemptuously aside by Plotinus was scrupulously gathered and studied by Iamblicus and his followers. The exponents of this late Neoplatonism thus gradually ceased to be philosophers, since they renounced the hope of arriving at divine contemplation by means of the reason and became instead to a greater or less extent hierophants, magicians, thaumaturges, and evokers of the gods. Because they knew how to discover the divine hidden in the cosmos, they dedicated themselves to the task of bringing that divinity to light (θεαγωγία), and they thus performed "theurgy," that is, divine work (θεουργία). The term also passed over into Latin (*theurgia*; cf. St. Augustine, *De civ. Dei*, 10. 9–10).

31. Syrian Neoplatonism had various offshoots. For us, the most important was the Pergamine school founded by Iamblicus' disciple Aedesius. He in his turn had as disciples Chrysantheus, Eusebius of Myndus, Priscus, and Maximus, all of whom had connections with Julian the Apostate. Eunapius, the author of the *Lives of the Sophists*, was also under the influence of this same school.

Among all these Neoplatonicians, Julian showed the greatest reverence for Iamblicus and Maximus. He describes the former as "a truly godlike man, the third after Pythagoras and Plato" (*To Priscus* — Wright, 3:4). He is "the inspired Iamblicus," who in his writings has reached "the highest wisdom that man can achieve," so that "no one can say anything more perfect than he, not even if he should toil long at the task and say much that is new. For in so doing he will naturally stray from the truest knowledge of God" (*Helios*, 157cd). As for the latter, Maximus, he is described by Julian, though not specifically, as the guide *par excellence*. To settle a question, it was sufficient to make an appeal to Maximus: "He said it" (αὐτὸς ἔφα — *To Theodore*, 452b).

Both ethically and spiritually Neoplatonism and Christianity were, of course, essentially different; but under certain aspects they did bear a superficial resemblance to each other. Various individuals, as Justin Martyr and St. Augustine witness for themselves, passed over the bridge of Neoplatonism on their way toward Christianity. St. Augustine, who had some interest in Porphyry's nontheurgical doctrines (*De civ. Dei*, 10. 21–32), states that an unnamed Platonist repeatedly expressed the desire that the beginning of St. John's Gospel, "In the beginning was the Word, and the Word was with God," etc., should be written in letters of gold and set up in a prominent place in all the churches (*ibid.*, 10. 29). There are good reasons for believing that this Platonist was the rhetorician Marius Victorinus, the translator of Porphyry's *Isagoge* into Latin, whose conversion so greatly influenced Augustine's own (*Confess.*, 8. 2). Although he had received the rare honor of a statue erected to him in the Forum Traianum at Rome, he subsequently fell under Julian's ban forbidding Christians to engage in teaching. Nevertheless he preferred, as St. Augustine tells us (*ibid.*, 8. 5), to abandon the teaching of words than to renounce the Divine Word, the Logos of Christianity (§ 170).

Contrary to what it had done for Justin Martyr, Marius Victorinus, Augustine, and others, Neoplatonism, instead of attaching Julian more closely to the Christianity which he already professed, violently separated him from it. But this was the theurgic Neoplatonism of Iamblicus and not the Neoplatonism of Plotinus.

32. In Nicomedia, Julian, who was now largely his own master, could do as much as he pleased, being careful, of course, not to arouse the suspicions of Constantius. He was at this time a fully developed young man of twenty years, though handicapped by a number of physical and moral defects. His physical appearance and, to some extent, his moral character have been described for us by three eyewitnesses: Ammianus Marcellinus, Libanius, and Gregory Nazianzen, though it should be kept in mind that in some details these descriptions may reflect a somewhat later period than that of his stay in Nicomedia.

Ammianus states that Julian was of medium height, with a beard that ended in a point, and endowed with bright eyes of striking beauty (*venustate oculorum micantium flagrans* — 25. 4. 22). He had elegant eyebrows, a perfectly straight nose, a rather large mouth with a loose lower lip, a neck somewhat bent, and large, broad shoulders. The same Ammianus notes elsewhere (22. 14. 3) that the rabble at Antioch called him a Cercops (one of a race changed by Jupiter into apes), since being of low stature and having a beard like a billy goat's, he spread his broad shoulders as he advanced with great strides through the streets. He lost his beard just before his nomination as Caesar (cf. § 63); during his campaigns in Gaul he kept his beard shaved like the ordinary soldiers (cf. Ammianus, 17. 9. 7), though he let it grow again after his proclamation as Augustus. Julian himself joked about his beard and his untidy apperance, as is evident from the whole of his *Misopogon* ("Beard-Hater"), in which he ironically answers his Antiochian critics.

For his part, Libanius states that as a student at Athens Julian was constantly surrounded by young men and old, by philosophers as well as by rhetoricians. Though his speech was admirable, it was at the same time modest: he quickly blushed at whatever he said, and this bashfulness was a source of delight to all (Libanius, 18. 29–30).

33. Gregory Nazianzen saw Julian's character mirrored in his external appearance and describes it in great detail.

Gregory had been suspicious of Julian since his first acquaintance with him at Athens. Impelled by a double motive, the prince had come there with the emperor's permission shortly after the death of his brother Gallus. The first of these motives was praiseworthy: to get acquainted with Greece and attend the schools there. The second, known only to a few, was to associate secretly with pagan priests and quacks, since he was not yet confirmed in his impiety. Although Gregory was not inclined to prophecy, he divined Julian's character even at this time. His irregular habits and many strange mannerisms had furnished the clue. Gregory could foresee that nothing good was to be expected from the weaving head, the wild, wandering eyes, the shifty feet, the nostrils breathing hate and scorn, the proud and contemptuous lineaments of the face, the paroxysms of uncontrolled laughter, the constant changes of opinion without apparent reason, the breathless speech and disordered, senseless questions interlaced with answers no more to the point. But why go into such particulars? These premonitions had been realized. There were those who could remember that he had exclaimed at the sight of Julian's peculiarities: "What a monster the Roman empire is nourishing within itself!" (5. 23–24.)

34. Obviously each of these three authorities speaks from his own point of view like three artists painting the features of the same person from different perspectives. Ammianus is moderately favorable, Libanius enthusiastic as usual (but this means little), and Gregory decidedly adverse and hostile. The flashing eyes depicted by Ammianus (see also 15. 8. 16) are of little importance for a psychological evaluation of the subject; the agreeable modesty noted by Libanius is of even less value; but this is not the case with the traits furnished by Gregory. Since he was well informed, he could have painted a faithful portrait. But was it impartial and objective? It would be hard to deny that he paints at times with too broad a brush. But is its total effect a portrait or a caricature? A psychiatrist could determine whether the work, prescinding from the historical subject, is probable, or whether it contains evident absurdities. A historian must strive to find confirmations or negations of the particulars in his other sources.

Julian's habitual nervousness, for example, which manifested itself in unexpected outbursts of joy toward his friends is witnessed by Libanius. Ammianus (22. 7. 3–4) thought that the boisterous way in which Julian greeted his former teacher Maximus of Ephesus, who visited him after he had become Augustus, was unbecoming to the emperor.

Julian as a rule wrote at a feverish pace and rarely revised what he had written. His works as a consequence carry the same pitch of excitement, the same sudden shifts in thought noted by Gregory in his conversation. As for the perpetual turmoil of his emotions, this is indirectly attested by Julian himself. When deprived of his friend Sallustius, he deplored the fact that he had lost in him his best guide and adviser: "Where can I find in the future such a well-disposed friend as you? With whose guileless and complete frankness shall I now be sustained? Who will now give me wise counsel, correct me with affection, give me strength for noble deeds without arrogance and conceit, and speak freely to me after removing the sting from his words?" (*To Sallustius*, 243c.) Other resemblances to the portrait may be found in the way in which Julian attacked different problems, but it would be premature to record them here. Gregory, therefore, may speak as an adversary, but his testimony cannot be rejected *in toto* on this account.

35. Julian's studies at Nicomedia proved to be profitable, but after a time he had no more to learn from his teachers. He then received from Constantius a new permission, or rather an extension of the old (§ 21): he could travel wherever he wished, accompanied by a small retinue appointed by the emperor to watch his movements (Eunapius, 474). Julian then left Nicomedia for Pergamum, a city in Asia Minor situated to the north of Ephesus and to the east of the island of Lesbos.

Through the efforts of the Attalid dynasty, Pergamum had become an important center of Hellenism, though not of the same rank as Alexandria or Antioch. Still it was there that Julian betook himself. Why? There can be no doubt that it was consequent to the new spiritual experiences at Nicomedia. There he had not only followed the lectures of Libanius through the notes taken down by his friends, but, what was of even greater significance, he had entered into very close relations with groups of Neoplatonic theurgists. His first vague suspicions that the light he was seeking was to be found in theurgy (§ 24) had become a profound conviction which gradually penetrated and gave fiber to his whole being. In it he finally found what he had sought elsewhere in vain.

At Pergamum, Julian did not find Iamblicus, who had died years before (§ 29), but his eminent disciple Aedesius. Here it will be sufficient to follow the substance of Eunapius' account (474–475), adding some brief explanations. "At that time Aedesius was very advanced in years and failing in bodily strength." His chief disciples

were Maximus, Chrysanthius, Priscus, and Eusebius (§ 31). After he
had once been admitted to Aedesius' company, Julian refused to leave
him, since, "like those who in the legend are bitten by the 'thirsty-
serpent,' he wished to gulp down open-mouthed large draughts of his
learning. To obtain this he kept sending Aedesius gifts worthy of a
king, but Aedesius would not accept them, and having summoned
the young man he said: 'You are indeed ignorant of my soul though
you have heard me speak many times.'" Then he added that since
he was so old and feeble it would be better for Julian to turn to his
faithful disciples for guidance along the right path. In giving this
advice, Aedesius may have been influenced by fear of the possible
consequences of association with a prince of royal blood if Emperor
Constantius, who kept an eye on the young man, learned of it. Still,
since he did not want to reject completely the promising pupil, he
encouraged him with the following words: "Once you have been
admitted to their mysteries [the wisdom and learning of Aedesius'
disciples] you will be utterly ashamed to have been born and to be
called a man."* The mysteries, in fact, were supposed to lift the
initiates far above human nature. "I would that Maximus were also
here," the old philosopher continued, "but he has been sent to
Ephesus. I could say the same of Priscus, but he also has sailed for
Greece. Of my companions, Eusebius and Chrysanthius are still here.
If you will study with them, you will spare me this burden in my
old age."

36. Julian followed this advice and for some time listened to the
lectures of Eusebius and Chrysanthius, but there was a notable difference between the two since Chrysanthius, like Maximus, was completely dedicated to the occult sciences and theurgy, while Eusebius
"avoided precise rational distinctions and the artifices and subtleties of
dialectic when Maximus was present, whereas, when Maximus was
absent, he shone as a star with a light like the sun's, so great was the
eloquence and charm that flowered forth in his discourses. . . . After
his exposition Eusebius would add that these were the only true
realities, whereas the deceits of magic and witchcraft were the works
of prestidigitators, insane men led astray into the exercise of certain
earthly powers." In other words, Eusebius had a very poor opinion
of the theurgy of Maximus, though he took pains that it did not

---

* This echoes Porphyry's famous observation on Plotinus: "He was like one who
was ashamed that he was in a body" (ἐῴκει μὲν αἰσχυνομένῳ ὅτι ἐν σώματι εἴη — Life
of Plotinus, 1).

reach him. Julian, who had heard such opinions expressed by Eusebius on several occasions, wanted an explanation. He privately asked Chrysanthius, Maximus' twin soul, for one: "If the truth is in you, my dear Chrysanthius, tell me plainly the meaning of this epilog to his exposition." Chrysanthius, being on his guard, advised him to have recourse to Eusebius himself. Julian followed the advice and received the following explanation: "Maximus is one of the older and more learned disciples. On account of the grandeur of his nature and his superabundant eloquence he despises all rational proofs in these matters and impetuously plays the part of a madman." And to prove his point Eusebius narrated the following incident.

A short time before, Maximus had invited Eusebius and others of his friends to the temple of Hecate. After he had told them that he would show them how far he surpassed ordinary men, he burned a grain of incense and recited a hymn to himself. Then it happened. The statue of the goddess first began to smile and then seemed to laugh out loud. Those present were alarmed, but Maximus tried to calm them by saying that the torches which the goddess held in her hands would soon burst into flame. And they actually did. According to Eunapius, Eusebius then concluded his account: "'We departed struck dumb for a time by that spectacular wonder-worker. But do not marvel at any of these things any more than I do, counting the purification of the soul through the use of reason as the thing of greatest importance.' But when the most godly Julian heard this, he said: 'Farewell, keep to your books, you have shown me my man.' And when he had said this he kissed the head of Chrysanthius and set out for Ephesus."

37. This account clearly reveals Julian's state of mind at this time. There are no reasons for doubting the reality of Maximus' display of his powers. If its account produced the exact opposite of what Eusebius had intended, the reason is that Julian was little attuned to "the purification of the soul through the use of reason" which Eusebius advised, but was, on the other hand, very anxious to contemplate those marvels which Eusebius discounted.

It would be historically false to maintain that the phenomena which occurred in the temple of Hecate were a complete fraud. We might perhaps pass such a judgment on them today, but for a Neoplatonic theurgist they were revelations of the divinity which the medium had succeeded in capturing with his wisdom. If for a theurgist, as we have already seen (§ 30), the divine was invisibly diffused throughout the whole cosmos like a primordial electric wave, the action which succeeded in capturing this wave, that is, whatever induced the divine to reveal itself, was a legitimate theurgic activity. And to obtain such a revelation one could have recourse to all the then known physical, chemical, and optical laws. But one could also enrich and complement the picture with additional props which would enhance the desired theurgic effect. Why did amber attract to itself little pieces of straw? And why did heliotropes feel the call of the sun, while the moonworts remained under the spell of the moon? Why did saltpeter mixed with powdered charcoal produce such thunderous effects? And why did the Valerian rhizome (the Greek φῦ?) send forth such a nauseating stench? The obvious answer to such questions was that there existed laws of "sympathy" and "antipathy" between these various things and the celestial principles from which they depended. The theurgists drew inspiration from this ideological foundation, which they partly intuited and partly strove to integrate with the secrets of their profession. When they made use of saltpeter, sulphur, colophony (Greek pitch), and other elements from their repertory in preparing for a revelation of the divinity, they were acting in perfect conformity with their own principles. Since they employed elements provided by the divinity, their manipulation was actually no fraud in their eyes.

38. Such a program was not exactly new. A half century earlier the Augustus Maximinus, who in a number of ways was a predecessor of Julian in his fight against Christianity, had gained the highest repute for the statue of Zeus Philios (Friendly Jupiter) erected at Antioch by Theotecnus, the "curator" of the city. Before the statue, secret initiatory and magical rites were performed. From its mouth descended oracles which stirred up a persecution of the Christians until one finally came forth ordering their complete expulsion from the city and its environs (Eusebius, 9. 3). After his defeat by Licinius, Maximinus was eager to take revenge on the pagan priests who had pushed him into the disastrous war, and among the first victims was Theotecnus. Priests and prophets of the temple were imprisoned and tortured. They then revealed the secret mechanism in the statue that made it seem to talk. It was all a clever contrivance of Theotecnus (ibid., 9. 11. 5–6).

It is not known if Julian was aware of this incident which had occurred decades before in Antioch, but even if he had known it, his faith in theurgy would not have been shaken. This is supported by

Libanius' observation (13. 11) that "a certain spark of the mantic art" which Julian discovered while seeking the truth caused him to lose his hatred of the ancient gods, and, as a consequence, he remained "docile to the mantic oracles." This information supplied by Libanius is not only in harmony with Julian's habitual state of mind, but it is also confirmed by details preserved in other historians. A rereading of the *De magia* of Apuleius (rather than his *Metamorphoses*) to extract the cold historical facts from this "most fulsome and eloquent oration" (*copiosissima et disertissima oratio* — St. Augustine, *De civ. Dei*, 8. 19) would be extremely useful for evaluating the general pagan attitude toward occultism some two centuries earlier.

39. At Ephesus Julian came under the direct influence of Maximus. He stayed there for some time and completed a regular course of studies in theurgy (Eunapius, 475). There he must also have been officially initiated into the theurgic mysteries, an event not recorded for us by a pagan but by his adversary, Gregory Nazianzen (cf. § 33).

Julian descended into a subterranean sanctuary closed to the common people in the company of a clever conjurer, a theosophist rather than a philosopher. Such individuals practiced a kind of divination that required darkness and subterranean demons to foretell the future. As Julian advanced farther and farther, he encountered terrors increasingly numerous and alarming — strange sounds, revolting exhalations, fiery apparitions, and other such prodigies. Since he was taking his first steps in the occult sciences, the strangeness of the apparitions terrified him. He made the sign of the cross. The demons were subdued and all the visions disappeared. Julian regained courage and began to advance. Then the dread objects started to reappear. The sign of the cross was repeated and they again disappeared. Julian wavered. The director of the initiation at his side explained: "We loathe, but no longer fear them. The weaker cause has conquered!" Convinced by these words, Julian was led on toward the abyss of perdition. What he later heard and did only those know who have undergone such initiations. At any rate, from that day he was possessed (Gregory Nazianzen, 4. 55–56; cf. Theodoret, 3. 1).

If the setting is here more grandiose than it was under Theotecnus, this may be attributed to the greater refinement of theurgic technique acquired in half a century of use. We may also presume that the high rank of the initiate would have flattered the mystagogue so that he carried out the rite in a flawless manner.

III. TROUBLED YEARS

§§ 40–42. Mystical Tendencies.   §§ 43–48. Political Consequences, and Apostasy From Christianity.   §§ 49–50. Fall
of Gallus and Julian's Peril.   §§ 51–52. On the Way to
Milan.   §§ 53–54. Como and Athens.   §§ 55–56. Julian,
Eusebia, and Helena.

40. Julian's total adhesion to theurgy marks the denouement of his own spiritual tragedy. Hence, it will not be out of place to trace the course of this inner conflict with what evidence we have at our disposal.

The slaughter of his relatives must have been a severe shock to Julian as a child (§ 4), but its full consequences appeared only later when, having passed through adolescence into the full consciousness of maturity, he tried to discover the motives behind this horrible crime and to identify those responsible for it. As we have seen, when he was able to speak freely (§ 5), Julian attributed the responsibility for the murders to Constantius himself. Since this was his conviction, it was natural that his rancor should be concentrated on the emperor, but this only aggravated him the more and increased his desire for revenge.

This hatred for the all-powerful Constantius was bound to extend to every facet of his being, beginning with his adherence to Christianity. Julian was driven to hate this religion not by any philosophical or abstract reasons but by the fact that his murderous cousin was a Christian.

Whether it was due to his spiritual make-up or to his reading of the Neoplatonists, when Julian began to think for himself, his mental outlook was that of a mystic, much more intuitive and enthusiastic than reasoned and calm. In his *Hymn to Helios*, written some six months before his death, Julian reviews his early years and reveals some intimate secrets that give us an insight into the hidden recesses of his mind: "I am a follower of King Helios [the sun god to whom in his early years his uncle Constantine the Great had been much attached, and perhaps even before him, Constantius Chlorus], and of this I have at home with me most certain proofs.* But this much I can say without sacrilege: From my childhood a great longing for the rays of the god encompassed me, and from my earliest years my mind was so completely enthralled (την διάνοιαν ἐξιστάμην) by the etherial light that I not only longed to gaze steadfastly at the sun but also, whenever I walked forth at night under a clear and cloudless sky, casting aside all else, I gave myself up to the beauty of the heavens, paying no attention to what anyone said to me or what I was doing myself. I was thought to be too curious and too attentive to these matters, and some even thought that I was an astrologer, though at the time my beard was just beginning to grow. And yet, by the gods, never had a book on astrology come into my hands, nor did I yet know at all what it was" (130b–131a). This confession shows that Julian even as a child was easily aroused and influenced by anything novel or striking in nature. And from the Neoplatonic point of view, such phenomena were no less connected with theology than they were with cosmology (§ 30).

41. It should, therefore, be no surprise to find Julian as a mature man firmly convinced that he was in direct relationship with the gods, who guided and admonished him in the most critical periods of his life. At Athens, in 355, after he had been nominated Caesar (§ 61), in fear and trepidation he turned for light and assistance to the goddess Athena, lifting up his hands toward the Acropolis. The goddess heard his prayer, bringing to his side "guardian angels from Helios and Selene" (To the Athenians, 275b). Not long after this he begged the gods to tell him in a dream whether he should send a letter to Empress Eusebia in Milan or not (§ 63); and, in his own words, "they warned me that if I sent it, I would incur a most shameful death. The gods are my witnesses that what I here write is true" (ibid., 275cd).

In 360, when the mutinous troops proclaimed him Augustus at Paris, the gods again intervened (§ 128). When he was uncertain about what he should do, he 'prayed to Zeus for a sign' (cf. Odyssey, 3. 173) through an opening in the wall in an upper room of his palace. "Then indeed he gave one to me and ordered me to yield and not to oppose myself to the will of the army" (284c).

---

* There is here some ambiguity in the text: τούτου δὲ ἔχω μὲν οἴκοι παρ ἐμαυτῷ τὰς πίστεις ἀκριβεστέρας, which may have reference to a chapel dedicated to Helios in the imperial palace at Constantinople, or to his initiation into the Mithraic mysteries.

To these data furnished by Julian should be added those preserved for us by his friend Ammianus Marcellinus. According to this historian, the night before Julian's proclamation as Augustus he had a vision of the guardian spirit of the state (*genius publicus*). It chided him for his reluctance to accept the proffered dignity and threatened to abandon him forever if he again refused to accept it. The ultimate source of this information had, of course, to be Julian himself, and Ammianus specifically prefaces his account by stating that "the emperor had told his more intimate friends about the vision" (*iunctioribus proximis rettulerat imperator . . . visum* — 20. 5. 10).

The *genius publicus* was again seen by Julian the night before he died (§ 208). With his mind in a turmoil because of the terrible developments of the Persian campaign, the emperor had stayed in his tent meditating upon a philosophical work. Suddenly "he saw rather dimly, as he confessed to his friends, that form of the guarding spirit of the state which he had seen in Gaul when he was rising to the dignity of an Augustus, but now with both its head and cornucopia veiled, sorrowfully passing out through the hangings of his tent" (25. 2. 3 — cf. § 208). Here again, as is obvious, Julian is only our real source of information. Certainly none of those friends, worn out by the hunger and toil of the preceding months, to whom he revealed the vision would have been found that night in his tent. Only the emperor weighed down by his responsibilities, but supported by his philosophy, was keeping watch.

42. Julian's conviction that he was in contact with gods and under their protection gradually increased to the point that he was convinced that they had chosen him for some extraordinary tasks. An attack on the Cynic Heraclius, which he composed in 362, contains an allegory on his family's history. His relatives had abandoned the worship of the gods, but he had been personally chosen by Zeus to repair this apostasy and the damage it had done throughout the empire. Helios, at Zeus's bidding, outlines the program to be followed: " 'You must return to earth and cleanse away all impiety and entreat me and Athena and the other gods for our assistance' " (*Against Heraclius*, 231d). When he wrote this (cf. § 147), Julian was certainly not thinking of the program announced centuries earlier by the Messianic servant of Yahweh (Isa. 49:1–6), though as a young lector he could have read it in the Christian assemblies (§ 16). Still, as a matter of fact, the two programs are nicely balanced. Just as the

Messianic herald had been chosen to bring back to Yahweh all the offspring of Israel and to carry the message of salvation "even to the farthest part of the earth," so Julian would have to go "over all the land and sea" (234b) to bring back to the worship of the gods all the peoples of the empire who had been corrupted by the Christianity of Constantine. It is interesting, however, to note that Athena, to facilitate the execution of the program entrusted to Julian, exhorts him in words taken right out of the New Testament: "Be sober and watch" (233a). It is the same exhortation that had been used by St. Peter (1 Peter 5:8) and by St. Paul (1 Thess. 5:6). Thus the pagan goddess, though for a contrary end, gives the same advice as the Christian apostles.

Was this pagan Messianic program exclusively religious? Not in the modern sense of the word, since it also involved politics as well. In the interpretation given to it by Julian and his supporters, it could be called "religious" in that they had set up as their goal the restoration of idolatry within the constitutional framework of the empire. This, to be sure, had been the traditional policy of the Roman Empire down to the time of Constantine: the veneration paid to the gods constituted the very foundation of the state, and all activity within the res publica was in some way or other connected with their official cult. Not even Galerius in his edict of 311 had denied this traditional Roman concept. He had granted, it is true, freedom of conscience and of worship to the Christians (denuo sint Christiani), but only to the extent of their being tolerated; they were not yet put on the same level with the pagans. The real revolutionaries in this field were Constantine and Licinius with their Edict of Milan in 313. This edict, while it did not recognize Christ as God, ceased to give recognition to the traditional gods of the empire, making no distinction for the present or for the future between the religions of the empire, and treating both pagans and Christians as equal in all things.

The pagans, still very numerous throughout the empire, were hostile to the Edict of Milan. They regarded it as being destructive to the very fabric of the state, and from their point of view they were right. But objectively they were wrong in that they did not realize that the empire was no longer the sacred institution it had been during the republic or even during the time of Augustus, and that practically it had been "laicized." At any rate, since Constantine was all powerful, especially after his final victory over Licinius, they had to bow their heads and postpone their hopes for more favorable times. But when Julian, still a student at Constantinople, appeared on the political horizon, those who were waiting for a restoration of idolatry had their hopes renewed (§ 22). These aspirations became more lively after 351, when Julian, returning to Nicomedia, began to enjoy a certain liberty of action.

43. From numerous friends with whom he kept in contact either personally or through letters, Julian learned of the widespread hopes placed in him. Through them he anticipated the realization of the program entrusted to him by Helios, and he conscientiously set about co-operating with his divine vocation. Since his brother Gallus at this time had great authority as Caesar, Julian was besieged with requests to mediate various types of business, and he readily lent his assistance to such petitions.

Almost by accident we know that he traveled several times in Ionia to secure favors for his friends; that he interceded with Araxius, a high magistrate who had been his fellow pupil, on behalf of a certain Carterius; that twice within the space of two months he went to Phrygia to protect the property of "the admirable woman Arete" from her neighbors' greed, even though he was weak from an illness brought on by earlier journeys; and that he took the side of a foreign sophist who was almost unknown to him and thus opposed one who was bound to him by ties of blood and friendship (To Themistius, 259cd). This final case merits particular attention since the unnamed person opposed by Julian could have been his brother Gallus, whose administration was not at all popular. But the matter is not certain.

Libanius, who was better informed than any others, describes the results of this multiple activity and the consequent fame accruing to Julian in the following fashion: "His fame spread far and wide. All the friends of the Muses and of the other gods came to him, some by land and some by sea, being anxious to see him, to associate with him, to speak with him, and to hear him. Once they reached him, it was not easy for them to depart, since Julian treated them like a siren not only with his words but also with his natural charm. Because he had a great capacity for affection, he taught others to love him in return. Thus they became so attached to him that they could not leave him without distress." All sensible men prayed that the young man might come into power so that he could prevent the collapse of the civilized world and remedy its ills. "I would not say that he disapproved of such prayers, for I will not make such a pretence on his behalf. They certainly were his own desires, but he wanted them not out of a love of show or of power or of the purple, but rather in order that through his own labors he might restore to the people what they had lost, and in particular their worship of the gods. What afflicted his heart most were the temples in ruins, the feasts not celebrated, the priests in exile, and the treasures of the temples distributed among the insolent" (Libanius, 18. 20–23).

Despite Libanius' habitual exaggerations, what he here says of Julian should be accepted, including the expressed desires of his friends and sympathizers. These aspirations not only harmonize with Julian's state of mystic exaltation (§ 42), but they are also evidenced by historians who, in contrast to Libanius, were not in sympathy with his pretentions. The Christians, Socrates (3. 1) and Sozomen (5. 2), note that Julian's first imperial ambitions were stirred up by the theurgist Maximus of Ephesus (§ 36; cf. Theodoret, 3. 1); and, considering the moral character of the theurgists, this is quite probable.

44. But this activity, conducted though it was with circumspection, was too extensive to escape completely the notice of Julian's superiors, among whom were the Augustus Constantius, busy at the time suppressing revolts in the West (§ 20), and the Caesar Gallus, who ruled over the area (§ 21) in which Julian was traveling about. Though crude and vicious, Gallus still clung to Christianity. Since the Augustus who had raised him to the purple was an Arian, this was the heresy to which Gallus himself subscribed. To show oneself faithful to the cross and opposed to the gods of Olympus had, under the circumstances, many practical advantages. But one harsh day Gallus realized that his brother was thinking about a restoration of idolatry and even secretly working for it. The least the Caesar could say was that the harebrained Julian had acted most imprudently. Constantius already had enough reasons for being worried about Gallus without the addition of a charge of failing to watch over his brother. Something had to be done to bring Julian to his senses, and Gallus decided to try persuasion rather than make use of threats and violence.

He had as his faithful consultant in ecclesiastical affairs Aetius of Antioch, a man whom he had once almost condemned to death but whom he later took into his confidence. Aetius, whom the orthodox Christians nicknamed "The Atheist," was the founder of the sect known as the Anomoeans, the most radical of the Arians. The Arian historian Philostorgius (3. 27; 4. 8; 6. 7; 9. 4) and the orthodox historians Socrates (2. 35) and Sozomen (5. 5) furnish us with some details about his life and teaching. There is also extant a short letter sent to him by Julian (*To Aetius*, 404bc). Since Aetius was an able dialectician, Gallus sent him to Julian to turn him away from his idolatrous projects. A cordial sympathy seems to have arisen between the two, but in the end Julian deceived Aetius into thinking that he was still a faithful adherent to Christianity, hiding of course his true sentiments. In the *corpus* of Julian's writings there is a letter addressed to him by Gallus in which the latter expresses his happiness on learning of Julian's religious attitude from Aetius. Almost all modern critics, however, consider this letter to be apocryphal, regarding it as the product of some unknown but well-informed Christian.

This same letter also asserts that Aetius had assured him (Gallus) that Julian was assiduous in visiting Christian oratories and celebrating the feasts of the martyrs. Despite the dubious character of the text, this part of it is true. Socrates, Sozomen, and Gregory Nazianzen all affirm that at this time Julian kept up the external appearance of being a Christian. Nevertheless, his withdrawal from Christianity, at least in the secret of his conscience, was already complete and definitive. He confesses this himself in a letter written at the end of 362 in which he states that he had "walked along the road" of the Christians "till his twentieth year," but that now "with the help of the gods" he had walked along another "for twelve years" (*To the Alexandrians*, 434d). This enables us to fix his apostasy in the year 350 or 351, that is, at about the same time that he was immersing himself in the theurgy of Maximus of Ephesus (§ 39).

45. Julian's religious hypocrisy was well known to those who shared his hopes and sentiments. Libanius, referring to this period, says that Aesop, if he had wished to tell a new fable, would not have spoken of the ass that hid itself under the skin of a lion, but of the lion that hid itself under the skin of an ass (18. 19). The lion naturally enough was Julian. As a point of controversy the application is ingenious, but, historically speaking, Julian's own observation is more significant. During the reign of Constantius, "because of the universal fear one could lawfully conceal the sounder opinions about the gods" (*On Christian Teachers*, 423c), that is, one could lawfully conduct oneself as a Christian exteriorly while remaining interiorly a pagan. Julian laid down this rule on the principle of human loyalty, in whose

name he here wished to speak; but it is precisely in the name of loyalty that no explanation can be given for Julian's contention that it was lawful in the time of Constantius to don the Christian skin of an ass. Was it perhaps because there was a "universal fear"? If it was, then the lauded loyalty was merely a matter of pure opportunism, solely to "save one's skin," the real skin, that is, and not the one of which Libanius was speaking. Historically, then, it is necessary to recall that very many during the "great persecution" of Diocletian a few decades earlier had seen herds of these Christian asses exterminated. Without donning the false skins of lions, and openly showing their real skins of asses, they had allowed themselves to be massacred. Consequently, Libanius may have given utterance to a very clever defense of paganism, and Julian may have stated a norm of pagan morality, but both are in conflict with the teachings of historic reality.

46. What kind of Christianity did Julian abandon? Was it Arianism or orthodoxy? It should be remembered that up to this time Julian had been under the influence of Christians who were all at least tinged with Arianism: his mother Basilina was probably an Arian (§ 2); Eusebius of Nicomedia, his first guardian, was a stanch advocate of the heresy (§ 8); Constantius, who controlled the destinies of Julian and his brother Gallus, was an Arian; so also was George of Cappadocia, the bishop whose library Julian had used (§ 15); and, finally, Aetius, who had attempted to reconvert Julian at Gallus' behest, was also an Arian (§ 44).

In spirit no less than in dogma, Arianism was opposed to Christian orthodoxy. It may be said in general that the typical representatives of Arianism were cold logicians who exhausted themselves on abstract speculations about the Logos, but who paid little attention to the religious and moral edification of their associates. The "salvation of one's soul," which had occupied Porphyry and the earlier Neoplatonicians so much (§ 29), was reduced by the Arians to dialectics about the Logos. Still speaking in general, these typical representatives of Arianism were extremely anxious to secure the favor of the imperial court and to draw up schemes for propagating their party by political means, but they almost never manifested any real pastoral care for their flocks. True, it must be admitted, they also had propagandist aims among non-Christian peoples, but their real object was to render their own party more numerous and extensive than that of the orthodox. In other words, practical Christianity counted for little. A typical representative of this mentality was the Aetius already mentioned. He had the reputation of being a great dialectician. Still extant is his treatise *On God Unbegotten and Begotten*, which attempts to demonstrate the fundamental principles of Arianism in forty-seven brief statements. He seems to have written some three hundred skeletonlike tracts of this kind.

As for the orthodox, limiting ourselves to Julian's contemporaries, it should be sufficient to name Athanasius, Basil, Gregory Nazianzen, Gregory of Nyssa, and John Chrysostom, most of whom were well known to him. Their polemical works against Arianism, their exegetical, hortative, ascetical, and other spiritual writings are still classics of Christian thought, while their various foundations to provide for the social welfare and general assistance of their flock (§ 19) can serve even today as models for imitation.

47. Julian, who in his own way was seeking for the "salvation of his soul," withdrew disillusioned from Arian Christianity. He then fancied that he could find it in the theurgy of Maximus of Ephesus. It would be interesting to know what Julian's decision would have been if, instead of being under the influence of Eusebius of Nicomedia, George of Cappadocia, and other Arians, he had come into intimate contact in his early youth with Athanasius or Basil or other orthodox Christians of the same caliber. No one, of course, can say what would have happened in such an hypothesis, but it is certain that Christianity would have appeared to him in a far different light than it actually did.

Even in his later years, this confusion between Arianism and orthodoxy weighed upon him. When he refers to Christianity in his writings, he does not succeed in distinguishing between the two and charges both Arians and orthodox with being "Galileans," that is, non-Hellenes. For him the irreconcilable dissension between the two groups, each claiming that it alone represented genuine Christianity, was a spontaneous manifestation of the hatred connatural to Christianity itself. He allegedly knew from experience that "there are no wild beasts so hostile to mankind as are most Christians in their hatred for each other" (Ammianus, 22. 5. 4). This judgment is perhaps less exaggerated than it seems when the unheard-of cruelties perpetrated by the Donatists in Africa and by some Arian sects in other areas are brought to mind, but Julian of course erred in branding all Christians with the ferocity of these heretics.

48. Even among the orthodox Julian could see things which repelled

him in his pursuit of "salvation." In the larger cities the high standards of Catholic conduct had suffered a more or less serious decline. From the year 383 or 384 comes the well-known letter of St. Jerome, To Eustochium (Ep., 22), which paints a very dark picture, undoubtedly exaggerated, of the life of the Christians, and especially of the clergy at Rome. From about this same time are a number of decrees against vagabond monks and clerics who, particularly at Rome, wandered about in search of legacies and inheritances (Cod. Theod., 16. 2. 3).

Even more revealing is the description given by Ammianus Marcellinus of the bloody conflict which evolved about Damasus and Ursinus for possession of the episcopal see at Rome. This honest pagan and friend of Julian then goes on to say: "I do not deny, keeping in mind the vain show of city life, that those who are eager for such a thing should strive with all the force of their eloquence to obtain what they seek; for when they have obtained it, they will be so free from care that they are showered with the gifts of matrons, ride seated in carriages, wear elegant garments, and serve such lavish dinners that their banquets surpass the tables of kings. These men could be really happy if they would despise the greatness of the city, with which they hide their faults, and live like some provincial bishops, whose great temperance in eating and almost total abstinence in drinking, poverty in dress, and downcast eyes commend them to the Eternal Deity and to His true worshipers as pure and reverent men" (27. 3. 14–15). For the city of Rome Julian never had any particular affection, but this did not hinder his being informed of what was happening there, especially since it was the principal seat of the Christianity he hated. All this, as a consequence, furnished him with added reasons for massing into one general condemnation the whole of Christianity, both Arian and Catholic.

49. In such a fashion almost four years had passed, when the clouds which for some time had been gathering on the horizon broke into a storm lashing down upon Gallus. As Caesar, which he had been from the year 351 (§ 21), he had not acted at all well. His private life was frivolous, completely taken up with gladiatorial shows and games in the circus. Escorted by his satellites, he wandered about Antioch at night in search of bloody adventures. In his public life his abuse of power and cruelty rivaled that of his wife Constantina (Constantia), the widow of Hannibalian (§ 5). This daughter of Constantine the Great is described by the circumspect Ammianus as "a Megaera [one

of the Furies] in mortal guise . . . no less thirsty for human blood than her husband" (14. 1. 2). Thanks to his generals, Gallus gained a number of victories over the brigands of Cilicia and the rebellious Jews of Palestine, where he destroyed Tiberias and Diocaesarea. But neither the fulsome flattery directed to him by Libanius nor the influence of his wife could protect him from the consequences of his conduct. Thalassius, the prefect of the East, sent grave reports to Constantius, who began to suspect that his cousin Gallus was a conspirator intent on becoming Augustus. Thereupon, with feigned sweetness, as though he wanted to treat of affairs of state, he invited him to Milan. But Gallus was skeptical about the invitation and with the approval of Constantina he took revenge by slaying a number of high officials at his court. The emperor continued to treat him kindly but insisted that Gallus accompanied by his wife, Constantius' own sister, should make his appearance at Milan. The two felt constrained to obey, but they hoped that Constantina's presence would have some weight on the emperor's decisions. She set out before Gallus, who remained at Antioch, but when she arrived in Bithynia she was seized with a violent fever and died.

Gallus was badly shaken by her death since he lost in his wife his sole defense against the well-founded wrath of Constantius. He set out, but stopped for some time in Constantinople to preside at the solemn games in the circus. This cynicism only increased Constantius' suspicions. To remove any possibility of a revolt the emperor gradually withdrew all the troops stationed in the areas through which Gallus had to pass. When he arrived at Poetovio in Pannonia, the tragicomedy finally ended. Gallus was arrested, deprived of his insignia as Caesar, and taken under guard to Flanona, a village near Pola. Here toward the end of 354, he was decapitated. At Pola itself, in 326, Crispus, the son of Constantine the Great, had been killed by order of his father. We have already seen (§ 12) the judgment which Julian passed upon his unfortunate brother.

50. Gallus' fall did not directly involve Julian, but it had grave repercussions at this time and later. For the present, Constantius' new victim took his place with that group of apparitions which had relentlessly fixed themselves on Julian's mind ever since the slaughter of his relatives (§ 5). For the future, it was instinctively felt that the execution was an implicit warning to the surviving brother, who had lived so long with the victim. It is true that Julian had not won any public

honors and traveled freely about the East visiting friends and scholars, but these very Eastern connections could prove harmful to him. Just as Gallus had come to know the religious crisis that Julian had experienced (§ 44), so the imprudence of one or other of Julian's confidants could reveal to Constantius the number of those who saw in Julian a candidate for the purple (§ 43); and if this happened, the candidate would not be long in joining his brother and the others.

Constantius actually did receive reports on Julian's conduct, but these were regularly manipulated by the cloud of courtiers, flatterers, and spies that surrounded the emperor. Gallus' fall was at once exploited by these intriguers. They hastened to offer their advice to the Augustus, ostensibly to prevent a repetition of a similar occurrence, but in reality to further their own interests by removing possible rivals. The great excogitator of these plots was Eusebius, *praepositus cubiculi*, or "grand chamberlain." At Milan the names of the most eminent persons who had been connected with Gallus were reviewed, and summonses were issued for their appearance. Very soon, as Ammianus observes (15. 3. 1), "bands of soldiers were brought from the East together with many courtiers, their limbs wasting in chains" as they waited their sentence.

Shortly before this, a different type of precaution had been taken against Julian. Toward the end of 354 he received an imperial command to appear at Milan. Since respect was still due to him as the emperor's cousin, a small official escort was furnished him and permission to choose his own route. He could travel where, and visit the sites he wished, provided that within a certain time he showed up at Milan.

Julian took advantage of this liberality to visit a place he had loved from the time when as a boy he had first studied Homer, the site of ancient Troy. His ship having sailed out through the Dardanelles headed south and coasted along the shore, passing between the mainland and the island of Tenedos. Shortly after navigating this narrow strip of water he landed at Alexandria Troas, from where a good road led to Ilium, the successor of ancient Troy; and toward it Julian directed his course.

51. The account of this visit is contained in one of the most lively and interesting letters he wrote, and it still has a special archaeological value (*To a Priest* — Wright, 3:48–54). Although the letter refers to events which took place at this time, that is, in 354, it was written much later, about the middle of 362.

Having left Alexandria Troas early in the morning, Julian arrived in Ilium a little before noon. One of the first to greet him was the local bishop, an Arian named Pegasius. This prelate had already adopted a double religious standard not unlike that of Hecebolius (§ 22). Later, during Julian's reign, he completely abandoned Christ to follow the god Helios. Julian readily accepted his offer to guide him in a tour of the city since he was anxious to see the state of the temples. We may leave the description of the tour to him: "Hector has a shrine there housing his bronze statue in a small little temple. Opposite this, in an open court, has been set up a statue of the great Achilles. If you have seen the place, you will certainly recognize what I am saying. You can hear from the guides why the great Achilles was set opposite Hector and takes up the whole of the unroofed court. I found that the altars were still kindled, I could almost say ablaze, and the statue of Hector glistening from the oil with which it had been anointed. I therefore looked at Pegasius and asked: 'What is the meaning of this? Do the people of Ilium offer sacrifices?' My real purpose was to make a cautious inquiry about his own views. 'And what is strange,' he replied, 'about their serving a brave man who was their own citizen, just as we do the martyrs?' It was not a good comparison, yet his intention, considering the times, was civilly expressed. Then what happened? 'Let us go,' he said, 'to the precinct of Athena of Ilium.' With great eagerness he led me there and opened up the temple, and just as if he were calling me to be a witness he showed me all the statues in a perfect state of preservation, nor did he act at all like those impious men [the Christians] are wont to do, making the sign on their impious foreheads, nor did he hiss to himself as they do. For this is the height of their theology: to hiss at demons and to make the sign of the cross upon their foreheads. These are the two things I said I would tell you, but a third comes to my mind which I shall not fail to mention. This same Pegasius also accompanied me to the shrine of Achilles which I had heard he had demolished. He approached it with the greatest reverence, as I saw with my own eyes, and showed me the tomb intact. I have heard from those who are now hostile to him that he also used to supplicate and worship Helios in secret."

To understand the import of this letter, it must be kept in mind that it was written by Julian as the high priest of paganism to show that he had acted properly in accepting Pegasius into the pagan priesthood and offering him his protection even though he had been a Christian bishop. Such benevolence was rendered legitimate by Pegasius' previous conduct to which his protector here alludes.

52. After he had finished his visit to Troy, Julian again took up his voyage for Milan. When he arrived at court, he found a state of terror raging. The prisoners that had been brought to Aquileia were gradually processed and punished with harsh sentences of death or exile. At Milan a double accusation was brought against Julian himself, one that he had left Macellum without permission (§ 21), and another that he had conferred with Gallus (§ 22). He vigorously defended himself against both accusations and received a favorable verdict. Still, though he was not condemned, he was not allowed to go free, much less to have an audience with the emperor. Eusebius and the other courtiers who were dictating the imperial policy feared that such a meeting might effect a union of their two minds. If Constantius became aware of Julian's outstanding gifts, he would begin to esteem him. For seven months Julian had to follow the emperor in his various changes of residence (*To the Athenians*, 272d). Although he was kept carefully under guard, still a certain respect was shown him because of his relationship with the Augustus. We know that he wrote a number of letters to Themistius (*To Themistius*, 260a). These were naturally very brief since they had to pass through the courtiers' censorship, but they had a very practical end. Although he was a pagan, Themistius was a favorite of Constantius. Julian's letters to him could thus serve as a personal commendation.

Despite all this, Julian's fate hung upon a thread which could break any day. Held in the dark about everything, he could do nothing but wait passively, preparing himself for any event that might develop in that obscurity. Then, quite unexpectedly, a beam of light burst out of the darkness.

53. At this time Constantius had Eusebia as his wife. She was his second spouse since he had had as his first Julian's half sister (§§ 5, 21). Eusebia, who came from a noble Macedonian family, was beautiful, cultured, and refined. Constantius was greatly in love with her, and because of her intelligence and extraordinary tenacity he was frequently influenced by her in his decisions. But in the midst of such great blessings Eusebia had the misfortune of having no children, although both she and Constantius ardently desired them both for their own comfort and for the good of the dynasty.

The empress suddenly began to show a lively interest in Julian's fate and sought means to assist him. The first obstacle to remove was the barricade which the courtiers had raised between him and Constantius. This the empress was able tactfully to do: the emperor granted an audience to his cousin. From then on Julian entered into normal, if not precisely cordial, relations with him. This favorable outcome to the negotiations, which could have been neither short nor easy, is attributed by Julian to the assistance of "the fair and virtuous Eusebia" (*To the Athenians*, 273a).

Though Julian makes passing references to Eusebia in his other writings, our chief source of information with regard to her is the encomium which he composed in her honor. Ammianus Marcellinus also provides us with certain other details. Julian's encomium may not seem to be of much value if we take into account the fact that he also composed at least two in honor of the empress' husband, for whom he certainly had no esteem whatever. Nevertheless, despite the necessarily eulogistic tone of the work, we may well believe that the praises he directed to the empress were as sincere as they were merited.

At Constantius' bidding, Julian took up his residence at Como (Comum). Though the city had many natural attractions and had even been the birthplace of Pliny the Elder, it afforded no opportunities for serious study. This was disconserting to Julian who was anxious to live in a place where he could continue his beloved inquiries and which would not be far from his masters in theurgy. When the vigilant Eusebia became aware of Julian's desire, she obtained permission for him to retire to a small piece of property in Bithynia which he had inherited from his mother's family (§§ 8, 11).

54. But another storm broke unexpectedly. In the summer of 355 various rumors reached the court that Africanus and Marinus at Sirmium in Pannonia (Mitrovica in Yugoslavia) and Silvanus in Gaul were plotting against the emperor. The accusations were largely calumnious, but the court, which lived on suspicions, was seriously alarmed. Under the circumstances it seemed unwise to allow Julian to continue his journey toward Bithynia and the adjacent territories where he was already known and esteemed (§ 43). Therefore he was ordered to settle in Greece (*To the Athenians*, 273cd). But Greece meant Athens, and to see Athens for the first time meant for Julian the consummation of all his desires.

Who suggested to Constantius this substitution of Athens for

Bithynia? Since it was a move that both calmed the fears of Constantius and delighted Julian, it is not hard to believe that Eusebia was ultimately responsible. He remained at this center of Hellenic civilization from about August to October, 355.

Eusebia's protection of Julian was also manifested in many other ways, but, before going on to these other benefactions, we must examine the mutual esteem which Julian and Eusebia had for each other. This brings us to speak also a little ahead of time of Julian's wife, Helena.

55. In the beginning of November, 355, Constantius appointed Julian "Caesar" and sent him at once to govern Gaul. Julian was at this time twenty-three years old, and the emperor, to bind him more closely to his own cause, gave him his half sister Helena (the daughter either of his father Constantine or of his mother Fausta) in marriage. The wedding took place a few days after Julian's election as Caesar (§ 65). Such marriages, between blood relatives, easily justified by dynastic considerations, were frequent among the descendants of Constantine. This time such reasons surmounted the circumstance that the bride was several years, perhaps five or six, older than her spouse.

In Julian's austere life, the only women who appear linked with him are these two: his wife Helena and the empress Eusebia. On only three occasions does Julian make mention of his wife: once, to praise the empress who had arranged his marriage with Helena and had presented him with precious wedding gifts (*Eusebia*, 123d); a second time, to note in passing that his wife had lived with him during his governorship in Gaul (*To the Athenians*, 284c); and, finally, to declare that the letters which he wrote to his wife were so chaste and respectful that they could be read by all (*To his Uncle Julian* — Wright, 3:102). Moreover, these references to Helena are all made with the greatest coldness, almost as if he were dealing with a stranger. Empress Eusebia, on the other hand, is always mentioned in Julian's writings in terms of lyric praise; and, in his encomium of her, Julian expressly represents her as a celestial apparition (§ 65).

Despite these contrasts, the two princesses not only had frequent dealings with Julian but even with each other. Various rumors concerning them have come down to us, and, whether well founded or not, they must be taken into consideration. Both died young, and almost contemporaneously, that is, in the winter of 360–361, when Julian's rebellion against Constantius was coming to a head. Three years before, in 357, they had taken a trip to Rome together, since Constantius, who was paying a visit to the Eternal City with Eusebia, had insisted that Helena should accompany them. But a grave scandal was circulated about the two princesses. The following account of it is given by Ammianus Marcellinus (16. 10. 18–19), our chief source of information in this matter.

From her marriage with Julian, Helena had had a child in Gaul that died at birth. It was said that the death was not accidental but deliberately provoked: Eusebia, still sterile and jealous of Helena's fertility, had bribed the midwife to kill the child "so that this most valiant man [Julian] should have no offspring" (*ne fortissimi viri soboles appareret*). Moreover, after this crime the evil machinations continued. When the two princesses were together in Rome, Eusebia gave her sister-in-law a slow poison that could cause the abortion of any pregnancy, but which, instead, finally killed her. Further rumors even blamed Julian for his wife's death: she had been poisoned by a physician in his service. This last gossip was propagated by a certain Polycles, former governor of Phoenicia, who claimed that he had as his source of information Elpidius, prefect of the praetorium under Constantius in 361 and Julian's old rival in Gaul. All these accounts are emphatically denied by Libanius in a brief work, *To Polycles*, written shortly after Julian's death.

56. In the face of rumors so serious and of such a delicate nature, a modern historian stands perplexed. Even taking into consideration the mentality of the times and the general character of the protagonists, it is practically impossible to distinguish truth from calumny, a definite fact from the infinite slanders floating about the court.

That Eusebia was a most diligent defender of Julian has already been seen, and subsequent events will bring this out even more clearly. That Julian was a hearty admirer of Eusebia is proved by his encomium of her, even taking into account the conventional laudatory style of such exercises. But none of this proves that there was anything blameworthy in their mutual relations.

In Julian's favor is the fact that his writings and his habitual conduct furnish us with the portrait of a man completely alien to all amorous intrigues. Still this portrait, accurate in itself, does not furnish a peremptory proof extending to each and every action of his life.

On the other side, in Eusebia's favor was the very rigid court etiquette which demanded extreme reserve in dealing with anyone foreign to the imperial gynaeceum, as is shown, for example, by the first public audience she granted to Julian (§ 65). But this also is not a definitive proof, since the Byzantine court mushroomed with hidden intrigues. If the known conduct of Julian and Eusebia in their dealings with each other is above suspicion, there is certainly no reason for placing any credence in Helena's supposed abortion and her subsequent death by poisoning. Here in all probability we are dealing with a complete fiction maliciously spun out of the calumnies circulating among the courtiers. The provocation for this slander was perhaps furnished by the sad and solitary figure of Helena, a princess almost a stranger to her husband, overshadowed by Eusebia, and alien to the intrigues and rivalries of the court. The tragic fate of her mother Fausta, the wife of Constantine, seems almost to have been perpetuated in her own career. Constantine had her executed at about the same time that he had ordered the death of her stepson, his own son Crispus. The real motives for this double crime are not given by the ancient historians, nor have they been discovered by modern scholars despite their various hypotheses. A motive, however, was immediately found by the courtiers and the common gossips of the time. The tragedy was seen as a repetition of the myth of Phaedra and Hippolytus, in which the stepmother is represented as being in love with her stepson. No such rumor was spread about Helena; rather, she was held to be the victim upon whom fell the consequences of the alleged adultery of her husband with Eusebia. Such tragic tales easily capture the minds of the unsophisticated, but they are works of pure fantasy.

We may conclude this account of the two princesses with the final notice appearing in our chief source: Julian "sent the remains of his deceased wife Helena to Rome, to be laid to rest in his villa in the suburbs on the Via Nomentana, where her sister Constantina, formerly the wife of Gallus, was also buried" (21. 1. 5). This is the so-called "Mausoleum of St. Constantia," not far from the tomb of the martyr Agnes. The Constantina, or Constantia, here named, the former widow of Hannibalian, is the one whom Ammianus himself had described as "a Megaera in mortal guise . . . thirsty for human blood" (§ 49).

Eusebia, the wife of Constantius, had died at almost the same time as, or shortly before, Helena. Thus another moral link binding Julian to the emperor was broken. Notwithstanding his great love for his deceased wife, Constantius does not seem to have been overwhelmed by his loss, since a short time later, at the beginning of 361, he married his third wife, Faustina. It was a marriage most likely demanded by dynastic considerations (§ 139).

IV. FROM ATHENS TO GAUL

§§ 57–60. Stay at Athens. Initiation Into the Pagan Mysteries. §§ 61–68. Election as Caesar. §§ 69–71. Departure for Gaul.

57. Arriving in Athens, Julian probably imagined that he would be there a long time instead of the three months he actually remained there (§ 54). He describes the sentiments he experienced on entering the city in the following terms: "Going to Greece, when all thought I was an exile, did I not praise my good fortune as though some great feast were being celebrated, and did I not say that the change was most delightful to me, and that, as the saying goes, I had gained thereby 'gold for bronze, the price of a hundred oxen for that of nine' (*Iliad*, 6. 236). So happy was I to have exchanged my own hearth for Greece, even though I possessed there no field or garden or cottage" (*To Themistius*, 260ab).

Julian's stay at Athens did not alter his general outlook, but rather confirmed his secret convictions. The cultural life of the city had become increasingly sterile. Rhetoric rather than philosophy reigned in the schools. Prohaeresius, a Christian Armenian, was the leading exponent of the art, followed by Himerius, a pagan of Prusa in Bithynia. To the citizens in general and the many students who flowed to Athens from all parts of the empire, the observation made by St. Luke some three centuries earlier was still applicable: "Now all the Athenians and strangers that were there employed themselves in nothing else but in telling or in hearing some new thing" (Acts 17:21). They were living on the memories of the glorious past, but they did little or nothing themselves to measure up to that past. They talked about Plato, but they substituted theurgy for his teaching; instead of speculating about his eternal ideas, they were engrossed with the trivialities to be heard in the agora. The student life, mixing together as it did young men of different languages, customs, and religions, was intense. Boisterous and colorful traditions accompanied a student from

the time of his entrance into a given school up to his final departure
from the city. Basil of Caesarea and Gregory Nazianzen (§§ 19, 33, 39),
who were students at Athens at this time with Julian, and who later
with Gregory of Nyssa comprised the famous triad of the Cappadocian
Fathers, were Christians like the rhetorician Prohaeresius. But the
Christian element cannot have been too strong since the city was
tenaciously pagan and remained so for many years to come.

58. From the little information still extant about Julian's activity in
Athens, it seems that he kept aloof from the noisy life of the city
and perhaps even from the lecture halls, finding his chief interests
instead in the famous monuments of earlier times and in the company
of those whom he enjoyed. He perhaps lived with Celsus, a friend
of Libanius; but, from the detailed account which Gregory Nazianzen
gives of him, it does not seem that he avoided the company of
Christians. If he occasionally visited the churches, as he did later,
his sole purpose would have been to elude Constantius' surveillance.
His real interests lay with those who shared his spiritual aspirations,
that is, with the Neoplatonists and especially the theurgists.

As might be expected, Julian was soon surrounded by a secret clique
which aimed at the restoration of Hellenism, the confutation of the
"Galileans," the securing of the imperial throne for a true worshiper
of the gods of Olympus, and its eventual reconsecration to these
same gods. Did not Julian have the potentiality of becoming such a
great benefactor? In short, what Julian's presence had already effected
in Constantinople was repeated here, but in a more ample fashion
(§ 22). The eager expectation that centered about Julian at Athens
is explicitly attested by Libanius (18. 29 ff.). He represents Julian surrounded by young and old, by philosophers and rhetoricians, and even
favored by the special protection of the gods, who knew that he would
restore the ancient institutions to their pristine glory. But Julian,
gentle and almost timid in his dealings with everyone, opened up his
heart to only a few. If, in accord with his mystic convictions, Julian
encouraged the secret hopes of his followers (§ 42), he checked any
public manifestation of their zeal. If Constantius became aware of
of what was going on, he would summon him at once to the court at
Milan. And if this happened, the outcome would not be as happy as
that of a few months before (§ 52). Meticulous care was therefore
absolutely necessary.

59. These external exigencies did not weaken Julian's inner convic-

tions in the least. He continued his mystic and theurgic activities. Here some prudent conjectures must supply for a lack of precise information. Julian had learned from Aedesius, whom he had met in Pergamum, that his disciple Priscus "had sailed for Greece" (§ 35). It is therefore most probable that Julian became acquainted with Priscus at this time in Greece. He soon became his devoted friend and, later on, one of Julian's most venerated teachers, almost on a par with Maximus of Ephesus, who had initiated him into the magical arts (§ 39). Both Priscus and Maximus were present at Julian's deathbed (Ammianus, 25. 3. 23), and there are still extant letters of Julian to Priscus in which he invites him to come and visit him in Gaul. When speaking of him, Eunapius (481) represents him as solemn and lordly in bearing, slow and hieratic in speech, and chary of the company of others, all of which traits were sure to impress Julian.

For one who was at Athens, it was relatively easy to be initiated into the mysteries celebrated at Eleusis some eleven miles away. Many famous Romans, including several emperors such as Hadrian, Lucius Verus, Marcus Aurelius, and Commodus, had, as a matter of fact, been initiated there. The Lesser Mysteries, which were held in the spring, and the Greater Mysteries, which were conducted in the early autumn, re-enacted the myth of the "two goddesses," Demeter (Ceres) and Kore (Persephone). The chief minister of the rite was the "hierophant," a member of the clan of the Eumolpidae, which traced its origins to Thrace. His was the duty of "showing the sacred things." A number of preliminary ceremonies were performed in the open air: the public procession of the initiates to the sanctuary at Eleusis, their purification in the bay of Phalerum, and other secondary rites; but the culminating part of the ritual, which lasted for three days, took place in the interior of the sanctuary under the most strict secrecy. Throughout the centuries this secret was so scrupulously kept that even today we know very little about the ceremonies.

As for Julian, the information furnished by Eunapius (476) permits us to affirm that he had dealings with the hierophant of the time, and that this relationship was so close that Julian "drew from him large draughts of wisdom." Eunapius had himself been initiated into the Eleusinian mysteries "by this most godlike hierophant," and on this account he could not reveal his name. Using these two notices as premises, we may conclude that Julian also underwent the initiation at Eleusis. Nevertheless there may still be some doubt about this because of that part of the rite which was held in the open and within the view of the general public. We cannot forget that the emperor kept a watchful eye on Julian. If Constantius had learned through his spies that his cousin had taken part in the mysteries, would he not have interpreted it as an open provocation and unholy disobedience? At any rate, given the scarcity of our information, it may be presumed that the ever cautious Julian acted in such a way that he was not delated to the emperor.

60. There can be no doubt, on the other hand, that Julian was initiated into the mysteries of Mithra. Where and when this took place is not known, but it was probably when he was governor of Gaul. In various writings he alludes to his Mithraic consecration, though of course with the reserve required of an initiate. We have already seen one of these passages in his *Hymn to Helios* (§ 40), a god practically identified with Mithra by Julian; but more important is another passage in his seventh oration in which he alludes to the third of the six steps of the Mithraic initiation, that of "soldier" (*Against Heraclius*, 234a). Also, up in Olympus, Hermes gives Julian a knowledge of his "father Mithra" (*Caesars* 336c), and he expressly reminds him of his "commandments," that is, the obligations assumed by the initiates. On numerous occasions during the later course of his life Julian was to be seen following out the duties and conforming himself to the *esprit de corps* of Mithra's soldiers.

It must be noted, however, that Julian in accordance with the custom of his age and, in particular, with his own mystic mentality, frequently confused the person and attributes of individual gods, though continuing to call them by their respective names. The *Hymn to Helios*, for example, actually deals with Mithra, since he had come to be considered as an equivalent to the sun god, who in turn was the highest manifestation of the Supreme One of Plotinus. A similar syncretism is encountered in the *Hymn to the Mother of the Gods*, the Magna Mater Cybele, in which the god Attis receives more considera-tion than Cybele. Julian's thought with respect to such syncretism and to mythology in general is further revealed in his sixth and seventh orations, *Against the Uneducated Cynics* and *Against the Cynic Heraclius*, written less than two years before his death. Although they were put down swiftly (the *Hymn to Helios* was written in three nights — 157bc), they were not casual works. Julian had spent long nights reading and meditating over the matter expounded therein.

Hence, these tracts, including the hymns, represent a kind of *summa* of Julian's theology.

Nevertheless, succeeding pagan philosophers paid no attention to the *summa* since the system of the theological emperor had no significance for them.

61. Julian was in Athens less than three months when a sudden order bade him return to Milan and present himself at court. The command was naturally anything but welcome. He states himself that he wept copiously at his departure, lifting up his hands toward the Acropolis and imploring the goddess Athena not to abandon him (*To the Athenians*, 275a). It is true that such sentimental leave-takings were common among aristocratic youths when they said good-bye to their friends and companions before setting out for their homes, but, in Julian's case the emotion may have been increased by the recollection of his occult activities in Athens and by the possibility of having to render an account of them to Constantius. His brother's tragic end of hardly a year before must have filled him with tearful presentiments even though, as time was to prove, any storm clouds that had appeared on the horizon had already been dissipated by his vigilant protectress, the empress Eusebia.

62. At this time the empire was in a condition quite similar to that in which it had been at the beginning of the year 351, when the revolts of Magnentius, Vetranio, and Nepotianus endangered the empire from within while the Persians threatened it from without (§ 20). Not long before Julian's recall, Gallus (§ 49), Africanus, Marinus, and Silvanus (§ 54) had been a source of worry to Constantius. Moreover, the Persian threat showed no signs of abating, and the barbarians in the West could not be checked in their devastating incursions into Gaul. But additional troubles were gathering about Constantius because of his mania for meddling in theological questions. This involved him in a quarrel not only with the ancient and irrepressible adversary of Arianism, Athanasius of Alexandria, but also with Pope Liberius. In Rome, Liberius not only had the strong support of the people, "who heartily esteemed him" (*qui eius amore flagrabat* — 15. 7. 10), but also that of many Roman senators. These latter, envious of the many privileges being granted by the emperor to the rival senate in Constantinople, took the part of Liberius if for no other reason than that they saw him at odds with the Augustus. The matter ended with the pope's arrest and deportation to the imperial court at Milan.

Some remedy had to be found for the mounting difficulties, and Constantius, either as the result of his own reflection or at the suggestion of others (§ 68), came to the same conclusion reached before his appointing Gallus as Caesar (§ 21): he should associate a blood relative with himself in the supreme command. Such a one would be able to help him rule the empire and would at the same time effectively shut off from the succession any nonrelated aspirants to the throne. This time the candidate for the office of Caesar could be none other than his cousin Julian.

When Constantius revealed this project to the imperial council, all the courtiers, as is recorded by Ammianus (15. 8. 2), were hostile to it. They feared that they would lose their influence and even be denounced by the future Caesar for their past and present misdeeds. But since these arguments could have had little effect with the emperor, they opposed the appointment on the ground that the office of Caesar should not be re-established after the sad experience with Gallus. Nevertheless, all the flattery which they lavished on the emperor failed to stop the project since Eusebia "all by herself stubbornly opposed them" (*obstinate opponebat se sola regina* — 15. 8. 3), stressing the fact that a relative had to be preferred to anyone else (*anteponi debere propinquum*). The struggle therefore was not so much between the counselors and Constantius as between the counselors and Eusebia. It cannot be said that Constantius himself was entirely satisfied with the outcome. Although he yielded to the arguments of his wife and adopted the plan, he soon deprived it of any substantial meaning.
63. Some ancient historians (Eunapius, 476; cf. Zosimus, 3. 1; Libanius, 18. 36 ff.) assert that Constantius elected Julian as Caesar to expose him to grave reverses in his government of Gaul and thus be rid of him forever. But it would be reasonable to ask if Constantius had no other means of removing Julian from the scene except that of paying the enormous price of a Roman catastrophe in Gaul. Such gossip, it may be supposed, was provoked by the absurd position in which the new governor found himself immediately after his election.

Julian made the journey from Athens to Rome not knowing what to expect. Perhaps the lot he least foresaw was the one waiting for him. When he arrived at Milan and took up his residence in a suburb, the clouds of uncertainty must have quickly scattered. But here it will be well to read Julian's own account of the course of events: "Now from the first moment of my arrival from Greece, Eusebia of blessed memory kept showing me the greatest kindness through the service of her eunuchs. When after a little her husband returned — for the problem of Silvanus had been settled — I was at last given access to the court and, as the saying goes, 'Thessalian persuasion' was applied to me. For when I firmly refused to associate with the people in the palace, some of them, just as if they had gathered in a barber's shop, cut off my beard and threw over me a military cloak and transformed me, as they thought at the time, into a very ridiculous soldier. For none of the trappings of these wretches suited me. And I did not walk as they did, looking about and strutting along, but gazing upon the ground as I had been taught to do by the pedagog who had reared me [§ 9]. At that time I provoked their laughter, but a little later their suspicions, and then their envy was kindled to the utmost. . . . When I came to Milan I lived in one of the suburbs. There Eusebia frequently sent me messages manifesting her good will toward me, and she bade me write confidently about whatever I desired. Thereupon I wrote her a letter, or rather a petition, containing prayers such as these: 'May you have children for heirs!' 'May God grant you such and such, but send me home as quickly as you can!' Then I began to fear that it was not safe to send a letter to the royal palace addressed to the emperor's wife. I therefore entreated the gods to inform me during the night if I should send the letter to the queen; and they warned me that if I sent it, I would incur a most shameful death. The gods are my witnesses that what I here write is true. It was on this account, then, that I refrained from sending the letter" (*To the Athenians*, 274c–275d). This is one of the instances already noted (§ 41) in which Julian felt that he was in contact with the gods and directly guided by them. But this night he strengthened his mystic conviction with long reflection, weighing the reasons both pro and con. In the end, following the example of Socrates, he entrusted himself to the will of the gods who had placed before him two alternatives but had also indicated to him their own preference. Consequently, "I consented to yield. And very soon I received the title and robe of Caesar" (277a).

64. The election was thus made and accepted. There only remained the public investiture. This ceremony, which is minutely described by Ammianus Marcellinus (15. 8. 4–17), was carried out at Milan on

November 6, 355. Julian had only recently entered upon his twenty-fourth year. Less than twelve months before, his brother and predecessor in the office had lost his life. (§ 49).

The ceremony was solemn. The army, which was spending the winter at Milan, was assembled with its eagles and legionary standards drawn up in array about a lofty tribune. The Augustus mounted the tribune, leading the new Caesar by the hand. They were followed by the highest officials. Constantius, who liked to speak in public, and who on this occasion was anxious to explain his project to the soldiers and gain their approval, addressed them as the "excellent defenders of the state" (*optimi rei publicae defensores*). His discourse ran as follows: Though the recent rebellions have been crushed, there still remains the barbarian threat against Gaul. Meanwhile he is himself being called by other exigencies to far-distant lands. What should he do? He suggests that the soldiers should give their approval to the election of his cousin as Caesar, whom he cherishes for his modesty, connection by blood, and the industry he has begun to display. At this moment a confused murmur of voices induces the speaker to pause. All say that the proposal has come not from a human mind but from the Supreme Deity, and that it is an omen for the future. The speaker then ardently bids the exemplary young man to ascend to his destined honor since those present are in favor of it. The elect is then invested with the purple. The soldiers show their joy. The new Caesar, on the other hand, appears "somewhat sad and drawn in face" (*contractiore vultu submaestum*). The speaker finally concludes his discourse with a further exhortation to his "most dearly beloved brother" (*amantissime mihi omnium frater*). With "nearly equal power" (*suppari potestate*) to that of the emperor, he will share in the latter's toil and dangers. He will console the afflicted Gauls and lead the troops against their enemies. As the crisis demands, he should set out boldly and show himself to be a brave commander of brave men. In his trials he may depend upon the emperor's steadfast affection and assistance. The two will fight together so that, being of one mind, with God's help they may govern the pacified world with piety and moderation.

The conclusion of the discourse was received with immense applause and a terrifying crash (*horrendo fragore*) caused by the soldiers beating their shields against their knees. (When they beat them with their lances it was a sign of grief and anger.) Their enthusiasm was general, though there were a few who did not approve the choice made by the Augustus. We are not told who these few were. They probably were not members of the rank and file, but higher officers who believed that the election of the new Caesar would impede their own careers. At the end of the ceremony, Julian took his place in the emperor's carriage and was drawn with him to the palace. But in the midst of all the jubilation, Julian was apprehensive and whispered a verse from Homer: "Purple death and mighty destiny gathered him in" (ἔλλαβε πορφύρεος θάνατος καὶ μοῖρα κραταιή — Iliad, 5. 83), where there is a play on πορφύρεος — the color of blood and of royalty.

And, as a matter of fact, how could he have forgotten on this occasion the fate of his brother Gallus?

65. After the conclusion of these solemn ceremonies there were, as the emperor had already noted in his speech, various urgent matters to be attended to before Julian could depart for Gaul. First, his marriage with Helena was celebrated (§ 55). The Augustus and the Caesar, who were already connected by blood, thus became relatives also by marriage. There is no proof that before this time Eusebia and Julian had ever met, despite their regard for one another and their mutual exchange of letters (§ 53 ff.). Since the imperial gynaeceum was closed to practically everyone, it must have been all the more impenetrable to a stranger who did not dwell at court. But this norm was now no longer applicable. Julian, who had been elected Caesar and had become a relative by marriage, now dwelt under the same roof as the Augustus (To the Athenians, 274d). Since he was now directly dependent on the Augustus, how could he be refused a public audience with the Augusta? His present status thus had to be regulated according to court protocol.

At the emperor's own invitation the audience did, in fact, take place, though it is quite possible that it had been first suggested by the empress. Julian has left us a description of this meeting: "When I first came into her presence, it seemed to me as if I saw a statue of Prudence erected in a temple. Reverence possessed my soul, and I kept my eyes fixed upon the ground for a rather long time until she bade me take heart. 'Certain things,' she said, 'you have already received from us, and, if God wills it, you will receive others, if only you prove to be faithful and honest toward us.' This is about all I heard; for she said nothing more, although she knew how to make speeches not at all inferior to those of the most gifted orators. Departing from this audience, I was completely enthralled and quite beside myself, since it seemed to me that I had heard Prudence herself speaking, so soft and honeyed were the words that ever since have been enshrined in my ears"(*Eusebia*, 123ac).

Julian then records some of the benefactions made by the empress, beginning with those conferred shortly after the audience, that is, his wedding gifts and the presents he received for his journey into Gaul. "Do you want us to tell you in detail what she did after this and list all the benefits she bestowed upon us? Or should we, taking them altogether as she did herself, describe them in general? Should I mention how many friends of mine she assisted, and how, with the emperor, she arranged my marriage? Or perhaps you are eager to hear also the list of her gifts to me: 'Seven tripods, untouched by fire, and ten talents of gold and twenty caldrons' (*Illiad*, 9. 122–123). But I do not have time to fritter away on such details. Still, it will perhaps not be out of place to recall for you one gift which especially pleased me. She gave me books of excellent philosophers and historians and of many rhetoricians and poets, since I had brought very few of these with me, being deluded by my hopes and desires of very soon returning home; and she gave me so many of these at once that even my desires were satisfied, although they are insatiable in such matters. Consequently, in the matter of books, Gaul and the country of the Celts appeared to me to be a Greek shrine of the Muses. Since I habitually returned to these gifts whenever I had any leisure, it is impossible that I should forget their gracious donor. And even when I take the field there is something which follows me as a provision for the expedition, an account of a campaign written long ago by an eyewitness" (*Eusebia*, 123c–124b).

66. But the words of an intellectual empress such as Eusebia are one thing, and the deeds of an emperor of such a tortuous mind as Constantius are quite another. No sooner was Julian lodged at court with the authority of Caesar than he noticed that the imperial palace was in reality a poorly disguised prison and that his role of Caesar only made him subject to the direction of others.

Julian gives a description of his stay at court in which it is easy to recognize the residue of his old rancor, but despite its obvious exaggerations it is substantially true: "What a great slavery ensued, and, by Hercules, what a great and terrible fear for my life hung over me every day! Locks on the doors, guards to watch them, the hands of the servants examined for fear that one of them might bring in a note from my friends, strangers for servants! Only with difficulty did I succeed in introducing into the court four of my own domestics for my personal service, two lads of tender age, and two who were older. Only one of these knew of my attitude toward the gods, and he assisted me in secret as far as he could. I had entrusted my books to the care of a certain physician who had been permitted to leave home with me because it was not known that we were friends. He was the only one of my many loyal friends and companions at hand. And I was so alarmed and apprehensive that even though my friends wished to come and visit me I very reluctantly turned them away. For though I longed to see them, I feared to be a source of disaster to them and to myself" (*To the Athenians*, 277ac).

This important autobiographical notice requires some explanation. Of the four domestics, the one who secretly shared in Julian's idolatrous worship was Euhemerus, of whom we know only that he was a native of Libya (Eunapius, 476). The other confidant was Oribasius, about whom we have more information (*ibid.*, 498–499, etc.), and who will reappear later. It is noteworthy that for his idolatrous worship at Milan and later in Gaul, Julian surrounded himself with a secret coterie just as he had done at Athens (§ 58). The secrecy was certainly a prudential measure to elude Constantius, and it was balanced by his continued visits to Christian churches. But Julian did not perceive that in narrating such affairs he furnishes at least a partial justification for Constantius' suspicions, who was concerned not only with his political but also with his religious conduct.

67. Meanwhile, final preparations for his departure into Gaul were being made. Haste was imperative since repeated reports, one worse than the other, kept coming in. At last news came that Colonia Agrippina (Cologne), the principal city of Germania Secunda, which had been held in a tight siege by the barbarians, had been taken and destroyed. The calamity, however, was kept secret at court for fear of the harm which could arise if it were divulged.

One of the most urgent matters was a clear definition of the powers and duties of the Caesar being sent out to repair the Gallic losses, but here Constantius wavered, refusing to make any precise statement. This recalls his earlier sudden change of attitude toward Julian, whom he had received joyfully upon his arrival at Milan and then treated as a prisoner of state immediately after investing him as Caesar. To clarify his own position, particularly since the counselors assigned to him were not suitable, Julian tried to make the sphinx speak. Going up to the emperor, he grasped his right hand and knees like a suppliant and begged for written rules as to what he should do (*To the Athenians*, 282ab; cf. 20. 8. 14). But he accomplished nothing: the sphinx refused to speak.

Constantius, as a matter of fact, did have a plan, but through fear of repercussions at court he wished to reveal it gradually: Gaul should be liberated by generals chosen by himself and not through Julian's efforts. The Caesar should only wear the purple; he should not conduct any campaigns or interfere in military matters. In other words, he should play the part of a "puppet Caesar." This arrangement was clear to Julian, who realized that he had "assumed the purple only externally" (*specie tenus purpuratus* — 20. 5. 4) and that he had been sent "not so much as a commander of the garrisons as a subordinate to the generals there. For letters had been written to them and express orders given that they should watch me as carefully as the enemy lest I should attempt to start a revolt" (*To the Athenians*, 277d).

68. How could such a ridiculous state of affairs have come about? Simply through the conjunction of various opposed forces. First of all, there was the support of Eusebia which had brought about Julian's election (§ 62). Second, there was the aversion of the courtiers and generals to this election. And, finally, in addition to this aversion, there was the obvious fact which Constantius could not have failed to take into account — the utter lack of experience for leading armies and governing vast territories in this young man, who up to this time had had no other occupation than his books. Would it not be wise first to submit him to a short probation, even if it were disguised? Constantius, therefore, adopted an expedient which aimed at bringing about at least a certain amount of harmony among the various conflicting forces.

Ammianus notes in general that Constantius was too devoted to his different wives (*uxoribus . . . nimium quantum addictus* — 21. 16. 16). This observation is particularly important in Julian's case since Eusebia, his protectress, was certainly the most conspicuous of Constantius' three wives. Constantius had created Julian a Caesar to please his wife, but he was not entirely happy about the election. He had no particular liking for his cousin, and he knew that he was not liked by the courtiers and generals. He did not think that he was ready to assume such heavy responsibilities. The only solution seemed to be to reduce Julian to a puppet Caesar. With Julian as Caesar, Eusebia was satisfied; with him acting only as a puppet, the courtiers and generals were satisfied; as dependent upon them, there was no fear of his making mistakes through inexperience. Constantius, as a rule, split up power to obtain a balance of forces. This furnishes us with a further explanation of his treatment of Julian as a prisoner of state after his investiture as Caesar. It also gives a further explanation of why he was denied any real authority in Gaul and left to the mercy of high officers and officials. The suspicion of some secret plot and consequent rumor that Constantius sent Julian to Gaul to destroy him (§ 63) were bound to develop from the patently absurd position in which the new Caesar found himself.

No, there was no plot — only too much interference on the part of the imperious Eusebia (*obstinate opponebat se sola regina* — 15. 8. 3; cf. § 62), and too much yielding on the part of the uxorious Constantius.

69. The day for Julian's departure for Gaul finally arrived. It was December 1, 355. Constantius, who was an expert in saving appearances and in court protocol, as a token of respect accompanied the departing Julian to a place marked by two columns lying between Laumello (Laumellum) and Pavia (Ticinum — 5. 8. 18). Thence Julian directed his course toward Turin (Augusta Taurinorum), and there he was informed of the fall of Cologne (§ 67). It was indeed a sad beginning. Sorely stricken (*maerore perculsus*) by this unlucky portent, he was frequently heard whispering to himself that his election as Caesar "had gained him nothing but the prospect of death under more trying circumstances" (15. 8. 20). As the days passed, Julian could see ever more clearly the tragic situation in which he had been placed. Nominally, as the sole Caesar, his rank in the empire was second only to the Augustus; actually, he had a minimum of authority. In the tetrarchy as originally conceived by Diocletian, there had been two Augusti, each assisted by a Caesar — one Augustus with his Caesar for the West, a second Augustus and a second Caesar for the East. But later troubles, and especially Constantine's advent, had largely brought about the abandonment of this theoretical institution. At this particular period, Gallus had been the last Caesar in the East, and now, succeeding him in the West, was his brother Julian. Officially, then, he ruled over Britain, Gaul, and Spain, but others were the real governors.

The army of Gaul had been under the command of Ursicinus, who had decisively quelled the revolt of Silvanus (§ 54); but soon the forces were entrusted to Marcellus, the master of the cavalry. He was not a good officer, but in Constantius' eyes he had the advantage of being born in Pannonia, that is, far from his present post of command, and of being able to spy effectively on Julian. However this may have been, Ursicinus was still left at his side as an observer.

Julian describes Florentius, the prefect of the praetorium in Gaul, as a corrupt official (*To the Athenians*, 282c). On the occasion of his election Julian had asked Constantius for experienced and honest assistants, but the Augustus, as Julian observes, "at first gave me the greatest knaves, but when only one of them, the most ribald of the lot, had accepted, and that with great alacrity, and none of the others consented, he reluctantly gave me a truly outstanding man, Sallustius, who, however, because of his virtue, immediately came under his suspicion" (*To the Athenians*, 281d).

Who was the ribald character who accepted the post so readily? Perhaps it was Pentadius (§ 113), but we cannot know with certainty. Sallustius, on the other hand, is well known to us. As quaestor, he was Julian's stanch assistant (§§ 76, 105, 114), and for all his life a faithful friend.

70. To compensate for the lack of higher directives, precise rules were laid down for the new Caesar in matters of less moment. With his own hand Constantius wrote out a small book containing a list of what should be served at Caesar's table, as if the Caesar were a young student leaving home for the first time. But Julian discovered that the booklet allowed too much waste and shortened the list, restricting himself to foods that were common and cheap (16. 5. 3). Further, an exact surveillance was exercised over him in matters of finance. The general rule was that the Caesar should always be without sufficient funds. If he had large sums at his disposal he would be able to use them to gain personal favor with the soldiers for an eventual revolt against the emperor. Lest this should happen, he was watched with childish meticulousness, so much so that one day, after he had given a very small coin to a soldier so he could get a shave, he was denounced as a corrupter and an instigator of the troops by Gaudentius, a notary (*notarius*) who occasionally acted as a spy for Constantius. But the tables were eventually turned. After Julian became emperor, Gaudentius paid for this denunciation and his other crimes with his own life

(17. 9. 7; cf. 21. 7. 2; 22. 11. 1). Some relief from these oppressions was given to Julian by Ursulus, the *comes sacrarum largitionum*, or superintendent of the treasury. On his own authority he ordered his assistants throughout Gaul to give Julian whatever he requested. By a tragic irony of fate Ursulus was executed almost immediately after Julian's election as emperor, an act which caused the honest Ammianus to exclaim that, "Justice herself seems to me to have wept for the death of Ursulus, accusing the emperor of ingratitude" (*imperatorem arguens ut ingratum* — 22. 3. 7; cf. 25. 4. 19). In his journey into Gaul, Julian, by his own account, was accompanied by a detachment of three hundred and sixty troops (*To the Athenians*, 277d). Libanius reduces this number to three hundred soldiers of the very poorest type (18. 37; cf. 12. 44). Julian observed that the only thing these soldiers knew was how to pray, which seems to indicate that they were Christians (Zosimus, 3. 3). The detachment was, therefore, not a reinforcement which Julian was leading to imperiled Gaul, as might be deduced from his own words, but rather his personal escort as Caesar. These were the only troops he had under his direct command. The others in Gaul were attached, as we have seen, to Marcellus and Ursicinus and were not subject to Julian's authority.

71. The journey, contrary to every expectation, proved to be easy and even pleasant. It is probable that the detachment commanded by Julian crossed the Alps at Monginevra, but whether it was here or elsewhere, a passage over the Alps at this season, when December was already advanced, was not as a rule easy. Now, however, the air was like spring, bright with that sun which beams down upon the Alps when the sky is clear.

Shortly afterward Julian entered Vienne, capital of Gallia Viennensis, where he was received by the inhabitants with lively manifestations of joy. The streets were decorated with garlands of branches and green crowns. All acclaimed the new Caesar as one who would again lift up the region from its abject and squalid state. From various incidents that marked his arrival, they drew happy auguries. In the first place, the resplendent sun was a clear forecast of his future glory. Further, a wreath of green boughs, detaching itself from on high and falling down upon the Caesar as he passed beneath, confirmed the glorious forecast, since all were sure that the wreath had been tightly bound to its support and should not have fallen. Finally, an old blind woman, having asked who had come and learning that it was the Caesar Julian, exclaimed that he would soon restore the temples of the gods (15. 18. 22). If this last episode is substantially true and not one of the later legends, the secret with which Julian had surrounded his own convictions (§§ 58, 66) must have been violated by some associate, and the vibrant hopes of his supporters must have been diffused far indeed.

The joy of the people was certainly sincere. Many of those celebrating his arrival could easily remember the reign of Constantine, under whom, protected by the pax Romana, they had lived so long undisturbed. The first years of Constantine's successors had not been equally serene. The three and a half years of the usurper Magnentius which followed (§ 20) loosed a veritable scourge upon the land. Now, under such clear and happy auspices, this new descendant of Constantine had arrived. Who could not rejoice and see in him one who would bring back prosperity to Gaul, restore the pax Romana, and be another Constantine?

V. IN GAUL

§§ 72–74. Gaul and Rome. §§ 75–76. Julian's Task in Gaul.
§§ 77–79. First Military Actions. §§ 80–82. Campaign of
the Year 357. Marcellus and Eutherius. §§ 83–86. Barbatio.

72. Gaul had now stood for centuries under the domination, and within the orbit, of Roman civilization. But during the third century the barbarian populations settled across the Rhine beyond the boundary (*limes*) of the empire had become more effectively organized and powerful, and they were beginning to constitute a real threat to the Roman territories. In 257, the Franks and Alemanni broke through the *limes* and flooded areas as far as the Alps and the Pyrenees, sacking and destroying everything they found in those rich regions. After Emperor Gallienus had gradually driven them back across the Rhine, the Romans methodically set about fortifying the Rhine frontier; but the project had not been completed by the year 275, when the same Franks and Alemanni renewed their previous invasion on an even larger and more devastating scale. This new invasion practically transformed the stricken areas into wastelands sown with ruins. Emperor Probus thereupon intervened and, after a series of long campaigns, reconquered several scores of the cities that had been occupied by the barbarians. He was then, about the year 278, honored with the title of *Germanicus maximus*. In 285, under Diocletian, there was a revolt of the Bagaudae (cf. Ricciotti, *Martyrs*, pp. 9–10), caused largely by the desperate straits into which the peoples of the plains had fallen.

Then slowly the country began to recover its former prosperity. Maximian, who had conquered the Bagaudae, strengthened the frontier on the Rhine, taking up his own residence at Treves (Augusta Treverorum or Treveri) so that he could keep an eye on the barbarians outside, and the Gauls within, the province. But in the meantime other problems were arising. The wretched condition of the fields, which had provoked the revolt of the Bagaudae, caused in turn a falling off of the population and an extension of the large estates

Roman Gaul
and the
Rhine

MILES

0   100   200

BRITANNIA

TEUTONI

SAXONES

FRISII

FRANCI

ATTHUARII

CHAMAVI

Rhenus Fl.

Colonia Traiana
(Kellen)

BATAVI

TOXIANDRI

SALII

Mosa Fl.

Novaesium
(Neuss, Nys)

Juliacum
(Jülich)

Colonia Agrippina
(Cologne)

Bonna (Bonn)

BELGICA II   GERMANIA II

Mosa Fl.

Rigomagus
(Remagen)

Antennacum
(Andernach)

Confluentes
(Coblenz)

ARDUENNA M.

TAUNUS M.

SILVA HERCYNIA

Vingo
(Bingen)

Moguntiacum
(Mainz)

Moenus Fl.

Augusta Treverorum
(Treves)

Mosella Fl.

Borbetomagus Vangionum
(Worms)

Durocortorum Remorum
(Reims)

BELGICA I

Divodurum
(Metz)

GERMANIA I

Noviomagus Nemetum
(Spires)

Lutetia Parisiorum
(Paris)

Durocatalaunum
(Châlons-sur-Marne)

Decempagi
(Dieuze)

Saliso (Selz)

Brocomagus
(Brumath)

Argentoratum
(Strasbourg)

SILVAE (BLACK FOREST)

ALEMANNI

Danubius Fl.

Augustobona Tricasium
(Troyes)

Tabernae
(Saverne)

VOSEGUS M.

MARCIANAE SILVAE

Rhenus Fl.

Agendicum Senonum
(Sens)

SENONES

L. Venetus
(Lake Constance)

Brigantium
(Bregenz)

Autessiodurum
(Auxerre)

Sequana Fl.

Augustodunum
(Autun)

Visontio
(Besançon)

Augusta Rauracorum
(Augst)

RAETIA I

GALLIA LUGDUNENSIS

Cabillonum
(Chalons-sur-Saône)

SEQUANI

L. Lemannus
(Lake Geneva)

HELVETII

ALPES (ALPS)

AQUITANIA

Rhodanus Fl.

Augusta Praetoria
(Aosta)

GALLIA

Mediolanum
(Milan)

Lugdunum
(Lyons)

Vienna
(Vienne)

Segusio
(Susa)

Padus Fl.

Augusta Taurinorum
(Turin)

CISALPINA

Laumellum
(Laumello)

Ticinum
(Pavia)

Matrona
(Monginevra)

(*latifundi*). The poor migrated from the land, which had proved so unproductive for them, while the rich bought it up at ridiculously low prices. The general disorder and scarcity of provisions were aggravated by the presence of the military garrisons. After the forts along the *limes* had been damaged by the barbarians, the troops normally stationed there had been withdrawn farther back into Roman territory, where there was a scarcity of everything. The poorly provisioned, and worse paid, soldiers satisfied their wants by looting and sacking the territories they were supposed to be protecting.

73. Despite all this, thanks to the industry of Constantius Chlorus, conditions continued to improve. He held the Franks, the Alemanni, and the wily usurper Carausius at bay. At the same time he devoted himself to the social and economic restoration of the Roman territories. He rebuilt Autun (Augustodunum), which had been practically destroyed during the revolt of the Bagaudae, and erected in the center of the city a large hall for a school of rhetoric. This and similar structures rising elsewhere, and particularly at Treves, brought back many Gallo-Romanic students, to the great advantage of the cultural and social life of the country. A number of financial measures taken by Diocletian such as his reform of the currency and his Edict on Prices (*Edictum de pretiis*) had had little or no effect on the economic conditions in Gaul. A slow but constant improvement, however, was produced by the relative security regained for the Rhine frontier, where Constantine, successor to his father Constantius Chlorus, kept a diligent watch over the barbarians.

Together, Spain, Britain, Germany, and Gaul constituted one of the four prefectures of the Late Empire. These areas were, in turn, subdivided into dioceses and provinces, which increased in numbers with the passage of time. Ammianus Marcellinus (15. 11. 1–18), who gives a list of the Gallic provinces (Belgica, Lugdunensis, Viennensis, Aquitania, Narbonensis, etc.), also mentions with high praise their principal cities and towns.

Meanwhile, as was inevitable, the barbarians were making a peaceful penetration into the Roman territories and intermingling with the local populations. This was often due to the Romans themselves. Colonies of a mixed civil and military character were established and designated by their ethnic names of "Gentiles" and "Laeti," though other designations were also employed. The army also made use of squadrons composed entirely of barbarian auxiliaries. They were largely drawn from various tribes of Franks, such as the Atthuarii and Chamavi, stationed along the lower course of the Rhine, particularly on the right bank. At the same time these Franks were entering the civil service in ever increasing numbers, and some attained very high posts in the government.

The progress of restoration was interrupted by Magnentius' usurpation of the title of Augustus (§ 20). Because of the heavy taxes and hardships of every kind imposed upon the people during the three and one half years that he was in power, his reign had the same effect upon the country as a prolonged foreign invasion. The barbarians profited by the internal confusion created by Magnentius and later by Silvanus to penetrate the *limes* of the Rhine. Even before 354, Chonodomarius, the king of the Alemanni, had crossed the frontier, devastating the land on the opposite side of the river. This was followed by a sham truce. The next year the same Alemanni, after making an alliance with the Franks and the Saxons, renewed their activities with the intention no longer of making simple predatory raids but of carrying out a wide and stable conquest.

74. Julian has left a description of the country as it was a few months after his arrival in Gaul: "The number of towns whose walls had been destroyed was about forty-five, and this does not include citadels and minor fortifications. The barbarians were in control of the land on our side of the Rhine from its sources to the ocean. Those who were settled nearest to us were as much as three hundred stadia (about thirty-five miles) from the banks of the Rhine, and an area three times as wide had been left deserted by their raids, where the Gauls could not even pasture their cattle. Moreover, there were certain cities abandoned by their inhabitants near which the barbarians were not yet established" (*To the Athenians*, 279ab). The accuracy of this description is confirmed by contemporary writers (Libanius 18. 33–35; Ammianus 15. 8. 1; *Panegyrici Latini*, 8. 7, etc.) and by recent archaeological investigations which have laid bare the material conditions of the posts at this time.

Everything indicates that this section of the large Gallic prefecture was in a state of bankruptcy. From Augst (Augusta Rauracorum) toward the north, the Rhine had been crossed in numerous places by the barbarians. They were now settled on a strip along the left bank of the river some thirty-three miles in width and stretching to the sea. Still deeper within the earlier Roman territory was a barren and devastated area. All the cities that had been erected in Germania Prima and Germania Secunda along the left bank of the Rhine had been lost. Cologne (Colonia Agrippina) had fallen some months earlier (§ 67), and this disaster was followed by the loss of Bonn (Bonna), Coblenz (Confluentes), Mainz (Moguntiacum), Worms (Augusta Vangionum), Spires (Augusta Nemetum, or Noviomagus), Seltz (Saliso), Saverne (Tabernae), Brumath (Brocomagus), and Strasbourg (Argentoratum).

75. The task of remedying this state of bankruptcy belonged officially to Julian as Caesar, but, as we have already seen (§§ 67, 68), a higher authority had determined that he should be only a figurehead. The actual direction of affairs, particularly those of a military character, was to be in the hands of others. Further, as has been previously observed, Julian's antecedents were those of a widely read student, not of a courageous warrior or strategist versed in the arts of war. At this time he was probably little experienced in drawing a bow or fencing with a sword; and, as for strategy, although he would have been familiar with the works of the great masters of strategy and of the ancient historians, all his knowledge was theoretical, which in this particular field is something far different from actual practice.

Julian, who was a sharp critic of himself, recognized at once his own deficiencies, and he promptly set about remedying them. He began with the most rudimentary of military exercises, that is, with learning how to march in step to the sound of the soldiers' flutes. As he underwent this training, the old man in him would occasionally rebel, and he would repeat the saying: "A pack-saddle is put on an ox; it's certainly no burden for me" (*Clitellae bovi sunt impositae; plane non est nostrum onus* — 16. 5. 10). But we may well believe that these exercises did not last long and that Julian got but a smattering of them. Much more serious cares were to occupy the new Caesar.

At Vienne, where he had taken up his residence after his arrival in Gaul (§ 71), Julian found a court and administrative center of great importance. It was the chief city of the province and the surrounding dioceses, and to it flowed the business of the neighboring regions. A good military road left the city and, passing through Lyons (Lugdunum), continued toward the north, with branches for Reims (Durocortorum Remorum) and Paris (Lutetia Parisiorum) toward the north and west, and for Strasbourg (Argentoratum), Mainz (Moguntiacum), Cologne (Colonia Agrippina), and the other cities on the Rhine toward the north and east. Since the immediate disposition of the troops, now in winter quarters, depended upon Marcellus and Ursicinus (§ 69), and the ultimate direction of both military and civil affairs was reserved to Constantius, the new "puppet Caesar" at Vienne could have played only a minor role in governing the province.

76. Julian realized that he was a novice in civil administration just as he was in military matters and that he needed a practical apprenticeship. Taking advantage of the enforced leisure of winter, he set about gaining the necessary experience. Consequently, during the winter of 355–356 Julian was very active. In the words of Ammianus (16. 2. 1), he passed a "busy winter" (negotiosam hiemem). While in the morning he may have practiced marching in the open to the sound of the flutes, he must have spent the rest of the day inside discussing various problems with government officials. Here, fortunately, he had an excellent guide at his elbow in the person of Sallustius, whom we have already mentioned among the assistants assigned to him by Constantius (§ 69).

Secundus Saturninus Sallustius (or Salutius) was a man of outstanding ability. Of Gallic origin, he was nonetheless thoroughly imbued with the civilization of Rome. He was cultured, upright, faithful to duty, and much experienced in administrative affairs. Though he was a pagan, he was no persecutor of Christianity. As quaestor to the Caesar Julian, he played rather the part of a loving teacher, and in this he resembled in some measure Julian's early pedagog Mardonius (§ 9). The comparison is one which Julian himself made (To Sallustius, 241c). Sallustius knew how to enlighten and encourage his apprentice and, when the occasion arose, how to restrain and correct him. And Julian readily accepted the intervention of this new guide just as he had accepted that of Mardonius (§§ 10, 13).

At the beginning of 356, Constantius made Julian his colleague in the consulship (16. 1. 1.). This high magistracy involved him in the emperor's religious policy, since he now had to countersign the decrees of the Augustus. This must have proved on occasion to be a bitter task for Julian with his secret pagan convictions. Though Constantius was a stanch supporter of Arianism against the Catholics, he was still an implacable foe of paganism. His law of April, 356, which sanctioned the death sentence for anyone convicted of having sacrificed to, or having adored, idols, was countersigned by Julian (Cod. Theod., 16. 10. 6), probably only a few hours after he had himself performed

secret acts of pagan worship with his faithful Oribasius (§ 66). But
we have already seen that Julian believed that a lion could properly
hide under the skin of an ass at such times. Fortunately, the law was
not rigidly enforced. About this time Hilary of Poitiers (§ 122), the
great Western champion of orthodoxy against Arianism, was compelled
to go into exile. Constantius ordered this banishment at the request
of the Arians, and its executor was almost certainly Julian. But, from
a passage from Hilary himself (*II Ad Constantium Aug.*, 2), it seems
that this order was carried out with reluctance and was the source of
various troubles to the executor himself.

77. In the late spring of 356, the barbarians came out of their wooded
retreats and began to stir about. While he was still in Vienne, Julian
received from different quarters threatening notices of their activities,
and he finally learned that a powerful force had pushed as far as
Autun (Augustodunum), where the danger was most serious. The fall
of this noble and industrious city would have been an enormous loss.
True, it was protected by walls and guarded by a military force, but,
as Ammianus reports, the walls had been "weakened by the decay of
centuries" (*carie vetustatis invalidos*), and "the soldiers who made up
the garrison were sluggish from inactivity" (*torpente praesentium militum manu* — 16. 2. 1). The imminent peril brought out the discharged
veterans living in the vicinity, and they, joining up with the active
troops as best they could, resisted the onslaught. Meanwhile, Julian
gathered some troops together and set out for the imperiled city. His
arrival there on June 24 caused a rapid dispersal of the barbarians.

This initial success augured well for Julian's future military career.
Though there had been no real encounter with the enemy, he was
anxious for one. Setting out for Reims, where the strength of the army
was concentrated, he passed through the territory about Auxerre
(Autessiodurum) at the head of a detachment of *cataphracti* and
ballistarii,* taking a road that was shorter than usual, but dangerous
and exposed to ambush.

The experienced Ammianus criticizes this march as having been
risky; but Julian's audacity, strengthened perhaps by his recent success,
paid off, and he arrived safely with his detachment at Auxerre. From

---

* The *cataphracti* (or *cataphractarii*, or *clibanarii*) were cavalrymen who together
with their horses were protected by breastplates. The *ballistarii* were soldiers in
charge of the *ballistae*, machines employed in hurling large rocks. They were thus
for all practical purposes the artillerymen of antiquity.

here, after he had given a short rest to his troops, he continued on toward Troyes (Augustobona Tricasium, or Tricasae). Turning aside from some and routing others of the hostile swarms that attacked him on the way, he finally arrived at Troyes; but his coming was so un-expected that, while the barbarians who were besieging the city scat-tered far and wide, those within the city remained for a time doubtful as to whether or not they should open up the gates to him (16. 2. 7). After a short stay at Troyes, he hurried back to Reims, where he found the army with its two generals, Marcellus and Ursicinus (§ 69).

It seems that the two commanders had hitherto taken the various disasters quite calmly. Julian's arrival, however, aroused them from their lethargy. A council of war was at once held with respect to future operations. After this council, Julian appears in Ammianus' account (16. 2. 9 ff.) as the mind directing the maneuvers, the true com-mander in chief. Had there perhaps occurred a shift in the hierarchy of command so that the two generals were now working in subordina-tion to Julian? There is no documentary evidence for this hypothesis, but the future course of events leads us to believe that there was. Whether it was due to his recently acquired dignity as consul or to the personal prestige which he had acquired through his bold march from Vienne to Autun, from thence to Auxerre, to Troyes, and finally to Reims, these old generals must have come to the conclusion that the fledgling officer was not to be underestimated, and that he knew how to play his part well; and, what was even more significant, he was not only consul, but also cousin of the Augustus and the protégé of the empress.

78. What was to be the objective of the new campaign? The general staff already had a strategic plan which it had to accept and carry through since it had been approved by the emperor. The nub of the plan was to maneuver to the west of the Rhine with two armies: one was to march down the west bank of the river pushing the barbarians back toward the north or forcing them to withdraw to the opposite bank; the other was to advance from the center of Gaul and take the retreating barbarians on the flank. The plan was not very practicable because the barbarians could never be pinned down and the two armies engaged in the maneuver were too far distant from each other and without adequate communications. The plan had the further disadvan-tage of taking into account only the area of the Middle Rhine, par-ticularly that lying to the north of Metz (Divodurum) on the Moselle

River (Mosella) and Strasbourg, where the Alemanni were stationed. No military operations were envisaged for the regions north of Cologne to the sea, where Frankish tribes such as the Atthuarii and the Chamavi (§ 73) were located, even though many of these barbarians were inclined to come to terms with the Romans.

In July, 356, Constantius made a short excursion out of Raetia toward the Black Forest (*Marcianae silvae*) to begin the project of encircling the barbarians, but the maneuver was never completed. The barbarians retreated into their impenetrable hide-outs, and Constantius gave up their pursuit, especially since they indicated that they were ready to come to terms. In Gaul the matter was carried on with greater energy. The army stationed at Reims headed for Strasbourg to cooperate with Constantius' forces, but these did not appear.

During this march upon Strasbourg, Julian learned a valuable lesson. His column of troops was marching boldly and rapidly (*solito acrior miles*) beneath an overcast sky through a region that had been poorly explored. But at Dieuze (Decempagi), about halfway between Metz and Strasbourg, the barbarians unexpectedly broke out of an ambush laid on both sides of the road and cut the column in two, separating the rear guard from the two legions in front. The rear guard defended itself from the attack. The noise of the fray caused the troops which had already passed to return to the assistance of the others. In a short time the barbarians were driven off; but from that day, as Ammianus notes, Julian always made provisions against traps set along the line of march or at the crossing of streams, showing himself to be "cautious and deliberate, which is a special merit in great leaders" (*providus et cunctator, quod praecipium bonum in magnis ductoribus* — 16. 2. 11).

79. The strategy of the barbarians was, in fact, peculiar. After invading a civilized territory, they were reluctant to occupy the cities. They preferred to live on their outskirts, or, even better, in the fields. Accustomed as they were to living under the open skies or in the dense forests, they looked upon the cities as if they were cemeteries, abhorring these large groups of buildings "as if they were tombs surrounded by nets" (*ut circumdata retiis busta* — 16. 2. 12; cf. 31. 2. 4). This observation of the ancient historian probably has reference to their custom of binding the sepulchers of women who had died in childbirth with nets through fear that they would otherwise come to take away their still surviving children. At any rate, their peculiar avoidance of the abandoned towns was a great asset to Julian in his reconquest of the

region: the barbarian occupation was dangerous and destructive, but not massive and deep-rooted. To dislodge it, he only had to disperse the barbarian forces scattered in the open, without having to besiege or storm strongly fortified sites. This was true for the cities already mentioned (§ 74) located on the Rhine from Strasbourg to Mainz, all of which were controlled in this fashion by the barbarians.

Directing his course in this direction, Julian, after routing a band of barbarians that had attacked him, took possession of Brumath (Brucomagus) in the Vosges mountains. The way was thus open for him to march either east toward the Rhine or toward the north. But simply to reach the Rhine would have been useless. Since Constantius' army had not appeared in that area, the execution of the projected joint maneuver of the two armies would have been impossible. Moreover, it was getting near the time when the troops normally retired to their winter quarters.

But here Julian, either on his own initiative or because of some unknown commission from the emperor, repeated what he had done at Reims. He prolonged the campaign. He was thus able to exploit both areas open to him, that is, to approach the Rhine and to march to the north. Going east first to the Rhine, he then headed north along the left bank of the river.

The advance was relatively easy since no barricades had been set up to check the army. No resistance was offered at Coblenz, called "Confluentes" ("Confluence") in antiquity since near it the "Moselle flows into the Rhine" (amnis Mosella confunditur Rheno), nor at Remagen (Rigomagus), nor at the single tower standing near Cologne (16. 3. 1–2). Once in Cologne, Julian showed a willingness to come to terms with the Franks farther to the north, who had been terrified by his rapid advance. After the barbarians had accepted Julian's conditions, aimed primarily at keeping them at peace until the renewal of the campaign in the following year, he led his army to Troyes (Augusta Treverorum or Treveri) and from there to Sens (Agendicum Senonum), where he set up his winter quarters.

80. In the following year, 357, the military operations had to be renewed since the preceding campaign, even though it had not fared badly, had made no substantial and lasting gains. Proof of this was the fact that at the beginning of the year, when it was still winter, the barbarians were very active, showing up at different places within Gaul on predatory raids.

Julian the Apostate.
Ancient Statue in the Louvre at Paris (Alinari).

Battle Scene.
From the Arch of Constantine at Rome (Alinarr).

Mithraic Sacrifice.
Ancient Sculpture From the Vatican Museum (Alinari).

Constantius II.
Colossal Bronze Head in
the *Museo dei Conservatori*
at Rome (Alinari).

Battle Scene.
From an Ancient Sarcophagus in the
Museo Ludovisi at Rome (Alinari).

This winter, like the preceding one, proved to be very tiring for Julian. Upon his shoulders, as Ammianus observes (16. 3. 3), weighed the entire burden of both present and future operations. For the present, he had to redistribute the armed garrisons among the sites most seriously threatened. For the future, in view of the new campaign, he had to store up stocks of provisions, very few of which were to be found on the spot.

The necessary dispersal of his troops greatly reduced the forces which Julian had under his direct command at Sens. Since he had repeatedly sent detachments of troops to one area or another, it finally came about that he was even without the assistance of the *scutarii* and the *gentiles*, who made up his personal bodyguard. These were barbarian auxiliaries, the former armed with shields, the latter mounted on horseback. All this was known to the barbarians who were roaming about sacking the countryside, and who got their information from deserters and from spies within the city. The situation seemed ripe for a bold stroke: the city should be taken by storm and the Caesar and all his staff captured.

But Julian's reaction was like lightning. The gates of the city were barricaded in time, and sections of the walls which could not be trusted were immediately repaired. As the siege continued, he could be seen both day and night inspecting the walls, and he showed himself at the battlements "boiling with anger" (*ira exundante substridens* — 16. 4. 2) that the scarcity of his troops hindered him from making a sortie. After the siege had lasted for thirty days, the barbarians finally withdrew disheartened, "muttering (*mussitantes*) that their plan to blockade the city had been vain and foolish."

The barbarians had done all they could to further their own interests, but the same could not be said about Marcellus, officially the commander in chief of the army (§ 69), for the Romans.

81. Although Marcellus had been near Sens with a Roman garrison during the assault on the city, he had made no effort whatever to assist it or to rescue the Caesar shut up inside. The reason for this unheard-of conduct may easily be found in the general's attitude toward Julian's intervention at Reims (§ 77) and his subsequent march on Cologne (§ 79). The senior officer must have thought that matters for the forward young man had thus far gone too well, with his bold march to Autun, Auxerre, Troyes, Reims, and finally to Cologne. Now that he had ended up in a trap, it was so much the worse for him. Let him free himself without relying upon the commander in chief, whom he

had thus far ignored. It would be too bold to say that Marcellus' neglect was prompted by a hope of gaining favor with Constantius. With Julian's election to the consulship (§ 76) and the conferring of other subsequent favors, the emperor seems to have abandoned his project of keeping Julian as a "puppet Caesar" (§ 67). But if Marcellus actually had fostered such hopes, the action immediately taken by the emperor shows that they had no foundation. The conduct of the general had crippled the current campaign and had outraged one who was both a consul and cousin of the Augustus; and Constantius was no monarch to treat lightly the demands of office and kinship. When he learned what had happened, he deprived Marcellus of his rank and position.

Marcellus, however, did not give himself up for vanquished. Fully aware of the power of the parties at court and of the ever suspicious mentality of the emperor, he resolved to recoup his loss by preying on Constantius' distrust. He accordingly went to Milan with a well-laid plot against Julian. Having entered the court with great hue and cry (*strepens ac tumultuans*), as is usual with those who try to bolster up a poor case with a good deal of bluster, he was admitted into the imperial council (*consistorium* — 16. 7. 2). There he expounded his thesis, emphasizing his words with many gestures. He portrayed Julian as one who was craftily setting his wings for flight, and, as he spoke, he shook all over and waved his arms as if he were actually flying.* But this time the accusation, even though it was acted out, had no effect. Julian, in fact, as soon as he heard of the departure of Marcellus, had sent the eunuch Eutherius, his *praepositus cubiculi*, or grand chamberlain, to Milan to counteract the intrigues of the deposed general.

82. The portrait of this Eutherius which Ammianus (16. 7. 3–8) has drawn for us with great sympathy and fidelity is that of a man rarely found in such surroundings; but, as his eulogist observes, "among brambles roses spring up" (*inter vepres rosae nascuntur*). Scrupulously honest, anxious to be of help to everyone, and prudent (*plenusque iusti consilii*), Eutherius had earlier served in the court of Constantine, then in that of Constans, and had finally passed on to Julian's, over whom he had an unusual amount of authority, so much so, in fact, that he occasionally criticized him for a certain levity of conduct, which he attributed to his Asiatic education. Eutherius' defense of Julian on

---

* It is curious to note that in speaking of himself Julian also used the same rhetorical figure. In *Against Heraclius* (235b), he confesses that he had been "winged with great external advantages" (cf. § 13).

this particular occasion was simple. After he had obtained the audience
which he had requested, he showed that Marcellus' accusations were
false, that the general had deliberately refrained from assisting the
besieged Caesar, and that Julian solely by his own efforts had with-
stood the barbarians. He concluded by offering his own head as a
guarantee that the slandered Caesar would as long as he lived be a
faithful servant of the one who had elevated him.

In the end, Marcellus was relegated to his place of birth, Sardica
(Sofia), and thus disappeared from public life. But was this due solely
to the efforts of the excellent Eutherius? Considering the care with
which Empress Eusebia watched over Julian's affairs (§ 53 ff.), we should
not be surprised if some credit was due to her; but there is no extant
record to that effect.

We do, however, have a document, or rather two of them, which
permit us to take a peek behind the general scene. When Eutherius
came to Milan, he probably brought with him two works which
Julian had composed during the winter of 356–357. These were the
two encomia, panegyrics, or eulogies, written by Julian during his toil-
some nights (cf. § 116), one in honor of the emperor and the other
in honor of the empress. It may be that Constantius had suggested to
Julian that he might send the panegyric of himself, perhaps also hint-
ing at another for Eusebia. However this may have been, Julian could
have himself thought of sending the one for Eusebia. Such writings
were in a sense hack works, mediocre as literature, but demanded by
that artificial luster which, for a lack of true glory, had to surround
the imperial court. It was no great task for Julian to spin out these two
orations, mixing in an abundance of flattery, since this was precisely
what their recipients expected. If they were received at this time, their
effect was immediately evident. Whereas Marcellus was sent into exile
in Sardica, Julian succeeded him as commander in chief in Gaul. Undoubtedly both provisions were fair, but it would be interesting to
know the exact influence on Julian's promotion exercised by the two
panegyrics, and particularly by the one dedicated to Eusebia.

83. This change of supreme command in Gaul took place at the
beginning of spring in 357 (cf. *Letter to the Athenians*, 278d). Ursicinus, Marcellus' assistant (§ 69), also left Gaul for a new post on the
Persian frontier, taking with him the historian Ammianus Marcellinus,
who from this time on ceases to be a witness of Julian's deeds in the
West (16. 10. 21). As second in command to Julian, Constantius sent

Severus, the master of the horse, whom Ammianus describes as brave and experienced (*bellorum usu et maturitate firmato*). With these changes, the situation in Gaul began to clarify and take definite shape. But not even then did Constantius completely renounce his usual technique of setting one commander against another. In the plan for the coming campaign, he introduced another actor as an antagonist to Julian. This was Barbatio. The Augustus was obviously not disposed to put all his trust in Julian if, after placing him in charge of the army, he chained his feet with this unprincipled character.

Barbatio, who had been the count commander of Gallus' household guard, had played a cruel and important role in the murder of Julian's brother (§ 49), and he was certainly more suited for devising court intrigues than for leading an army. Still to him, as master of the infantry, Constantius entrusted the second army which was to act outside of Gaul in consort with Julian's army within the province. For the coming campaign the same strategic plan as that of the preceding year was adopted (§ 78), namely, to use the two armies in a pincers' movement to encircle the barbarians. The separate forces were to move simultaneously, Julian's coming from the west, and Barbatio's from the southeast.

After the operation had begun, Barbatio advanced through Raetia as far as Augst (Augusta Rauracorum) with an army of twenty-five thousand men. From there he should have continued his course, crossing the Rhine and pushing north. Instead, he carried through neither of these two maneuvers, either because of the resistance of the barbarians, which must have been most persistent, or because of his own negligence, which was no less perverse.

84. At this juncture an unforeseen peril loomed up. A flood of barbarians belonging to the tribe of the Laeti poured out of the Black Forest and drove a wedge between the two armies. With the force of an avalanche they reached the walls of Lyons (Lugdunum). The gates of the city were barricaded just in time, so the barbarians scattered through the fields in search of plunder. When news of this disaster reached Julian, who was with his army in the area of the Vosges mountains, he moved swiftly to take the looters on the flank and recover the booty. For this purpose he sent three contingents of cavalry toward the south to shut off the roads leading from the Vosges and Jura mountains to the Rhine. In this area the operation was a complete success. The plunderers were killed and the booty recovered in its entirety. Other

squadrons of cavalry commanded by the tribune Bainobaudes and Valentinian, the future emperor, pushed farther south until they almost reached the line held by Barbatio. They had foreseen that other raiders would attempt to cross the Rhine at this point. But here the barbarians managed to escape, thanks to the protection of Barbatio, who ordered Julian's cavalry to withdraw. The pretext for the order could have been that the Caesar had no right to interfere in the territory assigned to another, but the actual motive was Barbatio's desire to let Julian know that he was a chain tied to his feet. Certainly many of his supporters at court, who were also adversaries of Julian, expected Barbatio to act in this manner.

At the end of May, Constantius had to leave Rome in haste, where he had gone together with Eusebia and Helena (§ 55). He betook himself to Sirmium, where the threat of the barbarians on the Danubian frontier was serious. But he still kept at a distance from the actual danger, being much more concerned about favoring the Arians than about defending the empire from the barbarians. Barbatio thus felt that he was free to deal with Julian as he wished, not bothering in the least to take part in the pincers' movement against the barbarians in Gaul. Still he sent to Constantius a report on his repulsion of Julian's cavalry. This "cowardly and persistent detractor of Julian's reputation" (ignavus et gloriarum Juliani pervicax obtrectator — 16. 11. 7) stated that Julian's officers had come to corrupt the soldiers under his command.

85. Despite his colleague's hostility, Julian continued the operation on his own. He first set about suppressing the barbarian bands that were active to the east of Vosges. They had defended themselves by barricading the already difficult mountain roads with enormous trees which they felled across them and by taking shelter on the small islands of the Rhine in this area. To reach them, Julian needed boats. He had none of his own, but Barbatio did. He asked for seven of these, but Barbatio, in answer to the request, burned all he had. Meanwhile, the barbarians on the islands watched this contest between the two commanders, a delightful spectacle to their eyes, heaping clamorous insult upon the Romans, and particularly upon Julian. But he refused to give up. Having learned from some prisoners that the river at this season could be forded at various points, he sent bands of auxiliaries under the command of the tribune Bainobaudes (§ 84) to attempt a passage, making use of anything that floated. The first echelon of auxiliaries

succeeded in reaching the nearest island. They slaughtered the men, women, and animals; then, finding the hollowed tree trunks used by the barbarians for boats, they manned these and continued their hunt on the other islands. At the end of the expedition the Romans returned safe and loaded down with booty. The barbarians on the islands that had not been assailed, seeing that they were no longer safe, crossed with their possessions to the right bank of the Rhine.

Barbatio continued his harrying tactics. He stopped a column carrying provisions to Julian, took what he wanted, and burned the rest. But Julian was already getting provisions from another source. Since the routed barbarians had left their crops intact, and these were now ripe, he sent his soldiers out to reap them. He was thus able to restock his army for some time and lay up stores of food for the fortresses.

The soldiers, as was to be expected, attentively followed the contest between the two leaders, but were unable to fathom the secret motives behind it. When they saw Barbatio burning heaps of provisions which had been brought from afar with great effort, they wondered if he were crazy or simply carrying out the orders of the emperor. As for this second alternative, Ammianus adds with a touch of malice, "up to the present time no answer has been given" (usque in id temporis latuit — 16. 11. 12). But this did not prevent the legionaries from drawing their own conclusion, which was crude enough: the Caesar, inexperienced in military matters, had not really been sent to repair the damages wrought by the barbarians in Gaul, but rather to meet a tragic end on the field of battle.

Despite these internal and external difficulties, Julian carried to completion a project strategically important for the future. At Saverne (Tabernae), to the northwest of Strasbourg on the edge of the Vosges mountains, had formerly stood a Roman fortress of great strategic import for the control of the area. It had since been dismantled by the barbarians. Julian, convinced of its importance, quickly rebuilt the fortress and then stocked it with provisions sufficient to last the garrison a year.

86. One day Barbatio remembered that Julian was not his sole adversary. Since he had also to take some measures against the barbarians, he planned to cross the river by himself and establish his army on the left bank of the Rhine. According to Libanius, this was consequent to an order which he had received from Constantius. The Augustus and his courtiers were eagerly waiting to hear Barbatio's report of a great

victory obtained without the help of Julian. As a matter of fact, there was a great victory, but for the barbarians and not Barbatio.

As described by Libanius (18. 50 ff.), Barbatio began by stringing together a bridge of boats for the passage of the river; but when everything was ready, the barbarians, who had been watching the operation from a distance, shoved a huge number of giant tree trunks into the stream. The logs carried down by the strong current smashed against the boats and sank them. The ties connecting the boats were broken, and the whole bridge ended up in the water. With the collapse of the bridge, Barbatio's military schemes collapsed as well. He concluded that it was better to put everything off until the campaign of the following year and led his troops into winter quarters. This had the further advantage of leaving Julian and his army, which numbered scarcely half that of Barbatio, to face the barbarians alone. He could now perhaps suffer that solemn catastrophe which his well-wishers at court, no less than Barbatio, so eagerly anticipated.

Perhaps the general was already beginning to console himself for the loss of the bridge with such reflections as these when a horde of barbarians, "outstripping by their great speed any rumor of their coming" (16. 11. 14), hurled itself upon the rear guard of the army, routed it, and then pursued the fugitives to Augst and even beyond. Loaded with booty taken from the Romans, the barbarians returned to their own land. Barbatio, on the other hand, "distributed his soldiers in their winter quarters as if he had made a successful campaign" (although it was still summer); and, as Ammianus shrewdly concludes, "he returned to the emperor's court to draw up an accusation against Caesar, as was his custom." This was, in fact, his real field of battle, and one from which he usually returned victorious.

VI. THE BATTLE OF STRASBOURG

§§ 87–89. Events Leading up to the Battle. §§ 90–95. The Battle. §§ 96–98. The Pacification of the Regions Along the Rhine.

87. Barbatio's shameful and disastrous retreat had widespread repercussions among the various barbarian tribes, where it was considered as an auspicious beginning of greater troubles for the rapacious Roman intruders. The hour had finally come to drive out those who claimed to bring peace, but who in reality created only a desert, as had been observed more than two and a half centuries before: *ubi solitudinem faciunt, pacem appellant* (Tacitus, Agricola, 30). On both the left and right banks of the Rhine the civilization of Odin should now replace that of Rome.

There was need, however, of acting in concert. Seven chiefs of the Alemanni, whom Ammianus calls "kings," but who in reality were only chieftains, or ethnarchs, of various tribes or clans, accordingly assembled near Strasbourg. These were Chonodomarius, Vestralpus, Urius, Ursicinus, Serapion, Suomarius, and Hortarius. The most influential of these was Chonodomarius, a worthy adversary of the Romans, having conquered the Caesar Decentius, brother of Magnentius (§ 20), and just recently Barbatio. He was the absolute ruler of the Alemanni, and the other chieftains were guided by his decisions. Immediately after him came his nephew Serapion. According to Ammianus, these two "possessed more authority than the other kings" (*potestate excelsiores ante alios reges* — 16. 12. 23). He then describes them separately as they appeared in their subsequent battle with the Roman forces: "Chonodomarius, who was, in fact, the evil instigator of the whole disturbance, rode before the left wing with a flaming red plume fixed in his helmet. He was a bold man who relied on the great strength of his arms, a towering figure wherever the heat of battle was anticipated; sitting erect on his foaming steed, he towered over the others, holding in his hand a javelin of terrible size; conspicuous in his gleaming armor, he was a more energetic soldier and skilled leader than any of the others. The right wing was led by Serapion, who was still a youth with down on his cheeks, but whose ability outstripped his age. He was the son of Mederichus, the brother of Chonodomarius, a man of utmost treachery as long as he lived. He was so named because his father, who had been held as a hostage for a long time in Gaul and had been initiated into certain Greek mysteries, had changed the name of his son, which in his native tongue had been Agenarichus, to Serapion."

Immediately after this account of the commander in chief, Ammianus describes the major staff and the army of the barbarians: "These were followed by the kings next in power, five in number, and then by ten princes and a long series of nobles, and thirty-five thousand armed troops of various tribes serving partly for pay and partly under the terms of a reciprocal alliance."

88. On the eve of the conflict Julian's chances for success did not seem favorable. Abandoned by Barbatio, he could count only on his own troops, which totaled in all about thirteen thousand men (16. 12. 2), that is, less than half of the thirty-five thousand barbarians mentioned above by Ammianus. But the disparity in numbers was largely compensated for by the courage and equipment of the Roman legions. Even the auxiliaries incorporated into the Roman troops, such as the Batavi, Aeruli, Petulantes, Gauls, were brave and well trained. Nevertheless, recent events, especially the defeat of Barbatio, must have had a baneful influence on the army's morale, and there must also have been some discontent among the soldiers from the exhausting labors entailed in fortifying and supplying their positions. There was, moreover, the anxiety caused by the uncertainty of the future. If the imminent conflict with the barbarians, who were already massing their forces along the Rhine, turned out badly, there would not only be the loss of a battle but also the immediate collapse of Roman rule in those areas. All the tribes scattered from the Alps down to the sea and from the Rhine to the east as far as the Hercynian Forest would pour out of their hiding places, rushing down in a flood upon the Roman territories.

The matters that worried Julian, on the contrary, were a source of encouragement to the barbarians, who received accurate information on whatever happened in the Roman sector. Finally a deserter, a Roman *scutarius* who had passed over to the enemy to avoid punishment he deserved, furnished the barbarian chieftains with information about the status of the Roman troops and their relative positions in battle. Weighing all these factors, the barbarians were confident of victory.

But they first made an essay of diplomacy, of which they had had some experience with the Romans. Sending a number of envoys to Julian, they ordered him to withdraw from the left bank of the Rhine. To prove the justice of their demands, they produced letters from Constantius in which the emperor recognized their control over the region (Libanius, 18. 52; cf. Socrates, 3. 1; Sozomen, 5. 2). These were letters written by Constantius to obtain help from the barbarians at the time of Magnentius' revolt (§ 20). Julian was fully aware of this aspect of Constantius' policy, blaming him on a subsequent occasion for being "too ready to conciliate the barbarians" (*To the Athenians*, 280b; cf. 286a). Thus it seems that he did not doubt the authenticity of the letters but rather looked upon them as being no longer in force. However this may be, he took no account of them. "Laughing at the presumption of the barbarians" (*fastus barbaricos ridens*), as his only response he kept their envoys under guard while he continued his work on the fortifications, and did not free them until after his victory (16. 12. 3; cf. 17. 1. 1). Having failed in their diplomatic endeavors, the barbarians completed the mustering of their troops on the right bank of the Rhine and began to cross the river.

89. Julian watched until the enemy had arrived in large numbers on the left bank so that he might engage them in a decisive battle and at the same time catch them with the river at their backs and with no easy means of escape. It was the height of summer in the second half of August, when the crops waving in the fields were ripening (16. 12. 19). One morning, when the sun was already high, Julian marched with his army from Saverne in the direction of Strasbourg. The infantry advanced slowly. Its flanks were protected by squadrons of cavalry, among whom were the *cataphracti* and the *sagittarii* (§ 83, note), described by Ammianus as a "formidable branch of the service" (*formidabile genus armorum* — 16. 12. 7). The army marched along the heights flanking the roads and occupied prominent positions since the whole region was under the eye of the enemy spies and at every step they could encounter ambuscades. The distance between the place of the Romans' departure and the barricades of the barbarians was estimated by Ammianus (16. 12. 8) as "fourteen leagues, that is, about twenty-one miles."

For some hours the march continued without incident. About mid-day Julian called a halt and assembled the army for an exhortation. A summary of the harangue has been preserved by Ammianus (16. 12. 9-12), who used Julian's own commentaries as a source for the speech which he drew up according to the canons of classical historiography. In the discourse, Julian does not aim at arousing but rather at checking the enthusiasm of his soldiers. He draws their attention to the fact that the day is somewhat advanced. All are weary from the march and are beginning to feel the heat of the day. Moreover, they are advancing along difficult and treacherous paths against an enemy that is rested and well fed. In such conditions would it not perhaps be better for the soldiers to check their eagerness for battle and pass the night in the shelter of a camp so that they might engage the enemy the following day rested and refreshed?

But even before Julian finished speaking, the soldiers gave vent to their impatience, showing their determination to attack at once by beating their spears against their shields (§ 64). Florentius (§ 69), the prefect of the praetorium, supported the demands of the soldiers by pointing out that the barbarians could disperse and make their escape, and that the enthusiasm of the soldiers for the fray might change into a rebellion if they decided that the Caesar wished to deprive them of a certain victory. Julian yielded to these arguments, or pretended to yield to them, if he had not himself deliberately provoked this manifestation, and ordered the army to take up the march again.

90. But almost immediately a new incident occurred which seemed to corroborate the fears of the commander in chief. Ammianus describes it as follows: "The army moved forward and approached a gently sloping hill covered with grain already ripe not far from the banks of the Rhine. From its top, three mounted scouts of the enemy galloped off and hastened to their own troops to announce the approach of the Roman army. But one enemy foot soldier unable to keep up with them was captured through the alertness of our men. He declared that the Germans had been crossing the river for three days and three nights" (16. 12. 19). The news was not encouraging since the Romans had not foreseen that such a numerous passage would have already been effected. But it was too late to change their plan. Since they could no longer take the enemy by surprise, they had to set to work at once. When they saw the enemy masses advancing, the Romans drew up their ranks and took their position "in a solid line, like an impreg-

The Battle of Strasbourg

MUNDOLSHEIM

Aqueduct

Ill R.

Rhine R.

OBERHAUSBERGEN

← SAVERNE

ROMAN BATTLE LINE
1. Severus
2. Julian
3. Reserves

BARBARIAN BATTLE LINE
4. Chonodomarius
5. Serapion

STRASBOURG

Rhine R.

nable wall" (*velut insolubili muro fundatis*), and waited for the signal for combat.

For the course of the battle, the account given by Ammianus, which depends on Julian's commentaries, must be compared with, and supplemented by, that of Libanius (18. 55 ff.), who used these same, and perhaps other sources. Archaeologists of the area have identified with some degree of certitude the site of the battle. It would be a little north of Strasbourg on a rise in the ground, with Mundolsheim to the north, Oberhausbergen to the southwest, and the stream Ill to the east. At the foot of the elevation extended a little valley almost hidden to sight, and a little farther to the left an aqueduct ran through a depression in the ground containing dense swampy vegetation. Traces of this aqueduct seem to have been found.

When the trumpets sounded, the Romans issued from behind the rise in the ground and moved toward the enemy in the following formation. The main force of the cavalry composed the right wing. Julian was in command at the center with the infantry and a part of the armed cavalry (*cataphracti*). Severus (§ 83), with more infantrymen, was in charge of the left wing. A strong battalion of infantry was placed in formation behind the first line, ready to intervene wherever it was needed. This Roman alignment had been communicated to the barbarians by the Roman deserter (§ 88), so they logically drew up their own line to oppose it. On their left wing, which was commanded by Chonodomarius himself, they concentrated their cavalry, reinforced by bands of infantrymen. Fixed bands of infantrymen arranged so as to form a wedge with the point turned toward the Romans were placed in the center. The right wing of the barbarians commanded by Serapion could not be seen since it was hiding in ambush in the swampy vegetation of the depression crossed by the aqueduct.

91. The first contact between the two armies was made by the archers. From both sides clouds of arrows and javelins were released. Severus, in the meantime, was advancing with the left wing toward the hidden enemy. He reached the edge of the depression but then, suspecting an ambush, halted.

This delay was harmful since it disrupted the order of the advance. Julian, protected by two hundred cavalrymen of his personal escort, came up. Passing through the ranks, he "flew past the missiles of the enemy" (*hostium tela praetervolans* — 16. 12. 29), directing brief but burning exhortations to his men. Reanimated they began the advance again.

In the meantime, trouble broke out in the ranks of the enemy. Alemanni infantrymen stirred up a noisy protest, urging their leaders to descend from their horses and fight on foot on equal terms with the infantry. The reason for this demand was their fear that if events should turn out badly the horsemen would gallop off, abandoning the infantry to its fate. This democratic, but unmilitary, imposition was accepted by Chonodomarius and the rest of the leaders. They immediately acquiesced "since none of them doubted that theirs would be the victory" (16. 12. 35). The battle was then engaged. No better description of it can be given than that preserved in Ammianus:

"Missiles were hurled for a time, and then, running forward with more haste than discretion and wielding their weapons in their right hands, the Germans flew at our bands of cavalry; and as they hideously gnashed their teeth and raged even more than usual, their flowing locks made a terrible sight, and a kind of madness flashed from their eyes. Our soldiers resolutely protected their heads by putting up their shields, and with sword thrusts or the hurling of javelins terrified their adversaries with the threat of death. At the very climax of the battle, when the cavalry had massed themselves in a strong position, and the infantry were stoutly protecting their flanks by making a barrier with their shields joined fast together, thick clouds of dust arose. Then there were various maneuvers as our men alternately fought back or gave ground, and some of the most skillful barbarian warriors tried to force their enemy back by pressing with their knees. But with great determination they came to hand-to-hand fighting, shield-boss pushed against shield-boss, and the sky re-echoed with the shouts of the victors and the falling" (16. 12. 36–37).

92. At this point the conflict was still fluid. The left wing under the command of Severus continued to advance, but the Roman horses on the right, under the weight of the entire barbarian cavalry, unexpectedly broke rank and fled (*praeter spem incondite discesserunt*). But when they found shelter "in the bosom of the legions" (*gremio legionum*) they wheeled about and renewed the battle.

As they were re-forming their line they were again unnerved at seeing their commander slightly wounded and another of their company slip over the neck of his horse that had fallen under the weight of its armor. They would have trampled on the infantrymen had these not been drawn up in such a tight array that it was impossible to break through their ranks. When Julian perceived that the cavalry was looking solely for safety in flight, he dashed up on his horse and checked them. One of the fleeing tribunes, recognizing the standard of his personal escort, a purple dragon fixed to the top of a long lance, was struck with fear and rode back to the battle. With a mild rebuke, Julian then succeeded in turning back the others.

The attack on the center continued with the utmost violence. After routing the Roman cavalry, the Alemanni had turned toward the infantry. For a long time the battle raged on equal terms (*pugnabatur paribus diu momentis*). To help the burdened line, Julian ordered the troops which he had wisely left in reserve to advance from the sides. The courageous auxiliaries, the Cornuti and the Bracchiati, who had proved their mettle in many other battles (*usu praeliorum diuturno firmati*), had the custom, probably borrowed from the Germans, of launching the *barritus*, or battle cry. According to Ammianus, this was "a shout produced at the height of the combat, beginning with a low murmur which gradually increases like waves dashing upon the cliffs" (16. 12. 43). The cry was launched; the conflict thickened; missiles were hurled in every direction; dust clouded the vision; weapons slashed blindly at weapons; and bodies crashed against bodies. To strengthen their position and, at the same time, to keep themselves separated from the enemy, the Romans adopted the *testudo*, joining their shields together in a barrier resembling the shell of a tortoise. The barbarians, thrown into confusion by their own violence and anger, flamed up like fire (*in modum exersere flammarum*) and hurled themselves at the *testudo*, endeavoring to break it up with repeated strokes of their swords. Thereupon the Batavi and Regii, "a formidable band" (*formidabilis manus*), came up to reinforce the Romans. Darts, javelins, and iron-tipped reeds were hurled. Breastplates were pierced with swords, but the two sides still seemed to be equally matched. The Alemanni had the advantage of height and strength; the Romans were obedient from long experience. The former were "savage and undisciplined"; the latter "calm and cautious." The Romans "relied upon their courage"; the Germans "placed their confidence in their great size." In the end, the balance was broken, and Roman discipline prevailed over the reckless fury of the barbarians.

93. A final effort was made by a courageous band of noble barbarians. With a sudden attack they succeeded in breaking through the first line of the Roman legions. But then they found themselves confronted by the legion of the Primani, who, still intact, "stood their ground fast and firm like towers." The clash of the two forces reminded Ammianus of the gladiatorial contests between the *murmillones* and the *retiarii*, in which the former, protected by a shield and helmet, riddled their adversaries with wounds as these latter tried to entangle them in their nets. The dead and wounded piled up in front of the legionaries. Finally, worn out and broken by their calamities (*fessi tot aerumnis*), the barbarians turned and fled, pursued by the Romans, who seized the javelins of their adversaries and thrust with them when their own swords were bent or lost.

It was a total collapse, and all that could, fled toward the Rhine. When they reached its bank some attempted to swim across it; others entrusted themselves to their reed shields or other objects that chanced to be floating by. When Julian ordered the Romans to refrain from pursuing their foe into the water, they halted on the bank and hurled darts at the fugitives. As Ammianus observes (16. 12. 57), it was like being present at a spectacle in the theater, since the Romans, who now had nothing to fear (*iam sine metu*), could see the terrible plight of their enemies.

The commander in chief, Chonodomarius, who is not mentioned during the whole of the battle, reappears at the end after his forces had been defeated. Cautiously withdrawing from the heaps of cadavers and followed by his numerous attendants, he fled toward the river where he had wisely stationed boats for just such a contingency. With equal prudence he wound up his face with a rag so as not to be recognized. But as he approached the river, his horse slipped on the muddy slope. The chieftain, although stout, got up at once, and fled to a neighboring knoll. The Romans who were standing along the bank recognized him, and a tribune with his cohort set out in pursuit. When they surrounded the wooded height to which he had fled, he surrendered of his own accord. Three of his closest friends and two hundred attendants did likewise. His old arrogance, once he was captured, vanished abruptly. Surrendering to others, he was pale, stammering, far different from the *miles gloriosus* of a few hours before. And in this, Ammianus observes, he acted like a typical barbarian — "humble in adversity and haughty in prosperity" (16. 12. 61). A little later he was haled before his conqueror. In the Caesar's presence he first bowed down and then prostrated himself upon the earth, asking for forgiveness. Julian treated him kindly and told him to take heart (*bono animo esse est iussus* — 16. 72. 66), and on this moderation the conqueror rightly prided himself (*To the Athenians*, 279c).

Chonodomarius nevertheless met a sad end. Out of deference he was sent by Julian to the Augustus. His life was spared by Constantius, who sent him to Rome where he remained a prisoner of honor in the *castra peregrinorum*, situated between the Caelian and the Palatine hills. There perhaps St. Paul had earlier been kept in custody when he was sent in chains to Rome. From his confinement the unfortunate prisoner could have had a view of the Colosseum and the Arch of Constantine. Pining there in the squalor of his prison for the shady Germanic forests, he died of consumption (*morbo veterni consumptus est* — 16. 12. 66).

94. In the battle, which lasted a long summer's afternoon, two hundred and forty-three Roman soldiers and four officers were killed, among whom were Bainobaudes, a tribune of the Cornuti (§§ 83, 85), and

Innocentius, a tribune of the armed cavalry (*cataphracti*). The losses of the barbarians were ascertained at six thousand dead on the field of battle, but no estimate could be made of those who drowned in the river. "Incalculable heaps of dead," Ammianus reports (16. 12. 63), "were carried off by the waves of the river." Libanius (18. 60), who fixes the number of enemy dead at eight thousand, agrees substantially with Ammianus. Zosimus (3. 3), who enumerates sixty thousand killed and as many more put to flight, certainly reflects popular exaggerations.

After the victory, the soldiers, vibrant with enthusiasm, saluted the conqueror as Augustus. But Julian resolutely rejected these acclamations and reproached the soldiers for their rashness (*agentes petulantius*), swearing that he had no hopes and no ambitions for so great an honor. The report may be true, and Ammianus perhaps records it to prepare his readers for Julian's actual proclamation as Augustus at a somewhat later date. Such an elevation was not likely at this time. In comparison with Constantius' authority, Julian's was still too weak and too contemned by the courtiers to hope for so much. Moreover, acclamations of this type were frequently no more than popular manifestations of enthusiasm. During the siege of Jerusalem in the year 70, for example, the Roman legions proclaimed Titus as emperor (Josephus, *Jewish War*, 6. 6. 1; cf. Suetonius, *Titus*, 5), even though the reigning emperor was his father Vespasian.

What effect did the news of this victory have at court? In the first place the success was attributed to Constantius, but too much insistence should not be placed on this since it was then the custom, as it had been before, to accredit the emperor with every successful military action (cf. *To the Athenians*, 279c).

The fact was, however, that it was Julian who had effectively conquered the enemy and freed Gaul from imminent danger. Since this could not be denied, the courtiers devoted themselves to blackening his character with calumny and facetious irony. The true conqueror, the *victor*, had been the emperor. Julian was only *Victorinus*. In his reports to the court this miserable dwarf trumpeted aloud high-sounding victories, but he was really only working for his own glory and to further his own ambitions. His victories were far from definitive, and his part in them was insignificant. As time passed and Julian's successes brought him increased fame, the sarcasm of his enemies at court grew in scope and bitterness: "This nanny-goat and no man [a reference to his shaggy, unkempt appearance] is becoming obnoxious with his victories" (*in odium venit cum victoriis suis capella, non homo*). He was a "talkative mole," "an ape dressed in purple," "a Greekish pedant," and "of a lazy, timid, shady character, tricking out his actions with fine words" (cf. 16. 12. 67–68; 17. 11. 1).

95. Julian's achievements hung like a cloud over Constantius, and both he and his courtiers, past masters in the art of flattery (*adulandi professores iam docti*), did their best, as Ammianus observes, to dispel it: "There are declarations filed away in the public records of this emperor in which he vainly boasts and exalts himself to the skies. When this battle was fought near Strasbourg, he was distant a forty days' march. Nevertheless in his description of the engagement he falsely asserts that he arranged the order of battle, stood among the standard-bearers, and drove the barbarians headlong. He also states that Chonodomarius was brought to him, but with rank ingratitude he says nothing about Julian's glorious deeds, which he would have buried in oblivion, except that fame was unable to be silent about his great accomplishments, even though many people would have obscured them" (16. 12. 70).

Obviously, the split between the two cousins was growing wider and deeper. All that was needed was a minor crisis for it to become complete and irreparable.

96. With the victory of Strasbourg, the campaign of the year 367 could be considered ended, since autumn was approaching and communications again were becoming difficult. But Julian was not entirely satisfied with the excellent results already obtained; he wished to consolidate them before withdrawing into winter quarters. The left bank of the Rhine in the area of Strasbourg was indeed tranquil, but it was so much tinder that could easily be kindled by sparks coming from the opposite side of the river. It was therefore necessary to continue operations beyond the Rhine to protect even its nearer side. With this end in view Julian prolonged his military campaign.

Before leaving the area about Strasbourg, he buried all the dead and set at liberty the barbarian envoys who had come to deal with him before the battle (§ 88). He then withdrew to Saverne (Tabernae). Here the soldiers expected to take their winter's rest; but instead, after sending the prisoners and the booty to Metz (Divodurum), Julian ordered them to set out on the march for Mainz (Moguntiacum). The soldiers grew angry at the command, protesting and grumbling like Napoleon's "grumblers" (*grognards*) of later days; but Julian, with his winning eloquence (*facundia iucunditateque sermonum*) and, in particular, by his own example, since he never asked his soldiers to perform a task he would not himself undertake, persuaded them to set out (17. 1. 1–2).

After reaching Mainz, they crossed the Rhine on a pontoon bridge. The barbarians, who believed themselves to be safe from attack on the other side of the river, were terrified and sent envoys to conclude a treaty. But then they changed their minds and threatened to clear the land of the Romans with a war of extermination. As his only answer, Julian, in the early hours of the night, sent eight thousand soldiers in swift boats twenty stadia (about two and one third miles) up the Rhine to put to fire and sword everything that they found. At the break of dawn Julian advanced with his legions toward the hills farther on, where the barbarians had assembled in large numbers. But when the legionaries reached the heights, they found no trace of the enemy. Instead, they saw great columns of smoke in the distance rising up from the places seized by the soldiers from the boats. And it was these same columns of smoke that had caused the disappearances of the barbarians from the hills. Seeing their villages on fire, "they abandoned the ambuscades which they had prepared for our forces in narrow, hidden places and fled across the river Main [the Moenus, which here emptied into the Rhine] to assist their relatives and friends" (17. 1. 6). The Roman cavalry was then brought in and a methodic advance was executed into a region which was not only rich in animals and agricultural products, but also furnished with "homes . . . carefully constructed in the Roman manner" (*domicilia . . . curatius ritu Romano constructa*), which shows that even the barbarians had begun to esteem and imitate the civilization of their foes. After the Romans had freed all of their captured countrymen, they destroyed everything they could.

97. They advanced ten more miles, but then the scene changed. Ammianus states that "they came to a forest fearful for its forbidding shade" (17. 1. 8; cf. § 8) where, according to information obtained from a barbarian deserter, "there were many of the enemy concealed in secret tunnels and wide-branching trenches, ready to rush forth at a favorable moment." That the deserter gave such information may well be, but it must have been deliberately exaggerated to terrify the Romans. The description which Ammianus gives of this area smacks of that legendary halo which as far back as the time of Julius Caesar

had been formed about the Hercynian Forest much farther to the east, though its name had been extended to other regions across the Rhine. This particular forest must have been located on the slopes of Mt. Taunus, a woody height a little to the north of Mainz, known today as Höhe.

Despite the disconcerting information furnished by the deserter, the Romans, following Julian's example, began to advance through the tangled undergrowth. But they soon found the paths barred by felled holm oaks, ash, and enormous firs. Moreover, the difficulties were greatly increased by cold. It was the end of autumn, and a heavy snow had fallen. But even in the face of such conditions, before retiring, Julian pushed on to a little fort on the Neckar River. This bastion, which was located on the site of the modern city of Ladenburg, had been constructed three centuries before by Trajan, but it was now in ruins. Julian repaired and reinforced it, and stocked it with provisions. This assertion of authority impressed the barbarians, who, having learned their lesson from their recent experiences, considered it more prudent to come to terms with such an energetic leader than to provoke him. A number of barbarian envoys appeared humbly petitioning for a treaty. A ten months' truce necessary to build up the fort's defenses was agreed upon. Three kings of the Alemanni were then sent to officially conclude the peace. This was granted on the condition that they leave the fort untouched and restock it with provisions whenever necessary. The treaty was confirmed by the oaths of the three kings according to their own rites and ceremonies, and it was subsequently maintained to the letter, "fear holding their treachery in check" (metu perfidiam frenante — 17. 1. 13).

98. When the reports of Julian's new successes arrived at court, they found his adversaries still in their old frame of mind. The facts could not be denied, but they were subjected to hostile interpretations. Why did the Caesar attempt such grave and perilous undertakings in Gaul? His detractors found an answer: "Because he preferred to die fighting gloriously rather than to be slain as he expected like a condemned criminal, as was his brother Gallus" (17. 1. 14). This contention of the courtiers should be compared with the somewhat similar judgment attributed to Constantius (§ 63), and with the one which Julian had had about his own fate when he departed for Gaul (§ 69).

The time finally came to withdraw into winter quarters. But instead, another incident occurred. The army, whose advance guard was commanded by Severus, set out on the road passing through Cologne and Jülich (Juliacum) on its way to Reims and Paris. But, near the Meuse it ran into bands of Frankish looters plundering Germania Secunda. Taken by surprise, the barbarians shut themselves up in two small forts on the banks of the river. Ammianus says there were six hundred of them; Libanius says a thousand. Julian had his legionaries surround the two forts, but he did not dare an all-out attack because of the difficult terrain. There was nothing else to do but to prolong the siege until the men surrendered from famine. A cold December came on, and the Meuse began to freeze over, offering a means of escape to the barbarians. To remove this possibility, Julian had his soldiers row up and down the stream from dawn to dusk in the small vessels which the Romans maintained on the rivers marking the boundaries of the empire. In this way they broke up the ice as it began to form and prevented the barbarians from taking advantage of a few moonless nights to make their escape. The besieged held out for a good fifty-four days with "unbelievable tenacity" (*incredibili pertinacia*), and only surrendered in January "when worn out by hunger, sleeplessness, and extreme desperation" (*inedia et vigiliis et desperatione postrema lassati* — 17. 2. 3). They were sent to Constantius, who treated them well and enrolled them as able auxiliaries among his troops.

The surrender occurred in the nick of time for Julian, since a large number of Franks were already on the road, coming to the assistance of the besieged. When they learned that it was all over, they made no further effort (*nihil amplius ausa*) and turned back. After he had distributed his troops in their various quarters, Julian withdrew to Paris, there to pass the rest of the winter.

VII. IN THE NORTH OF GAUL

§§ 99–100. The Campaign Against the Salii and Chamavi.
§§ 101–102. Discontent in the Army and Activity Across the
Rhine. §§ 103–104. Campaign of the Year 359.

99. The winter at the beginning of the year 358 was the first of those
which Julian passed at Paris, and he spent this time largely in making
preparations for the furtherance of his military projects. The campaign
of the preceding year had been successful, but the results had not been
definitive. Many other operations had to be completed before Roman
Gaul could be regarded as free from danger. But the site of the new
general quarters, Paris, in itself forecast the future field of activity. It
would certainly be farther north than it had been in the preceding year.

The general conditions were as follows. As a consequence of the
previous campaign, the upper and middle courses of the Rhine, from
the Alps to just north of Cologne, no longer gave cause for concern,
but the same could not be said about the lower Rhine, from Cologne
to the sea. The tribes stationed between the Meuse, the Rhine, and
the sea, controlled the approach to the sea, which was of great importance to the Romans. Whereas up to the present the army had
been provisioned with grain from Aquitania far to the south, provisions
could also be brought from Britain across the sea and up the river.
But to take advantage of this route there was, first, need of a good
fleet and, second, of a free passage on the Rhine to the sea; and both
of these were lacking.

Julian, as he notes in his own words, succeeded in providing the
first requisite: "A large fleet arrived from Britain. I assembled a fleet
of six hundred ships, four hundred of which I built in less than ten
months, and I brought them all into the Rhine, no small task because
of the attacks of the neighboring barbarians" (*To the Athenians,*
279d–280a). If Julian had a fleet of six hundred ships and had constructed four hundred of these himself, he must have found two
hundred of them already built. But these were probably in a wretched

state of repair, the old hulks of the German and Britannic fleets, rotting away at different docks. Whatever they were, the majority must have been barges or landing craft rather than regular warships.

Florentius, the prefect of the praetorium, provided in his own way for the second exigency, the free passage of the boats on the Rhine (§ 69). Coming to terms with the barbarians, he agreed to pay two thousand pounds of silver for the right to sail on the river. When Emperor Constantius was informed of the treaty, he ratified it and ordered Julian to pay the sum "unless it seemed absolutely disgraceful" to him to carry out the agreement (To the Athenians, 280b). Though Constantius had previously shown his willingness to enter into such pacts with the barbarians, Julian was of a different mind and completely rejected this new project. As his only answer he took the field, even though his rations for the campaign had not arrived from Aquitania. Anticipating the usual time for beginning military operations, he left Paris in the late spring of 358 and moved rapidly to surprise the barbarians, who were not expecting an attack for another two months. Hardtack (buccellatum — 17. 8. 2) was baked from his reserve stocks of grain and a sufficient quantity to last twenty days was distributed to each of the soldiers.

100. Julian's first goal was the area west of the Meuse River, where for a long time the Frankish tribe of the Salii had been settled next to the Toxiandri. The Salii, surprised by Julian's coming, since they were of the opinion that he was still in his winter quarters, offered no resistance. After some hesitation they accepted a treaty which placed them under Roman rule. Julian then advanced toward the east. Crossing the Meuse he attacked the Chamavi, who dwelt between the Meuse and the Rhine.

The campaign against the Chamavi was bloody, since they had been settled only a short time on the left bank of the Rhine and were looked upon by the Romans as invaders. After mentioning his campaign against the Salii, Julian refers to this attack in the following terms: "I drove out the Chamavi, capturing many cattle and women with their children. And I so terrified them all and caused them to tremble at my approach that I received hostages from them at once and obtained a safe passage for my provisions" (To the Athenians, 280bc). Nearly everything was put to fire and sword, as we may gather from other historians who furnish us with more details (Libanius, 18. 75; Zosimus, 3. 6–7; Eunapius, Fragment, 12 — Dindorf; but cf.

17. 8. 4–5). The legates of the Chamavi came to discuss a treaty; Julian asked for hostages, among whom was to be the son of the king. The legates replied that he already had too many hostages in the prisoners he had taken and, at any rate, they could not bring back to life those who had died in battle, among whom had been the king's son. At this juncture Julian had the prince brought forth. He promised to treat him well, but he still kept him as a hostage (Zosimus, 3. 7). The valuable prize had not been captured by the Roman soldiers but by a barbarian named Charietto who had recently entered the Romans' service. This Charietto was a giant of extraordinary courage (*mirae fortitudinis* — 17. 10. 5), something of a highwayman and adventurer who, surrounded by other barbarians of the same stripe, plundered his own countrymen at night and by day worked on behalf of the Romans for the rewards they gave him. In this way the Chamavi were also induced to come to terms. They agreed to withdraw from Roman territory and never set foot upon it again.

The regions to the west of the lower course of the Rhine could now be considered safe. The area to the east of the river was still a source of some worry. The barbarian kings who, unlike Chonodomarius, had escaped from the battle of Strasbourg had sought refuge there (§ 87), and they were undoubtedly planning revenge. Julian would have liked to attack them at once, but he had to deal with an unexpected development, a military revolt.

101. Julian had hitherto requested much of his men, perhaps too much: curtailment of their winter's rest, forced marches, exhausting labors in constructing defenses, dangerous treks through unexplored regions. The soldiers had endured these hardships chiefly because of their attachment to their leader and the support which they received from his example. He slept only a few hours; at night he personally made the rounds of the guard posts of the encampments to assure himself that all was in order; he ate very little, and the food he did eat was of the poorest, taken sometimes while standing like a common soldier (25. 4. 4–5). All this won the esteem and affection of his men, but there were still two things about which they were extremely sensitive: their purses and their stomachs. When these were empty, the soldiers lost their enthusiasm and became morose and reticent even in the face of a normally inspiring example. Partly without realizing it, and partly without being able to avoid it, Julian had irritated the

soldiers on both these counts and had thus occasioned their revolt.

Even earlier there had been several occasions on which the soldiers manifested their discontent (§§ 88, 96), but this time it was more extensive and serious. When Julian finished restoring three small forts overlooking the Meuse and was girding himself for a renewal of the war, the soldiers refused to endure any further tasks or dangers without food and pay. And they had good reason for their refusal. The reserve supplies of food carried by the soldiers were dwindling before their eyes (§ 99), while for a long time the pay and bonuses customarily distributed to the troops had not even been mentioned. For provisions Julian had hoped to make use of the crops of the Chamavi, but these had not yet ripened; as for the pay of the soldiers, he had no special funds and Constantius had sent none (§ 70). The soldiers became furious and, as is noted by Ammianus, they began openly to slander their general in a frankly military fashion: "They called him an Asiatic, a contemptible little Greek (Graeculus), a swindler, a fool with only a show of wisdom . . . and kept bawling out such words as these: 'Where are we being dragged, robbed of hopes for a better lot? For a long time we have endured the very bitterest kinds of hardships from snow and piercing frost; but now, and what a crime it is! when we are on the point of destroying the enemy, it is by hunger, the most cowardly form of death, that we are wasting away. And let no one think that we are fostering a revolt; we protest that we are only speaking for our lives. We do not ask for gold and silver, which we have not been able to touch or to see for a long time, since they have been denied us as if we had been convicted of undertaking these many labors and toils against our country' " (17. 9. 3–5). Ammianus, who was no mean judge, states that the complaints were just, but he later adds that the commander in chief succeeded in bringing matters back to normal "with various types of flattery" (non sine blanditiarum genere vario — 17. 10. 1).

The favorable outcome of this incident indicates the enormous credit which Julian had with his soldiers. They could quarrel with him briefly over matters of food and money, but in the depths of their hearts they were sincerely attached to him.

102. Even though Ammianus was at this time no longer in Gaul but in the East (§ 83), his references to Julian's financial straits should not be questioned (see also 25. 4. 12). Still they should not be taken

too literally: Julian enjoyed the secret help of Ursulus, the superintendent of the treasury (§ 70), and was even able to offer a cash reward for every enemy head brought to him (Libanius, 18. 45).

After order had been restored the campaign again got under way. The troops headed for the Rhine and crossed the river on a pontoon bridge, but here another unforeseen incident and further difficulties occurred. Severus, master of the cavalry (§ 83), ceased to take any interest in the expedition. He may have been sick and worn out by his previous efforts, or perhaps harboring some secret resentment against Julian; but whatever it was, he suddenly lost all his former energy, and instead of encouraging his troops he began to hold them in. He even reached the point of threatening the guides for advancing too rapidly, persuading them to say that they were unfamiliar with the roads. The advance naturally slowed down almost to a halt. Fortunately the news of this internal crisis did not reach the barbarians, who were daily expecting the outbreak of hostilities.

A little farther on, in fact, Suomarius, who ruled over an area north of the Main near Mount Taunus and had taken part in the battle of Strasbourg with the other kings (§ 87), made an unexpected appearance. "Formerly haughty and intent on destroying the Romans" (ferox ante saeviensque in damna Romana), he now begged for peace on bended knees (17. 10. 3). It was granted to him on the explicit condition that he free his Roman prisoners and furnish his former enemy with supplies.

Then it was Hortarius' turn, another king, whose domains were situated to the south of those of Suomarius. Since Hortarius had no intention of submitting, the contest was here more difficult. Julian ordered the tribune of the scutarii, Nestica, and the highwayman, Charietto (§ 100), to track him down and capture him at any cost. A young Alemannus who had been taken prisoner was forced to act as a guide to the army. But the way proved to be difficult since the roads had been blocked with felled trees. Nevertheless, by making long and circuitous detours, the Roman forces eventually arrived at their goal. Thoroughly enraged, they began to lay waste the fields and homes and mercilessly slaughtered any who made a show of resistance. Terrified by what he saw, Hortarius surrendered and promised on oath to do whatever was asked him, beginning with the restitution of prisoners. But when it came to the execution of the agreement, only a few prisoners were returned, the greater number being held. Julian, who was familiar with this ruse of the barbarians, gathered the names of those still detained from those who had recently been freed. When he saw that only a portion of the prisoners had been returned, he refused to release four of the king's most loyal attendants. Hortarius then surrendered his other captives and was compelled to furnish material for rebuilding the cities. If this account of Ammianus (17. 10. 5–9) can be accepted in its entirety, it furnishes us with still another proof of the care and forethought which Julian lavished on his various undertakings.

The barbarians were unable to provide their conquerors with supplies of food, since all these had been destroyed during the war. With the advent of peace the wounds of so many troubled years began to mend; cities rose slowly from their ruins, and the repatriation of the Gallo-Roman prisoners caused a renewal of the economic and social life of the country.

Accounts with a number of barbarian kings who had taken part in the battle of Strasbourg still remained to be settled, but since the season was now advanced, it was necessary to put the reckoning off until the following year, 359. Julian therefore returned to his winter quarters at Paris.

103. On the renewal of activities in the spring, Julian began his campaign with a minute inspection and systematic rebuilding and restocking of the conquered territories, with a view to future operations. Granaries for the supplies coming from Britain were rapidly erected along the left bank of the Rhine. Along this same line, according to Ammianus, "seven cities were seized: Castra Herculis, Quadriburgium (Schenkenschanz), Tricensima (Kellen), Novaesium (Nuys), Bonna (Bonn), Antemnacum (Andernach), and Vingo (Bingen), where the prefect Florentius by a happy chance also appeared unexpectedly, leading part of the troops and bringing a store of provisions that could be used for a long time" (18. 2. 4).

The work of repairing and rebuilding was carried forward with alacrity. The Roman legionaries did not labor alone. They had the assistance of the barbarian auxiliaries, who as a rule were reluctant to perform such tasks. Men could be seen carrying on their shoulders beams of more than fifty feet in length, which the Rhenish forests produced in great abundance. Meanwhile, Julian had sent Hariobaudes, a tribune at large (vacantem tribunum) who had a thorough knowledge of the enemy's language (sermonis barbarici), into the area ruled by

King Hortarius, who had recently come to terms with the Romans. The purpose of his mission was to gather information about the dispositions of the neighboring Alemanni kings who had not yet submitted, but whom Julian intended to subdue. When the work of reconstruction had been completed and Hariobaudes had returned, military operations were begun without delay.

Severus, the master of the horse (§ 102), had died in the meantime, and had been succeeded by Lupicinus. Together with the prefect Florentius, who had just arrived, Lupicinus now had the direct command of the army. Both wanted to begin operations by crossing the Rhine at Mainz over the bridge which had been standing there since the time of Trajan. This, however, would have involved going through the territory of King Suomarius, who had surrendered only a short time before, and the inevitable infliction of damages by the troops. Julian was strongly opposed to the plan since he did not want to give Suomarius grounds for complaint or create unwarranted distrust among the other Alemanni who were still holding out. He therefore had recourse to a ruse.

He continued to march with his army up along the left bank of the river, while the barbarians followed him on the opposite bank, watching his every move by day and night. At a spot which seemed suitable for the maneuver, he had three hundred of his soldiers get into boats at the dead of night and cross the river in absolute silence. The barbarian troops in the meantime kept a watch on the fires in the Roman encampment, while their chiefs feasted at a banquet prepared by King Hortarius. As usual, the eating and drinking continued until the third watch of the night. As the revelers were leaving they met the Roman troops that had crossed the river. Both parties were taken by surprise. The barbarian chieftains fled on their horses, leaving their attendants on foot to be slaughtered by the Romans. This incident facilitated the construction of a bridge by the Romans on the other side of the river out of material which had already been prepared at a favorable site.

104. After crossing the river, the army spared the land of Hortarius but put that of the other kings farther on to fire and sword. When he arrived at the confines of the Burgundiones, Julian pitched camp. The sum total of these events broke the back of the barbarian resistance. The two brothers Macrianus and Hariobaudes were the first kings to sue for peace. They were immediately followed by

Vadomarius, who came to plead for himself and for Urius, Ursicinus, and Vestralpus (§ 87). An agreement was made at once with Macrianus and Hariobaudes. Vadomarius, whose lands lay about Augst, farther to the south, had had previous contacts with the Romans. He now produced a letter received from Constantius in which he was highly commended (cf. § 88). No immediate reply could be given to him since he was negotiating not only for his own safety but also for that of the other kings, who might not adhere to a treaty arranged through another. But these sent further envoys when they saw their homes and harvests going up in flames and their subjects being captured or slain by the Romans. They then obtained peace on the same terms as the others, beginning with the freeing of all the prisoners they had taken in their frequent raids (18. 2. 15–19).

The regions on both sides of the Rhine were now pacified; and, what was more, they were guarded by a chain of fortresses running from Raetia down to the sea. Some of the peoples were allies of Rome; others were forcibly maintained as subjects. The real support of the *status quo* was the army of Gaul, whose morale had been so effectively renewed by its commander in chief. Soberly and without exaggeration, Julian sums up the results of his campaigns against the Alemanni in the years 357, 358, and 359: "I crossed the Rhine three times while I was still Caesar. I requested and received from the barbarians twenty thousand persons who were being held captive on the far side of the Rhine. In two battles and one siege I captured a thousand prisoners,* and these were not of unserviceable age but men in the prime of life. I sent four levies of excellent infantry to Constantius, three more not so good, and two outstanding squadrons of cavalry. With the help of the gods I have now recovered all the towns, but by that time I had recovered fewer than forty" (*To the Athenians* 280cd).

---

* The two battles were those of Strasbourg (§ 89 ff.) and Toxiandria (§ 100). The siege was that of the two small forts on the Meuse (§ 98). The manuscripts read "a thousand" ($\chi\iota\lambda\acute{\iota}ovs$) for the number of captives taken, but this is too low. There is perhaps here a copyist's error.

VIII. JULIAN AS GOVERNOR OF GAUL

§§ 105–106. *The Antagonism Between the Military and Political Powers.* §§ 107–110. *Fiscal Program and Its Reform.* §§ 111–112. *Omens for the Future.* §§ 113–114. *Conflict With Florentius and Departure of Sallustius.* §§ 115–117. *Julian's Way of Life and Attitude Toward Christianity.*

105. Up until now we have examined only one aspect of Julian's rule in Gaul, his role as the head of the army. But if this was the chief element in his office, it was not the only one — he had also to function as civil governor and administrator.

We have already seen that at his coming he had found a highly complex administrative center at Vienne, but one upon which he could have very little influence since the emperor had destined him to be only a figurehead. Besides this, Julian was actually little acquainted with administrative procedures (§ 75). Nevertheless, since he was a realist with an observant and reflective mind, he was bound to become an able administrator just as he had become a successful general. With his election as consul and his reception of greater military power from Constantius (§ 76), he naturally received more authority in civil matters as well.

But this was the source of new difficulties. Between the two powers, military and civil, there had existed an old antagonism, particularly in Gaul where military exigencies were so compelling that they took precedence over the needs of the civil service. They were like two oxen kicking against each other, even though, like it or not, they had to be kept under a common yoke. Moreover, Gaul was in a state of economic collapse, not only from the barbarian invasions and the years of constant fighting but also from the heavy taxes, a hated burden which had been rendered even more oppressive by the greed and corruption of government agents. These aimed only at extorting money from the wretched populace with no thought of what could actually be paid, or the desperate straits into which the people had fallen, or helping them

116

recover through their own labors. Julian's gradual introduction into the secrets of public administration under the expert guidance of Sallustius (§ 76) and his own observation of the desolation of his subjects made him appreciate the severity of the problem.

106. His progress in solving it may be traced by comparing the two encomia he composed in honor of Constantius. We have already referred to the first, written toward the end of 356 (§ 82). In it, besides pompously enumerating Constantius' military exploits, Julian, as was mandatory, praises his shrewdness in civil government, but confines himself to vague and general statements. In this encomium, as a matter of fact, the orator had his eyes turned to recent literary models, especially those of Themistius and Libanius, and hardly at all on actual events, of which he had had little experience. But later, Julian himself felt dissatisfied with this effort which had perhaps been too hastily composed. Accordingly, at the end of 358, during his winter's leisure, he returned to the same theme and wrote *On the Heroic Deeds of the Emperor, or On Kingship.*

This is obviously a courtly panegyric. Nevertheless, the orator reveals in it his own personal experiences gained in two years as governor of Gaul. Many of the observations which he makes on the proper way to conduct civil and military enterprises come from what he had seen with his own eyes during that time. The whole, which takes the form of a series of general precepts, is naturally presented with the usual elegant flattery; but one feels at once that these precepts represent Julian's own very definite reaction to the sad examples of maladministration he had seen in Gaul. Particularly serious is the recommendation that the perfect governor should entrust "the business of state contracts to one who is just, kind, humane, and easily moved to pity, devising this means of protection for the weaker and simpler citizens, and for the poor against those who are strong, dishonest, wicked and so elated by their wealth that they violate and contemn justice" (*Heroic Deeds*, 90cd). If we may employ a modern metaphor, we have here before our eyes a picture taken in Gaul, but it is a negative, and not a positive print. Julian has perforce portrayed not the actual state of affairs, but rather what they should have been.

In this second panegyric is evident a certain positive rejection of the courtly world surrounding Constantius, but not, of course, of the emperor himself. We are reminded of one who canes the dog since he cannot cane the master. Further, when he treats of religious matters,

Julian uses expressions that sound strange coming from one who passed for a Christian writing to another who actually was a Christian. But this may be explained by Julian's actual state of mind, which is revealed in a clearer light in his essay, A *Consolation to Himself upon the Departure of the Excellent Sallustius* (§ 114). His hatred for Christianity and his rancor toward Constantius after a long suppression were beginning to explode.

107. The fiscal regime, more or less defective throughout the empire, was desperate in Gaul. The duty of collecting taxes fell for the most part upon the *decuriones municipales* and others who had the *munera civilia*, which were far more of a civic burden than honor. Out of respect for Christianity, Constantine had exempted the Catholic clergy from such duties. The distaste for such offices was intense, and almost everyone tried to escape them. In time the municipal curiae became almost deserted, and edicts had to be published forcing men to assume these offices.

Land taxes were periodically fixed by means of an *indictio*, that is, a per capita (*capitatio*) list of contributions, which roughly corresponded to the presumed income of a given zone divided up among its inhabitants. But because the rate of income was exaggerated or because wars or bad seasons interfered with the harvest, small farmers were seldom in a position to pay their *capitatio*, or, if they did pay it, did so at the cost of great hardship, particularly in the increase of their already heavy private debts. The rich, on the other hand, instead of paying, busied themselves with winning over the agents of the treasury with lavish gifts. They thus paid when and what they wished. In their turn, the tax collectors, who were past masters in the art of peculation, caused a large portion of the sums collected to evaporate along the numerous channels conveying them to the coffers of the state.

108. Julian's conduct, which was in sharp contrast with accepted practice, is outlined by Ammianus in the following terms: "Spending the winter in Paris after winning such renown through his victories, he laid aside for a time the cares of war and with no less solicitude made many provisions for the well-being of the provinces. He diligently saw to it that no one should be overburdened with taxes; that the powerful should not seize the property of others; that none should hold positions of authority whose private estates were being augmented by public disasters; and that no public official should stray from justice with impunity" (18. 1. 1).

Julian sought personally to remedy this last abuse by trying cases himself when they were particularly important or when they involved prominent individuals, "inflexibly distinguishing between right and wrong." Among the many instances which Ammianus could recall, he cites specifically that of Numerius, who a short time before had been governor of Gallia Narbonensis. He was now accused of embezzlement, and, as it seems, unjustly. Julian presided at the trial, which was open to all and conducted with unusual severity (*inusitato censorio vigore*). Numerius put up a solid defense. The prosecutor Delphidius, who had a cutting tongue, became exasperated at his own lack of evidence and at one point shouted: "Can anyone, exalted Caesar, ever be found guilty if it is sufficient to deny the charges?" "And can anyone," was Julian's retort, "ever be proved innocent if an accusation is all that is required to convict him?" (18. 1. 4.)

His rigor in punishing delinquents was tempered by a certain clemency. On one occasion he ordered that a man guilty of criminal assault should be exiled if found guilty. The girl's parents, who had desired the death penalty, registered a complaint, but Julian merely replied: "The laws may blame my clemency, but it is fitting for an emperor of a mild disposition to be superior to all other laws" (16. 5. 12).

He was more actively engaged in holding court during the winter months than in the other seasons of the year since military operations were then suspended. Whenever he was on the point of setting out on a campaign, many would come to him complaining about the wrongs they had received. Since he had no time to make a personal investigation, he would recommend them to the provincial governors; but later, when he had returned, he would inquire about the outcome of the various suits and would frequently "mitigate the punishment of the offenses with his native kindliness" (16. 5. 13).

109. To settle the thorny problem of taxes, Julian made a personal audit of the province's finances. Going over the figures, he found that the deficit was not due to excessive expenditures for the upkeep of his own frugal court (§ 70). He further discovered that it was impossible to increase the *capitatio* of twenty-five pieces of gold (*aurei*)*

---

* The aureus was a coin which could have different values depending upon its coinage and the current quotations. Originally it had had a weight of one fortieth of a pound of gold (about 8.15 grams), but with the passage of time this weight had greatly decreased, to even less than one seventy-second of a pound (4.55 grams), at which it was fixed by Constantine the Great in 312.

which was in force when he arrived in Gaul because of the wretched economic status of the country (16. 5. 14). There were others, on the other hand, such as Florentius, the prefect of the praetorium, who maintained that a supplementary tax (*indictionale augmentum*), which a law of the year 356 had permitted at the discretion of the prefects, should be imposed. This special tax provided that the quota left unpaid by the insolvent should fall upon those who had already paid their own quota. Julian declared that even at the cost of his life he would never permit this supplementary tax. And his decision was based on the solid argument that the provinces in which the supplementary impost had been collected had been reduced to extreme misery, as had happened in Illyricum.

The examination of the balance had shown Julian the weak point in the whole fiscal structure. The income from the ordinary taxes was sufficient, and more than sufficient, to take care of public expenses, provided it was collected in full. But this had not occurred since from time to time "indulgences" (*indulgentiae* — 16. 5. 15) were granted, that is, cancellations of taxes that were in arrears. It might be thought that this was an advantage for all in general, but actually it was only to the advantage of the rich, "since, as is generally known, the poor are constrained to pay all their taxes without any easement as soon as the collectors come around" (16. 5. 15). The rich, on the other hand, by making a deal with the collectors, succeeded in putting off their large payments until a new indulgence was granted; and, consequently, no further mention was made of them, to the great loss of the treasury.

Other sources of waste were the exemptions granted to special taxes due from particular areas. Only the prefect of the praetorium Florentius knew where the taxes were drained off instead of flowing into the coffers of the state. If Julian publicly accused him of avarice (§ 69), this must have had reference to the collection of taxes.

110. On the basis of the conclusions of his examination, Julian decided against increasing the *capitatio* and quashed the project of a supplementary impost. Instead, abolishing all indulgences, he insisted upon the full payment of taxes in arrears and the proper handing over of the special tributes.

Touched to the quick, Florentius in his turn rejected Julian's proposals. They argued at length over the fiscal policy to be adopted. Florentius based his claims upon the recent law permitting a supplementary impost. Julian, with the figures in his hand, pointed out that the new tax was not necessary. When the prefect presented the project for the new impost neatly drawn up, Julian would not even read it, but threw it to the ground instead. Florentius finally had recourse to the emperor, but Constantius merely attempted to straddle the issue. He advised Julian to be more conciliatory and less distrustful of his prefect. Julian replied that it would be most gratifying if the ordinary taxes could be collected, but that it was absolutely impossible to even think of other extraordinary taxes. This ended the controversy. Julian was victorious, and the project of the supplementary impost was abandoned.

Subsequent events showed that Julian was right. A short time after, with the firmness characteristic of men possessed by an idea, "contrary to precedent" (inusitato exemplo — 17. 3. 6) he obtained from the prefect the administration of the province of Belgica Secunda, still prostrate from the calamities of the recent war, with the proviso that no agent of the prefect or the governor should compel anyone to pay the supplementary tax. The result of this experiment was that the taxpayers freed from further anxiety paid their dues even before the appointed date.

It is to Julian's credit that the fairness and humanity he showed in the matter of the taxes won the esteem of his tenacious adversaries Gregory Nazianzen (4. 75) and Ambrose (De obitu Valentiniani, 21). During the course of his governorship of Gaul he succeeded in reducing the capitatio from twenty-five to only seven aurei per head. Nevertheless, it must be noted that in the East, as Augustus, he was less scrupulous about granting tax exemptions than he had been in Gaul. Among the numerous proofs (testimonia plurima) of his liberality in public administration, Ammianus cites his many condonations of old taxes (remissa debita multa diuturnitate congesta — 25. 4. 15). This does not mean that he indiscriminately pardoned all arrears, but only that he made partial remissions according to places and circumstances (cf. Misopogon, 366d–367d; Cod. Theod., 11. 16. 10).

111. What were Julian's real feelings during this contest for the amelioriation of conditions in Gaul? For this we possess a document which, although not certainly authentic, is most probably so. It is a letter written in 359 to his faithful Oribasius (§ 66) then at Vienne. In it Julian bewails the conduct of a high functionary of the court whom he does not name, though almost all modern scholars are of

the opinion that the reference is to Florentius. The letter also reveals how firmly Julian was convinced of the imperial mission entrusted to him by the gods (cf. § 42) and hints at his plans for the future.

Oribasius had informed Julian of a dream he had had which seemed to bode ill for Constantius. Julian, who was himself most attentive to dreams, was deeply impressed. A little later he had a somewhat similar dream which he reported in turn to Oribasius: "I think that this time, if ever, you have seen clearly into the future. For this very day I also have seen something of the same sort. I thought that a lofty tree had been planted in a very large banquet hall and that it was bending down toward the ground, while from its roots there rose up another small, young and vigorous tree. I greatly feared that someone in uprooting the large tree would pull up the small one as well. And, as a matter of fact, when I came near I saw that the tall tree was lying stretched out upon the ground, while the small one was standing upright above it. Seeing this I said in alarm: 'What a misfortune for the tall tree! There is danger that not even its shoot will be saved.' Then one who was entirely unknown to me said: 'Look attentively and take heart. For since its root remains in the earth, the smaller tree will not be hurt and will be rooted even more solidly than before'" (*To Oribasius,* 384cd). The allegory is perfectly transparent. The great tree is Constantius, and the little tree is Julian himself, his blood relative. But it is important to note that allegories of this kind, even if they are sometimes found in Greek authors (cf., for example, Herodotus, 1. 108), are found more frequently and strikingly in that Sacred Scripture which Julian as a lad had read in church to the people (cf. Ezech. 17:3–24; 19:10–14; 31:3–18; Dan. 4:7, 23; §§ 16, 19).

112. The letter then continues: "So much then for the dreams; God knows to what they lead. As for that accursed eunuch (μιαροῦ ἀνδρογύνου), I would be glad to know when he said these things about me, whether it was before he met me or after. Let me know whatever you can." From our present state of information, the courtier here mentioned could hardly have been any other than Eusebius, the all-powerful chamberlain of the emperor and the instigator of many of his misdeeds (§ 50). The opprobrious term here used by Julian could have reference to his office of "eunuch." It would not have been applicable to Florentius.

With some break in the thread of its logic, which may indicate that some names have been suppressed or that the text has been retouched,

the letter continues: "As for my relations with him [presumably Floren-
tius], the gods know that often when he wronged the provincials I
kept silence, though it did not behoove me, turning a deaf ear to some
of the charges and refusing to admit others, distrusting some and
attributing others to his associates. But when he asked me to share in
such infamy by sending me those shameful and completely abominable
reports to sign [presumably the project of the law for the supplementary
tax; cf. § 110], what was I to do? Was I to keep silent or to oppose
him? To do the former was foolish, servile, and hateful to the gods; to
do the latter was just, manly, and liberal; but such a course was not
open to me at the time on account of the cares that oppressed me.
What then did I do? In the presence of many who I knew would
report it to him I said: 'This man will certainly revise his reports completely, for they are dreadfully out of line.' When he heard this, he
fell so short of acting prudently that he did things which, by heaven,
no temperate tyrant would have done, and that too when I was so near
him. In such a matter what was a man who was a zealous student of
the teachings of Plato and Aristotle to do? Should I have looked on
while the wretched people were being handed over to thieves, or should
I have aided them to the best of my ability, for they were already
singing their swan-song because of the impious devices of men of this
sort? At least it seems to me to be a disgrace that while I punish my
military tribunes for deserting their posts — and indeed they ought to
be put to death at once and not even given burial — I should myself
desert that post which I have received for the defense of such unfortunates, since it is my duty to fight against such thieves, especially when
God is fighting on my side, for it was He who placed me here"
(384d–385d).

113. It may well be that while writing these last words Julian was
reflecting on the thought expressed by Socrates in his *Apology:* Just as
he had not run away from the posts assigned to him by the generals
of the army, so he could not abandon the station that had been assigned
him by God (28e). Or it may have been that he was inspired by
his conviction that he was a spiritual soldier of the god Mithra
"who fought with him" (§ 60). He concludes his letter with a respectful thought for Sallustius, of whose company he had recently been
deprived.

This collection of allegories and presentiments, whether pertaining
to Julian or to the Constantinian dynasty, is of great importance for

evaluating what Julian did a few months later. The revolt at Paris, which made him an adversary of, and eventually the successor to, Constantius, was not a bolt from the blue but something that had been presaged by the storm clouds mentioned in this letter. Oribasius, to whom it is addressed, will appear as a disguised but highly important actor in the events at Paris (§ 131).

But even before Julian's victory in the matter of the supplementary tax, Florentius had set about isolating him by removing his most efficient counselor, Sallustius (§§ 76, 105). For such an enterprise he found ready allies in the high dignitaries at court. Julian describes them as "notorious sycophants hired against me" (282bc), and he occasionally mentions Pentadius (§ 69), Gaudentius (§ 70), and Paul. We have already met the first two, and it should be sufficient to add here that Pentadius was quite probably the mastermind in the plot, just as he had earlier had an important part in the murder of Julian's brother Gallus (§ 49). It is still possible, however, that the ultimate sponsor of the whole conspiracy was the grand chamberlain Eusebius (§§ 50, 112), particularly since Julian vaguely hints at another whom he does not name. Paul was "a native of Spain, a poisonous snake, whose appearance beguiled his real character. He was extremely clever in scenting out secret paths along which to carry others to their ruin. . . . He was nicknamed 'the Chain' for his baneful habit of implicating others" (Ammianus, 14. 5. 6–8).

114. The conspiracy conducted by such clever and powerful individuals had its full effect. The final blow was struck by a letter addressed by Florentius to the court of the Augustus in which he accused Sallustius of exciting the Caesar against him. The immediate occasion for the charge was afforded by Julian's refusal to accept jurisdiction in a criminal trial for peculation which had been brought before Florentius. Florentius had been bribed by the defendant, and when the matter became known he tried to get Julian to judge the case, supposing that he would also side with the defendant, even though he was guilty (Libanius, 18. 84). In the imperial council Florentius' complaints received the support of the conspirators. The upshot of the business was that Sallustius, relieved of his office as quaestor in Gaul, was recalled to court. His successor was Lucillianus (*To the Athenians,* 282c). These events occurred in the first months of 359.

This painful separation from Sallustius reminded Julian of his earlier separation from his dear Mardonius (§ 76). To console himself he wrote a work entitled *A Consolation to Himself upon the Departure of the Excellent Sallustius*. It is a sincere composition, not burdened with the usual tearful affectations, even though it followed the pattern established by Sophistic literature for this genre. The author speaks to himself, but he knows full well that others will be listening to him, not only Sallustius, but also his enemies at court. References are made to, and examples cited from, classical antiquity through the medium of Plutarch. He recalls the days spent together with Sallustius in the midst of various trials, their pure and upright friendship, their constant co-operation in all that was good, and unwavering opposition to evil (241cd). He finds no fault with Constantius, but strongly condemns his courtiers, those "sycophants" who often "shoot their arrows at you, or rather at me, aiming to wound me through you" (242a).

There is nothing in the essay directly in favor of the worship of the pagan gods, though it may include a veiled attack on Christianity: "In philosophy . . . the Greeks alone reached the summit, for they sought truth through reason as nature requires, not permitting us to pay attention to incredible tales and absurd miracles like most of the barbarians" (252b). This statement makes one pause since it resembles so many others made by Julian, particularly in his work *Against the Galileans*, in which the Christians are treated in the same fashion. In Julian's mind, the material for his future polemic against the Christians was being elaborated, just as his will was hardening in its aversion to Constantius.

115. Despite all these military and civil occupations Julian did not neglect "the salvation of his soul" (§§ 46, 47) and the beloved studies that were so intimately connected with that salvation. The time available for this was scarce, but he succeeded in prolonging it by leading an austere life and clinging to a strict routine.

The well-informed Ammianus furnishes us with important data on Julian's workday. There does not seem to have been much difference between the periods when he was in residence at court and when he was in the field, since even on the last night of his life, when the Persian expedition was collapsing into a dismal ruin, Julian continued to read and meditate in his tent by the light of a lamp. Even the presence of his wife Helena at Paris (§ 55) could not have notably changed the order of his day (cf. *To the Athenians*, 284c). In the words of Ammianus, "he divided the night into three parts: one for rest, one for the affairs of state, and one for the Muses. . . . He woke up as often as he wished without any mechanical means, and he always got up after midnight, not from a feathered bed or silken spreads glittering with varied hues, but from a rough blanket and rug which the common people call *susurna*. Then he prayed in secret to Mercury, whom the teachings of the theologians have shown to be the swift intelligence of the universe arousing men's minds to activity; and despite such a great lack of material things he paid great attention to all his public duties. And after he completed these difficult and serious tasks, he would turn to the exercise of his intellect; and it is unbelievable with what great eagernesss he sought out the high knowledge of all the principal things and, as if in search of some sort of nourishment for a soul climbing to higher levels, ran through all the phases of philosophy in his learned discussions. And yet, though he gained a full and exhaustive knowledge of these matters, he did not neglect more humble subjects, making a moderate study of poetry and rhetoric (as is shown by the pure elegance and dignity of his speeches and letters) and the varied history of domestic and foreign affairs. Besides all this he was also sufficiently fluent in speaking Latin. . . . These, then, were the nightly indications of his self-control and his virtues" (16. 5. 4–8; cf. 25. 4. 2 ff.).

116. It was a pleasure for Julian to read and write by lamplight, either because he felt more alone and at ease at such a time, or because he was then imitating his ancient models. He must certainly have read that the adversaries of Demosthenes had caustically contended that his orations smelled of the lamp; and to the lamp Julian himself remained faithful up to the eve of his death.

The purity of his morals was known to all. "He was so conspicuous for his undefiled chastity that after the death of his wife [Helena, who had died prematurely — § 56] it is well known that he never gave a thought to love. . . . Even his most confidential servants never accused him of any suspicion of lustfulness, as often happens" (Ammianus, 25. 4. 2–3). It is true that grounds for such an accusation are apparently found in two letters purporting to be addressed by Julian to Sopater and Iamblichus respectively (Wright, 3:212–214; 3:252–262 [416c–420a]). In these letters reference is made to "my children," but the authenticity of the first is suspect and the second is certainly apocryphal. And even if the first is from Julian's own hand, the expression may easily be taken as a metaphor.

Instances of his temperance in the use of food have already been cited (§§ 70, 101), and these could be multiplied. Another proof of his moderation in eating is shown by the fact that even though it was a common custom throughout the empire to induce vomiting after a solemn banquet, Julian never indulged in the practice. The only instance of the sort that might be cited was when he became ill from a brazier which had been brought into his room. It had been a severe winter, and the Seine "was carrying down slabs like marble . . . so that it seemed likely they would form a continuous path and bridge the stream" (*Misopogon*, 341c). Julian had steadfastly refused to let his domestics heat his room; and when he finally did permit them to bring in a few coals, he fell asleep and became poisoned by the fumes.

This extraordinary austerity is not to be explained simply by the admiration which Julian fostered for the ancient philosophers and their teachings. It undoubtedly had a firm religious foundation. It was a real mystic asceticism leading, as he believed, to his prized "salvation." Its inspiration may easily be found in the Mithraic mysteries (§§ 40, 60). 117. What was Julian's attitude toward Christianity? For ten years he had been alienated from it (cf. § 44), and the separation was now complete. But this was true only as regards his internal convictions: in his external conduct, he adopted without scruple the principle that "because of the universal fear one could lawfully conceal the sounder opinion about the gods" (§ 45); and he not only concealed his real opinions — he publicly manifested their very opposite. A few months later, during the revolt against Constantius, "in order that he might win the favor of all men and be opposed by none, he pretended to be an adherent of the Christian religion from which he had much earlier secretly withdrawn. Having a few sharers in his hidden activities, he gave himself up to haruspicy and auguries, and all the other practices which the worshipers of the gods have always performed. And in order that this might remain concealed at the time, on the festival day which the Christians celebrate in the month of January and call the Epiphany, he entered their church and departed after praying to their divinity in the usual manner" (*sollemniter* — 21. 2. 4–5). This took place on January 6, 361, at Vienne in Gaul.

There on the preceding November 6, Julian had celebrated the fifth anniversary of his election as Caesar. About this same time also his wife Helena had died (§ 55).

IX. THE REVOLT

§§ 118–120. Diplomatic Skirmishes Between Constantius and Persia.   §§ 121–122. Arians and Orthodox; Athanasius, Hilary, Lucifer of Cagliari.   §§ 123–124. The Persian Peril. §§ 125–126. Demand for Troops From Gaul; the Legal Question.   §§ 127–128. Reluctance of the Soldiers to Depart.   § 129. Advice From the Gods. Julian Allows His Election as Augustus.   §§ 130–131. Background of the Revolt.

118. Up to the beginning of 359 the relationship between Julian and Constantius seemed to be normal, but it was only so in appearance — beneath the ashes a fire was burning. In an inscription from the baths of Spoleto reconstructed by Constantius after a fire in 358 (Dessau, *Inscriptiones Latinae selectae*, 739), the "most victorious" Caesar is mentioned with the Augustus. But because of personal losses and public reverses such a mark of courtesy would not have been shown a few months later. During this period Constantius suffered the loss of his wife Eusebia, Julian's great protectress, and of his sister Helena, Julian's wife (§ 55). These deaths removed from the scene two precious bonds which could have sweetened much of the bitterness and attenuated much of the rivalry that existed between the two cousins.

Relations with Persia were also worsening and causing anxiety to Constantius. After their indecisive battles with the Romans (§ 20), the Persians had not given up their hopes for revenge, aiming particularly at a reconquest of the territories lost at the time of Diocletian. Although King Sapor continued to press against the Roman frontier, he had made no all-out assault against it, since he was himself assailed by various peoples on the eastern frontier of his empire and by internal difficulties. His position was similar to that of Constantius, who was harassed by the barbarians along the Rhine, by the Sarmatae along the Danube, and internally perturbed by his distrust of Julian.

A short time after Sapor conducted a campaign against the Chionitae, the Gelani, and other tribes threatening his eastern frontiers, Constantius did the same against the Sarmatae. All this occurred between the end of 357 and the early part of 359. The two colossi, the Persian and the Roman empires, seemed to be eager to rid themselves of secondary conflicts in order to settle accounts between each other. In the meantime, they kept the *status quo*, without either formal peace or effective war.

When matters reached this stage Flavius Strategius, later called Musonianus, decided to do something about them. He had enjoyed a long administrative career culminating in his appointment as praetorian prefect for the East (cf. Ammianus, 15. 13. 1–4; 16. 9. 2–3), and he asked himself if it would not be to the mutual advantage of the two rivals to come to some definite and fixed agreement. Such an undertaking would be anything but easy, but Musonianus knew that if he could establish contact between the two parties and further the negotiations, he was bound to gain the highest credit with Constantius.

119. To reach King Sapor, Musonianus got in touch with Tamsapor, a high-ranking governor of Persian territories bordering on those of the Romans. Musonianus suggested that he should present Sapor with the opportunity of signing a regular peace treaty with the Romans. In this way the Persian monarch would obtain the double advantage of securing his western frontiers bordering on those of Rome and freedom of action against the rebels to the east. Tamsapor reported this to his sovereign, who was far off warring against the rebels; but in order to gain credit with him, as Musonianus hoped to gain it with Constantius, on his own authority he added some clarifications and explanations: Constantius was in desperate straits because of wars and troubles within the empire. Therefore his only aim was to obtain a peace to his own advantage.

Needless to say, Sapor also interpreted the proposal in the same fashion when he read Tamsapor's letter. He looked upon the Roman offer as a positive indication of internal weakness (*non nisi infirmato imperii robore temptari talia suspicatus* — 17. 5. 2). Led by this conviction, Sapor did not reject the proposal but assumed a haughty air, making it appear that it was through his condescension that he took the offer under consideration.

The matter fluctuated while representatives of both parties kept up the negotiations until finally, in the first months of 358, a message from Sapor reached Constantius. Sapor thus directly intervened in

the matter which up to then had been handled only through intermediaries. "I, Sapor, King of Kings, partner of the stars, brother of
the sun and moon, to Caesar Constantius, my brother, send hearty
greetings." After citing this introduction, Ammianus gives what is likely
a résumé rather than the exact text of the message, having previously
noted that the Persian ruler "imposed grave conditions without relin-
quishing the least bit of his native boastfulness" (*nusquam a genuino
fastu declinans, condiciones posuit graves* — 17. 5. 2). The King of
Kings ordered the Romans to abandon the conquests made at the
expense of his grandfather five decades earlier during the reign of Diocletian, and, withdrawing from Armenia, to restore Mesopotamia to
the Persians. As a matter of fact, as an heir of the Achaemenids, he
could have asked for much more, that is, for all the territory as far as
the Stridon River and Macedonia, but since from his youth he had
valued moderation (*ubique mihi cordi est recta ratio*), he limited himself to these requests. If they were not granted, he would advance the
following spring with all his forces as far as he thought proper.

120.   During these long negotiations, false and exaggerated rumors had
spread through Roman circles, stirring the imagination of the courtiers
and petty politicians. If Tamsapor believed that Constantius was
already at the end of his rope, at the court of Constantius it was
believed that Sapor was at the end of his, and ready to beg for mercy.
When, on January 1, 357, Constantius was proclaimed consul for the
ninth, and Julian for the second, time, the orator Themistius pronounced a discourse in the senate at Constantinople in praise of the
emperor. In it, after recalling the triumphs gained by Constantius in
the West, he declared that the invincible Augustus, even though he was
in Gaul, constrained the Persians to ask for peace, and that he himself
a short while before in Antioch had seen Persian messengers come
to beg for it (57a). These messengers were probably members of
an embassy carrying on the negotiations between Musonianus and
Tamsapor.

In the midst of these lively expectations, there fell instead, like a
ball of fire, Sapor's message to Constantius. It was no humble petition
for peace! The King of Kings, partner of the stars, and brother of
the sun and moon spoke like an absolute ruler and ended his message
with a veritable ultimatum: either accept these demands or make
preparations to withstand an all-out attack within a short time.

Sapor's letter was examined in the imperial council, and, after long consideration (*litteris diu libratis*), the Augustus replied: "I, Constantius, victorious on land and sea, ever Augustus, send greetings to my brother Sapor." Refraining from general statements and anything that pertained to the old controversies, Constantius simply disavowed the negotiations that had been conducted up to this point. Without his approbation (*me inconsulto*), they had been undertaken on a private basis by the praetorian prefect with one of Sapor's generals through certain obscure individuals (*per quosdam ignobiles*). Further, Constantius was strong and sure of himself. He did not intend to break the peace, but he was resolved to defend what was his own (17. 5. 9–14).

Despite this positive language, Constantius wished to leave a way open for further negotiations, and this time official. A few days after sending his reply, he hastened the departure of three ambassadors with letters and gifts for Sapor, but also with the secret commission to impede the Persian preparations for war in whatever way they could. But their efforts proved to be fruitless, and after a long stay with "the most obstinate king" (*obstinatissimum regem*), they returned empty-handed (17. 14. 2).

Sapor wasted no time. When he had equipped a powerful expedition of about one hundred thousand men, he advanced toward the Roman territory. The Romans for their part had not restored and strengthened their line of defense along the Euphrates. Only at the last moment, when the enemy was on the move, were barricades erected at Amida (Diarbekr) on the right bank of the Tigris and a few other places. More effective was their forethought in so completely devastating the land opposite Edessa and Carrhae that in the whole territory between the Tigris and the Euphrates no growing crops were to be seen (*nihil viride cerneretur* — 18. 7. 4). This scorched-earth policy forced the Persian king to go much farther north to cross the Euphrates. The Romans therefore set up their defense also in the north with its center at Amida. Sapor raged unsuccessfully against this city defended by seven Roman legions and auxiliary troops for more than two months, and only at the high cost of thirty thousand slain did he succeed in capturing it on October 6, 369. A minute report of the siege and fall of the city is given by Ammianus, an eyewitness of the events (§ 83). It is one of the most vivid and informative of this period of Roman history.

121. The Persians' capture of the city was for the moment little more than a Pyrrhic victory. Because of the losses endured and troubles

within the realm, King Sapor had to withdraw in the fall into his own territory. This tacitly implied that he would resume the struggle the following year, and this presumption was confirmed by numerous deserters who told the Romans of the great preparations being made by the King of Kings. Constantius, therefore, had to make counterpreparations, which consisted chiefly in reinforcing the frontier of the Euphrates and particularly in assembling great numbers of well-trained troops. Constantius, who was well aware of the crisis, was already preparing to move from Sirmium to Thrace in order to be near the Persian frontier. Nevertheless, his caesaropapistic mentality was agitated to nearly the same extent by the sharp and bitter attacks which the various Arian movements were making on orthodoxy. These were creating a religious crisis in which he felt obliged to intervene as the patron of Arianism.

At the Council of Rimini in July, 359, there were assembled more than four hundred bishops, of whom scarcely eighty favored Arianism, while all the others were orthodox. Nevertheless, despite this small majority, Constantius maneuvered his agents so well that they held the orthodox majority at bay. A delegation of the orthodox members of the council received by Constantius in Thrace ended up signing a protocol on October 10 which lent itself admirably to an Arian interpretation. This signing took place at a stopping place near Adrianopolis called Nice, or Nicaea, and this name was later used extensively by the Arians to deceive the ignorant, as if it were a matter defined by the great Ecumenical Council of Nicaea in 325. The other counselors who remained at Rimini were induced to yield through the violence which the praetorian prefect Taurus exercised over them for many months.

The similar Council of Seleucia, which began on September 27, numbered about one hundred and fifty Eastern bishops. Here the interests of caesaropapism were upheld by Leonas, quaestor of the sacred palace. Here also, although the orthodox had a three-to-one majority, the tricks and insults of Constantius' representative first troubled the waters and eventually brought about the capitulation of almost all to the wishes of the Arian emperor. From this moment began the disastrous descent of orthodoxy, culminating in the Council of Constantinople which began in January, 360.

To the totality of these events St. Jerome refers when, not without a touch of rhetoric, he states that "the whole world groaned and was surprised to find itself Arian" (*ingemuit totus orbis et Arianum se esse miratus est — Altercatio Orth. et Lucif.,* 19).

122. Despite these unexpected victories, the prevalence of Arianism was more apparent than real. When the imperial favor and the play of interests which permitted the Arian leaders to obtain the most conspicuous episcopal sees for themselves would come to an end, the swollen sails of the movement would immediately collapse. The great majority of Christians remained orthodox. The outstanding orthodox bishops had been banished and persecuted in various parts of the empire, but everywhere they had carried on their earnest battle against the prevailing heresy.

During his almost fifty years as bishop, Athanasius was to be seen at his see in Alexandria, at Tyre, Treves, Rome, and among the ascetics of the Egyptian desert. Eluding the imperial authorities, he constantly enjoyed the open or secret support of the enemies of Arianism. During his peregrinations he wrote works of various types, especially tracts dealing with the Arians or Emperor Constantius in order to defend his own personal conduct or to denounce that of his adversaries.

Hilary of Poitiers, the Athanasius of the West, performed a similar task. At the time of his baptism, about 345, he was married and had a daughter, Abra. A fervent Christian and then a priest, it was not long before he was made bishop of Poitiers. Since he was very strongly opposed to Arianism, Constantius sent him into exile in Asia Minor (§ 76); but there also he showed such diligence against the Arians that they persuaded the emperor to order him back to his own country since he was "a disturber of the peace in the Orient" (Sulpicius Severus, *Historia Sacra*, 2. 45). After his return, Hilary assailed the emperor in a violent "invective," *Contra Constantium Imperatorem*, in which he assembled, almost as in an anthology, the most frightful parallels from Sacred Scripture and ecclesiastical history. Did Constantius perhaps believe that he had sinned less than the ancient Jews? He certainly had not: the Jews had spilt the blood of Zacharias, but Constantius had betrayed Christ Himself. Hilary addressed him as he "would have addressed Nero, Decius, or Maximian." The emperor is a precursor of the antichrist, the instrument of his dark plots. Though this invective was written in 360, it was not published until after Constantius' death.

The most unusual and delightful of these anti-Arian polemicists is Lucifer of Cagliari. His Latin is plebeian, replete with idiomatic expressions of his native Sardinia. His writings are of great interest to philologists, just as his Biblical citations are important for the history of the Latin text of the Bible prior to St. Jerome. Lucifer did not have a speculative mind. He was essentially a fighter who hurled himself into the middle of the fray, a pamphleteer who would not come to terms with anyone, not even with the orthodox who held opinions different from his own. After he was sent into exile by Constantius, he traveled for six years through Syria, Palestine, and the Thebaid; but during his stopovers he regularly bombarded the emperor with short essays which he had delivered personally to him. The titles of these *opuscula* reflect their contents: *No Pacts with the Heretics; The Apostate Kings; On St. Athanasius, or No One Ought to Judge and Condemn Another in his Absence; Pardon Ought Not to be Given to One who Sins Against God; It is Necessary to Die for the Son of God.*

123. After meeting his counselors in Thrace (§ 121), Constantius directed all his energies to the Persian question. Since he believed that he had solved the military and religious problems of the West, he was of the opinion that he not only could, but he also should, take full action against the Persians. The war about Amida, even though it had been most damaging for the enemy had, as a matter of fact, provoked endless criticism of the sovereign and his staff in the empire. Were the very costly fortifications and garrisons along the Euphrates only to serve as convenient targets for the enemy? Would it not be much better to anticipate their attacks and carry the war into Persian territory as had been done in the glorious times of Trajan and Galerius?

All this was evident, but the fact that the war could not be carried on in those boundless regions beyond the Euphrates without a very large army and without the assistance of still more numerous allies was also evident. But manpower was the one thing that was most lacking. Fifty thousand combatants at the most could be counted in the East. Few or none could be withdrawn from the garrisons in Illyricum and on the Danube, always under the threat of barbarian invasions. And even if levies were made in these regions, they would produce very little. There was no other recourse except to turn to Gaul, but here the problem became precarious for other reasons.

Militarily, after Julian's last campaign, Gaul could be said to be at peace. To be sure, toward the end of 359 bands of Picts and Scots had penetrated Roman territory in Britain, but this did not represent a serious threat. Julian moreover had sent against them his master of cavalry, Lupicinus, with the Aerulian and Batavian auxiliaries and two divisions of the Moesi, which had been more than sufficient. In the rest of Julian's territory all seemed quiet. It was only natural, then, that the emperor should look for military assistance from this peaceful quarter.

Yet precisely here was to be found the man about whom the emperor did not feel at ease. The old distrust with which Constantius regarded Julian must have become somewhat weakened, but it had never been completely lost. At court there was no lack of individuals who took every occasion to revive it. Chief among these was the praetorian prefect Florentius (20. 4. 2). To the old trick of giving a malicious interpretation to all of Julian's actions in the emperor's presence, there was now added a new one which aimed at producing the same effect but by opposite means: Julian was extolled as a military and civil leader; he was the sole savior and restorer of Gaul (Mamertinus, *Grat. act. Juliano*, 4). On the suspicious Constantius these grandiloquent eulogies naturally had the effect of vinegar poured on an open wound.

124. Faced with these internal and external problems, Constantius made his decision. Troops should be brought from Gaul for the imminent campaign against Persia. The chief motives behind this decision were, first of all, the very pressing need of troops in the East; second, the absence of any threat of war in Gaul, where the barbarians had abandoned all aggressive tactics (Zosimus, 3. 8); and, finally, the fame of the courageous Gallic troops who were said never to turn their backs on the enemy (*I Constantius*, 36b), and who, moreover, a short time before in the siege of Amida (§ 120) had given proof of admirable heroism (19. 6. 3 ff.). These were patent reasons, and they certainly gave an appearance of regularity and justice to Constantius' decision. But were there no other secret motives that might have had a particular influence upon Constantius?

We have already observed that Julian had the mystic conviction that he was under the direct guidance of the gods and had received from them a great religio-political mission for the Roman Empire. Moreover, there were many in the East and perhaps also in the West who were aware of this conviction and who approved it (§§ 42, 43, 45, 58, 66, 71), and there had been the recent exchange of letters between Julian and Oribasius full of presentiments (§ 111). These various hopes and aspirations were too widespread to escape the notice of Eusebius, Paul the Chain, Gaudentius (§ 113), and other spies at court, always ready to report their suspicions to Constantius. Further, Julian's victories had rekindled the enthusiasm of his secret supporters in the East, where prayers were being offered that at least a portion of the benefits granted by the gods to Gaul would be granted also to the eastern portion of the empire (Libanius, 14. 41).

Constantius could have easily concluded that a notable dampening of all these hopes centered on Julian would be achieved by making him militarily weaker, and this could be done by withdrawing troops from Gaul and sending them against the Persians (cf. Ammianus, 20. 4. 2). In this way his suspicions about his cousin could be concealed behind the apparent strategic interests of the empire.

125. After reaching his decision, Constantius sent his orders to Gaul through the tribune and secretary Decentius. A comparison of Julian's account of this episode (*To the Athenians*, 282c ff.) with that of Ammianus (20. 4. 2 ff.) reveals some minor divergencies. According to the former, the emperor "wrote letters slandering" Julian "and threatening destruction to the Gauls," but he does not state to whom these letters were sent. Further, the emperor ordered Lupicinus and Gintonius to withdraw from Gaul and take with them the larger and more experienced part of the army, giving an express command to Julian not to oppose this in any fashion. That the emperor sent this order to Lupicinus is easily explained by the fact that he did not know that at this time Lupicinus was no longer near Julian but in Britain (§ 123).

Ammianus makes no reference to any letters sent by Constantius to belittle Julian. Further, he makes no mention of Gintonius by this name. He specifies that the troops to be transferred were the Aeruli, Batavi, Celts, Petulantes, and an undefined number of other infantrymen taken in lots of three hundred from each of the other divisions of the army. Moreover, for this purpose Julian's chief squire, Sintula (who must correspond to the Gintonius named by Julian), was commissioned to take the best of the *scutarii* and *gentiles*, who formed part of Julian's personal bodyguard, and send them off at once to the emperor.

Quantitatively, the total number of troops to be dispatched to the East may be estimated at about a half of the soldiers at Julian's disposal; but qualitatively, this half was worth considerably more than the remainder who were to stay in Gaul. This must suffice for the substance of the command. As for the way in which it was communicated, it is necessary to note that it was directed to Lupicinus and

Sintula (or Gintonius), both of lesser rank than Julian and subject to him. Absolutely speaking, it cannot be denied that the emperor, as the supreme authority in the state, had the right to skip over a higher official and give orders directly to a lower one, but *summum ius, summa iniuria* — a right pushed to its extreme may prove to be a very grave injustice. It may even be asked if it was to Constantius' own interest to apply at this time his *summum ius* in such a delicate matter, when there was need of great tact and prudence. Here also Constantius must have listened to the suggestions of Julian's enemies, his counselors at court.

126. There was, further, a legal question pertaining to the auxiliaries enrolled in the Roman army. When Julian came to know the destination of the companies that were to leave the country, he recommended that "those men who had left their homes across the Rhine and had come to him on the condition that they should never be led to regions beyond the Alps should not be forced to undergo such a hardship; for he declared that it was to be feared that the barbarian volunteer soldiers, who were often accustomed to come over to our side under such conditions, might on learning this be kept from doing so hereafter" (Ammianus, 20. 4. 4). Poorly informed as we are today, we have no right to question these statements of Julian and Ammianus. It is important to note, moreover, that they speak of the auxiliaries who had been enrolled after they "had left their homes across the Rhine," and not of those coming from the nearer side of the Rhine, who strictly speaking were Gauls. The least we can say is that an agreement not to expatriate the troops was frequently unobserved, either with the consent of the enlisted auxiliaries themselves or because of other reasons that now escape us. We have already seen that a mixed populace of Gauls and barbarians, from which the Romans made unconditioned forced recruitments, dwelt along the lower course of the Rhine (§ 100). Thus, even those auxiliaries who fought so valiantly against the Persians at Amida (§ 120) must almost certainly have included soldiers who were not of Gallic descent. The same must also be said of the army which hardly a year later Julian was to lead against Constantius. In this army there were undoubtedly many auxiliaries of barbarian origin. And yet these auxiliaries at Amida and those that followed Julian, as far is known, left their countries without any reluctance. The personal attachment which the auxiliaries had for Julian does not adequately explain their readiness to leave Gaul and join him in his

expedition against Constantius. We have seen them deriding and rebelling against him for much lesser reasons, such as their *crumenae* (purses) and their stomachs (§ 101). How, then, was Julian ever able to bring about such a change of policy that some months later he could lead the auxiliaries who, in his own words, "should never be led to regions beyond the Alps," thousands of miles beyond them? From the information at hand we may conclude not only that the narrative of the events has been muddied, but that the rapid change from a reluctance to leave their country on the part of the auxiliaries to a ready enthusiasm for the campaign was the result of hard and secret labors.

When Decentius arrived at Julian's court in the beginning of 360, Lupicinus, the principal addressee of Constantius' letter, was in Britain. Consequently, he had to give it instead to Sintula. When Decentius informed Julian of the orders he had brought, the Caesar, "leaving all to the will of his more powerful associate" (*potioris arbitrio cuncta concedens* — 20. 4. 4.), made only one objection. He did not believe, as we have already seen, that the auxiliaries should be expatriated against the terms of their contract. Nevertheless, foreseeing the discontent of the troops when they learned of the order for their departure, he was anxious to consult the praetorian prefect Florentius, who was at Vienne gathering provisions. He wrote and urged him to return to Paris, adding that if he would not come, he would himself relinquish the emblems of his office, preferring to meet death under the command of another than to be responsible for the ruin of the province (20. 4. 8). Such grave words show that Julian felt he was facing a crisis. Florentius, on the other hand, who was in touch with his friends at court, refused to have any part in the changing course of events. He stayed at Vienne, leaving Julian to extricate himself from his difficulties. This in itself was an indication as to which of the two contestants Florentius would support when an open conflict broke out. 127. Sintula, the secondary recipient of Constantius' orders, eager to show his compliance with them, collected the troops which had been assigned him and set out on the road. This seemed to augur a favorable outcome for the emperor's commands, but he soon suffered a reverse that made matters worse than they had been before.

What happened is best described by Julian himself: "I waited for Florentius and Lupicinus to arrive; for the former was at Vienne, the latter in Britain. There was in the meantime a great excitement among all the civilians and soldiers, and someone wrote an anonymous letter to a neighboring town addressed to the Petulantes and Celts, as these legions are called, full of accusations against Constantius and lamentations about his betrayal of the Gauls. The author of the letter, moreover, bitterly complained of the disgrace I had suffered. When this letter came, it moved all the chief supporters of Constantius to urge me in the strongest terms to send the troops away at once before similar letters were scattered among the other legions. And indeed there was no one there of those who seemed to be well disposed toward me, but only Nebridius, Pentadius, and Decentius, the latter of whom had been sent for this very purpose by Constantius. And when I said that we ought to wait for Lupicinus and Florentius, no one listened to me; but they all declared that we should do the very opposite, unless I wished to add this as a further proof and evidence for the suspicions already entertained about me. And they added this: 'If you send away the troops now it will be your work, but when the others come Constantius will give the credit to them and not to you, and you will be blamed'" (*To the Athenians*, 283ad).

Ammianus' account agrees for the most part with Julian's, which he used along with other secondary sources. He is more precise in stating that the anonymous letter was secretly thrown on the ground near the standards of the Petulantes, and that among many other things it contained the following: "We indeed are being driven like condemned criminals to the ends of the earth, and our dear ones whom we freed after murderous battles from their former bondage will once again be slaves of the Alemanni" (20. 4. 10). The letter was brought to Julian and discussed in his council. But it seems that different copies of it were circulated with practically the same text (cf. Zosimus, 3. 9). This could create the suspicion that there was a secret organization directing the propaganda.

128. Seeing that the situation was going from bad to worse, Julian sought a remedy for it. He gave orders that the departing troops should be accompanied by the wagons of the imperial post which had brought their wives and children so that their leaving would be less painful. Then, following the advice given him by the emperor's supporters, he began to think about writing directly to him, but first he waited for affairs to jell.

After the decision for the departure of the troops had been made, it was necessary to determine a place of assembly. Julian was anxious to exclude Paris to avoid any violent manifestations on the part of the relatives of the departing troops. But Decentius and the others sent by Constantius insisted upon Paris, confident that the presence of the high civil and military functionaries would check the anger of the troops. Julian yielded to their opinion and agreed that they should assemble at Paris.

As the soldiers gradually abandoned the encampments, their families, lodged in neighboring villages, became alarmed and tried to intervene. If the description given by Libanius is to be taken literally, it would seem that at any moment they expected a repetition of the recent barbarian invasions (18. 95). Mothers brought up their infants and entreated their husbands not to abandon them and did everything in their power to detain them. It may be noted that these complaints corresponded to those contained in the anonymous letter dropped on the ground near the legionary standards.

When the first platoons began to arrive, Julian went out to meet them in the suburbs of the city. He greeted them cordially, praising those whom he personally knew and reminding them of the brave deeds they had performed. He encouraged them to continue to be well-disposed to the emperor, who would reward them for their sacrifices. In the evening he invited their officers to supper and asked them if they had any requests to make. All went well, and his guests left saddened at the thought that through an adverse fortune they were being deprived not only of the land of their birth but also of such a mild ruler (20. 4. 12–13).

At this point it is necessary to listen to Julian himself, since he furnishes us with psychological data that no one else can give. "The legions arrived, and I, according to custom, went to meet them and urged them to continue on their way. They halted for one day, and until that time I knew nothing of what they had planned; I call to witness Zeus, Helios, Ares, Athena, and all the other gods that no such suspicion even came near me until that very evening. About sunset, when it was already late, I learned what was going on; and immediately the palace was surrounded and they all began to shout, while I was still considering what I should do and feeling very little confidence. My wife was still alive (§§ 15, 56), and I had happened to go to an upper room near hers to rest alone. From there I then prayed to Zeus through an opening in the wall. And when the shouting grew still louder and all in the palace was in a horrible state of confusion,

I 'entreated the god to give me a sign; and thereupon he showed one to me and ordered me' (Odyssey, 3. 173–174) to yield and not to oppose the will of the army. Yet even after I had received these signs I did not yield at once but resisted as long as I could, and would not accept either the salutation [as Augustus] or the crown. But since I could not overcome so many by myself alone, and the gods, who willed that this should be, urged on the soldiers and softened my resolve, about the third hour or so some soldier or other gave me a necklace, and I put it on my head and returned from there to the palace, as the gods know, groaning in my heart" (To the Athenians, 284ad).

129. Ammianus' account agrees substantially with that of Julian's although it gives several additional details (20. 4. 14 — 5. 10). After the dinner given to them by Julian, the officers returned to their lodgings. But here they became extremely agitated, and in their excitement seized their weapons, ran to the palace, completely surrounded it, and hailed Julian as Augustus even though he refused to show himself to them before daylight. On this same night Julian received another mystic communication quite distinct from the one he had experienced while praying to Zeus through the opening in the wall. In this communication the guardian spirit of the empire (genius publicus) appeared to him in his sleep and reproached him as follows: "For a long time, Julian, I have been secretly watching the forecourt of your house, desiring to lift you up to a higher rank, and I have often gone away as though rebuffed. If I am not received even now, when many men share my opinion, I shall depart sad and dejected" (20. 5. 10; cf. §§ 41, 208).

Strengthened by this new illumination from on high, Julian came out in the morning to address the soldiers; but when he attempted to reconcile them to the commands of the emperor, they refused to listen and began to revile him with abuse and insults. He was thus forced to yield (assentire coactus est — 20. 4. 17). He was then raised up on a military shield and proclaimed Augustus. To complete the ceremony he had to be crowned. The crowd asked him to produce a diadem. Julian replied that he had never had one. They then asked for a necklace or coronet of his wife. But this aroused Julian's superstitious fears: it would be an evil omen to be inaugurated with a woman's jewelry. They then looked about for one of the frontispieces with which the cavalrymen adorned the heads of their chargers. But Julian did not approve of this either. Finally, a certain Maurus, a standard-bearer of the Petulantes, removed the neck chain which he wore as a carrier of the dragon (the standard of the cohorts) and placed it on Julian's head. Thus all was in order. The newly elect, following an old tradition, then promised five gold coins and a pound of silver to each of the soldiers.

Julian had now cast his die. Later he declared that the thought which most afflicted him at the time was that "of not seeming to be obedient to Constantius to the end" (*To the Athenians*, 285a). Despite the enthusiasm of his soldiers, Julian was troubled with anxiety, "and foreseeing the future with quick intuition" (*futuraque celeri providens corde* — Ammianus, 20. 4. 19), he kept to himself within the palace. In the meantime, according to Julian (Ammianus makes no reference to the matter), the supporters of Constantius were attempting to win over the soldiers with bribes. When a rumor spread through the army that Julian had been killed, the soldiers became so enraged that they rushed into the palace. They were finally calmed when they saw Julian in the council chamber dressed in the official garb of an Augustus. They then withdrew. Julian adds that only with the greatest difficulty did he succeed in saving the supporters of Constantius from the vengeance of the soldiers.

When these events became known to the troops under Sintula, who had already set out on the road (§ 127), they reversed their steps and returned to Paris. The next day Julian held a grand review of the whole army on an open plain. Having mounted the tribune, which was surrounded by the legionary standards, he referred to his election as Caesar, reminded the soldiers of their joint campaigns, and warned them that promotions in both the civil and military services would henceforth be determined solely by personal merit. The soldiers of the lower ranks, who for a long time had not shared in the honors and awards granted to the others, struck their shields with their spears and shouted their approval. The warning about promotions was put to an immediate test. The Petulantes and Celts, who had been stanch supporters of Julian, requested a special favor for their commissaries. But when their petition was refused, they withdrew without being offended or depressed.

Seeing the bad turn which affairs had taken in Gaul, first Decentius, and then Florentius departed for the court of Constantius (20. 8. 4, 20–21). When Julian learned of the latter's departure, he sent after him by the public courier service his relatives and personal effects which had been left behind in Gaul.

130. The scenes which we have thus far witnessed upon the great stage of history have not all run smoothly (cf. § 126). It should therefore be to our advantage to go behind the stage in search of some explanation.

We have already seen that Julian, besides fostering an inveterate rancor for Constantius (§ 40), had a mystic conviction of being chosen by the gods to renew their worship. We have also seen that many others shared in this conviction, and that Julian was himself aware of the hopes that were placed in him (cf. the references in § 124).

But was this radiant dream to remain a vague hope without effective realization? Certainly not: as the faithful soldier (miles) of his father Mithra (§ 60), he was obliged to fight bravely so that at the end of his life he might repeat the words of the Christian apostle: "I have fought a good fight" (2 Tim. 4:7). He had to exert himself to the utmost, especially now when Constantius' hold on his throne seemed to be slipping.

Still, it was an immense undertaking, and Julian's mystic temperament had need of a manifest confirmation to bring him to act. But the means for such a confirmation were at hand. Despite his many duties as governor, Julian had kept his esteem for those who had instructed him in theurgy and the mystery religions. He had even brought two of them with him into Gaul (§ 66), while through letters he kept in touch with others, among whom was the eminent hierophant of Eleusis who had initiated him into the Eleusinian mysteries (§ 59).

An historian who is very favorable to Julian tells us explicitly that after his reconquest of Gaul, "he summoned the hierophant from Greece, and after he had performed with his assistance certain rites known to themselves alone, he was aroused to throw off the tyranny of Constantius. Oribasius of Pergamum and a certain Euhemerus, a native of Libya, which the Romans in their language call Africa, were their accomplices in this" (Eunapius, 476).

131. We have already seen that Oribasius shared in Julian's secret worship of the gods and like him had received omens pertaining to Constantius' imminent ruin (§§ 66, 111–112). At this time he was writing at Julian's request a great medical encyclopedia. In its original draft it comprised seventy books, but it was later abridged by its author. Not much of it is extant, but the little that survives includes the intro-

duction dedicating the work to his patron Julian. Oribasius, as Julian's friend and client, was an important person in Gaul and could travel about at will. When Julian addressed his letter to Oribasius, he sent it to Vienne since that is where he was staying. Not all of his efforts, therefore, were taken up with his medical writings; a good share of them must have been directed toward the realization of those politico-religious ideals he had taught Julian and which they discussed in their correspondence. The same type of activity must have been carried on by the other secret friends that Julian had brought with him to Gaul. Had these friends of Julian formed a secret conspiracy to influence the soldiers before the rebellion at Paris? What caused such a radical change in the troops that they were eager to follow Julian in his expedition to the East against Constantius, whereas they had refused a few months earlier to cross the Alps (§ 126)? Who wrote and distributed the anonymous sheets found near the standards and in the camps (§ 127)? The fact that there is no direct evidence that Julian was personally involved in these events is not surprising. But this lack of direct evidence should not make us forget what Eunapius has told us about Julian's secret meetings with Oribasius and his other colleagues, and that it was Oribasius "who made Julian emperor" (Eunapius, 498).

X. FROM PEACE TO WAR

§§ 132–137. Negotiations Between Julian and Constantius: Letters and Envoys.   §§ 138–140. Preparations on Both Sides.   §§ 141–142. The March to Sirmium.   §§ 143–144. Rebellion at Aquileia and the Occupation of Nish (Naissus). §§ 145–147. Letter to the Philosopher Themistius.   §§ 148– 149. Reaction of Constantius and His Death.   §§ 150–151. Julian Elected Augustus; He Moves to Constantinople. The Court at Chalcedon.

132. Julian, therefore, had crossed his Rubicon; but if Julius Caesar knew perfectly well where he was going when he crossed his fatal stream, the same cannot be said of his successor. Ammianus tells us that "Julian was in a state of anxiety, dreading the outcome of the recent events; for after carefully considering the matter from various aspects, he was certain that Constantius would never consent to what had been done, since he stood low in the emperor's esteem as being base and contemptible" (20. 8. 2).

And, as a matter of fact, the vision which Julian could have had of his own future, whether proximate or remote, was anything but favorable. If there were a few bright spots on the horizon, the rest was darkened with clouds. In the highly probable event of war Julian could count only on his troops in Gaul, and even about them he had some doubts. But what were they in comparison with the forces of the other three quarters of the empire which Constantius could muster in the field against him? Where would he find provisions for the army of Gaul? How would he overcome their reluctance to leave their own country (§ 126)? True, he had gained much secret sympathy in the East, but in the event of an open break the majority would undoubtedly side with Constantius; and among these would be the hordes of state employees and others dependent upon the public treasury who looked upon Constantius as the son and legitimate heir of the great Constantine. Constantius' Christianity was practically an extension of the

145

Arian heresy which Constantine had unsuccessfully attempted to stifle at Nicaea, and this certainly did not recommend him to the orthodox. But neither, on the other hand, did they have any surety about Julian's own beliefs. Except for the members of his secret coterie, very few knew anything about his projects in favor of idolatry, whereas on Christian feasts he could be seen going to church to perform his devotions (§ 117). To conclude, then, had it been a question of betting on one or the other, few indeed would have placed their money on the man from Gaul.

133. Although Julian may have had an impetuous and mystic temperament, he could conduct himself with calmness and precision when the occasion demanded it. As he had done earlier during the rebellion at Paris, so now he carefully weighed the pros and cons of his position. He reached the conclusion that he should keep his eyes upon developments and gain what time he could. From the outset he resolutely rejected the idea of a complete break with Constantius by recourse to arms. On the contrary, if he entered into direct negotiations with the emperor, new factors favorable to his own aspirations might emerge with time. He began to seriously consider the suggestion made by Constantius' supporters before the rebellion at Paris of writing directly to the emperor (§ 127).

Recent events had considerably increased Julian's stature. He could now address Constantius as an Augustus clothed in the purple which he had received from his soldiers. It is true that there were many points at which the two were at complete odds, but these were the very problems which needed airing to see if some compromise could be found. So far as our evidence goes, Julian had not as yet officially informed Constantius of developments in Gaul; but he knew perfectly well that the emperor had heard of them from the different functionaries who had fled to him from that province. Julian, on his part, had never denied Constantius' supremacy in the empire, nor had he made any personal requests of him. Consequently, it was quite proper for him to write directly to Constantius to inform him of what had happened and to receive instructions from him for the future. There was no need to adopt the attitude of one asking for a favor or begging for pardon. It was sufficient to treat of concrete matters, examining past events and drawing conclusions for those to come.

134. Moved by such considerations, Julian wrote a letter to Constantius, the rough contents of which have been preserved for us by

Ammianus (20. 8. 5–17). The letter, in a respectful and even deferential tone, describes the events that had occurred and, in general, manifests a desire to come to a peaceful settlement. It is neither timid nor arrogant. It consistently recognizes Constantius as the supreme ruler of the empire and simply asks in return a recognition of the new ruler in Gaul. On the practical level, Julian shows himself still bound to Constantius and interested in the general welfare of the empire. He declares that he is willing to send Spanish horses for the Persian war and the *gentiles* and *scutarii*, who had earlier set out under the command of Sintula (§§ 125–127), and these would be reinforced by "some young men of the Laeti, a barbarian tribe stationed on this side of the Rhine, or at least by those who of their own choice come over to us" (20. 8. 13). The specific mention of the provenience of the troops seems to refer implicitly to the problem of the expatriation of the auxiliaries, which had furnished the spark for the rebellion at Paris (§ 126). As for the civil and military officials in Gaul, Julian states that he will accept whomever Constantius nominates as praetorian prefect, but he intends to reserve to himself the choice of the rest since he is anxious to have assistants whom he can trust.

In this letter, Julian succeeds in repressing his own feelings except where he begins to lecture Constantius, exhorting him to be on his guard against the calumnies of his courtiers (*nec . . . sussurrantes perniciosa malignos admittas*). He then goes on to remind his cousin of the fact that they are united by ties of blood and by their high position (*qui caritate sanguinis et fortunae superioris culmine sociamur* — 20. 8. 11). Probably more out of prudence than out of deference, Julian signed the letter simply as Caesar and not as Augustus (*To the Athenians*, 285d).

As a further mark of courtesy, Julian sent the letter by two messengers esteemed by Constantius. One of these was Pentadius, who, however, should probably not be identified with the emperor's confidant of the same name (§§ 69, 113). The other was Eutherius, whose earlier mission to the imperial court on Julian's behalf had ended so happily (§ 82). There were hopes, then, that the two envoys could make the contents of the letter less bitter.

135. According to Ammianus, Julian entrusted another secret document for Constantius to the two envoys. No one was allowed to examine the contents of this mordantly reproachful letter (*obiurgatorias et mordaces*), and even if it had been permitted, it would not have

been proper to publish them (*nec si licuisset, proferre decebat in publicum* — 20. 8. 18).

How far can this report, given only by Ammianus, be trusted? If the stinging contents of the letter were eventually known to Ammianus, this is no proof that he learned about them while Constantius was still alive. The emperor died within a few months, and many secrets hitherto buried in the imperial archives could have come to light. The authenticity of the second letter has recently been questioned on the grounds that its bitterness would have been in obvious contradiction to the deferential and conciliatory tone of the first. In other words, Julian would be tearing down with the second letter what he had tried to build with the first. But such a doubt does not seem to be justified. In the first place, Julian was naturally so impetuous that he did not always succeed in controlling his feelings. Second, he was spiteful, always anxious to get the last word in an argument, and not above using contempt and sarcasm to humiliate his adversaries. Such traits are revealed in many of his works — especially in the *Misopogon, Against the Galileans, Against the Ignorant Cynics,* and *Against the Cynic Heraclius.* Psychologically, then, there are no reasons for denying the fact that Julian could have written both letters, assuming a different attitude in each. In the first he speaks as a politician who, not wishing to appear as yet as an open enemy of Constantius, temporizes for practical reasons and writes a letter which can be read by anybody. In the second he writes as a polemicist, as an orphaned cousin persecuted for many years who at last gives vent to his spleen, yet still has the courtesy not to broadcast his personal animosity. There are, accordingly, no real reasons for doubting Ammianus' positive statements about the second letter.

136. Taking the two letters, the envoys set out on the road. They had hardly left Julian's sphere of influence and entered into that of Constantius when they encountered continual obstacles placed in their way by the authorities. Since they came from Julian, they were covertly detained (*oblique tenebantur* — 20. 9. 1). Sticking tenaciously to their goal, however, they finally reached the Bosphorus. After crossing the strait, they pushed on to Caesarea in Cappadocia, where Constantius was living at the time, in the same general area where Julian had passed his early adolescence (§ 12).

The two messengers were admitted into the emperor's presence and given permission to present their letters. No sooner were they read than the emperor broke out in a rage (*ultra modum solitae indignationis excanduit* — 20. 9. 2), so much so, in fact, that they feared for their lives. Without questioning them or even permitting them to speak, the emperor ordered the two envoys to leave; but later, having regained control of himself, he set about weighing the two threats growing up about him, the danger from the Persians in the East and that from Julian in the West. Which should he meet first? After listening to the advice of his counselors he decided to give priority to the Persians. They seemed to be the more dangerous and immediate threat; against them, moreover, a plan of action was already in progress. Julian, on the other hand, was not as powerful as the King of Kings, and, further, in his letters he had shown that he was anxious to reach an understanding, which could indicate that he sensed his own weakness.

In the end, Constantius came to the same conclusion that Julian had already reached: it was necessary to gain time. To take his answer back to Julian he passed over the two who had come from Gaul and sent posthaste instead the quaestor Leonas, who had so ably seconded the caesaropapism of Constantius at the Council of Seleucia (§ 121). According to Ammianus, the letter which Leonas carried to Julian contained the following principle points (20. 9. 4–5): If Julian cared anything for his own safety and that of his friends, he should set aside his arrogance and assume no more authority than he had as Caesar; for the office of praetorian prefect, the filling of which Julian had himself left to Constantius, he nominated Nebridius, Julian's quaestor; he appointed the secretary Felix as master of offices; and he made other appointments as well, overriding Julian's desire to fill these lesser posts with men of his own choosing.

When Leonas arrived in Paris, he thought it best to adopt the same authoritarian tone as that of the letter which he was delivering, but he was quickly disillusioned. He was received with respect, but when in the course of his first audience he ventured to chide Julian for his ingratitude toward Constantius, he was sharply answered: "And who left me an orphan as a child if it was not my father's murderer?" Such recollections served only to exasperate the old wound (Zonaras, 13. 10).

But to this answer, already too revealing, Julian added another even more significant since it was given through the lips of others. The following day Leonas was conducted into the camp, where he found a great crowd of soldiers and civilians assembled to hear him. These were the men who had elected Julian Augustus and who now had to be informed of the further development of events. He asked for the scroll containing Constantius' edict and began to read it in a loud voice. When he came to the place where the emperor, condemning what had been done at Paris, declared that the authority of Caesar was sufficient for Julian, from all sides terrifying shouts of "Julian Augustus!" arose.

Leonas could do nothing but return to Constantius and tell him about Julian's second imperial election at which he had himself assisted. He also carried with him a letter from Julian to the emperor telling what had occurred. As for the new appointments, Julian accepted Constantius' nomination of Nebridius as praetorian prefect, as he had agreed he would. He rejected, however, the emperor's candidate for the master of offices and named instead Anatolius. There remained the post of commander in chief held by Lupicinus, who was now busy in Britain (§§ 103, 123, 125). Even before receiving Julian's first letters, Constantius had named Gomoarius as his successor. But Julian had his own motives for distrusting this haughty and arrogant officer. He therefore sent an agent of the police to Boulogne (Gesoriacum) to stop anyone going to Britain who might spread the news of his recent quarrel with the emperor. On his return after finishing the campaign in Britain, Lupicinus was arrested with three others (20. 9. 9; *To the Athenians*, 281a).

137. Although all these factors increased the ever widening rift between the two cousins, Julian does not seem to have as yet abandoned the idea of coming to some sort of an agreement (Ammianus 21. 1. 1 ff.). We know that he not only wrote several letters at this time to Constantius, but that all the legions dependent upon him also addressed letters to the emperor entreating him to accept an amicable settlement (*To the Athenians*, 285d–286a). Obviously, such entreaties could not have left Gaul without the consent, or perhaps even the prompting, of Julian.

As for Constantius, it can at least be said that if he did not accept Julian's proposals, he was certainly relieved by the lull in the dispute. Julian tells us that Constantius sent him "a certain Epictetus, a bishop of Gaul, to offer me guarantees of my own safety" (*To the Athenians*, 286c), that is, personal immunity, on the condition, of course, that he abandon his pretenses and make his due submission. We have no further knowledge of this Epictetus, though some scholars by reading "bishop of Centumcellae" (Κεντουμκελλῶν ἐπίσκοπον), the modern

Civitavecchia, for "bishop of Gaul" (τῶν Γαλλιῶν ἐπίσκοπον) have identified him with Constantius' ardent Arian collaborator of the same name. But whoever he may have been, his embassy was a complete failure, as had been that of Leonas before him.

Almost the whole of the year 360 passed in these diplomatic skirmishes. Foreseeing that an open clash was almost inevitable, Julian was anxious to finish his consolidation of Gaul, since the course of events might soon take him far from that part of the empire. To the north was located the Frankish tribe of the Atthuarii (§ 73) who had often troubled the Roman territories with their incursions. To check these infiltrations and at the same time to keep his soldiers in trim for the uncertain morrow, toward the end of the summer Julian conducted a campaign against them. A rapid campaign, marked by far-flung pillaging and a great slaughter of these raiders who believed themselves to be safe in their practically unknown and impervious recesses, spread terror through the Atthuarii and the neighboring tribes (20. 10. 1–2). Julian then returned, examining the forts on the Rhine as far as Augst (Augusta Rauracorum). Having recovered there some lost territory, he turned to the right and came to Vienne. There he set up his winter quarters, celebrating on November 6 the quinquennial games to commemorate his election as Caesar dressed in a magnificence he had never adopted before (21. 1. 4).

The substitution of Vienne for Paris is easily explained by its proximity to the Alps and to the roads leading to the east. In other words, this move was a further provision against the uncertain morrow. And such likewise was Julian's participation in the feast of the Epiphany, January 6, 361, in the church of the Christians. We have already seen that he took part in the feast "in order that he might win the favor of all men," even though in secret he was accustomed to perform various acts of pagan worship (§ 117). But Julian, who despised Christianity, was concerned lest he leave at his back, if he had to depart for the East, sparks of a revolt, particularly among the Christians.

138. Still, not even Gaul itself was entirely free from danger. During the winter, at the beginning of 361, a new incident occurred, as regrettable to Julian as it was unforeseen. Swarms of Alemanni coming from the domains of Vadomarius made a sudden raid on the regions bordering on Raetia, thus breaking the earlier treaty that their chief had made with Julian (§ 104). Against the invaders Julian sent the Celts

and Petulantes under the command of Count Libino, but the poorly led expedition had an unfortunate ending. Libino was killed and the auxiliaries were dispersed near the *oppidum Sanctionem* (the modern Säckingen). Roman sentinels captured a messenger bearing a letter from Vadomarius to Constantius containing among other things the implication that Julian needed to be watched: "Your Caesar lacks self-control" (*Caesar tuus disciplinam non habet* — 21. 3. 5). But in his letters to Julian he constantly addressed him as "lord, Augustus, and god" (*dominum et Augustum appellabat et deum*). Having thus ascertained Vadomarius' treachery, Julian did not trouble his army with a regular campaign but contented himself with paying back the chieftain in kind. After luring Vadomarius into Roman territory with a courteous invitation, he had him seized and sent far off into exile in Spain. Soon after, a modest military expedition avenged the death of Libino and pacified the agitated area.

There was a rumor abroad that Constantius in his desire to harass Julian had persuaded Vadomarius to order the raids. Ammianus records this rumor without necessarily subscribing to it (*si famae solius admittenda est fides . . . si dignum est credere* — 21. 3. 4–5). Julian, for his part, alludes several times to secret agreements between Constantius and the barbarians (§§ 88, 99), but these accusations were voiced in anger when he was at war with the emperor (*To the Athenians*, 280b, 286ab). Perhaps in this matter it is better to imitate the reserve of Ammianus.

It is certain, on the other hand, that Constantius, even though he was at the other end of the empire, was worried about Gaul and making preparations against Julian. He ordered large quantities of grain to be stored in the cities bordering on Gaul and in the area about the Cottian Alps. Julian claimed that the barbarians who had received the letters bearing Constantius' demands brought them to him along with others from Taurus, the praetorian prefect of Italy (*To the Athenians*, 286b). The emperor further sent Gaudentius, who had been spying on Julian's activities in Gaul, to Africa to guard the coasts lying opposite Aquitania and Italy and secure the transport of grain from there to Rome (21. 7. 2–4).

To strengthen his army, particularly with a view to the war with the Persians, Constantius took other more ample measures. He made new levies of troops to fill out the deficiencies in the legions, increased the number of squadrons of cavalry, requisitioned beasts of burden

and materials for war, and imposed heavy contributions on all classes
without distinction (21. 6. 6).

Julian naturally took similar measures, although on a lesser scale
because of his more limited resources. He notes himself (*Misopogon*,
360c) that the Gauls not only ventured to take up arms on his behalf,
but that they also furnished him with large sums of money, and when
he would have refused it, they almost forced him to accept it. Less
voluntary seem to have been the provisions to which he refers in another
passage: "I thought that I ought to add to my forces the most powerful
tribes and supplies of gold and silver, to which I had a perfect right"
(*To the Athenians*, 287a). "The most powerful tribes" refers to the
recruiting of auxiliaries from both sides of the Rhine (§ 126). The
"supplies of gold and silver" seems to refer to taxes imposed upon the
various subject tribes.

139. Now everything was ready. The only thing needed to generate
the deadly spark was for the two charged poles to come together. But
they were separated by an enormous distance — the whole central area
of the empire. Which of the two would make the first move toward
the other?

Constantius was much occupied with the Persians since even after
the loss of Amida (§ 120) the Roman fortunes had not improved.
During the year 360 he had entertained Arsaces, the king of Armenia,
and had received his oath of continued fealty. With a powerful force
in the fall of the same year he attempted to conquer the city of Bezabde
lying on the left bank of the Tigris, but the expedition failed in its
purpose. The city held out, and Constantius had to withdraw into
Syria to pass the winter at Antioch (20. 11. 32). Here at the beginning
of 361 he married Faustina (§ 56). There can be little doubt that this
third marriage was largely dictated by the hope of offspring not realized
in his two earlier marriages, particularly since he was eager to avenge
himself on his cousin Julian. At this same time Constantius named
Florentius, who had fled from Gaul (§ 129), praetorian prefect in
Illyricum; and he further appointed him as consul for 361 along with
Taurus, the praetorian prefect in Italy (§ 138).

At the beginning of July, 361, Julian saw that his hour had come.
The space separating him from Constantius was vast indeed, but the
way through it was almost unimpeded since most of its defense forces
had been withdrawn by Constantius for his war against the Persians.
Julian was thus able to tell his soldiers that Illyricum was without

important garrisons (21. 5. 6). But it was of the utmost importance to act with speed, thus adding the element of surprise to the initial advantage, as the great generals of all times from Alexander the Great and Julius Caesar to Napoleon have done.

Still, there was one aspect of the great decision about which Julian did not feel perfectly at ease — that of religion. If the gods had entrusted him with a great mission (§§ 124, 130) and with their interior inspirations had for years guided him toward its fulfillment, if during the crucial rebellion at Paris he had received a direct admonition from Zeus and later a visit from the *genius publicus* stirring him to action (§ 129), why was he not now, at the most critical hour of all, favored with some celestial communication which would reassure him in the step he had taken? On the other hand, he may have thought that the gods were not obliged to reveal their pleasure in an extraordinary fashion when this could be known through ordinary means. At least he so acted. After entrusting the whole matter "to the gods who see and hear all things," he offered sacrifice for his departure and received favorable omens for it (*To the Athenians*, 286d). Ammianus adds the further particular about Julian's departure that, being "uncertain about his soldiers' loyalty" (*incertus de militum fide* — 21. 5. 1), he propitiated Bellona with a secret rite before addressing his troops.

Bellona was an ancient Roman goddess of war, but by this time the primitive concept of this divinity had been contaminated with oriental beliefs and her worship had developed into rites of phrenetic exaltation. Since Julian was attracted to such rites, it is not surprising that he had recourse to a divinity of this type. But it is remarkable that he was still uncertain about the loyalty of his troops. He may have felt a distrust for the Christians among them who, whether they professed their faith openly or only in secret, could not have been few. Even Jovian, for example, who was to succeed Julian some months later, was a Christian.

140. After assuring himself of the support of the gods, Julian went on to secure the support of his men. From a stone tribunal he directed to the assembled army a vibrant discourse (21. 5. 2–8), calling to mind their past successes, laying out his plans for the future, and invoking the assistance of heaven. In this latter he wisely skirted the religious problem by referring only to "the will of the God of heaven" (*arbitrio dei caelestis*) and to "God's support and yours" (*deo vobisque fautoribus*), formulae which could offend neither pagans nor Christians.

The discourse still further inflamed the minds of his soldiers, who received it with shouts of approbation and, when ordered to do so, took the usual oath of allegiance to their commander "under pain of dire execrations" (*sub exsecrationibus diris*), putting their swords to their throats to show that they were ready to lose their lives for him. The only one who refused to take the oath was the new praetorian prefect Nebridius (§ 136), who did not wish to turn his back upon his benefactor Constantius. The soldiers became infuriated and wanted to kill him, but Julian saved his life and gave him leave to retire to his property in Tuscany. All the other dignitaries took the oath.

Julian then set about reorganizing the high command (Ammianus, 21. 8. 1). He appointed Nevitta master of the cavalry, Jovius quaestor, Mamertinus to the treasury (*largitiones curandas*), and Dagalaif prefect of the household troops. As for the office of praetorian prefect, Ammianus states that Julian "leaving Augst [*Augusta Rauracorum*] . . . sent Sallustius, who had been promoted to prefect, back into Gaul and ordered Germanianus to take the place of Nebridius" as praetorian prefect. This Sallustius is not to be identified with Julian's earlier friend (§ 114) but with Flavius Sallustius, consul in 363 (23. 1. 1). As for Germanianus, who later appears as praetorian prefect in Gaul (26. 5. 5), it seems that at this time he was acting as an adjutant to Sallustius since the latter must have been busy with preparations for the coming campaign.

In planning his attack, Julian sought to add confusion to surprise in the enemy camp. The advance should therefore be carried out not only as rapidly as possible, but it should also be directed along three different routes so that the enemy at the very outset would get the impression of the approach of a crushing force, and would not take into account from whence it came and where the principal attack would be launched. Julian had, as a matter of fact, only twenty-three thousand men at his disposal, a very small number even for those times, and especially for such an undertaking as this. He divided them up into two principal groups, each comprising about ten thousand men, placing one under the command of Nevitta and the other under Jovinus and Jovius. The rest, about three thousand men, he kept for himself. After making this division of the army, he gave written instructions for the order of march (*per tesseram edicto itinere* — 21. 5. 13) and set out at once for Pannonia.

Nevitta was to cross through Raetia and Noricum, and then descend into Pannonia following the course of the Danube. The troops of Jovinus and Jovius were to cross northern Italy and then head for the Danube. Julian with his own small force set out for the same goal, marching first through the Black Forest (*Marcianae silvae*). The juncture of the three armies was to take place at Sirmium (Mitrovica in Yugoslavia), the capital of Lower Pannonia, on the Save River, which flows into the Danube.

The passage from the "cold war" to open hostilities had immediate repercussions in the legislation of the empire. Hitherto Julian's name as Caesar had been found with that of the Augustus Constantius, but for May 19, 361, there is a law promulgated in Constantius' name alone (*Cod. Theod.*, 2. 20. 1; cf. *Cod. Justin.*, 3. 29. 9).

141. Ammianus, no mean authority in military matters, quite properly observes that Julian "rashly committed himself to a doubtful fortune" (*temere se fortunae commisit ambiguae* — 21. 5. 13) when he set his expedition in motion, though it may well be that the word *temere* in this particular context does not have its usual pejorative meaning of "rashly," but the more positive meaning of "boldly," "without hesitation." Nevertheless, from various aspects the expedition undoubtedly appeared rash, and was recognized as such by Ammianus when he refers to its "doubtful fortune." The smallness of the invading army, the distance from their own bases, the uncertainty of the obstacles which they would encounter, the reception they would get from the people, and many other intangibles were so many reasons for challenging any hopes for a successful outcome of the campaign.

The ancient historians, such as Libanius, Mamertinus, and Zosimus, who report the progress of the troops, were all supporters of Julian. Ammianus, who would have given an impartial account of the expedition had he accompanied it, was in Asia at this time (§ 83) and had to depend on others for his knowledge of it. Since unfortunately there are no longer extant any primary sources giving a neutral or hostile account of the events, all of our information is burdened with the general prejudice that it has at least unconsciously been "adapted." A somewhat similar case is afforded by the battle of Marengo. In the official "adapted" report, which received subsequent retouchings, Napoleon appears as the guiding genius of every maneuver, whereas in reality he gained the victory unexpectedly after suffering a severe repulse. Desaix's unforeseen arrival rescued Napoleon from the plight into which he had already fallen, just as Constantius' unforeseen death brought a happy ending to Julian's expedition which, after a propitious beginning, was heading toward disaster.

We have no information about the advance of the forces under Nevitta and Jovinus until their arrival in the environs of Sirmium. The passage through northern Italy, where Julian had foreseen ambuscades and other obstructions (Ammianus, 21. 8. 4), seems to have been achieved without striking a blow. The surprise tactics created the intended panic. At the first appearance of the invaders, Taurus, praetorian prefect in Italy, fled and, passing through Illyricum, took with him Florentius, who was prefect there (§ 139).

With respect to the advance of Julian's small force we are better informed, thanks to the later accounts of Mamertinus, a member of the band. But too often he is carried away by his enthusiasm, not rising above his office of panegyrist (cf. *Gratiarum actio Juliano*, 6–7). According to him, Julian's march proved to be difficult at first as he made his way through the rugged paths of the forests, but it subsequently changed into a triumphal sailing down the Danube. The people flocked together at his passage — the Romans on the right bank to acclaim him, and the barbarians on the left to gaze on him in wonder and to bend their knees in terror. Prescinding from the rhetoric, we may conclude that the advance toward Sirmium was extremely rapid, as was necessary and intended. While on land, Julian led his army "in forced marches" (or, possibly "in a long line" — *porrectius ire pergebat* — 21. 9. 1). Then, having arrived at a spot where the Danube was navigable, he ordered his soldiers to get into the numerous boats which they found there. According to Ammianus, these were discovered by chance, but more probably they had been collected by Julian's advance agents. They then began to sail downstream.

142. Instead of halting to receive the homage of the tribes along the banks, Julian kept on his way with the greatest possible speed and secrecy (*quantum fieri potuit, ferebatur occulte*). When his fleet arrived at Bononea (Bonmünster?), a small town nineteen miles north of Sirmium, he disembarked his soldiers. Since it was a night poorly lit by a waning moon (*senescente luna*), it must have been about October 10.

Despite Julian's speed and secrecy, some news of his coming had already reached Lucillianus, a brave officer who had fought against the Persians and who, after holding various responsible posts, had received the military command of Pannonia with his residence at Sirmium.

There he immediately ordered his troops to assemble. Then, thinking that a few days would pass before Julian appeared upon the scene, he calmly went home to rest. He was sleeping soundly, just as the prince of Condé had done the night before the battle of Rocroy, when he was abruptly aroused by loud shouting about his bed. With startled eyes he saw that he was surrounded by unknown soldiers who ordered him to get up and follow them. Julian, scarcely disembarked, had sent Dagalaif (§ 140) ahead with a picked band to bring Lucillianus to him whether he wanted to come or not.

After he had been kindly received by Julian, the disconcerted count regained courage and attempted to show his gratitude by giving his captor some opportune advice: "Very rashly have you, general (*imperator*), ventured with so few into another's territory." To this Julian replied with a bitter smile: "Save your advice for Constantius, for I have offered you the emblem of majesty [the royal purple given to kiss at the beginning of an audience] not as a counselor, but in order that you might cease to be afraid" (21. 9. 8).

The head of the resistance being thus removed, no further opposition was offered. Julian entered the city and was joyously received by its inhabitants. The following day he staged a chariot race, hoping that the favorable reception given to him at Sirmium would be imitated by the other cities he would meet on his way. But on the third day, urged on by the constant need of haste, he resumed his march. About this time, perhaps even at Sirmium, he was rejoined by the armed forces of Nevitta, which had passed through Raetia and Noricum. With the addition of these reinforcements Julian's small band of soldiers was increased more than threefold.

In addition to the forces brought up by Nevitta, Julian now had at his disposal the newly surrendered garrison of Sirmium, consisting of two legions and a cohort of archers; but he distrusted these soldiers, who were in reality deserters and who could at any moment also abandon him. They could not be left at their post since there was the danger that they might form a conspiracy with the natives. Where could he send them? Julian thought of Gaul, an area sufficiently distant from Constantius, but Gaul was at peace and had no need of reinforcements. Still, to justify the move, after he had left Sirmium he sent orders to the two legions and the cohort to depart for Gaul "on the pretext of urgent necessity" (*per speciem necessitatum urgentium* — 21. 11. 2).

143. This time, however, the exact opposite of the Paris revolt occurred. The disgruntled soldiers took to the road. As they advanced, stirred up by the tribune of the cavalry Nigrinus, they became more and more dissatisfied. When they arrived at the upper extremity of the Adriatic, they barricaded themselves in Aquileia, "a well-situated and prosperous city surrounded by strong walls" (21. 11. 2) which, although it had frequently been besieged in the past, had never been taken. After entering the city, the rebels at once set about reinforcing the gates and towers. This bold act created a reaction in favor of Constantius which was to spread throughout Italy. The native population seems to have supported the revolt not so much because it favored the emperor, but because it feared his vengeance after Julian's defeat, which all expected.

This revolt was highly inimical to Julian, who needed to protect his rear. It represented, moreover, the beginning of a conflagration which could spread rapidly throughout the West. To quench the first flames, he ordered Jovinus, who was coming up with his troops (§ 140), to turn toward Aquileia and reduce the rebels to obedience, assigning him reinforcements for this purpose.

The attack on the city began at once, but with no success. As time passed the siege became a blockade, but those in the city still resolutely held out. When the first reports of Constantius' death reached them, they had no effect since they were believed to be false. Only later were the rebels convinced by a special envoy sent by Julian that Constantius was really dead and that he was now the sole Augustus. Then the usual popular reaction occurred. The gates were thrown open and the leaders of the rebellion surrendered. Nigrinus was burned alive; a few others were condemned to death; the rest escaped punishment.

Meanwhile, after the three-day halt at Sirmium, Julian had resumed his advance toward Constantinople. Marching down along the Danube, he entered Moesia, whose southern boundary bordered on Thrace. In its turn, Thrace was bounded on the south by the Propontis (the Sea of Marmara), on which was located the capital, Constantinople. Julian had thus accomplished nearly half of his journey. But the final stretch was the most dangerous. Thrace was well fortified with military posts and included such strong cities as Philippopolis and Adrianopolis, which had to be passed before the capital could be reached. Further, though it was easy to enter into Thrace, it was anything but easy in a strategic war to withdraw from it. The approach was the chain of mountains extending from Mount Haemus on the east to Mount Rhodope on the west. There was only one pass across this chain, and that was through the valley of Soucis. Although this pass offered few obstacles to those descending from Moesia, it was extremely difficult to negotiate on the way up from Thrace, even when there were no troops to defend it (*etiam nullo vetante* — 21. 10. 4).

After scouting the pass, Julian concluded that it was foolhardy to advance farther. He therefore limited himself to occupying it with a garrison under the command of Nevitta. When he had done this, he withdrew to Nish (Naissus), which Ammianus describes as "a well-stocked town" (*copiosum oppidum* — 21. 10. 5), and which was therefore suitable for passing the winter.

144. Though Julian's stay at Nish was not long, it must have been laborious. Military and political problems demanded his constant attention. With regard to his expedition, he could do nothing more than hold the positions he had occupied on his way to Constantinople and await for those events which had been favorably forecast by the gods. Politically, he had not only to establish a certain amount of order in the territories already dependent upon him, but also to find ways of winning over the people in the territories controlled by Constantius.

Julian's epistolary activity during the whole of the expedition was most intense. From a passing observation in a letter addressed to his uncle a few days after the emperor's death, we know that it was written with his own hand since all of his secretaries were busy, and that, too, after "the third hour of the night" had begun (*To his Uncle Julian,* 382b). He not only wrote to his friends with whom he wished to keep in touch but also to public corporations, cities, and territories whose good will he wished to secure.

Passages from these letters reveal his state of mind at this highly critical period. In another letter written shortly after the death of Constantius to his revered master, the theurgist Maximus of Ephesus (§ 36 ff.), he refers to the preceding months of anxiety: "May Zeus, great Helios, mighty Athena, and all the gods and goddesses be my witnesses how I trembled for your safety on my way down to Illyricum from Gaul! And I kept inquiring of the gods, though I dared not do this myself, for I could not endure to see or hear anything such as one might have imagined would be happening to you at that time, but I turned this over to others. And the gods did in fact show plainly that you would have to undergo certain trials, but nothing terrible, and that none of the plans of the impious would be carried out" (*To Maximus*, 415ab).

These consultations about the future were continued throughout his stay in Illyricum. According to Ammianus, "in the midst of his great activity in Illyricum, Julian was constantly examining the entrails of victims and watching the flight of birds in his eagerness to know how matters would turn out; but he was embarrassed by ambiguous and obscure answers and remained uncertain about the future" (22. 2. 1).

In time Julian was comforted by better portents. Aprunculus, a Gallic orator skilled in haruspicy, "finally told him what would happen" (*ei tandem . . . nuntiavit eventus*). This soothsayer, who had accompanied Julian on his expedition, found a double membrane about the liver of a sacrificial victim. There could be no more doubt: the expedition would have a happy ending. Nevertheless, even after this decisive proof, Julian was hesitant, since "he feared that things agreeable to his own desires were being invented, and he was therefore sad" (22. 1. 2). But a new omen made everything clear. At the very moment that Constantius was dying in Cilicia a soldier, while giving his hand to Julian to help him mount his horse, slipped and fell prostrate on the ground. Julian, immediately interpreting the accident as having reference to himself and Constantius, cried out: "The man who raised me to my high estate has fallen." If the two events actually occurred at the same time, as Ammianus asserts, it would have been November 3, 361. Nevertheless, "even though he knew these were favorable signs, he remained within the confines of Dacia as if standing fast upon his guard, and even so he was sore afraid; for he did not think it wise to trust predictions which might perhaps have their fulfillment in opposite effects" (22. 1. 3).

145. Two typical aspects of Julian's character appear in this context: fervent mysticism and cold calculation, ample play for omens and sacrificial offerings but exact attention also to the realities amidst which one had to work.

Julian must certainly have weighed his own position, and when he did he must have discovered that the balance was not at all in his favor. While clinging to the mountain chain overlooking the valley of Soucis, he knew that beyond the pass Constantius was assembling a great force to hurl at him in an all-out attack. Since there was no returning from the plains of Thrace, to descend from the pass with his modest force was equivalent to descending into a tomb. He would be able to maintain himself at Soucis itself as long as the rebellious soldiers in his rear at Aquileia did not break through Jovinus' blockade or a new revolt did not break out elsewhere (cf. 21. 12. 21–22). And this did not even take into account the fact that the ever-restless barbarians on the other side of the Danube could take advantage of the rivalry between the two Augusti to fall upon the Roman provinces.

Confronted by these harsh realities, Julian tried to strengthen his position by favoring his subjects and by making new appointments. Mamertinus, who had already been assigned to the treasury (§ 140), became prefect of both Italy and Illyricum. He was further designated consul for the following year with Nevitta, the general guarding the pass of Soucis. Having met the historian Aurelius Victor at Sirmium, Julian summoned him to Naissus, named him governor of Pannonia Secunda and erected a bronze statue in his honor. As prefect of Rome, to replace Tertullus, he chose the senator Maximus, preferring him to Symmachus, who in Ammianus' opinion was more deserving of the post (21. 12. 24). These two, Symmachus and Maximus, on their return from an embassy to Constantius ordered by the Roman senate, visited Julian at Naissus and were received by him with great honor. The precise object of their visit to the two rivals is no longer known.

During this same period Julian attended to the general public welfare. Walls, aqueducts, and other works were restored; measures were taken to reactivate the municipal curiae, which were almost deserted (§ 107). Further, as had already happened in Gaul (§ 110), taxes were lessened in some regions, and stores of grain were collected for Rome, which had begun to suffer from the hostile activity of Gaudentius in Africa, Rome's traditional granary (§ 138).

Julian took no less care to arouse the sympathy of the people through his writings. One of his temperament, who dictated his works in a rapid and turbulent fashion, could not have failed to avail himself of this means of bringing entire groups over to his side. As a consequence, in the two or three months preceding the death of Constantius, besides his private correspondence, Julian sent letters to various cities in Illyricum, Macedonia, and Greece, as well as to the Roman senate and to the Athenians. This last is the only one that has been preserved.

Ammianus furnishes us with some information about the letter to the Roman senate, which was, according to him, "a sharp oration full of invective, in which he accused Constantius of certain disgraceful acts and faults" (21. 10. 7). In this letter, as in his secret letter to Constantius some months earlier (§ 135), Julian was again unable to control his impulsiveness. The "conscript fathers," who still maintained a sincere regard for the traditions of aristocratic dignity, received Julian's letter with great displeasure, and at a certain point they cried out in unison: "We ask you to respect your own great benefactor" (*auctori tuo reverentiam rogamus*), that is, Constantius. From this it may be argued that Symmachus and Maximus had set out on their embassy to the East before the arrival of the unfortunate letter; otherwise they would not have extended their journey to include its author.

Julian was not disturbed by the hostile reception given to his letter, perhaps because he did not realize how damaging such indignation was to his cause. Shortly afterward, as Ammianus continues, "he attacked the memory of Constantine as an innovator and disturber of ancient laws and of customs handed down from antiquity, openly charging him with being the first to bestow the fasces and consular robes upon barbarians" (21. 10. 8). In this, as Ammianus immediately notes, "he showed neither good taste nor consideration." Julian should have at least avoided doing what he had censured so bitterly, but a short time later he raised to the rank of consul Nevitta, a Gaul by birth and much less deserving than the men whom Constantine had raised to the highest magistracy. His boorishness was bad enough, but what was even more intolerable was his cruelty in high office.

146. As has already been observed, of the various public letters sent by Julian at this period, only the one addressed *To the Senate and People of Athens* has come down to us. It is a competent work containing many important autobiographical details, the general veracity of which cannot be challenged; but the same cannot be said about the many accusations hurled at various individuals. It is a highly personal defense of Julian's own activities, and from the very beginning its aim of winning over the Athenians is perfectly obvious. In it Julian strives to arouse their sympathy by enumerating the trials he has suffered from his childhood, contrasting these ills which he has received from Constantius with his own dedication to duty and slowness to assert himself. He recalls the excellent proof that he had given of himself in Gaul, assures them that he had stayed entirely apart from the revolt at Paris, so much so, in fact, that at the time he "was terribly ashamed and ready to sink into the ground at the thought

of not seeming to obey Constantius to the last" (285a). In the conclusion of the letter he declares: "And even now if he cared to be reconciled, I would be content with what I now possess" (287a). Since this letter was composed about two months before Constantius' death, it must be concluded that at this time he was still disposed toward an agreement with the emperor.

Such a conciliatory attitude seems to be ruled out by Ammianus (21. 10. 7), who states that Julian believed it impossible that Constantius would ever be induced to come to an agreement. This observation is connected with his account of Julian's letter to the Roman senate, and hence comes from about the same time as the letter to the Athenians. But it seems hardly necessary to reject either Julian's attestation or Ammianus' notice: both may be true, since at this crucial period the highly excitable Julian (§ 34) could have passed rapidly from hope to fear. There was even a rumor abroad that Julian proposed to end the contest by uniting his army with that of Constantius and leaving them the right to choose between the two, a project with so little to support it as to appear incredible.

At this point we must take into consideration a very different work, Julian's letter to the philosopher Themistius, about which there is a serious question of chronology. Some scholars maintain that it was composed shortly after Julian became sole ruler, which agrees with the manuscript tradition attributing it to "the emperor" Julian. Others believe that it was composed much earlier, between the years 355 and 356, when Julian, as Caesar, began his government of Gaul. Although there are weighty reasons on both sides, the first opinion seems the more tenable.

Themistius was a prominent man, a pagan but not hostile to Christianity, a friend of Constantius and the author of a number of panegyrics in his honor. He had even recommended freedom of conscience and religion in a discourse *On Clemency*. He had for a long time been in correspondence with Julian (*To Themistius*, 259d–260a; cf. 253a, 266d); and when the latter became governor of Gaul, he exhorted him to take up the active life without, however, disowning philosophical speculation. After Julian became emperor, Themistius returned to the same theme and renewed his earlier exhortations. Julian answered him with the letter which has come down to us.
147. Morally, it is the best of Julian's writings. Deferential to his distinguished friend, Julian makes much of his advice but he does

not hesitate to give reasons for his own views. In writing to Themistius, Julian must certainly have had in mind many other cultured readers into whose hands the letter would eventually come, and who would thus have the opportunity of knowing the outlook and proposals of the new emperor.

The figure of the *optimus princeps* contemplated by Julian as his model for inspiration is substantially that traced by Plato, whose work *On the Laws* is frequently cited. "It seems to me, at any rate, that the task of ruling is something more than human and that, as indeed Plato too used to say, a king needs a more divine nature" (φύσεως δεῖσθαι δαιμονιωτέρας — 260c). And in another place, commenting on the exhortations he had received from Themistius, he observes: "With your recent letter you have increased my fear and made the contest appear in every way more difficult, saying that I have been assigned by God the same position formerly occupied by Heracles and Dionysus, who, being at once philosophers and kings, purified almost all the earth and sea of the ills infesting them [§ 42]. You bid me free myself from every thought of rest and repose in order that I may fight in a manner worthy of my destiny. And, in addition to these examples, you remind me of the legislators such as Solon, Pittacus, and Lycurgus, and you say that men today rightly expect greater things from me than were achieved by any of these. Coming upon these words, I was almost dumbfounded" (253c–254b). Consequently, Julian observes, if anyone, dismayed by the greatness of the task, should prefer the philosophical meditation and the "humble home" (δωμάτιον — 259b) of Socrates, he should not be blamed on that account. Past experiences have shown that he knows how to lead an active life himself, and he cites as examples his interventions on the behalf of different persons in Ionia and Phrygia (§ 43). But who deserves greater admiration, Socrates or Alexander? From Socrates came "the wisdom of Plato, the strategy of Xenophon, the courage of Antisthenes, the Eretrian and Megarian philosophies, Cebes, Simmias, Phaedo, and countless others, not to mention the offshoots from the same source, the Lyceum, the Stoa, and the Academies. Who indeed ever found salvation through Alexander's conquests? What city was ever better managed because of them, what private individual improved? You may find many who were enriched by these conquests, but no one made wiser or more temperate than he was by nature, if indeed he was not made more insolent and arrogant. On the other hand, all those who now are

saved through philosophy owe their salvation to Socrates" (264cd).
Worthy of the whole composition is the conclusion: "May God grant
me the greatest blessings and wisdom to match these blessings! For
I now think that I need help from on high (ἐκ τοῦ κρείττονος) most
of all, and also from you philosophers by every means at your disposal,
since I have shown myself to be your leader and champion in times
of danger . . ." (266d–267a).

148. At this time Constantius had moved from Antioch (§ 139) to
Edessa to be nearer the Persian peril, which seemed to be a graver
threat than Julian. During this period of waiting he learned that the
King of Kings had relinquished his campaign because of unfavorable
omens. Thus freed in the East, Constantius could concentrate upon
the West, and he decided to confront Julian with all his forces.

In Thrace, facing the valley of Soucis, he already had an important
contingent under the command of Count Marcianus. He now hastened
to send there the troops no longer needed on the eastern front, making
use of every means of conveyance at the disposal of the imperial post
for this purpose. Being a good orator, he did not let the chance of
addressing his assembled army slip by (21. 13. 10–15). He recalled
the benefits he had lavished upon Julian, the ingratitude he had
received in turn, and entrusted his soldiers with the task of punishing
the rebel with the help of the Supreme Deity (favore numinis summi
praesente). His vibrant discourse was received with enthusiastic demon-
strations analogous to those with which Julian's soldiers a few months
earlier had greeted his harangue (§ 140). There were shouts, clashings
of weapons, and ardent requests to be led immediately against the
rebel. The lancearii (lancers) and mattiarii (soldiers armed with a
small javelin called a mattium) and companies of light-armed troops
set out at once under the command of Arbetio. Constantius also
ordered the auxiliary Laeti under Gomoarius (§ 136), who had broken
with Julian, to oppose Julian's advance. At the earliest possible moment
he would himself rejoin the army in Thrace, bringing up the other
troops.

From the height of the Soucian pass, Julian was aware, and in part
had a view, of these preparations; and if up to this time he had been
torn between hopes and fears (inter spem metumque — 21. 13. 1),
from then on his hopes must have been on a constant decline. Shut
off in front, threatened from the rear by the rebels in Aquileia, far
from his bases of supply, and in enemy territory, the only thing he

could really hope for was some unforeseen break in fortune. And this break occurred — Constantius' death, which ended the contest by taking one of the two rivals from the scene.

Although our sources employ the customary convention of listing the various portents which foreshadowed the emperor's death, it was in reality altogether unexpected. Constantius was only a little over forty-five (Socrates, 2. 47; Sozomen, 5. 1; cf. Ammianus, 21. 15. 3, which must be corrected from the Christian historians) and had shown himself full of energy and activity almost to the end. Nevertheless, in his final months, perhaps because of the troubles of the empire, he had appeared somewhat unsound in mind. In his sleep he saw strange phantoms; he confided to his intimates that for some time he no longer perceived, as he had occasionally before, a mysterious being which he believed to be his guardian genius "assigned to protect his life" (*tutelae salutis appositus* — 21. 4. 2). Despite all this, and against the advice of his courtiers, toward the end of autumn he set out on the road from Antioch to join the army in Thrace. A final portent was given to him in the suburbs of the city. He saw a corpse of a man lying stretched out toward the west with its head torn off. Disregarding the omen, which could have been interpreted as foretelling his own "setting" (cf. the *contra occiduum latus extensum* of Ammianus, 21. 15. 2), he continued on his way; and, after reaching Tarsus, the birthplace of St. Paul, was stricken with a light fever. Convinced that the exertion of the journey would help him throw off his sickness, he kept traveling on the difficult roads leading to Mopsucrene, the last station of Cilicia at the foot of Mount Taurus.

The following day his fever became so high that he was unable to continue the journey. Since death was imminent, preparations were made for his baptism. Up to this time he had been a "clinic" (κλινικός) catechumen, that is, one of the many who waited to receive baptism on their deathbed. His father Constantine, who was baptized by the Arian bishop Eusebius of Nicomedia when he was already dying, had done the same. Equally Arian was Euzoius, the bishop of Antioch, who baptized Constantius. His death came on November 3, 361, after a long agony.

According to Ammianus (21. 15. 2), there was a rumor abroad that before his death Constantius had designated Julian as his successor. But this report is at variance with the accounts of other historians, and it also seems unlikely in that Constantius left his third wife with child (§ 139), whose dynastic rights he would probably have respected.

149. Ammianus describes the character of the deceased emperor at some length, enumerating both his virtues and his vices (21. 16. 1–18). Though he was himself a pagan, he makes an acute observation on the role of religion, that is, Arian Christianity, in Constantius' life: "Confusing the plain and simple religion of the Christians with an old woman's superstition, he stirred up much discord by subtle investigations instead of seriously trying to settle the points at issue. And as this spread more and more, he fed it with public disputations. Since throngs of bishops making use of the public beasts of burden hastened hither and thither to the synods, as they call them, while he sought to subject the whole ritual to his own will, he cut the sinews of the public carriers" (21. 16. 18).

Dynastic murders such as those which had taken place after the death of Constantine (§§ 5, 6) did not occur after Constantius' death. A move was made to elect immediately a new Augustus in opposition to Julian, but this plan seems to have been due, as many others before it, to the grand chamberlain Eusebius (§§ 50, 112, 113), who had everything to fear from Julian's coming to power (cf. Ammianus, 21. 15. 4). But since Eusebius himself must have had no small number of enemies, his plan fell through. Moreover, the very needs of the empire demanded Julian as Augustus: the barbarians were a threat along the Danube and the Persians along the Euphrates; Constantius' child had still to see the light of day, and even if it should be a boy (it was instead a girl), the empire would have to be ruled for long years through others, whereas the times required an energetic and warlike leader. Such reasons influenced the great majority of officials and functionaries to side with Julian.

To forestall any hesitancy, they sent the counts Theolaif and Aligildus as ambassadors to Julian to announce the death of Constantius and to invite him to come at once and claim the succession. Julian seems to have mistrusted the report at first, fearing that it was a ruse to lure him from his position in the Soucian pass into the perilous plains of Thrace. But then, reassured by a book of divination or, what seems more likely, by confirmation from other sources, he cast aside his diffidence, certain that his hour had come.

During these days Julian's soul was in a veritable tumult, tossed about as he was by a sense of relief, by new hopes, and by his thoughts for the future. His two letters already cited (§ 144) furnish some hints of this. He had finally obtained clear proof of the authenticity of the mission entrusted to him by the gods (§§ 42, 147). And since this had been effected by the gods themselves, he offered hecatombs to show his gratitude: "I openly worship the gods, and the majority of the troops accompanying me are pious [that is, they were pagans and not "impious" Christians]. I sacrifice oxen in public. As thank-offerings to the gods I have presented them with many hecatombs. The gods order me to purify everything as far as I can, and I obey them with a right good will" (*To Maximus*, 415cd).

"Since all my secretaries are busy, I have forced myself to write this to you with my own hand. I am alive, by the favor of the gods, and have escaped the necessity of either suffering or doing anything irreparable. The Sun, whom most of all the gods I entreated to assist me, and sovereign Zeus are my witnesses that I never prayed that I might slay Constantius, but rather that this might not happen. Why then did I come? I came because the gods expressly bade me, and promised me safety if I obeyed them, but they threatened me with what I pray no god may do to me if I stayed" (*To his Uncle Julian*, 382b).

150. Reassured by so many signs from the gods, Julian descended from the valley of Soucis, rapidly crossed Thrace, and, passing through Perinthus (Heraclea), arrived at Constantinople, which he entered on December 11.

The fame of his exploits in Gaul and his quarrel with Constantius, which had ended so unexpectedly and so fortunately for the capital, had made him a center of universal interest, and the people turned out en masse to greet him. It was partly due to the usual curiosity of a crowd, and partly to pride at receiving into Constantinople the first emperor born there, and whom, perhaps, some remembered having seen walking about the city as a boy. "For it seemed almost like a dream that this young man, who had just reached the prime of life (*adultum adhuc iuvenem*), of slight frame but conspicuous for great deeds, after the bloody destruction of kings and nations, had passed from city to city with unexpected speed, and growing in strength and resources wherever he went, like a rumor had easily gained possession of everything, and had finally received without any loss to the state the supreme power bestowed on him by heaven's nod" (22. 2. 5).

Meanwhile the court had decreed a solemn funeral for the dead

Augustus, and Jovian, who not many months later was to render a similar service for the dead Julian, had brought Constantius' body to Constantinople. There it was interred in the Church of the Apostles, the most sumptuous of the basilicas erected in that city by Constantine, and the one in which he had himself been buried. Julian, now in complete possession of his title of Augustus, attended the funeral services (Libanius, 18. 117 ff.; Zonaras, 13. 12). Wearing the imperial purple but not the crown, he appeared to be sorely stricken with grief. The senate then decreed the "apotheosis" of the deceased emperor, adding the usual title of *divus*. Julian made no objection to this, though a little later in his satire, *The Caesars*, he ridiculed this ancient Roman custom of "fashioning gods as others fashion puppets" (332d).

Julian now stood alone at the pinnacle of the empire, and he could without serious opposition bend his efforts to the accomplishment of the task entrusted to him by the gods. He had first to confront the problems that had risen in the past, examining the inheritance received from Constantius and correcting whatever mistakes had been made. It was impossible, of course, to bring Constantius into court, nor did Julian have any intention of attempting to do so, since he was resolved to show respect for his rival now that he was dead. But one could easily distinguish between the deceased Augustus and his surviving counselors, and call these latter to account. That this was Julian's state of mind is shown by a letter written toward the end of 361 to Hermogenes, a former prefect of Egypt: "Ah! how I have been saved against hope! Ah! how against my hopes I have heard that you escaped the three-headed hydra. Zeus be my witness that I am not speaking of my brother (τὸν ἀδελφόν) Constantius, since he was what he was, but of the wild beasts that were about him casting their evil eyes on all. They made him harsher than he was by nature, though this was in itself by no means mild, even if it seemed so to many. But since he is now one of the blessed, 'May the earth,' as the saying goes, 'lie lightly on him!' Nor should I wish, Zeus know it well! that these others should be unjustly punished; but since they are being accused by many, I have set up a court to try them" (*To Hermogenes*, 389d–390a).

This court, or "special commission," had to pass judgment on deeds committed under a different ruler and in a different political climate. It was to begin functioning in the last days of 361; and to give it an appearance of independence and neutrality, it was assembled at Chalcedon across the Bosphorus from Constantinople. Julian, of course, did not figure among the jurors, but the presidency of the court was entrusted to his friend Secundus Saturninus Sallustius (§ 114), who a little earlier had been named praetorian prefect of the East. If Sallustius was worthy of the post, the same cannot be said of Arbetio, the public prosecutor, whom we have already seen among Constantius' commanders in Thrace (§ 148). He was a wily opportunist, ever ready to change sails with the wind. Ammianus justly describes this man, who had earlier contributed to the ruin of Gallus and Ursicinus (14. 11. 2; 15. 2. 4; 20. 2. 2), as "always shifty and overweening" (semper ambiguum et praetumidum); and he rightly blames Julian for including him among the judges at Chalcedon (22. 3. 9). Mamertinus (§ 145) was another member of the court; Nevitta, Agilo, Jovinus, and other officers who acted as auditors represented the army.

The preponderance of the military caste on the tribunal did not augur well for the accused, who belonged primarily to the high court circles and the civil administration.

151. Palladius, a former official in Gallus' court, was the first to be tried. He was suspected (suspicione tenus insimulatum) of having lodged certain accusations against Gallus with Constantius. He escaped with a light sentence — banishment to Britain.

It was then the turn of Taurus, prefect of Italy, who was accused of fleeing to Constantius when Julian's troops invaded Italy (§ 141). This charge is immediately rebutted by Ammianus with the elementary observation: "What crime did he commit, if fearing a storm that had risen he fled to the protection of his emperor?". (22. 3. 4.) This same historian points out a tragicomic aspect of Taurus' trial. He happened to be still consul for the current year 361, and his condemnation "was read not without great horror" (non sine magno legebantur horrore) since the public protocol began with the words: "In the consulate of Taurus and Florentius, when Taurus was summoned to court by the heralds." This was tantamount to saying that one of the supreme magistrates had both cited and condemned himself. In his case also the penalty was not extreme: he was simply exiled to Vercellum (Vercellae).

A certain Pentadius, perhaps different from the one sent as an envoy by Julian to Constantius (§ 134), was accused of having set down in writing the interrogation of Gallus; but he stoutly defended himself and was acquitted as having simply carried out Constantius' orders.

Florentius, Julian's adversary in Gaul in the matter of the taxes (§ 110), later praetorian prefect in Illyrium, and now consul, received a summons, but he went into hiding with his wife. He was condemned *in absentia* for contumacy. Another Florentius, an Evagrius, a Saturninus, and a Cyrinus were exiled on charges no longer extant. Ursulus, Julian's former benefactor (§§ 70, 102), suffered a lamentable end, being condemned to death. We have already cited Ammianus' severe judgment on this case, in which he specifically calls Julian to task. This condemnation aroused general execration, and it seems that Julian, moved by this unfavorable reaction, sought later to prove that he had nothing to do with it and took pains to alleviate the financial penalties burdening Ursulus' heirs (Libanius, 18. 152).

Paul "the Chain" (§ 113) and Eusebius (§§ 50, 112–113) atoned for their evil deeds by being burned alive. The same fate befell Apodemius, who had certainly been deeply involved in the deaths of Silvanus and Gallus, but not without the connivance of Arbetio who was now acting as prosecutor (§ 150). Later, through the direct intervention of Julian, his old opponent Gaudentius (§§ 70, 138) and Artemius, a former military governor of Egypt who was now accused of atrocities, were put to death (22. 11. 1–2).

It was, therefore, a high court which passed a number of just sentences, and others which were obviously unjust, and which in general did not stay clear and independent of outside influences to the extent expected of a tribunal dealing with matters of such importance.

XI. JULIAN AS EMPEROR

§§ 152–153. Reforms at Court.   §§ 154–157. Restoration of
Idolatry.   §§ 158–160. Reactions and Victims.   §§ 161–
162. Julian's Ardor for Paganism.   §§ 163–165. Delusions;
Reform of the Pagan Priesthoods.

152. After repairing in this manner, whether for good or for ill, the mistakes of the past, Julian had also to provide for present exigencies, particularly the renovation of the imperial court in its constitution and activities. It was actually a worn-out institution in which there was very little worth saving and a great deal to repudiate.

When Diocletian established the tetrarchy in A.D. 293, he endowed the court, which stood at the summit of the empire, with a certain moral prestige. The dominating idea had been suggested by the religion of paganism. Four dynasts were to preside over the functions of the empire, two Augusti, and two Caesars, one for each of the Augusti; but Diocletian was to remain the chief Augustus. He was held to be endowed with a kind of sacred majesty, and had the title of *dominus* par excellence. In the East this title was used as an epithet of the divinity, but it had not been so used at Rome in the Early Empire since it normally designated an "owner" of slaves. The title was accompanied with appropriate external trappings: the Augustus dressed in purple garments hemmed with gold; he wore precious boots and a diadem gleaming with gems; subjects were admitted only rarely to his presence, and when they were granted an audience, they had to prostrate themselves and "adore" ($\pi\rho o\sigma\kappa\upsilon\nu\epsilon\tilde{\iota}\nu$) the divine majesty. Minute prescriptions regulated all civil ceremonies, and an interminable hierarchy of officials and courtiers descended from the throne of his majesty until they finally reached the level of common mortals (Ricciotti, *Martyrs*, pp. 15–16).

When Constantine became the sole successor of the tetrarchy, little change was made in the external façade of the court: the elaborate ceremonials remained in general what they had been before. Without formally being a Christian, Constantine, partly through conviction, and partly through political opportunism, favored Christianity and never deliberately opposed the sentiments of his Christian subjects. However, he did not abolish the official ceremonies since they had by this time lost their original pagan connotations and were now simply a matter of court etiquette. Even the ritual of "adoration" was retained, not, to be sure, in its religious sense, but merely as the supreme act of homage to the Augustus. As such, this practice could be, and was, observed by the numerous Christians in Constantine's court. His successor Constantius not only continued this tradition of impressing the people with such pageantry, but even added to it. When he appeared in his coach in public, he felt obliged to remain motionless, making no gestures, looking neither to the right nor to the left, but bearing himself as if he were a statue of a god (16. 10. 10; 21. 16. 7).

How many props were needed for all this external pomp and splendor, and how many parasites because of it wormed their way into the emperor's service may easily be imagined. Besides the regular military offices, there was an unending series of graded posts at court. These positions, for the most part, were richly rewarded without any commensurate responsibilities. But they seemed so indispensable to the luster of the Byzantine court that when they began to disappear as the result of Julian's reforms, many regretted their loss as a diminution of the empire's glory (Socrates 3. 1). The mentality behind this was akin to that which, in the ancient Semitic monarchies, measured the greatness of a ruler by the size of his harem. Though the figures furnished by Libanius (18. 130) cannot be taken literally, still they do give us some general idea of the numbers of such employees. According to him, in the court at Constantinople there were thousands of cooks, thousands of barbers, thousands of cupbearers, and eunuchs as countless as the flies in summer about a sheepfold. And there were "some who," in the words of Ammianus, "had grown fat on the pillaging of temples, and scenting out every source of gain . . . habitually laid hands upon the property of others" (22. 4. 3). Raised from abject poverty to enormous wealth, these individuals reveled at sumptuous banquets prepared in their luxurious homes. Through contacts with such courtiers, greed and avarice spread through the armed forces, to the ever increasing detriment of their morale.

On one of his first days at court, Julian summoned a barber for a haircut. The one who came for the task was so gorgeously attired that Julian exclaimed in astonishment that he had asked for a barber and not for one of the ministers of finance. Then, out of curiosity, he asked the barber how much he earned, and discovered that besides a high annual salary he received many other remunerations, including a daily allotment of rations sufficient for twenty men and twenty horses (22. 4. 9).

Julian rid himself of the *palatini*, that is, these palace parasites, by dismissing all who belonged to this class or could be included in it (*conversus . . . ad palatinos, omnes omnino qui sunt quique esse possunt removit*). Ammianus felt some sympathy for these unfortunates, feeling that Julian had taken too radical a step, but one "which could have been commended if he had retained at least those few who were known for their modest behavior and virtuous character" (22. 4. 2).

153. Despising the professional informers known as the *curiosi*, who had so irked him under Constantius, Julian avoided their service and reduced their numbers. Two of those dismissed thought that they could regain their former position in court by promising to reveal to the emperor the hiding place of the consul Florentius, who had been condemned to death *in absentia* (§ 151). On hearing this, Julian called them spies, as they deserved, and avowed that it was unbecoming for an emperor to use such devious methods to lay hands on a man hiding for fear of his life, and who perhaps had not long to wait for a pardon.

Nevertheless, since the court proved to be understaffed after these dismissals, Julian had to replenish it with men of his own choice. He was also eager to show deference to high state officials whenever there was an occasion to do so. On January 1, 362, when the two new consuls Mamertinus and Nevitta (§ 145) took possession of their office, Julian went on foot to the inauguration accompanied by other high officials. Ammianus notes that while some praised this show of humility, others regarded it as affected and cheap (*affectatum et vile* — 22. 7. 1). In defense of Julian, however, it should be observed that such an action was not unprecedented. Shortly afterward, Mamertinus staged the customary games in the circus, and, as was usual on such an occasion, a number of slaves were brought in for him to free. But Julian slipped here and pronounced the formula of manumission himself. When he was reminded that jurisdiction belonged to another on this particular day, he acknowledged his mistake and fined himself ten pounds of gold (22. 7. 1–2).

He showed a great deal of respect for the senate of Constantinople, which was animated with a certain spirit of rivalry toward that of Rome, even though in authority and renown it was at a much lower level. From this assembly Julian received the recognition of his imperial authority, and, in return, he granted it a number of privileges. Contrary to the earlier custom of Constantius, he did not summon the senators to his presence and compel them to stand while he imparted his instructions. Instead, he went himself to the senate and took part in the debates, inviting those present to remain seated.

In a number of extant letters of this period, he deals cordially with various individuals and even invites some of them to come and visit him. Notable among these latter were Eutherius (§ 134), the Christian rhetorician Prohaeresius (§ 57), a certain Basil, possibly but not certainly the future bishop of Caesarea in Cappadocia (§ 19), and others. But it seems that in general these invitations were received rather coolly, since apparently this was deemed the better part of prudence. Maximus of Ephesus, Julian's beloved master, visited him and was received with such effusiveness that it won the reproach of Ammianus, as we have already seen (§ 34). Together with Julian's other teacher Priscus, Maximus stood at his side during his last days (§§ 59, 209); Chrysanthius, on the other hand, although he too had been one of Julian's teachers (§ 36), consistently refused to join him, despite repeated invitations (Eunapius, 477–478).

154. These various cares were worthy of Julian's best endeavors, but in his own mind they certainly ranked below that highest and noblest of tasks entrusted to him by the gods, the restoration of idolatry. And it was all the more urgent in that one had only to look about to see that paganism was in full decline.

Under Constantine, despite his obvious propension for Christianity, the pagan temples had remained open and had continued to function. But they were in general in a rather sorry plight. Not only did the state show progressively less interest in them, but even many pagans looked with indifference upon their impending moral and material collapse. With the decline in the number of devotees, temple offerings also declined. Funds were no longer available for the support of the cults and for the material restorations required by the ravages of time.

From among the Christians occasional demands could be heard for the closing of the pagan temples, but Constantine did not listen to them (Eusebius, *De vita Constantini*, 2. 60). Only as an exception did he order the suppression of the temples of Aphaca in Palestine and Aegae at Heliopolis (Baalbek) in Phoenicia, but this was done in the interest of public morality to suppress the licentiousness long connected with these sites.

Under Constantine's immediate successors the status of pagan worship declined still further. Certain laws promulgated during the reigns of Constans and Constantius seem to have prohibited all pagan sacrifices, but their contents and significance are disputed. Further, it is certain that the suburban temples, which were connected with the games, and assemblies for processions, sacred banquets, mystery rites, and taurobolia, were not disturbed. At Ostia, the port of Rome, the prefect Tertullus (§ 145) under Constantius offered a solemn official sacrifice in the temple of the Dioscori to obtain the safe arrival of a fleet bearing grain to the city (19. 10. 4). Naturally, whatever laws were made against paganism were enforced with greater or less zeal according to the various regions of the empire, the temperament of the magistrates, and particular circumstances.

From various sides Christians continued to make requests for the closing of the pagan temples and the destruction of the idols. Under Julian, Marcus of Arethusa (§ 159) and George of Cappadocia (§ 158) not only advocated, but actually took measures to bring this about. Their zeal in this matter incurred Julian's displeasure. Even earlier a Christian writer had made such a proposal. This was Firmicus Maternus, a dilettante who wrote a little about everything — astrology, history, and finally even theology. His *De errore profanarum religionum*, which was published about 346 or 348, advised Emperors Constans and Constantius to bend all their efforts to the extinguishing of the last glowing embers of idolatry. This was to be done by destroying the temples and statues of the gods and turning their property over to the state treasury. But these self-appointed apostles of repression failed to gain a hearing, and the slow evolution of events continued on its course.

The matter, however, was eventually brought to a head by something of a more practical nature. Since the temples were becoming ever more deserted and even falling into ruins, they began to be used as a source of material for other buildings. Columns, statues, works of bronze and other precious materials, were being willfully abandoned to the first claimants. Constantine had already made extensive use of materials taken from old and decrepit buildings to erect his new city of Constantinople. It was even said in jest that the new capital stripped the other cities to clothe herself. Such a use of ancient materials may seem strange in an age like our own in which there is a high regard for archaeological sites. But such an esteem is a relatively recent development. Up to the sixteenth, and even into the seventeenth century, the ancient custom of erecting new buildings with ancient materials still prevailed. To limit ourselves to Rome, the normal places for contractors to obtain their materials were the Roman forum and that part of the outer ring of the Colosseum which had collapsed in the course of time, known as "the quarry." Stones taken from these sites were used at the height of the seventeenth century for the buildings erected by the Barberini. This practice gave rise to the famous pasquinade: *quod non fecerunt barbari, fecerunt Barberini* ("what was left undone by the barbarians, has been finished by the Barberini").

155. Julian's heart bled at seeing the decline of the temples, and even more from his realization of the fact that it was accompanied step by step by the moral degeneration of the pagan priesthoods. The worship of the gods now brought almost no material gain. To dedicate oneself to their service was to dedicate oneself to a life of misery and hunger. The unemployed priests, who were recognizable in public by their woebegone look, were compelled to find various means of supporting themselves. In his letters Julian occasionally deplores the fact that such individuals made up the courts of the civil magistrates, frequented wine shops, theaters, and even less worthy places, and allowed themselves to be caught in actions warranting public prosecution, while at the same time they appeared only rarely in the temples and even then did not know how to carry out their sacred chants and duties.

On the other hand, as Ammianus has already informed us (§ 152), many of the ancient revenues of the temples had gone to enrich high officials at court, and the few that remained were not sufficient for even the most urgently needed restorations. There was no way out: temple worship left to its own resources would never be able to regain its former position.

With the authority given him by the gods, Julian set about putting an end to this state of affairs. During the course of his gradual withdrawal from Constantius' authority, he had carried out pagan rites in honor of Bellona (§ 139) and had offered hecatombs to the gods (§ 149) contrary to the legislation then in force. But when he became the absolute ruler of the whole empire, "he laid bare the secrets of his heart and with plain and final decrees ordered the temples to be opened, victims to be brought to the altars, and the worship of the gods to be restored" (22. 5. 2). At the same time he had the foresight to accompany these "plain and final decrees" (*planis absolutisque decretis*) with a practical proof of his intent to grant full religious liberty not only to the pagans but also to the Christians. To this end, "he summoned to his palace the Christian bishops, who were at odds with each other, and the people, who also were divided into factions, and politely advised them to set aside their differences, and each without fear or opposition to observe his own beliefs" (22. 5. 3).

This principle, repeated on several occasions by Julian in his letters, was certainly equitable, but it must be added that it was in no sense his own personal discovery. The same principle had been sanctioned forty-eight years earlier by the famous Edict of Milan, through which liberty of conscience and of worship had been granted in equal measure to both pagans and Christians in remarkably precise terms (Ricciotti, *Martyrs*, pp. 189–193). Constantine and his subordinate Licinius had been the authors of this truly revolutionary edict (§ 42), and Julian, consciously or unconsciously, was inspired by it in his own decrees, though he elsewhere charges Constantine with corrupting the ancient traditions of the empire. An example of this may be found in his parable referring to Constantine in his work *Against the Cynic Heraclius* (227c ff.).

156. But this was not the whole story. After mentioning Julian's advice to the Christians, Ammianus goes on to explain his real motive for giving it. He granted freedom of conscience to all "in order that he might have no fear thereafter of a united populace, because such a freedom increased their dissensions, and he knew from experience that no wild beasts are so hostile to mankind as are most Christians in their savage hatred for one another" (22. 5. 4; § 47). We have already noted that this refers to the bloody attacks of the Donatists, Novatians, and various types of Arians upon the orthodox. Attention is therefore to be paid to Julian's playing on the dissensions within his enemy's ranks so as to fight according to the ancient rule, "divide and conquer."

In this manner he may have hoped to rid himself of Christianity, or at least to reduce it to extremes without himself appearing as an open adversary.

At any rate, from the very beginning of his religious policy, Julian remitted the sentences of all Christians who had been imprisoned or exiled under Constantius (Sozomen, 5. 5; Julian, *To the Citizens of Bostra*, 436b); and many bishops regained possession of their sees. If this return of their exiled leaders pleased the Christians, freedom of worship and the reopening of the temples pleased the pagans even more. Apart from the evidence for this furnished by Libanius, there are still extant from different parts of the empire dedicatory inscriptions honoring Julian as the restorer of the ancient religion.

But the laws granting universal freedom of worship would not of themselves have been sufficient to revitalize paganism had Julian not implemented them with other measures. In the first place, the old temples had to be reactivated, and others had to be built where none as yet existed. This latter was the case at the capital Constantinople, where only a few places of pagan worship could be found, and these in the narrow precincts of the older city. In the large new quarters erected by Constantine and his successors no pagan temples had been erected (Ricciotti, *Martyrs*, pp. 216–220). But the construction of such places of worship within the capital would have involved so many problems in the removal of already existing buildings and such an enormous expense that Julian could do little about it. He consequently turned his efforts toward the ancient temples.

Here also Julian was more or less inspired, but to an opposite effect, by what Constantine had done for Christianity. Just as his half uncle and father-in-law had decreed that Christian places of worship confiscated for the benefit of the public treasury during the "great persecution" (Ricciotti, *Martyrs*, pp. 191, 194) should be restored to their rightful owners, so Julian made every effort to reclaim the pagan temples which had passed to other uses. Rigorous means were employed toward this end. The new proprietors had to restore the sites as they were, or had to return the columns, statues, and other parts of the temples that had been removed; and at times they were compelled to restore or rebuild what had been torn down. The many complicated problems arising from attempts to execute these commands may easily be imagined; but Julian was convinced that he was acting generously in not punishing those who had exposed themselves to severe penalties by profaning res sacras, even though they had acted under an earlier administration with a totally different religious policy.

157. Similarly, he made no attempt to imitate Constantine's provisions for indemnities. Where Constantine had ordered that the recent owners should be fairly compensated, Julian gave no such instructions. And in this he was certainly not motivated by avarice, but rather by his esteem for paganism, which should not debase itself by granting such compensations.

The owners naturally defended themselves as best as they could from such financial losses. They refused to tell where the various claimed objects could be found. They held on to those that were found and paid no indemnities for what they failed to restore. The zeal of the claimants went at times to ridiculous lengths, as when they demanded that an entire building should be demolished to recover a column or a pair of capitals. Instances of this sort must have frequently been prompted by the private interests of individuals seeking to capitalize on the decrees. Intelligent pagans, public officials as well as private citizens, refused at times to have anything to do with these controversies, where it was often impossible, even with the best of will, to retrace the successive ownership of a given object. In such instances they may have had in mind the axiom possessio pro titulo est (or, freely translated, "possession is nine tenths of the law"), although Julian would not have considered this norm applicable to the goods of the temples. Still, the majority of the magistrates must have been more concerned about the peace of their districts than about the pagan zeal of the emperor.

The settlement of these practical matters, either because of their complexity or because of the extent of the areas involved, was necessarily slow. The decree for reopening the temples arrived at Alexandria on February 4, 362. This same decree must have had very little effect in the West since Constantius' laws pertaining to idolatry had left matters more or less in their status quo. At Rome, in Gaul, and in Spain, paganism was predominant. Numerous temples had continued to function freely. Pagan feasts, particularly the more popular ones, were celebrated regularly.

At Rome the faltering morale of paganism had its revenge. In former times an altar of Victory had stood at the entrance to the curia, and its corresponding statue was to be found at the rear of the hall. On entering the building the senators had been accustomed to burn a grain of incense on the altar. In 357, Constantius had ordered the altar removed to the consternation of the pagan senators, who regarded it as a symbol of Roman power; but now, in accordance with the terms of the new decree, the altar was replaced on its original site, and it remained there under the tolerant rule of the Christian Valentinian until the time of Gratian.

158. As might have been expected, a lively reaction set in to Julian's pagan activities, especially in the East, where Christianity was more deeply rooted in the masses. Attacks and counterattacks took place on one side and the other. In various places the pagans, believing that the hour had come for the Christians to pay for their triumph under Constantine and his successors, proceeded to rob and profane the churches. In return, the Christians, when they could, knocked down the statues of the gods.

There was no official persecution, but there certainly were Christians who suffered abuse and violence from the hands of pagans acting with the tacit approval of the authorities. At the most these intervened only to deplore an accomplished fact and not to punish it. At times they even found pretexts to justify the pagans and to declare that they had acted with reserve. In a word, there was a disguised persecution guided by the hand in power.

The cruelest example of this, mentioned even by Ammianus, was that connected with George of Cappadocia. This learned but grim individual, whom we have met before (§ 15), was an Arian bishop born to violence and intrigue. If Gregory Nazianzen summarily depicts him as a "Cappadocian monster," the pagan Ammianus states more precisely that, "forgetful of his calling, which counseled nothing but justice and mildness, he descended to the gruesome practices of the informers" (22. 11. 5). With the assistance of the magistrates serving under Constantine, he had usurped the episcopal see of Alexandria. There through his arrogance and avarice, and especially through the delations he sent to Constantius, he won for himself the hatred of the whole city. Detested by the orthodox, who recognized only the exiled Athanasius as their bishop, he was also cordially hated by the pagans, whom he sought to irritate at every opportunity. Having obtained permission from Constantius to erect a church on the site of an old abandoned Mithraeum, he deliberately exposed to public ridicule the emblems used at the initiation into the mysteries that were found there (Sozomen, 5. 7; Socrates, 3. 2). On another occasion passing with a great retinue before the temple dedicated to the genius of the city, he looked scornfully at the building and cried out, "How long will this tomb be left standing?" The temple was at the time thronged with worshipers, who, needless to say, were highly incensed by this outburst.

After three years of absence George returned to Alexandria, arriving in the city on November 26, 361, just as Constantius was setting out from Antioch to oppose Julian. Had he been able to foresee the immediate future, he would not have gone there to put himself into the hands of his enemies. A few days later, it was officially announced in the city that Constantius had died and that Julian had been elected as his successor (§ 149). The people rose up at once and threw George into prison. Less than a month later, on December 25, the dies natalis Solis Invicti ("birthday of the Unconquered Sun"), popular fury broke out again. George was snatched from prison and killed along with Dracontius, the superintendent of the mint, and Count Diodore. Dracontius was accused of having demolished a pagan altar, Diodore of having cut the locks of a number of children as a symbol of their consecration to God. The pagan mob made sport of the three bodies. George's was set on a camel; those of the other two were tied with ropes and dragged along the streets of the city. When they reached the bank, the mob burned the bodies and hurled their ashes into the sea for fear that the usual martyr shrines would be erected in their honor. Actually, such a fear in the present case was completely unfounded.

159. This outrage afforded Julian an opportunity to show his impartiality toward pagans and Christians by punishing the culprits whoever they might be. At first he thought of inflicting capital punishment (expetiturus poenas a noxiis ultimas), but he was soon dissuaded from this by his friends, and substituted for the death penalty a simple letter To the People of Alexandria (378c–380d). A surprising thing about this letter is the way it is addressed. Was the entire populace of Alexandria guilty of the triple murder? The orthodox Christians could obviously not be called into account since the disturbance had been caused only by the pagans and the principal victim was an Arian bishop. But to Julian's mind, the Christians deserved no consideration in such a case. The general tone of the letter is also surprising. At first Julian blames the Alexandrians not for the murders but solely

for having sentenced individuals to death without recourse to himself, since "all the gods, and above all the great Serapis, deemed it right that I should rule over the inhabited world" (378d). But then, placing himself on their level not as a judge but as an advocate, he finds excuses and attenuating circumstances for the crimes. He finally terminates his letter by saying that he is furnishing them with the very mildest remedy, that is, "words of admonition," since they are Hellenes of ancient lineage. This was the only punishment meted out for the macabre slayings.

Marcus, an old bishop of Arethusa, a small town in Phoenicia, was another victim of the disguised but growing persecution. This was the same Marcus who had rescued the infant Julian when other members of his family were being put to death (§ 7). He was denounced to the emperor as being responsible for the destruction of a temple and for mistreating pagans. He was ordered to rebuild the temple, but this he steadfastly refused to do. Judging from Julian's stand taken in the mob murder of George of Cappadocia, it might have been presumed that the emperor would himself inflict a sentence of death or some other severe penalty, without allowing the accused to fall a prey to the mob as George had done. But in such cases Julian shrank from a death sentence, since this would have removed the disguise from his system of a veiled persecution. Marcus' fate was precisely that which Julian had deprecated in the case of George. He was abandoned to the ferocity of the mob, which dragged him through the streets, tore out his beard, inflicted other torments, and then entrusted him to the refined cruelty of schoolboys, who amused themselves by piercing him with their styli. Finally, all lacerated as he was, he was smeared with honey and exposed to the stings of insects.

160. Christians were also put to death elsewhere, to punish them either for their acts of retaliation or for their attacks on idolatry. Among them were the priest Basil of Ancyra (Sozomen, 5. 11); the soldier Aemilian at Dorostorus in Moesia, who was burned alive (Jerome, *Chronicon*, Olymp. 285); and Macedonius, Theodolus, and Tatian, Christians of Meros in Phrygia (Socrates, 3. 15; Sozomen, 5. 11). At Caesarea in Cappadocia, near which Julian had received his early education (§ 12), all but one of the temples had been torn down by Constantius. The Christians believed that it was time to destroy the sole survivor, a temple to Fortune, but this turned out unfortunately

for them. Deeply hurt, Julian accused the few pagans in the city of failing to protect the temple. He confiscated all the ecclesiastical property within the city and its environs, imposed a fine of three hundred gold pounds on the people, enrolled the Christian clerics in the local militia, and threatened to continue his oppression unless the temple was rebuilt at once (Sozomen, 5. 4).

Such rigor, however, was not employed to punish acts of violence committed by pagans. These were deemed to be simple compensations, or legitimate retaliations, for the losses incurred by paganism under Constantius or even under Constantine.

Various sites in Syria and Phoenicia were desecrated by scenes of sacrilegious fury. At Emesa (Homs) the church was wrecked and a statue of Dionysus was placed on the altar. The Christian cemetery was torn up and set on fire. In the cities along the Palestinian coast from Gaza to Ascalon, and as far as Heliopolis, there were continuous outbreaks against the Christians accompanied by unheard-of violence. Churches were sacked, priests tortured, consecrated virgins violated. The stomachs of the victims were slit open and barley thrown into them to feed pigs. Studied parodies of the Christian liturgy were made to please the mobs. The local governors, knowing the attitude of the emperor, tolerated such crimes, regarding them as natural manifestations of popular feeling. In fact such outrages were even occasionally rewarded, as happened in the case of Maiuma, a small Christian city on the coast which served as the port of pagan Gaza. Maiuma had received its independence from Gaza and had enjoyed its own autonomy from the time of Constantine, but Julian, in order to punish it, again subjected it to Gaza. There was also the case of the governor who dared to punish the author of a riot in which Christians were slain: Julian intervened, punishing the governor in turn by removing him from office. In fine, the Christians constantly labored under the presumption of being malefactors.

At Bostra, capital of Arabia, a Christian by the name of Orion was haled before the governor Beleus. Under Constantius, when many idols in the city had been demolished, he had possessed great authority, and it was only natural that an attempt should be made to hold him retroactively responsible for their destruction. The accused, however, was defended by none other than Libanius, Julian's friend and teacher. He produced many witnesses and proved that Orion had neither destroyed the statues nor persecuted the priests, but rather that he had himself been persecuted and injured in a great many ways. It was an honorable exception to the general course of events.

161. Julian's anti-Christian activity and his open support of idolatry were the products of his own inner convictions; but his secret spiritual life, far from the sight of men, was also guided by these same convictions. Moreover, so great an inner fire could not have been maintained had it not been continually nourished by new material.

His father, the god Mithra, who had chosen him for this great enterprise, had accompanied him step by step along the arduous road ever since his consecration as his soldier (§ 60). None of the innumerable gods, which according to Hellenistic paganism were scattered throughout the entire cosmos, were excluded from his worship; but naturally he had his own particular protectors, among whom the most important was the god Helios (*Sol*, or Sun), the counterpart of Mithra. He has already told us, though with the reserve rigorously required of an initiate, that he had a place far from profane eyes where he worshiped this god in secret (§ 40). In the imperial palace at Constantinople, he had set up a little pantheon with altars dedicated to a multitude of gods; but, in addition to this, he had also set apart a special place there for the worship of his favorite god, a Mithraeum (Libanius, 18. 127), which in its essential lines must have been similar to the Mithraea which have come down to us from this time.

It is probable that in this Mithraeum, Julian, who had already been initiated into the first grades of the god's worship, was raised to the highest ranks, becoming in turn the guide and teacher of new initiates. One of these privileged individuals was the sophist Himerius, who expressed his thanks to Julian in a discourse. The theurgists Maximus of Ephesus and Priscus (§ 153), Julian's old teachers, must certainly have been visitors to this Mithraeum. From his first arrival at court Maximus had been a person of great influence, and there is no doubt that, with Priscus, his opinions had great weight in the decisions taken by Julian on religious matters.

From a hostile source, but still one which there are no reasons to doubt (Gregory Nazianzen, 4. 52), we have the account of Julian's attempt to purify himself from the last traces of his Christian baptism, a ritual which must have occurred at this time. From his childhood Julian had been taught that the first of the Christian rites impressed an invisible but permanent sign on the one who received it.

Very likely he did not believe this to be entirely false. His secret esteem for magic and the experiences which he had had under Maximus' guidance in the subterranean chamber at Ephesus (§ 39) gave him grounds for suspecting that the impious Galileans actually had a mysterious power enabling them to impress such a sign. Whatever it was, there was an easy and effective way to wipe it out. All that was needed was to undergo the rite of the taurobolium, that is, to take one's position in a trench and allow the blood of a bull slaughtered overhead to flow down over the body, particularly over those members most in need of purification. One who was so bathed came out of the trench completely purified and reborn for eternity (*in aeternum renatus*). For a Christian, the parts most in need of purification were the hands, into which the neophyte received the mystic bread of the Eucharist immediately after baptism. It is thus no surprise to learn from Gregory that Julian "washed his hands, purifying (ἀποκαθαίρων) them from the unbloody sacrifice through which we become partakers in the sufferings and divinity of Christ."

162. Julian and his fellow initiates were linked together with a bond of absolute secrecy. Naturally, among these chosen friends he found his special confidants, and he made use of them for the more delicate affairs of government (*To Theodore*, 452ab).

But neither the worship of Mithra nor the pantheon erected in the imperial palace could satisfy the longing for the divine which Julian felt within himself. Such was his frame of mind that he gradually became a missionary, first by his example and later by active proselytism. His private oratory within the imperial palace soon appeared inadequate. To further his missionary program, he provided as best he could for pagan places of worship within the city. We are told (Socrates, 3. 12; Sozomen, 5. 4) that he had an altar placed before the statue of Fortune erected by Constantine as an ornament in the city's public basilica, and that he himself came there to offer sacrifice. This aroused the indignation of Maris, bishop of Chalcedon. Though old and blind, this ardent supporter of Arianism and relentless adversary of Athanasius approached Julian intent on the sacrifice and called him impious and an apostate. Controlling his anger, Julian answered him with the sarcasm he was later to vent on the Antiochians in his *Misopogon*, assuring him that his God, the Galilean, would not restore him his sight. To this the old man replied that he deemed his blindness a blessing in that he did not witness such impiety.

With the passage of time, Julian's missionary zeal increased, spreading out beyond Constantinople. Wherever he thought it necessary, he provided sacrifices with countless victims, as pagan and Christian historians alike attest. Ammianus states that "he drenched the altars with the blood of too great a number of victims, at times sacrificing a hundred bulls at once, and countless flocks of other types of animals, and white birds* sought out on land and sea" (22. 12. 6). Sacrificial banquets regularly followed the slaughter of these animals. The soldiers took part in these, particularly the Petulantes and the Celts, who, thanks to their earlier support of Julian (§ 127), were now omnipotent. At the end of the feasting, this crowd of debauchers, gorged with food and reeling from the generous libations, had to be carried almost every day to their barracks on the shoulders of passers-by. These sacrifices and revels were particularly frequent at Antioch just prior to Julian's last expedition against the Persians, when it was more than ever urgent to propitiate the gods and probe the future by scrutinizing the entrails of victims. The city at this time was suffering from a scarcity of provisions (22. 14. 1), but for the sacrifices there was an abundance of everything. The only worry was that if Julian returned victorious from his expedition there would not be enough bulls in the whole empire for the thank offerings (25. 4. 17). Julian sought to remedy the shortage of grain, but the means he employed, while proving his good will, showed his inexperience as well (§ 177).

The cost of these continuous hecatombs was extremely high (Libanius, 18. 170), but through these expenditures Julian reached the height of his desires. Standing in front of a blood-stained altar and surrounded by heaps of quartered beasts in the center of a reddish bog, Julian was filled with delight: "He was called a slaughterer rather than priest (victimarius pro sacricola) by many who ridiculed the number of his victims . . . and though he took offence at this, he controlled his feelings and continued to celebrate the festivals" (22. 14. 3).

163. Still, in the midst of such great consolations, he could not but be disillusioned, and this disillusionment increased with the passage of time. In his enthusiasm he had expected hordes of pagans to come to him, bringing pagan worship back to its pristine splendor. Instead, the masses at first eyed him with a certain curiosity, but without being much impressed. Then he sought to gain a following by calling together

---

* A color of good omen, cf. Horace, Sat., 1. 7. 8; Suetonius, Galba, 1; Juvenal, 13. 141.

the pagan priests who in former times had presided over the sacred rituals, but the results were extremely meager. For the most part they remained aloof, either because they did not anticipate any real revival of paganism, or because they thought that Julian lacked a sufficiently strong political hold on the people for such a vast enterprise. And the laity were even more skeptical in the face of Julian's zeal. In the temples, after he had spent a long time with his tunic tucked up and sweating like a slave at quartering the victims, he would suddenly realize that almost all the spectators had quietly walked away.

It will be best to listen to his own account of a solemn festival in the temple of Apollo at Daphne near Antioch at which he happened to assist: "In the tenth month as you count — Loos I believe you call it — there is a feast founded by your forefathers in honor of this god, and it was your duty to be eager in your visits to Daphne. For myself, I hurried thither from the temple of Zeus Cassius, thinking that, if anywhere, I should there be delighted with your wealth and public spirit. And I pictured to myself, like a man seeing visions in a dream, what kind of a procession it would be, and the beasts for sacrifice, the libations, the choruses in honor of the god, the incense, and the youths of your city there about the precinct, their souls adorned with the greatest reverence for the god, and their bodies decked with white and splendid garments. But when I entered into the precinct, I found there neither incense, nor cake, nor sacrificial victim. For a moment I was amazed, and I presumed that I was still outside the precinct and that you were waiting for the signal from me, doing me this honor as the high priest. But when I asked what sacrifice the city was going to offer to celebrate the annual festival of the god, the priest replied: 'I have brought with me from my own house a goose as an offering to the god, but for the present ($\tau\grave{\alpha}$ $\nu\tilde{\upsilon}\nu$) the city has made no preparations'" (*Misopogon*, 361d–362b).

A modern reader may smile while reading this, but Julian was so grieved by the neglect of the feast that he sent an official rebuke to the senate of the city, which, however, also received it with a smile of indifference.

There was, however, no lack of individuals ready to profit by Julian's religious fervor, and among these opportunists there were even women. Ammianus notes that at the sacrifices "Julian presumptuously delighted in carrying the sacred emblems instead of the priests and in being attended by a band of women" (*mulierculis* — 22. 14. 3). That these women were models of virtue cannot be seriously sustained, especially in the light of the conduct of the soldiers sharing in the same rites. They were cheap profiteers who siezed the opportunities afforded by Julian to revel at little cost. There are other reports handed down to the same effect by Gregory Nazianzen and John Chrysostom. To be sure, these authorities were hostile to Julian, but precisely because of this they had to be on their guard to relate facts and not fiction. Moreover, they challenged witnesses still living to refute their charges. According to them, Julian was habitually followed by a train of prostitutes, libertines, and perverts who assiduously assisted at his functions. Further, since there was a lack of pagan priests, he chose to fill the vacant offices with adventurers and unemployed, and these made a fortune from their election. The consequences of this policy soon burdened Julian himself. He then undertook to raise the moral level of these ministers of the gods, but at the beginning he was more concerned with increasing their number. Worried by the general anemia of paganism, Julian availed himself of the support of women of doubtful reputation and others of the same stripe. But since he was himself of an austere temperament and certainly did not approve of the conduct of his clients, it would be unjust to accuse him of expressly favoring this rabble. His support was rather indirect in as much as he deemed these persons necessary for the restoration of paganism and the checking of Christianity.

164. In such a state of affairs, an intelligence as keen as Julian's was not needed to realize that matters would get worse with the passage of time. What was needed was a radical reform which would gradually elevate the dignity of the pagan priesthood to the level desired by the emperor. This was particularly necessary in that any impartial observer could easily see that the Christian priesthood, especially that of the orthodox, was infinitely superior to the pagan. It was precisely this sight of the Galilean priests adorned with gifts, not even the shadow of which existed in the priests of the gods, that caused Julian his greatest distress. And this was not solely the effect of recent events but of old and persistent memories going back to the time of his Christian education at Macellum (§ 15 ff.).

Prompted by such sentiments, Julian began to trace the first lines of a radical reform of the pagan priesthood in a series of letters beginning about June, 362, when he moved from Constantinople to Antioch. In recent years these have received the apt title of "pastoral letters," since they reveal his purpose of founding a real pagan church with himself as the supreme pastor.* We have already given a number of extracts from them showing their patent Christian inspiration (§ 18 ff.).

He interested himself in many details, hierarchy, doctrines, ritual, and all the rest, since the projected church would depend entirely upon him as *pontifex maximus;* but he was particularly concerned with the spirit which should animate the pagan priesthood. Consequently, he gave minute prescriptions with respect to the religious and moral conduct of the priests both in public and in private, even outlining the ascetic and devotional practices to be followed by individuals.

An organization of the pagan priesthood had, as a matter of fact, also been attempted some decades earlier by Maximinus Daia (Ricciotti, *Martyrs,* p. 178); but like Maximinus' own crude character, it was a hasty, superficial attempt aimed at gaining rapid credit for the class by drawing into it men of a prominent social position, but without taking into account their moral fitness. Julian, instead, desired in the first place men of moral standing. But if the general status of the pagan priesthoods was as has just been described, where was he to find them? For the higher offices, at least, he turned to his fellow initiates, the Neoplatonic theurgists, and the faithful followers of the god Mithra.

Thus we find among the newly elect the theurgist Chrysanthius, Julian's teacher, who had earlier declined the kind invitations of his august pupil (§ 153). He now accepted the post of *pontifex maximus* of Lydia, while his wife received a corresponding office. Chrysanthius seems to have exercised his duties without molesting the Christians. Another of Julian's protégés was Pegasius, bishop of Ilium, who had been his guide through that city (§ 51). This open apostasy is not at all surprising since, as we have seen, he was even at that earlier period more pagan than Christian. Others also followed the example of Pegasius. In their zeal for paganism they caused their past to be forgotten and made themselves currently most acceptable to Julian.

165. Drawing his inspiration in part from the Church and in part from the followers of Mithra (§§ 60, 161), Julian proposed to organize the pagan priesthoods into a regular hierarchy; but this project was only in its initial stages when he died. Over the priests of a city was

---

* Bidez has grouped these letters under the following numbers: 84, 85, 86, 87, 88, 89a, 89b. The first six of these letters correspond to letters: 22, 33, 32, 34, 18, and 20 in the third volume of Wright. The final letter is to be found in Wright, 2:296–338.

to be the archpriest; over the archpriests of a province was to be the *pontifex maximus* of the province, and at the head of the entire hierarchy was to be Julian, *pontifex maximus* of the empire and grand master of all the priestly corporations. And just as the higher clergy were to watch over the conduct of the lower, so Julian was to have supreme jurisdiction over all.

His authority was based not only on his capacity as *pontifex maximus* of the empire, a post he held in the highest esteem, but also on a special investiture which he had received from the gods. He speaks of himself in the following terms: "By the laws of our fathers I am *pontifex maximus*, and in addition I have only recently received the gift of prophecy from the god of Didymus" (*To an Official*, 451b). This was the Didymaean Apollo worshiped at Miletus, who had been consulted by Diocletian before he launched "the great persecution." Confident in his own authority, Julian rebuked whole cities, as he did in his letter to the senate and people of Antioch cited above (§ 163), or individual governors, as in the case of one whom he put under a kind of religious interdict for the space of three months (*To an Official*, 451c).

Above all, he demanded of the pagan priests zeal and a missionary spirit, praising those who, like the priestess Theodora, showed these traits (*To Theodora* [Wright 32, 33, 34 — 3:109–115]), and occasionally deploring the sloth of others. It is obvious that while making these admonitions he had in mind the noisome example of the priests of the impious Galileans, so superior to that afforded by the pagan priests. The letter which he addressed at the beginning of 363 to the archpriest Theodore, whom he had placed at the head of all the pagan priests in the province of Asia, can serve as a summary of these reforms ambitioned by Julian (*To Theodore*, 452a–454b). This, it is true, is a personal letter; but it seems to have served as the outline, or first draft, of an official document, a kind of encyclical which the supreme pontiff intended to publish. Other exhortations, rebukes, and directives of various kinds are contained in the letter addressed to Arsacius, *pontifex maximus* of Galatia (*To Arsacius*, 429c–432a).

Julian had many other projects in mind which he thought would deprive the Galileans of their monopoly on certain good works. Such, for example, was the material assistance which they gave to the poor, to travelers, to those in prison, and to single women without means of support. With all of these needy individuals the Christian bishops in some way or other were regularly occupied (§ 19). They even gave letters of introduction to travelers which they could use upon reaching their destinations. The Christians called all these undertakings "charity." Julian, on the other hand, called them "philanthropy," and regarded them simply as means of propaganda. Be that as it may, there was no denying their efficacy as propaganda, and he consequently resolved to found similar institutions. But these resolutions were never realized.

He even envisaged a kind of "Sacred Congregation of Rites" which would codify the rules for the various liturgical ceremonies and have a special section for chant and sacred music. He also toyed with the idea of sponsoring a series of lectures which would explain the hidden meaning of the "Hellenic dogmas" (ἑλληνικῶν δογμάτων). He was, in fact, convinced that if the works of Homer and Hesiod with their references to gods and men were properly presented and explained, the worshipers of the gods would find ample food for spiritual edification and a safe guide for their religious beliefs.

One cannot help but admire Julian's boldness in all these projects. He dared to take under consideration matters about which the pagan pontiffs before him had not cared in the least. In fact, if they had been confronted by projects of this nature, they would probably have looked upon them as the wild dreams of a fevered brain. Julian, on the other hand, believed that they were completely practicable. And history has proved him right, since they have been realized, not in the pagan milieu which he foresaw, but in Christianity where they were first conceived (§ 19).

XII. AGAINST THE CHRISTIANS

§ 166. Laws on Teaching. § 167. Freedom of Teaching in Ancient Rome. §§ 168–170. Julian's Legislation and Its Effects. §§ 171–172. Christians Forbidden to Hold Public Office.

166. As Julian elaborated his program for the restoration of paganism, he soon enough realized that its effects were rather nugatory. It was hard to reopen and restore the temples. The pagan priests were lazy and listless. Pagans of the higher classes ridiculed him when they saw him playing the part of a *victimarius*, all stained with blood and surrounded by women of easy morals, and libertines (§ 162). What was the source of this resistance? Julian pondered the matter and came to the conclusion that it had its origin with the Christians. Even prescinding from their religion, their social status was not inferior to that of the pagans, and often superior. Many of these infamous Galileans were cultured and learned. Through their cleverness they held high offices in the state and were leaders in their communities.

To Julian's way of thinking this was extremely bad. The credit which the Christians enjoyed was really not their own since it had been acquired through the study of "Hellenic letters," the sole font of human greatness. Consequently, it would be sufficient to dam up this source to cause the flower of Christianity to wither away. The Christians should be discredited by being deprived of their culture. They would thus be made powerless, and would no longer impede the restoration of paganism.

Nor could it be said that their rights would be thus infringed. Quite the contrary! Hellenic culture was the sacred and inalienable patrimony of those who believed in and worshiped the gods of paganism. By what authority did the Christians appropriate to themselves this patrimony and use it to their own advantage? They should give up what they had unjustly taken. They should no longer touch Homer and Hesiod. They should rest content with their crude evangelists and that fanatic Paul, and not profane the sacred inheritance reserved by the gods for the Hellenes. And this would not be an act of moral violence but one of strict justice.

In substance, this was the line of argument behind which Julian took refuge, but which no one would repeat today. It is common knowledge that there are scholars who have a thorough knowledge of the sacred books and the cultural heritage of the ancient Persians, Indians, Moslems, and others, but who do not believe in their religions. In other words, they know the container without accepting the contents. Julian, however, was unable to make this distinction since he pushed his mystic and Hellenistic principles to their ultimate consequences. For him, one who admired the brilliant cup of Hellenism had also to drink the nectar which it contained. Libanius shrewdly observes that Julian considered the literary monuments (λόγους) and the sacred rites of the gods to be like brothers to each other.

As a matter of fact, more than a century before, the great representatives of the Christian school at Alexandria had revitalized Platonic thought, and later Neoplatonism was the point of departure for a number of individuals who became renowned as Christian thinkers (§ 31). No Christian had then cried out at the scandal, and no pagan had asked that the reading of the works of the Platonists and the Neoplatonists be forbidden to Christians.

But Julian, confident in the mission entrusted to him by the gods, banned Christian teachers from the schools and attempted to impose a cultural ostracism on all of that belief. That which would have been offensive in any ruler was most offensive in one who was constantly appealing to ancient traditions. He either did not know, or would not admit, that his ban on culture was an act directly opposed to an age-old Roman conviction.

167. In early Rome, teaching had been entirely a matter of private initiative. The old Romans started with the principle that a father, inasmuch as he is responsible for the physical being of his son, should also have the right to his moral training. Consequently, even the state bowed to the authority of the paterfamilias, leaving him absolute arbiter in the education and instruction of his own son. In the De republica, Cicero rejects Polybius' accusation that the Roman constitution was deficient in this matter by noting that the Romans "had never wished for any system of education for free-born youths that was either definitely fixed by law or officially established or uni-

form for all" (*disciplinam puerilem ingenuis . . . nullam certam aut destinatam legibus aut publice expositam aut unam omnium esse voluerunt* — 4. 3).

During the first centuries of Rome the *paterfamilias* exercised this right of his *patris potestas* by personally instructing his son, being assisted at most by a slave known as a *litterator*. At times even affairs of state were subordinated to this paternal duty. With his own hand Cato the Elder wrote a book in large characters for his son to study. But this method of instruction, besides being rudimentary, could not become general. Lack of competence on the part of parents, family affairs, the increasing standard of culture, and various other factors brought about the opening of elementary schools for the sons of the well-to-do. These schools had their origins about the middle of the third century B.C., and they soon developed into three distinct types adapted to the age and attainments of the pupils.

The first of these was the *ludus litterarius*, which boys began to attend at about the age of seven. The course of studies was limited and monotonous — reading, writing, recitation, and a little arithmetic. The teacher's rod was poised menacingly above the backs of the boys curved over their writing tablets, ready to descend on the careless and leave them black and blue. *Plagosus* ("flogger") was the title given by Horace to the teacher Orbilius (*Ep.*, 2. 1. 70).

When a boy was about twelve he passed on to the second type of school where he received his lessons from a *grammaticus*. Here he was taught how to express himself (*ratio loquendi*) and how to interpret the authors he read (*enarratio auctorum*). Greek and Latin authors were studied alike even at Rome. With such exercises a boy's mind was opened up to a new horizon of widely divergent ideas, and he stored up the material which he would have to have at his disposal in the final phase of his formal education.

The third and highest type of school was that conducted by a *rhetor*, or teacher of eloquence. This was the one which opened up the way to high public careers. It also remained the most popular, though alongside it there also gradually arose schools of philosophy and medicine. In the former, instructions were given in Greek, in the latter in Latin.

Up to the time of Hadrian, the opening and maintenance of all these different schools was up to private initiative, always on the principle that the *paterfamilias* was primarily responsible for his son's education, and that he was consequently free to entrust it to others. However, even before Hadrian teachers had received occasional favors from different emperors. Vespasian was the first to assign to rhetoricians an annual salary of 100,000 sesterces from the public treasury. The first to enjoy such a grant was the famous Quintilian.

Even after the schools began to receive state assistance, they remained completely free both as to subject matter and the manner of teaching. Private schools also continued to function freely alongside those subsidized by the state and even proved to be successful rivals to them. Julian's friend Libanius, for example, at the outset of his career entered a contest at Constantinople for a subsidized chair of rhetoric. Even though he was defeated by another candidate, he opened up a school at the same time as his more fortunate rival and attained such great success that the latter's school remained empty. The authorities of Constantinople then replaced the teacher in the endowed chair with one who was very famous. But Libanius challenged the new occupant to a debate and showed himself to be so far superior to his new rival that those present carried him off in triumph.

The first great public school, the Athenaeum, was opened under Hadrian. It was almost like a university in that Greek and Latin rhetoricians were invited there to give connected series of lectures. From this time on, the state took increasingly more official interest in the schools, though the tenacious resistance of the private schools still continued for several centuries.

In the schools, particularly after the third century, religion was not a prejudicial factor for either teachers or students. One could believe in Jupiter or in Christ, have been initiated into one of the mystery religions or be a partaker in the Christian rites. This was no concern to the authorities in charge of the schools. Teachers who proved to be competent in their respective fields and students who showed that they were able and willing were alike admitted.

168. When Julian decided to move against Christianity on a scholastic level, his first measure so far as we know was the constitution *Magistros studiorum* of June 17, 362 (*Cod. Theod.*, 13. 3. 5; cf. *Cod. Justin.*, 10. 53. 7). But of even greater significance is the letter he wrote from Antioch explaining the constitution (*On Christian Teachers*, 422a–424a). Other notices have come down to us from the Christian historians (Zonaras, 13. 12; Sozomen, 5. 18; Socrates, 3. 16. 1; Theodoret, 3. 4), but it is not clear whether they are taken directly from Julian's legislative acts, or whether they are not rather inferences drawn from, and further elucidations of, these acts.

The constitution *Magistros studiorum* has an appearance of neutrality. Aiming at a proper nomination of public teachers, it requires of them professional competence and, above all, moral stature. To achieve this end it prescribes that a candidate for a post should be declared suitable by the local municipal curia through the unanimous vote of the more distinguished members, and that this declaration should be confirmed by the emperor.

The words of the decree, taken alone, could not be interpreted as a direct plot against any individuals or groups within the empire such as the Christians. But it is necessary to keep in mind that Julian was a member of the secret society of Mithra, that his principal advisers in religious matters were his confreres Maximus of Ephesus and Priscus (§§ 161–162), and that in such associations it was the rule to reveal only the more generic and vague aspects of one's thoughts, keeping hidden whatever was more characteristic and decisive. We obviously have an example of this procedure here: Julian's generic plan was set forth in the *Magistros studiorum*, but its specific interpretation was reserved for the letter already cited.

What is the real purport of this letter? Though the Greek text lacks a title and seems to be defective in a number of places, it seems to be a slanderous attack on the Christians and a justification of the measures taken against them, quite in keeping with Julian's vindictive temperament (§ 135). Taken in its totality, it has the appearance of a circular letter addressed to the magistrates and teachers in the East giving an explanation of the constitution *Magistros studiorum*. It would thus be a document similar to the one addressed to the archpriest Theodore (§ 165), but with this difference: the letter to Theodore was a draft for a future law, while this letter was a kind of commentary on a law already enacted. The following is a summary of it:

A good education does not consist in the ability to arrange words and phrases harmoniously but in a healthy condition of mind which distinguishes between good and evil. It is not honorable to think one thing and teach another, especially in matters of great importance. Anyone who acts in this way is like a huckster who cheats his customers with worthless wares. Teachers should be men of character and should not harbor opinions contrary to what they publicly profess. And this is particularly true of those who teach literature to youths, "whether they be rhetoricians, or grammarians, or still more if they be sophists." These latter, in fact, aspire to be not only teachers of eloquence but particularly of morality, and they maintain that political philosophy is their special field. "Did not Homer, Hesiod, Demosthenes, Herodotus, Thucydides, Isocrates, and Lysias receive all their learning from the gods? Did not some of them believe that they were consecrated to Hermes, and others to the Muses? I think it absurd that men who explain the works of these writers should dishonor the gods whom they honored." Still Julian does not wish to force anyone to change his opinions: those who do not believe in the gods should give up their teaching and cease to sell their own consciences for a few drachmae. If "it is true that hitherto there were many excuses for not frequenting the temples, and the terror that threatened from all sides excused men from revealing their truest beliefs about the gods" (§ 45), there is now no reason to fear but rather freedom for all. Therefore, let those who believe that these writers were in error "go to the churches of the Galileans to expound Matthew and Luke." They should not teach what they do not themselves profess. "A general ordinance to this effect is binding on religious and secular teachers, but any youth who wishes to attend school is not to be excluded," for there is always the hope that those who are in error may be cured of their malady.

169. Two categories of individuals are clearly envisaged in this document: those who teach literature to youths, "whether they be rhetoricians, or grammarians, or still more if they be sophists," who ought to believe in the gods, and those who attend the schools, for whom there was no such restriction. Christians could thus be admitted into the schools as students.

A number of Christian writers maintain that Julian removed Christians from the teaching of the classics with the secret aim of preventing them from drawing arguments from these authors to refute paganism. Many add that the prohibition not only affected the Christian teachers but that it also extended to the students, who consequently could no longer attend the schools (Rufinus, 1. 32; Socrates, 3. 12, 16; Sozomen, 5. 18; Theodoret, 3. 4). Though it is not impossible that Julian forbade the teaching of the pagan classics by Christians to prevent their drawing antipagan arguments from them, there is no proof that this was his actual intention. But even if this had been his aim, he would not have openly confessed it. The statement, therefore, is probably a conjecture of these historians. The alleged prohibition of Christian students' attending the schools is also most likely a simple deduction which these same historians drew from Julian's letter. They must have felt that such prescriptions imperiled the consciences of Christian students and prevented their attendance at these seedbeds of idolatry *in re* if not *in iure*. Some modern scholars have postulated the existence of another decree expressly prohibiting the attendance of Christians at the schools, but this is an hypothesis devoid of proof.

As to the teachers affected by these regulations, Ammianus names only the rhetoricians and grammarians (22. 10. 7); John Chrysostom adds also the teachers of medicine.

In the face of such orders a Christian teacher had either to deny his faith or give up the prominent position which he held in society. If he chose the latter course, he became a social derelict exposed to hunger and public pity. But this was precisely Julian's aim. The Christians were to lose their social standing. At the very most they could for a time be grudgingly tolerated in unimportant posts. There was to be no bloody persecution but rather a slow asphyxiation and inevitable paralysis. They did not believe in the gods? Well, then, they should gradually disappear from that Hellenic society which was the masterpiece of the gods.

170. We have no data for determining how many teachers abandoned their schools rather than give up their faith in Christ, but we may be sure that they were the vast majority. The remembrance of countless martyrs under Diocletian, Maximinus, and Licinius was still too fresh in their minds not to have had its effect. The two most striking cases were those of Marius Victorinus and Prohaeresius, whom we have already mentioned (§§ 31, 57). The African Marius Victorinus had been a follower of the Neoplatonism of Plotinus and Iamblicus and had acquired great renown in Rome by translating their works. The Hellenized Armenian Prohaeresius had achieved a similar success at Athens, and even in Rome a statue had been erected in his honor as to "the king of eloquence." If Marius' conversion to Christianity exercised such an influence on St. Augustine (*Confess.*, 8. 2), Julian's personal acquaintanceship with Prohaeresius at Athens must have left a profound impression upon him. For these two luminaries of the whole empire Julian was disposed to make an exception, permitting them to continue with their teaching without forsaking Christianity; but the two refused the offer and gave up their profession.

Even in pagan circles resentment against these provisions must have been extensive since Ammianus, although he was a friend of the emperor and a pagan, thought that Julian's measures against Christian teachers were "inhumane (*inclemens*) and ought to be buried in eternal silence" (22. 10. 7).

Still, surprisingly enough, there were Christians who looked on Julian's law as a boon to their coreligionists since it preserved youths from the danger of studying polytheistic writings (Socrates, 3. 16). Other Christians had recourse to an expedient of considerable ingenuity. They set about putting various episodes of the Bible into verse. They wrote tragedies, odes, epics, lyric poems, hymns, and even prose dialogues about the life of Christ and His disciples in imitation of the Socratic dialogues. In this way Christian teachers and pupils had at their disposal texts which conformed with the law. The two Apollinarises of Laodicea, father and son (the latter afterward became the leader of a heresy), distinguished themselves in this attempt. But the consequence was what could have been foreseen. The Greek classical texts could not be so literally replaced, and after Julian disappeared from the scene these compositions, which are no longer extant, also disappeared, without great loss to Christian literature (Sozomen, 5. 18; Socrates, 3. 16).

171. There still remained a large field for Julian's zeal. For example, if Christian teachers should no longer live by expounding Hellenic writings, was it proper for other Christians to make their living as civil or military servants of the empire? Was not the empire a creation of the gods ordained for the service of the gods? These parasitical Christians should withdraw from all public offices and cease to profit from this divine handiwork. Moreover, did not their Gospel forbid them to put their hand to a sword (Mt. 26:52)? Not only soldiers, but magistrates as well were continuously obliged to make use of the sword. Consequently, the Christians could not in conscience be engaged in either of these two spheres of activity as demanded by the spirit of Roman law.

As we are told by more than one ancient historian (Rufinus 1. 32; Socrates, 3. 13), Julian was constantly mulling over such thoughts. And, on the practical level, he sought in every way to exclude the Christians from public life and replace them with pagans. A short letter addressed to Artabius, governor of the district of Euphratensis, begins with the usual declarations of impartiality, but then it immediately changes its tone: "I declare by the gods that I do not want the Galileans to be put to death, or unjustly beaten, or to suffer anything else; but still I emphatically maintain that those who reverence the gods must be preferred to them. For through the folly of the Galileans nearly everything has been upset, whereas through the good pleasure of the gods we are all preserved. Wherefore, we ought to honor the gods and those who reverence the gods, both men and cities" (*To Artabius*, 376cd).

Elsewhere we find: "He often wrote to cities. If he knew that they favored Hellenism, he freely encouraged them to ask for the gifts they wanted. To those that were Christian he was openly opposed, being unwilling either to visit them personally or to receive ambassadors from them with their complaints" (Sozomen, 5. 3). And he was rigorous in carrying out his threats. On one occasion the inhabitants of Nisibis sent him an embassy entreating him for protection from an imminent invasion of the Persians. Though Nisibis was the city in which St. Ephraem had given admirable proofs of patriotism against the Persians, Julian replied that he would not receive the embassy, nor would he give any assistance to the city since all in it were Christians and the temples of the gods had not been reopened. He further stated that he would never set foot in that defiled city unless the inhabitants were first converted to Hellenism. From this it may be concluded that Julian regarded the pagans as being the primary, if not the sole, objects of his concern, and that he would not have been greatly displeased if a Christian city became the prey of the Persians.

The emperor's hostility to the Christian cities assumed a character of real fanaticism. Edessa was a profoundly Christian city of the empire. In 363, after Julian's death, many Christians who had been living in Persian territories fled there to preserve their faith. Among these was St. Ephraem Syrus, a refugee from Nisibis. On this occasion he wrote a lyric hymn of thanks to the hospitable city: "O Edessa, filled with chastity, filled with prudence and intelligence, clothed with wise judgment, girt with the loins of faith, armed with the truth that conquers all, may Christ bless all your inhabitants!"* So great was the rancor Julian felt for this city that during his last expedition against the Persians he would not even set foot in it (Theodoret, 3. 21; Sozomen, 6. 1). Nevertheless, taking advantage of an occasion offered by certain dis-

---

* A translation of the whole poem may be found in P. Schaff and H. Wace, *A Select Library of Nicene and Post-Nicene Fathers*, Second Series, 13 (New York, 1898), 132.

putes between the Arians and Valentinians at Edessa, he issued a decree of confiscation expressed in cheap irony against the Christians (*To Hecebolius*, 424c–425a). By means of this decree he deprived the Arians in the city of their property, turning over their money to his soldiers and the immovable goods to his personal treasury. It should be noted, however, that at this time Julian was in urgent need of funds for his Persian campaign.

172. The historian Socrates furnishes us with the following résumé of Julian's anti-Christian activity: "He gave orders that those who did not wish to abandon Christianity and offer sacrifice should not fight in his army, and that Christians should not be appointed provincial governors since, he said, their laws forbade recourse to the sword against those who had committed deeds worthy of death. Partly through threats and partly through bribes, he induced many to offer sacrifice" (3. 13). Here also, as Eutropius justly observes (10. 16), the persecution was not pressed to the point of shedding blood. In this matter Julian was very careful not to imitate his greatly despised Constantine, who had never excluded pagans from public employment. Many Christians sold their consciences to preserve their posts, particularly since special inducements were offered to outstanding individuals. These, however, were not always successful. Julian did not succeed, for example, with Caesarius, a highly esteemed physician at court and brother of Gregory Nazianzen.

Julian now appeared to be a prisoner of his own devices and unable to avoid the avalanche he had himself set in motion. He now realized that the consequences of his acts were more extensive than he had at first foreseen and that his own resources were not sufficient to cope with the obstacles in his way. But the raging fire that drove him on was not to be tempered. Several times the prudent prefect of the East, Sallustius (§ 150), and even Libanius attempted to restrain him. But how could the voices of men prevail against the voices of the gods which he heard echoing within his soul? Moreover, he was now too far involved to turn to the right or to the left. He had to go straight on to the very end, convinced in his own mind that time would prove him right.

XIII.   REFORMS AND WRITINGS

§ 173. Municipalities.   § 174. Highways. The Persian Question.   §§ 175–177. Julian at Antioch.   §§ 178–179. Daphne.
§§ 180–183. The Misopogon and The Caesars.   §§ 184–185.
The Hymn to King Helios; The Hymn to the Mother of
the Gods; Against the Ignorant Cynics; Against the Cynic
Heraclius.   § 186. Athanasius of Alexandria.

173. But Christianity was not the only problem weighing down upon
the empire. Even independent of Julian's religious notions, the threat
of the Persians pressed from without, while within the state various
long-standing problems waited for solution. Julian was convinced that
it was necessary to come to a reckoning once and for all with the
King of Kings. In the spring of 362, he began gathering supplies for
a powerful military expedition against the Persians (To Philip —
Wright, 3:105–107). As for the internal problems, Julian attacked them
with his usual energy, taking one up after the other in search of a
solution.

The framework of the empire had become loose and tottering at
many points, particularly in civic administration. The cities and towns,
which were the primordial cells of the state (§ 107), had many important public duties (munera civilia) to perform. Among the most
important of these were matters of finance and transportation. Under
Constantine, and still more under Constantius, the municipalities had
functioned poorly, largely because of a lack of manpower. To be a
member of a municipal curia was an extremely heavy burden, and since
it was regarded almost as a punishment, it was dreaded by all. The
decuriones municipales had to busy themselves with a little of everything without any remuneration. They had to collect taxes, requisition
produce for the state, conduct military levies, look after the garrisons
and police, and carry out other related duties. And for each of these
services they were financially responsible. If there were deficiencies in
the paying of the troops, the decurions had to make them up from

their own funds. To be sure, fraudulent compacts which enabled both parties to enrich themselves from a portion of the sums collected (§ 107) could at times be drawn up between the decurions and the high tax officials, but even then the burdens of the system rested upon the decurions.

Naturally every subterfuge was used to avoid becoming a member of a municipal curia. Many preferred to emigrate, to enter the service of powerful citizens almost as slaves, or to enlist in the army, rather than become *curiales*. Members of certain professions such as physicians endowed by municipalities and teachers were exempted from the office. In 313, Constantine extended the exemption to the clergy, but so many began to enter the service of the Church that a law was later passed prohibiting the decurions from taking orders.

In the first place, then, it was necessary to restaff the almost deserted *curiae* (§ 145) by withdrawing the exemptions. Julian began by conceling the exemption granted by Constantine to the clergy. He ordered bishops, priests, and monks, who were perhaps little suited for such an office, to take their places in the town councils. Merchants and industrialists, who were much more suited for the post, were also summoned in great numbers. Fathers of three sons, notaries of the imperial secretariate after fifteen years of service, police inspectors (*agentes in rebus*) at a certain point in their career, and some others had formerly been exempted, but such privileges were not as a rule recognized by Julian (22. 9. 12; 25. 4. 21). Those who had transferred their residence from one city to another were subject to the *munera civilia* only in the place of their actual residence, whereas formerly they had been obliged to serve in both places. In this way the curiae began to be restaffed. The one at Antioch, for example, received an increase of two hundred members, although many of these later proved to be completely useless. Similar excesses were committed in the election of *curiales* elsewhere (*Misopogon*, 367d–368b).

Some relief was found for the burden of taxes. Cities reobtained the right to impose municipal taxes, and they reacquired civic property that had not been legally alienated. Pamphilia, which was in a wretched condition, particularly benefited in this way. Old taxes that had not been collected were more or less generously condoned according to local conditions. But Julian, as a general rule, avoided a complete remission. An old question to be solved was that of the *aurum coronarium*. Although in principle this was a free-will offering in the form of a "gift" to the emperor, it was in reality an extremely burdensome tax because of the rivalry between the various cities and the servility shown toward the emperor. Julian reduced it to a modest sum. 174. The system of communication was also in disorder. From ancient times, the Romans had been masters of building and maintaining roads between one region and another. This network of highways, many traces of which can still be seen today, was primarily set up for the conveyance of troops and functionaries. Along the roads were erected stations or halting places (*stabula*) with appropriate personnel to maintain them for the change of animals and the lodging of travelers. Helena, the mother of Constantine and grandmother of Constantius, as a young woman served in one of these stations as a *mulier stabularia*. Abuses infiltrated into the transport system and multiplied rapidly. Not only state officials but many private individuals obtained permission to make use of the *cursus publicus* for their own personal interests. Constantius freely granted these permissions (*evectiones*) to the Arian clergy so that large numbers of priests and bishops favorable to his own views could assist at the synods where the doctrines he sponsored were to be sanctioned. The burden of all this service fell eventually upon the municipalities which had to furnish beasts of burden and fodder for the imperial post. The *cursus publicus* thus became a public scourge which Constantius had tried to remedy but to little effect.

With knife in hand, Julian began to cut away all this parasitic growth. Permissions for the *evectiones* were reduced: only those signed by the emperor or by the prefect of the praetorium were henceforth to be valid, although a modest number was also annually granted to vicars and governors. This parsimonious distribution of free passes, which was vigorously observed, delighted the provincials. Not only the usually laudatory Libanius praises the reform (18. 143–145), but even Gregory Nazianzen (4. 75). It must be noted, however, that in actual practice it proved to be excessive since it greatly hindered restocking the large provincial markets.

Even under the pressure of these occupations, Julian did not permit himself to be distracted from the grave Persian question. The preparations which he had already begun in the spring of 362 for his campaign against the King of Kings were being continually intensified, particularly since he planned on penetrating into the heart of the enemy's empire. According to Ammianus (22. 12. 2), he was on fire with his eagerness for war. Among his aims was that of obtaining, through a great victory, the title of "Parthicus." He rejected the advice of those few who counseled him to make a campaign against the treacherous Goths along the Danube, declaring that such an undertaking was beneath his dignity (22. 7. 8). A late tragic poet might perhaps have said of him that a mysterious sphinx was charming him from afar into the East and drawing him to his ruin; but the real sphinx was Maximus of Ephesus (Socrates, 3. 21) who had enthralled Julian with his theurgy (§ 36 ff.), had recently convinced him that he housed within himself the soul of Alexander the Great, and had assured him that he was destined to equal and even to surpass Alexander's deeds.

That Julian wished to imitate the famous Persian expedition of his predecessor Trajan was natural enough. But Libanius — whatever credence he may deserve — speaks of a projected campaign to the Indus, which would fit in with the suggestions of Maximus.

In his usual manner, Julian thoroughly studied every detail. By the middle of the summer of 362 he was nearly ready. He therefore headed toward the area of his future activity, moving from Constantinople to Antioch where he was to assemble his troops and supplies. But, in the meantime new complications arose.

175. Julian's state of mind at this period is described in the following manner by Ammianus (22. 9. 1): "But Julian, lifted up by his success, now had more than merely human aspirations, since he had been tried by so many dangers. Kind fortune, as if bearing an earthly horn of plenty, was now bestowing upon him, the undisputed ruler of the Roman world, all glory and prosperity, adding this also to the record of his former victories that as long as he was sole ruler he was not troubled by internal strife nor by barbarians crossing his frontiers; but all nations, laying aside their former eagerness for attacks as being disastrous and subject to punishment, were kindled with a wonderful desire of praising him." It was only natural that thoughts of Trajan and Alexander should continuously come to one in such a frame of mind. Was this not perhaps the triumphant carrying out of the mission entrusted to him by the gods?

In traveling, Julian passed through Chalcedon and Libyssa, where the tomb of Hannibal was preserved. He then went to Nicomedia, where he had lived as a youth (§ 23), but which a short time before had been destroyed by a terrible earthquake followed by a general fire. He was profoundly moved by the sight and gave generously toward the reconstruction of the city. He then satisfied his longing to visit the city of Pessinus, famous for its sanctuary to the Great Mother Cybele. There he offered sacrifice to this most honored goddess of the mystery cults. Finally, he headed straight for Antioch, where he was received by an immense crowd. It was the middle of July, when the feast of Adonis was being celebrated with by the erection of small artificial gardens and with rites recalling his death from a wild boar and his burial. These honors for Venus' lover, which had spread throughout the entire East, are justly called ancient by Ammianus (22. 9. 15). Much earlier they had been mentioned by Ezechiel (8:14) as practiced in honor of Tammuz (Adonis-Tammuz) by degenerate Jews in Babylon. The lamentations heard throughout the city could have been interpreted as an evil omen for the emperor's entrance, but he seems not to have heeded them.

In Antioch, Julian found his former teacher Libanius, who was invited to deliver a lecture for the occasion. The discourse (*Oratio* 13) glorifies Julian as a scholar, as a worshiper of the gods, and as governor of Gaul. It also extols the assistance he received from Maximus of Ephesus and the Neoplatonic theurgists.

176. Antioch was a great metropolis at definite odds with Julian's own ideals and sentiments. It was a frivolous, pleasure-seeking city, a melting pot of the ancient world for people of every race and religion. Christianity had won a place there almost immediately after its expansion outside of Palestine. One of the most zealous propagators of the new faith at Antioch had been St. Paul, who had been brought there by Barnabas in the year 43. A consequence of the great success of this missionary activity was that at Antioch the new believers were for the first time called Christians (Acts 11:26). At Antioch likewise, a few years later, occurred the dispute between Peter and Paul with respect to the retention of Jewish practices by Christians (Gal. 2:11 ff.). In Julian's day Christianity was predominant in Antioch (*Misopogon,* 357c), although its observance was often superficial. Pagan processions alternated with those of the Christians along the same streets. Pagan temples, old and new, functioned alongside the Christian churches. At times Christians on leaving their churches would stop to gaze at a pagan revel such as that held at Maiuma with its shameful nakedness.

The typical Antiochian affected an air of refinement and polished elegance. One should not take life too seriously but rather enjoy it to the full. That was everything. All the rest could be easily adjusted to this ideal. Possessed of such an attitude, the Antiochians naturally did not listen to anyone who had the temerity to admonish or instruct them. They had no need of tutoring. They did what they pleased, and freely criticized whom and what they pleased. But they also had their own peculiar propensities, produced in part by an exaggerated respect for antiquity and in part by their independent and reactionary temperament. Great numbers of the Antiochians had been baptized in Christ's name; and, though they frequently followed Aphrodite, they had a moderate attachment for Him. They had not been mistreated by Constantius despite his zeal for Arianism, and under him they had continued in their traditional ways. Hence, as Julian himself observed, they opposed his war upon the *Chi* (the initial of Christ's name) and regretted the loss of the *Kappa* (the initial of Constantius — *Misopogon*, 360d).

When Julian arrived at Antioch, it would have been the normal thing for the people to come out to meet him as they had done at Constantinople. But what they heard of him had aroused their suspicions. A scholar? a kill-joy? an ascetic? a careless dresser? a pagan zealot? None of these qualities exactly commended him to their sympathy, nor were they at all hopeful about any radical change in their new emperor.

177. From the very beginning Julian showed himself concerned with the practical welfare of the city. At the time of his arrival, Antioch, as the result of a poor harvest, was suffering from a lack of grain. As a remedy, Julian promulgated an official price list fixing a maximum level which was not to be exceeded. Technically, his remedy was extremely poor, although it had been attempted before by Diocletian with his *Edictum de pretiis* (*Ricciotti, Martyrs*, pp. 23–24). This time also, as under Diocletian, matters grew worse, since speculators caused the produce to disappear from the public markets. With a genuine but unenlightened generosity, Julian brought in large quantities of grain from various regions, even from as far off as Egypt, and paid for most of them out of his own personal funds (*Misopogon*, 369ab; cf. 350b–c; Ammianus, 22. 14. 1–2). But before the provisions could reach the small markets they were swept up by the heavy speculators. Ammianus states that Julian strove to lower the price of commodities in order to gain favor with the people (*popularitatis amore*), but he adds that when such a matter is not properly regulated it sometimes induces want

and famine (*inopiam gignere solet et famem*). The experience of
every age shows that Ammianus was right (cf. also Socrates, 3. 17),
but Julian did not recognize his mistake. As a consequence, serious
disputes broke out first with the senate, which had been largely
renovated (§ 173), and then with the Antiochians in general. The
people shouted in the theater that everything could be found, yes,
but at prohibitive prices (*Misopogon*, 368c). These controversies
furnished Julian with an abundance of material for his *Misopogon*.

The emperor was still further alienated from the people by his
religious policy. We have already seen the prodigality he lavished on
his pagan sacrifices, and this at a time of general want. The war
against the Persians was becoming increasingly imminent, and he felt
that he not only had to propitiate the gods with countless victims,
but that he also had to win the added favor of his oldest and most
trusted troops, the Petulantes and Celts, whose continual orgies at the
sacrificial banquets were a public scandal (§ 162). The Antiochians,
who saw the drunken soldiers being carried to their barracks after
these festivities, could not check their resentment; yet the benevolence
of the gods and the good will of his soldiers had more influence on
Julian than the attitude of the citizens. He made frequent visits to
various temples in and about the city, to those of Zeus Philios, of
Fortune, of Demeter, of Daphne (*Misopogon*, 346bc). His practices
of divination were multiplied. He examined the entrails of victims and
the flight of birds (22. 12. 7). His investigations extended even to
far-off Egypt where, after much searching, a new Apis (sacred bull) was
discovered, a lucky stroke which would bring great good fortune (22.
14. 6–7). Another omen was afforded by a swan that dwelt on a lake
near the temple of Zeus. One fine day during a sacrifice it unexpectedly
flew toward the east, as if to reveal the future source of Julian's
greatest glory.

178. Nevertheless, not all was bright and clear in the midst of these
eloquent auguries. About four and one half miles from Antioch was
located Daphne, a very beautiful site with groves, brooks, and a famous
temple dedicated to Apollo. There, about the year 172 B.C., the Jewish
high priest Onias III had taken refuge from his enemies, since it
enjoyed the right of sanctuary. Near the temple gushed forth the
spring of Castalia, from which the emperor Hadrian had learned of
his glorious future. It was therefore only natural that Julian should
also wish to consult this spring (22. 12. 8; Sozomen, 5. 19).

The site was thronged as a rule by youths in search of pleasure (according to a proverb no one should go to Daphne without a courtesan), and also by religious enthusiasts eager to consult the hordes of idols venerated there. Still, the wealth of the temples had declined under Julian's brother Gallus, who had shown his hostility to Daphne by neglecting to make necessary repairs in the temple and by seeking to counterbalance the crowds of pagans with crowds of Christians. He had erected a church in front of the temple of Apollo, enclosing in it the remains of St. Babilas, a bishop of Antioch who had suffered martyrdom under Decius. This shrine proved to be a ruinous rival to the pagan gods. It not only brought many Christians to the place but, after a certain time, the pagan gods became dumb and ceased to give their oracles.

Even before arriving at Antioch, the emperor had ordered his uncle Julian to set about restoring the temple of Apollo (*To his Uncle Julian* — Wright, 3:99). Moreover, since no one was as interested as he in hearing the mute oracles which in former times had gushed forth from every corner of Daphne, he inquired at Antioch about the reason for their miserable silence. From an expert in such matters, he learned that the reason for their silence was the fact that the site had been contaminated by dead bodies and must, therefore, be purified. The contamination had been principally produced by the remains of St. Babilas. Julian immediately gave orders that his body should be removed.

The order soon became known in the city. The Christians assembled for the removal of the relics and to show at the same time their hostility to Julian. The wagon bearing the reliquary was surrounded by a great crowd which accompanied it from Daphne to the cemetery at Antioch. The crowd sang psalms from the Bible, repeating especially those verses which decry the folly of worshiping idols and foretell the confusion of those who venerate them. This time Julian lost control of himself. He would have liked to renew the "great persecution" of Diocletian, but "since he could not do so on account of the imminent campaign against the Persians, he ordered Sallustius, the prefect of the praetorium, to arrest for capital punishment those who had been most zealous in singing the psalms. But the prefect, although he followed the religion of the Hellenes, did not approve of the order. Nevertheless, since he could not oppose it, he arrested many Christians and shut them up in prison" (Socrates, 3. 19; cf. Sozomen, 5. 20; Theodoret, 3. 6–7). A lad named Theodore was subjected to the cruelest kinds of torment but remained unmoved. Sallustius (§ 150) then referred the whole matter to Julian. This made him realize that the use of such means would cover him with ridicule and only increase the prestige of the Christians. Theodore and the rest were accordingly set free.

179. But the tragicomedy was not yet ended. During the night of October 22 of this same year, 362, the temple of Apollo caught fire and burned to the ground. The fire originated high up in the beams about the head of the acrolithic cult statue, a representation of Apollo Citharoedus carved of wood and marble by the Athenian Bryaxis. It spread from the beams to the statue and enveloped it in flames. Soon the head fell down on the torso of the statue already weakened by the fire and split it into two parts. The crash of the statue's head awakened those in charge of the temple and they rushed to the scene. The whole interior of the temple became a roaring furnace, and everything was consumed by the flames. The gleam of the fire and the news of the disaster brought many out from the city, Julian being among the first; but it was impossible to bring any assistance.

What was the cause of the fire? It was said to have spread from votive lamps kindled at the feet of the statue of the Cynic philosopher Asclepiades (22. 13. 3; *Against the Cynic Heraclius*, 224d). To discover the culprits Julian had the guardians of the temples scourged with rods and the priest of Apollo put to torture. Though these measures proved to be fruitless, he was himself convinced that the fire had been set by the Christians to avenge the translation of the body of St. Babilas (*Misopogon*, 361bc). Still his own conscience was at ease. From one of his mystic communications he had learned even before the fire that the gods had abandoned the temple. The Christians, consequently, could not boast that they had overcome the god. But the Christians, in their turn, pointed out that the fire had started high up in the temple. It was therefore a fire come down from heaven. Farmers in the vicinity even claimed that they had seen a stroke of lightning (Theodoret, 3. 11; Libanius, 60. 12; cf. John Chrysostom, *Contra Julianum*, 17; Philostorgius, 7. 8).

Presuming the guilt of the Christians, Julian ordered reprisals to be made far and near. He destroyed the chapels which the Christians had erected over the tombs of martyrs near the temple of Apollo Didymus at Meletus, of which he was the great high priest and prophet (§ 165). In Antioch itself he closed the principal Christian church and then robbed it of the precious furnishings it had received from Constantine and Constantius. This act of vengeance was carried out under the direction of his uncle, Count Julian (§ 177), who like his nephew had formerly been a Christian. The superintendent Felix and the treasurer Elpidius assisted in the undertaking. Count Julian even went so far as to foully desecrate the sacred table and vessels (Sozomen, 5. 8; Theodoret, 3. 8). Euzoius, the Arian bishop who had baptized Constantius on his deathbed (§ 148), protested and was slapped by the count for his pains.

Many other individuals and institutions suffered from Julian's reaction, but the evidence is often uncritical. On the other hand, if Lactantius had still been alive, he would have been able to add an appendix to his *De mortibus persecutorum* describing the calamities that befell Julian's assistants in his struggle against Christianity. These are recorded by pagans and Christians alike. To limit ourselves to the individuals connected with the events of Daphne, the superintendent Felix died shortly afterward from a violent hemorrhage. Count Julian came to an even more terrible end. He was stricken with cancer of the intestines. His wife, who had remained a Christian, told him frankly that his affliction was a warning that he should acknowledge his evil deeds. Heeding her advice, he vainly entreated his nephew to repair the wrongs done to the church at Antioch. He finally died after a long agony (23. 1. 4–5; Philostorgius, 7. 10; Sozomen, 5. 8; Theodoret, 3. 8).

As usual, the common people made sport of these events. Julian's official title on the public monuments was *Dominus noster Julianus Pius Felix Augustus*. As they looked at the inscriptions, the people, omitting some of the words, read the names aloud as *Felix, Julianus,* and *Augustus*, implying that Augustus (the emperor) would follow Felix and Count Julian to the grave. Julian himself was terrified by this highly significant omen, and events were to show that his fear was well founded (*terrebatur omine quodam, ut docuit exitus, praesentissimo* — 23. 1. 5).

180. After establishing himself at Antioch, Julian withdrew into complete retirement. Knowing that he was despised by the Christians and ridiculed by the pagans, he surrounded himself with a small company of intimate friends or, better, of "initiates," since they formed a small secret society. He describes the group as follows: "We are seven, strangers and newly arrived in your city, though indeed one of us is a fellow citizen of yours, a man loved by Hermes and by me, an excellent craftsman of discourses. We have no business dealings with anyone, nor do we tread any road that does not lead to the temples of the gods. Seldom do we go to the theaters, and even then not all of us" (*Misopogon*, 354c). As we have already seen (§ 24), the fellow citizen of the Antiochians was Libanius. The other six strangers were Maximus and Priscus, Julian's spiritual guides; Himerius (§ 161), and Oribasius (§ 131), members of the secret society; Sallustius, prefect of the praetorium (§ 150); and Anatolius, master of the offices.

Among these confidants Julian felt at ease, whereas in the city he met nothing but disappointment and disillusionment. He was fully aware of the gibes, jokes, and lampoons that circulated about him in the city. He was a hairy ape (§ 32) with the beard of a he-goat, always buried in books, with nails long and stained with ink. He ate "like a grasshopper" and slept "like a Vestal," and was only good for playing the butcher as he quartered hundreds of victims to his idols. In his *Misopogon*, that is, "Beard-hater," Julian makes a valiant attempt to appear superior to this mockery, but despite his seeming indifference the sallies pierced him like so many thorns. Ammianus has already told us (§ 162) that "he was indignant" at this ridicule, "although he kept silent and controlled his feelings." But Julian's character was too vindictive to suffer it long (§ 135). Toward the end of January, 363, his resistance broke down, and during the next few days he dictated his reply to the Antiochians. At this time he was occupied with many heavy cares of state and particularly with the intense preparations for his Persian expedition.

The *Misopogon* did not receive the approval of his friends and contemporaries. That Gregory Nazianzen disparaged it, is not surprising; nor is it remarkable that Libanius was less than enthusiastic, since he found too many things in it which hurt him both as an Antiochian and as a rhetorician. Another native of this city, Ammianus Marcellinus, expressed his disgust as follows: "He composed a prejudiced invective, which he called *The Antiochian* or *Misopogon*, listing the faults of the citizens, and exaggerating them in many instances" (22. 14. 2). Surprisingly enough, on the other hand, we find the Christian historian Sozomen (5. 19) describing it as "a very clever and beautiful piece of work."

181. Like almost all of Julian's writings, it was set down in a single draft without subsequent polishing or revision. The indisputable literary

merit of the essay stems from its author's profound convictions and intense feelings, and it proves the truth of Quintilian's observation: "Feeling and strength of mind make men eloquent" (*pectus est quod disertos facit, et vis mentis* — *Inst. orat.*, 10. 7. 15). In it Julian employs the rhetorical device of antiphrasis, a species of irony in which one says the very opposite of what is really intended. This style of argumentation by itself reveals Julian's sense of superiority and his disdain for his adversaries. In pretending to furnish the Antiochians with reasons and assist them in proving their thesis, he, the emperor, descends to their level, arguing as one might with hucksters in the public market. This literary trick, which leaves us cold today, irritated many of his ancient readers since it seemed to debase the dignity of the imperial office.

Ranking himself, then, among his adversaries so as to be able to assist them, Julian begins by disparaging his own physical appearance, then his boorish manners, clumsy ways, and pagan devotions. He passes nervously from one idea to another, mingling personal experiences of the past, current happenings, forecasts for the future — always pretending to be accusing himself and assisting his adversaries. We have already drawn precious autobiographical data from these burlesque confessions. Beneath the fun, however, seethed a galling bitterness and shudder of disdain painfully concealed under the literary convention — *in hilaritate tristis.*

Julian's satire, *The Caesars*, written toward the end of 361, was ranked higher in antiquity than the *Misopogon* as a literary work, and in recent years certain scholars have again expressed such a preference. But the general consensus of opinion today runs counter to this. Giacomo Leopardi, for instance, one of the world's great authorities on Byzantine literature, writes: "Wit of this type, as I have noted elsewhere, is peculiar to antiquity. An example of it was given by the Antiochians who said that the Emperor Julian wore a beard to give him courage. This witticism was enthusiastically spread throughout the city, and it prompted Julian to write a humorous and ironic work against the Antiochians. It is certainly elegant, and in its Attic and Lucianic jests it is infinitely superior to his *Caesars*. It is without sophistry in style or anything else, and without affectation even in expression, although elegant and rich, and this because the *Misopogon* is a work written to meet a challenge and is not a *tour de force* like *The Caesars*. The jest, however, which prompted the work, would seem today to be crude and in bad taste."* And in another place he notes: "Julian's age was completely sophistic, and so is he in all his other works, just as Libanius, Themistius, and his other famous contemporaries. But no one is a sophist when he speaks about himself and for himself and on an occasion that moves him profoundly.**

182. *The Caesars*, which was composed in Constantinople, has fared better, since it is more popular and more intelligible to those who are not acquainted with the historical background of the *Misopogon*. That Julian for this work borrowed from the writings of the Hellenized Semite Lucian of Samosata cannot be denied. Nevertheless, he makes his own original contributions, particularly where he treats of individuals close at hand. The manuscript title of *The Caesars* is *Symposium*, or *Kronia*, which is sometimes translated into Latin as *Saturnalia;* but this must be distinguished from another *Saturnalia* which he wrote, and which is no longer extant. This farce, which was composed while the high court of Chalcedon was functioning (§§ 150–151), parades the various deified emperors in review. They are criticized with that liberty of speech which was permitted on the feast of the Saturnalia held in honor of Saturn, or Kronos. It is in part a fantasy, in part a release of pent-up emotions in which Julian excoriates his predecessors. Only Marcus Aurelius, Julian's favorite, is spared.

For the feast of the Saturnalia, Romulus on Mt. Olympus offers a dinner for the gods, to which he invites the principal Roman "Caesars" and Alexander the Great. The throne upon which Zeus is seated is made of electrum, or something similar (307d). After the banquet has begun, the guests stage a contest to challenge Zeus's dominion over the world. Silenus, who acts as the court jester, frequently interrupts the debate with witty comments. The emperors appear in turn: the haughty Julius Caesar, the chameleon Augustus, the old satyr Tiberius, an unnamed "cruel monster" (Caligula). Then Claudius, Nero, Vindex, Galba, Otho, and Vitellius make their flitting appearance. These are followed by the "Egyptian miser" (Vespasian) and his sons, the libidinous Titus and criminal Domitian. An old man fair to behold makes a passing appearance (Nerva). Then comes Trajan burdened with trophies, but he is ridiculed by a vile insinuation of Silenus. The same insult is extended to Hadrian "always gazing at the heavens and prying into occult matters." There follow Antoninus

---

* G. Leopardi, *Zibaldone*, 4 ed., Vol. I (Milan, 1953), p. 88.
** *Ibid.*, p. 284.

Pius and his two adopted sons, Marcus Aurelius (here called Verus) and Lucius Verus (called Lucius). Though respect is shown for Marcus Aurelius, he is blamed for his errors in judgment with respect to his wife and son. Other emperors follow rapidly down to Diocletian, who is accompanied by his three colleagues in the tetrarchy, including "my grandfather Constantius" (315a). At the end Constantine makes his appearance with his sons and Magnentius.

As the gods get ready to examine the heroes that have been invited to the feast, Heracles suggests that Alexander the Great should also be introduced, even though he is not a Caesar, and the suggestion is approved. Julius Caesar, Octavian (Augustus), and Trajan are each told to argue their own cases since they were the greatest warriors. At the insistence of Kronos, the philosopher-emperor, Marcus Aurelius, is also invited to take part in the debate. Constantine, on the other hand, is only permitted to assist at it from the threshold since, "though he is not unwarlike, he is a slave to pleasure and enjoyment." Julius Caesar first gives a long nonsensical harangue on his military exploits. Alexander the Great becomes bored and is about to depart, but he is restrained by Heracles. At one point, Alexander breaks in and tries to speak about himself. This is followed by a self-glorification on the part of Octavian and Trajan. Marcus Aurelius finally concludes the debate. He simply appeals to his deeds, showing himself "admirable in other respects and wise above all others in knowing 'when it is necessary to speak and when it is fitting to keep silence'" (328d — the quotation is from a fragment of Euripides — Nauck, 417).

183. It would now be Constantine's turn to speak. And, in fact, he is haughtily waiting his chance, but it is clear that in comparison with the other leaders his achievements are ridiculous. Further, instead of paying attention to the peroration, he stands absorbed in contemplating Luxury, who is stationed far from the gods near the boundaries of the Moon. Constantine then speaks a few words to extol his victories, but Selinus interrupts him with the remark that those victories were like the little artificial gardens of Adonis (§ 175) which last only a few days.

Then there is a new examination, partly repetitious, of the contestants, each of whom must indicate the extent of his achievements. Constantine says that he had aimed at acquiring great wealth to satisfy his own desires and those of his friends, but Selinus interrupts him, saying that he had led the life of a "cook and a barber" (§ 22).

When the new examination has been completed, Zeus orders each one to choose a god as his own special protector. Constantine, failing to find among the gods one whom he could approach, runs toward Luxury. She embraces him, clothes him with showy, effeminate robes, and leads him to "Asotia" (which may be translated "Dissipation," but which is here probably better rendered by "Perdition" or "Atheism"). There too Constantine finds Jesus, one of her companions, who cries out for all to hear: "Whoever is a seducer, whoever is a murderer, whoever is unholy and infamous, let him come without fear! For I shall wash him with this water and he will straightway be made clean. And even if he should be guilty a second time of those same sins, I will make him clean again if he strikes his breast and beats his head" (336ab).

The farce concludes with a grave admonition directed by Hermes to Julian. Since he has given him knowledge of his father Mithra, Julian should keep his commandments (§ 60) and thus secure for himself during his lifetime an anchor of salvation and after death a benevolent god as his guide.

The new twist in the conclusion is remarkable. Up to this point the work is one continuous burlesque with jests and ridicule in keeping with the spirit of the Saturnalia, but at the very end it takes on an edifying and hortatory tone revealing the inner convictions of its author. The crude disparagement of Jesus and of Christian baptism serves as a contrast to the pious exaltation of the god Mithra.

184. Here it will be convenient to make a rapid survey of what are commonly held to be Julian's minor philosophical works. Actually, despite his many excellent gifts, Julian did not possess a truly philosophical habit of mind. He probably thought otherwise himself, but if so, it was only because he substituted Iamblicus for Plato, theurgy for reason. His opuscula, which were written at intervals of only a few months, are four in number and are all to be assigned to the year 362. They are as follows: *To King Helios; To the Mother of the Gods; Against the Ignorant Cynics;* and *Against the Cynic Heraclius.* The first two of these are known as "hymns," though they are written in prose as was customary at this time.

No definite philosophical system can be deduced from these works. What is best in them comes from the Neoplatonism of Iamblicus, but this is all mixed up with, and obscured by, various ideas which

Julian picked up from polytheism, astrology, and the mystery cults, especially that of Mithra.

The hymn *To King Helios* was composed at the winter solstice to celebrate the birthday of the Sun on December 25, and was dedicated to Sallustius, the prefect of Gaul. Julian's purpose in writing it was to provide a kind of breviary for the pagan church he ambitioned, which was to be based on state monotheism with the emperor as the *pontifex maximus*. From the Supreme One of Plotinus (§ 27), which presides over the Intelligible World, emanates the Intellectual Sun, which communicates its perfections to the gods. The Material Sun, the image of the Intellectual Sun, acts as the intermediary between the Supreme One and the Material World. Consequently, it also possesses a certain superiority over the other gods, which often appear only as different aspects of the Intellectual Sun, and of these the most worthy are Mithra and Helios (Apollo).

The "Mother of the Gods" is Cybele, the "Great Mother" of the Western mystery cults. The first part of this hymn tells of her transfer from Phrygia to Rome during the Second Punic War, but as the hymn progresses her companion in mythology, Attis, comes to the fore. Moreover, his attributes are largely confused with those of Mithra. This work, which was composed in a single night, plainly shows the defects of its origin. Nevertheless, it furnishes us with important data on the mystery rites, even though the philosophical explanations afforded by Julian are for the most part arbitrary.

185. *Against the Ignorant Cynics* and *Against the Cynic Heraclius* are polemics. In the latter, Julian expounds his ideas on mythology.

The ignorant Cynics are not the ancient philosophers, whom Julian respected, but those men of his own day who liked to go about unkempt, knapsacks on their shoulders and staff in hand, making a mockery of everything. Starting with the ancient Greek maxim "Know thyself," Julian rewrites the history of philosophy to show that Plato and Diogenes had a single end in view. A true follower of Diogenes ought not to be "shameless or impudent or a scorner of all things human and divine, but reverent toward the divinity like Diogenes, for he obeyed the Pythian oracle and did not regret his obedience. But anyone who imagines that his failure to visit the temples and to worship the statues or altars is a thing of impiety is in error, for Diogenes had no incense or means of libation or money with which to buy

them. But if his opinions about the gods were correct, that was in itself
enough, for he worshiped them with his soul, offering as I believe, his
most precious possession, the sanctification of his soul through his
thoughts" (199ab).

Against the Cynic Heraclius, which is somewhat similar to the work
just described, carries in the manuscripts the subtitle *How a Cynic
Ought to Act and Whether it is Proper for Him to Create Myths*. It
was occasioned by a lecture given by Heraclius which Julian attended
with Sallustius, Anatolius, and other friends. Heraclius was a skeptic
in religious matters, and he treated the pagan divinities without respect.
Julian was deeply incensed and at one point felt like rising and breaking up the meeting, but he checked the impulse out of deference to
the public and to avoid attributing too much importance to the orator.
His natural punctiliousness, however, could not let the incident pass
without a reply (§§ 135, 180). His answer contains various autobiographical details (§§ 13, 25, 42, 155), but where there are opportunities of discussing the hidden meanings of the mystery rites, Julian
does not avail himself of them, saying rather, "'I put an ox on my
tongue,'* since ineffable things must not be spoken" (218a). This, of
course, referred to the secrecy binding the initiates (§§ 40, 60). According to Julian, one must distinguish between thought and expression in
the myths. In the expression one may find much which seems paradoxical and unlikely, but it should not be rejected on that account.
"For what is incongruous in the myths guides us to the truth, that is,
the more paradoxical and prodigious the enigma is, the more it seems
to warn us not to trust simply to the bare words but rather to examine
diligently the hidden truth" (217c). Such a rule of interpretation had
already been employed by the Christian school of Alexandria, and particularly by Origen in his exegesis of Sacred Scripture, but on the
strength of far different principles and with a completely different
justification. Julian here bases his norms solely upon his own authority
as *pontifex maximus* of all paganism.

The comparison which Julian draws between the wandering Cynics
and the Christian "Apotactistae" (224ab) is curious. St. Basil also
speaks of these Apotactistae, or "Apotactitae," that is, "Renouncers."
He states that they were followers of the ancient heretic Marcion.
They led a very ascetical life, renouncing all property and even mar-

---

* This was a proverb used of the silence connected with some mystery (Theognis,
815; Aeschylus, *Agamemnon*, 36–37.

riage, and wandered about exactly like the Cynics. Orthodox Christians looked upon them as heretics and madcap fanatics. Under Theodosius they were even condemned by public law, but Julian, to support his own position, regards them merely as a special group within the Church. Addressing the Cynics, Julian observes: "I gave you a name long ago, and now it is time to write it down. The impious Galileans call certain individuals 'Apotactistae.' For the most part they are men who gain much, or rather everything, from all sides by making small sacrifices, and secure besides honor, throngs of attendants, and flattery. You act in a somewhat similar manner, except perhaps that you do not utter divine oracles" (224ab).

186. Despite his many achievements, there were a number of problems which Julian did not succeed in solving. Athanasius, the bishop of Alexandria, for instance, was a source of particular annoyance. This hardy prelate suffered his third banishment when George of Cappadocia took over his see. Even after George was killed (§ 158), Athanasius remained in exile until the death of Constantius, traveling about and visiting various centers of asceticism in the Egyptian desert. The famous Anthony of the Thebaid was a very close friend of his. On the strength of Julian's decree restoring liberty to all who had been exiled or imprisoned by Constantius (§ 156), Athanasius thought that he could return to Alexandria; and on February 21, 362, he again took possession of his see to the great joy of the orthodox, who honored his return with a public illumination of the city.

But Julian was of a different opinion: the general amnesty did not apply to Athanasius, who had been banished by so many imperial decrees; moreover, the bishops banished by Constantius had been granted permission to return to their countries but not to their churches (*Edict to the Alexandrians*, 398c–399a). Yet Athanasius was acting not only as the shepherd of his flock, he even held a council at Alexandria and strove to win over the semi-Arian Christians and pagans. This audacity prompted Julian to add a postscript "in his own hand" to a letter addressed to Ecdicius, prefect of Egypt: "I am grieved that my orders have been contemned. By all the gods, I would see and hear nothing more gladly done by you than that Athanasius, the infamous wretch who dared to baptize Greek women of noble birth during my reign, should be sent out of Egypt. Let him be driven forth" (*To Ecdicius*, 376bc)!

Athanasius was not at all disturbed. On October 24, he again set out for the desert and his friends the hermits, where Julian's agents could not discover him. To those who consoled him on his departure, he observed, "Have no fear: it is a small cloud that will soon pass." The Alexandrians sent a petition to Julian on behalf of their bishop, but again Julian was carried off by his natural belligerency. Instead of answering the petition with a dry and peremptory decree, he sent a letter treating a little of everything (*To the Alexandrians*, 432d–435d). He appeals to the lord Serapis, the ancient Hebrews, Alexander the Great, Ptolemy, the son of Lagus, Helios, the Sun, and Selene, the Moon, Jesus, who is not the Word of God, and others. He then orders that "contemptible little fellow" (ἀνθρωπίσκος εὐτελής — Athanasius) to be banished not only from Alexandria but from the whole of Egypt. Naturally, Athanasius and Julian each continued on his own way, but on August 13, 363, when Julian's death was announced in Egypt, Athanasius, who was at Antinoë, quietly took the road for Alexandria. The "little cloud" had passed, and Julian's successor, Jovian, with a deferential letter had recalled him from exile. The old champion of orthodoxy underwent still another exile under Valentinian, but in the end he died peacefully in Alexandria ten years after the death of Julian.

XIV. RECONSTRUCTION OF THE TEMPLE AT JERUSALEM AND THE LAWS ON FUNERALS

§ 187. *Julian's Attitude Toward the Jews.* §§ 188–189. *Projects for the Reconstruction of the Temple and Its Failure.* §§ 190–191. *Laws on Funerals.*

187. Julian did not foster a burning hatred for the Jews as he did for the Christians. He felt a good deal of sympathy toward them since their institutions contained a large measure of truth. To his way of thinking, the religion of the Hellenes, which amply provided for the tutelary gods of individual nations, was highest in the hierarchy of religions (*Against the Galileans*, 115d). Immediately after this religion came that of the Jews, whose chief defect was monotheism. In Julian's own words, "I desired to show that the Jews agree with the Gentiles except for the fact that they believe in one God. This is a characteristic point with them but foreign to us, since after a fashion we have all else in common — temples, sacred precincts, altars for sacrifice, purifications, and certain commandments, in all of which we differ not at all from one another, or only in minor details" (*ibid.*, 306b).

It is not necessary to pause here at this very empiric comparison. But even more strange is Julian's observation of a few lines earlier, that "the Jews in private (ἐν ἀδράκτοις) offer sacrifice, and even to this day everything they eat is sacred (ἱερά)." At best, this sacrifice could refer to the paschal lamb, but this had to be slaughtered in the temple at Jerusalem, which had been destroyed three centuries earlier. Outside Jerusalem the Jews had no sites where they could lawfully offer sacrifice, nor did they have "sacred precincts" and "altars for sacrifice." Julian, therefore, must have been misinformed, or he was speaking anachronistically, referring to a period centuries earlier.

But in Julian's designs, any such anachronism was to disappear. The ancient prescriptions of the Torah, or Hebrew law, regarding sacrifices should be revived and observed in their entirety. To this end, the

223

temple at Jerusalem, the only one recognized in the Torah, would have to be rebuilt and used again, even though for many decades Roman emperors had forbidden Jews to approach its ruins or even to set foot in Jerusalem.

Another advantage would accrue to Julian from the reconstruction of the temple: Christ's prophecy that there should not remain a stone upon a stone of all that great structure would receive a resounding refutation (Mt. 24:2). The high priest of the Hellenes would embarrass the God of the Galileans on His own terrain, making Him out to be a charlatan.

A letter *To the Community of the Jews* (369a–398a) attributed to Julian may substantially represent his thoughts even if it is apocryphal, as a number of modern editors maintain (cf. Sozomen, 5. 22; Socrates, 3. 20). Whatever its worth may be, Julian certainly had definite plans for the reconstruction of the temple at Jerusalem. A small fragment of an authentic letter addressed to the Jews proves this: "I will use all my zeal to make the temple of the Most High God* rise again" (quoted in Lydus, *De Mensibus*, 4, cf. Bidez, 1. 2:197). Another authentic letter also refers to the same project (*To a Priest*, 295c).

188. After he made his decision, Julian entrusted its execution to Alypius, a trustworthy individual who had governed Britain as vicar of the praetorian prefect. The events which followed would be almost incredible if they were not attested with substantial agreement by Julian's pagan friend Ammianus (23. 1. 2 ff.), by the Arian Philostorgius (7. 9), and by orthodox Christians such as Rufinus (1. 37–39), Socrates (3. 20), Sozomen (5. 22), Theodoret (3. 15), Gregory Nazianzen (5. 3–8), and others, such as the contemporaneous but distant Ephraem Syrus. But, to limit ourselves to Ammianus, one has only to read his account to see that it is completely independent of Gregory's. Moreover, since Ammianus had been present at Antioch and later took part in Julian's Persian campaign, he was well informed on the actual events, while he perhaps had no knowledge whatever of Gregory or his writings.

The announcement of the plan filled the Jews of the diaspora with enthusiasm. According to Ammianus, Julian allotted enormous (*immo-*

---

* The name "Most High God" must have been suggested to Julian by the rabbis who desired the reconstruction of the temple, but it stems from the El elyon of the Hebrew Bible (Gen. 14:18 ff.). Nevertheless it was also known to the Phoenician theogony of which Philo of Byblos speaks (in Eusebius, *Praep. evang.*, 1. 10; cf. Epiphanius, *Adv. haer.*, 1. 3. 40. 5).

dicis) sums for the enterprise. These were augmented by contributions of the patriarch of all Judaism and other voluntary offerings, including costly garments and jewels handed over for the purpose by Jewish women.

The work began with the clearing of the site of the ancient temple from the accumulated debris of centuries. This was found to the east of the ancient valley of the Tyropoeon, which divided the city into two parts, descending from north to south. The great basilica built on Calvary over the tomb of Jesus by Constantine some forty years earlier was not disturbed since it was located to the west of the valley (Ricciotti, *Martyrs*, pp. 224–226).

Toward the close of 362, violent earthquakes occurred along the Palestinian coast and in various parts of Syria leveling such cities as Gaza, Eleutheropolis (Beit-Jibrîn), to the southwest of Jerusalem, Nicopolis, to the west of Jerusalem, and Neapolis, near Samaria in the center of Palestine. In certain areas permanent changes were effected in the earth's crust. Elsewhere, the seas rushed in through great fissures in the earth. Jerusalem also suffered from these great tremors. Recently cleared portions of the temple area were at times littered with ruins caused by the earthquakes. On one occasion a violent tremor caused the collapse of a portico upon a large number of workmen, some of whom were killed, though others found refuge in a neighboring church.

189. Despite all this, the project was pursued vigorously. Here we must leave the account to our neutral witness, Ammianus: "But though Alypius pushed the work forward energetically, and though he was assisted by the governor of the province, frightful balls of flame kept bursting forth near the foundations of the temple and made it impossible for the workmen to approach the place, and some were even burned to death. And since the elements persistently drove them back, Julian gave up the attempt" (23. 1. 3).

Even today no real explanation has been given for these "balls of flame." It has been suggested that they were due to a seepage of petroleum, which is found in abundance about the Dead Sea. This sea, in fact, was called in ancient time the "Asphalt Lake," since masses of asphalt and bitumen frequently detached themselves from the bottom of the lake, particularly during times of earthquakes, and floated to the surface (Josephus, *Jewish War*, 4. 8. 4), as has since been seen in 1834, 1837, and 1927. But it must be kept in mind that the Dead Sea is more than twenty-five miles from Jerusalem, and further, that there is a great difference in altitude between the two sites. Jerusalem is 2500 feet above the level of the Mediterranean while the Dead Sea lies 1290 feet below it. A difference in height of some 3790 feet does not seem to support the hypothesis, especially when the mean depth of the Dead Sea itself is some 1080 feet.

After this failure, Julian had nothing to do but make a bold front in the face of his misfortunes. In a letter written early in 363, he openly refers to the failure of the undertaking, but only to draw from it conclusions favorable to his own pagan beliefs (*To a Priest*, 295cd). The Jewish prophets, he writes, inveighed mightily against the worship of idols, but what would they now say of their temple thrice destroyed and not yet reconstructed? Julian does not bring this up to cause offense, since he had himself intended to rebuild the temple, but only to show that idols and temples of every kind are perishable. The God of the Jews may be great, but He has not found worthy prophets and interpreters. The reason is that their souls have not been refined by a liberal education, and their eyes have not been purified by the light of study.

To sum up, whereas at the beginning Julian had diligently exerted himself on behalf of the Jews and their temple, he now abandoned them to their fate after disparaging their religion and culture.

190. Julian was still not satisfied with all this turbulent activity. His consciousness of the secret mission entrusted to him by the gods induced him to make a diligent inquiry to see if there were any further measures to be taken and any mistakes to be corrected in his struggle with Christianity. And he actually did find something sorely in need of remedy. It was the manner of conducting funerals.

Even today an individual may turn aside from a funeral procession that he sees coming down the street and head in a different direction. This is a very old superstition, and one that is almost always unconscious. At the time, and in the theurgic world in which Julian lived, such a fear was greater than it is today, but it was not unconscious, since cosmology and theology were used to explain it. The lower and darker elements in the human composite were controlled by the higher and clearer elements (§ 30); but when these baser elements were separated from the higher ones, they freely sent forth their baneful influences, contaminating everything in the vicinity. Consequently, scrupulous care was needed to preserve oneself from such contaminations, the worst of which was that which emanated from a cadaver.

In times past Julian had not himself observed such taboos. He had taken part in the obsequies of Constantius, even touching his sarcophagus (§ 149); and, further, as part of his restoration of paganism he had advised the pagan priests to imitate the Christians in their care for the graves of the dead (*To Arsacius*, 429d). But under the ever increasing influence of Maximus of Ephesus and other theurgists, he became scrupulous even on this point and strove to impose his rigorism on all. We have already seen the measures he took to purify Daphne from the contamination of the relics of St. Babilas (§ 178). At this same time in his writings he was beginning to disparage the Christian care for the dead.

According to Julian, the Christian churches, which were built as a rule over the tombs of martyrs, were nothing but loathsome mausolea (*Misopogon*, 344a), and the Galileans had done nothing but fill the world with tombs and sepulchers (*Against the Galileans*, 335bc). Although he does so only incidentally, Julian makes an archaeological allusion to the tombs of Peter and Paul (*ibid.*, 327b), which is of interest in the light of the excavation of St. Peter's tomb on the Vatican.

191. In this matter of funerals also, Julian partially concealed his motives. There are two extant documents reflecting his attitude. One is official, the edict of February 12, 363 (*Cod. Theod.*, 9. 17. 5; cf. *Cod. Justin.*, 9. 19. 5); the other (*On Funerals* — Wright, 3:190–196) is apparently a private document summarizing the juridical motives for the edict. The matter is, therefore, more or less analogous to that of the schools (§ 168). Here, as in the legislation on the schools, the real aim of the edict hardly appears in the official text, whereas its scope is clearly indicated in the private document.

Since men most versed in religious practices, Julian observes, believe that the most suitable time to honor the gods of the netherworld is at night, or at least after the tenth hour of the day (that is, a little before sundown), all funerals, including the translation of bodies, should from now on be carried out at this time. Life and death unfold on two different planes which must be kept perfectly distinct, especially since it is not known if the gods who rule the living rule also over the dead. Funeral rites carried out during the course of the day are a detriment to people occupied with the countless affairs of ordinary life and to those going to the temples of the gods to pray, especially when a funeral cortege passes before the open doors of a temple. All this is accursed, "since the gods are the authors of life and of all things the farthest removed from decay," and one may not approach them after seeing such a sight without being first purified from the stain. For a funeral procession to pass before an open temple while sacrificial rites are being carried out is even more abominable, since the proximity of the corpse and the lamentations of the mourners disturb the sacred ritual. Consequently, it has been ordained that bodies should be carried out between sunset and dawn: "Let the pure day be consecrated to pure works and to the pure gods of Olympus."

With such a decree, Julian secured Neoplatonic purity for the Roman Empire, but only for a few months. Some forty years later St. Augustine, without thinking in the least about Julian, was to write his little essay *De cura pro mortuis gerenda*, which is still today living and effective.

XV. THE PERSIAN CAMPAIGN

§ 192. Decision on the Campaign.   §§ 193–195. Against the
Galileans.   § 196. Military Preparations.   §§ 197–199. The
Expedition Gets Under Way. Detachment of Procopius and
Sebastian.   §§ 200–202. Advance to Ozogardane. First En-
counters With the Persians.   §§ 203–204. Toward Ctesi-
phon. From the Euphrates to the Tigris.   §§ 205–206.
Departure From Ctesiphon. Burning of the Fleet.   § 207.
Retreat of the Romans and the Persian Reaction.   §§ 208–
210. Julian's Death.   § 211. Sequel.

192. Meanwhile the days passed swiftly. The expedition against the
Persians was ready in every detail; all that remained was to initiate it.
Reports of the large-scale preparations had already crossed the frontiers
and reached the court of the King of Kings, stirring up first vague
apprehensions and then a real fear. The ruler of the Roman Empire
was now no longer the cautious Constantius, long on words and short
in action, but a young man of boundless energy who had tamed the
fierce barbarians of the Rhine, had crossed the whole Roman Empire
like lightning, and with a single stroke had seized its capital. Further,
offers of alliance and military assistance had come from various areas
toward which the expedition was heading (23. 2. 1), and war material
of every sort was being daily accumulated on the frontiers. Since the
danger was so serious, the King of Kings suddenly abandoned his
haughtiness. He sent a letter to Julian suggesting that they negotiate
their differences.

Even more unexpected was Julian's answer. After reading the letter
he tore it up in the presence of the Persian ambassadors and told them
that he would soon carry his answer in person to the King of Kings
(Libanius, 18. 164; cf. Socrates, 3. 19). The theatricality of this gesture
was perhaps deliberately planned as a warning to the king. Though
such an action was not new to the diplomacy of the times, many of
the courtiers disapproved of it since it made war inevitable (Ammianus
22. 12. 3).

That the undertaking was extremely dangerous was only too evident. Even prescinding from the ancient misfortunes of Crassus and Valerian, the former of whom was killed, and the latter made prisoner by the Persians, the fate of Galerius, who had been totally routed in his first Persian campaign and had with difficulty reached Antioch, was still recent. But even a successful expedition would entail incalculable burdens for the empire, and particularly for those areas which would be the theater of the war. The Antiochians, who would be the first exposed to its hazards, especially deprecated it, and the Christians were similarly averse. The Antiochians knew that Julian, angry at their attacks and insults, had decided to abandon Antioch and take up his residence at Tarsus if he returned victorious from the war (23. 2. 3–5). The Christians, on the other hand, feared that the emperor on his return would unleash a radical persecution (Theodoret, 3. 16; Gregory Nazianzen, 5. 9; John Chrysostom, *Contra Julianum*, 22). To placate Julian's anger many citizens and magistrates of Antioch called on him to bid him farewell as he set out on his expedition. Libanius himself acted as a peacemaker and sent the emperor a letter almost immediately after his departure. But all proved to be futile: the emperor harbored his rancor against the city which, as he had announced beforehand, but with a far different intent, he would never see again.

193. Was the motive determining Julian's decision for war only political? That political considerations were predominant is certain, but probably mixed in with them were others of a psychological nature. The great mission entrusted to him by the gods was proceeding slowly and with difficulty. Since the area to be purified in the Roman Empire was rotten with Christianity, would it not be better to move into virgin territory and there erect the citadel of the world's spiritual rebirth? When he would reappear as the triumphant "Parthicus," bearing within himself the soul of Alexander the Great (§ 174), the cause of the gods would be victorious also in the West. Libanius (18. 282) had already envisaged Julian as a missionary of paganism evangelizing the Persians, persuading them, even though they abhorred bloody sacrifices, to immolate victims to the gods of Hellenism and to send their sons to schools conducted by Greek rhetoricians and sophists. Was all this simply a flight of fancy? Possibly, except for the fact that at Libanius' back were Maximus of Ephesus and all the band of theurgists (§ 174), who had even greater influence over Julian than Libanius.

Before his departure for Persia, Julian found one more outlet for his hatred for Christianity. He delivered an attack on the "Son of the Carpenter" and His religion by writing *Against the Galileans*, a name he imposed on the Christians (Gregory Nazianzen, 4. 76) to give the impression that their origins were not only socially but also geographically obscure. It is curious to note that such geographical obscurity seems also to have bothered St. Jerome (*Ep.*, 129. 4). Julian makes a reference to his work against the Christians in a letter written toward the end of 362 to the heresiarch Photinus, bishop of Sirmium (*To Photinus* — Wright, 3:188–190), in which he states that he will unmask the doctrines of the Galilean God preached by Diodore of Tarsus.

In judging this essay we are unfortunately in the position of a sailor who has to describe a boat sunk at some distance from the shore with only the mast and a few other pieces of rigging rising above the surface. When in the middle of the fifth century the Christian court at Byzantium officially proscribed anti-Christian writings, copies of *Against the Galileans* gradually disappeared, as did the *True Discourse* of Celsus, written about the year 180, and the later work of Porphyry *Against the Christians* (§ 29). All that remains of these attacks on Christianity are excerpts made by other authors. In recent years scholars have collected these fragments and strung them together, but, as might be expected, only portions of the sunken hulls are thus revealed.

Almost all the fragments of *Against the Galileans* come from the refutation of the work written by Cyril of Alexandria a little before 440. But even of Cyril's work, which once comprised twenty books, we possess only the first ten, while of the last ten only fragments are preserved in the *catenae*, or anthologies. A few very small parts are also found in Theodore of Mopsuestia, Aretas, and several other ancient writers. Since it is practically certain that Julian's work was divided into three volumes, although St. Jerome speaks of seven, we can form an opinion of only about a third of the entire work, that is, what is taken into account in the ten surviving books of Cyril, all of which refer to Julian's first volume. A few fragments of Julian's second book are found in the *catenae*, but nothing at all has survived from the third. Moreover, Cyril expressly states that he passes over those passages injurious to Christ and repulsive to Christians. At times copyists did the same with Julian's other writings.

194. Julian must have begun drafting his arguments in the late summer of 362, toiling intensively during the long nights of the following winter "to refute," as Libanius says (18. 178), "those books which make the man from Palestine a God and Son of God."

But the general theme had been stored up in Julian's mind for many years. The raw material had been accumulated during the period of his Christian education at Macellum (§§ 15, 16). This had been ordered and elaborated for polemic purposes as he gradually withdrew from Christianity and progressed in theurgy (§ 36 ff.). Even when he was busily occupied with his duties as governor of Gaul, Julian's persistently inquisitive mind had mulled over this material, striving to discover aspects in it that would put in better light the mission he had himself received from the gods.

Given the present condition of the text, it is impossible to gain an adequate picture of the work. It seems that Julian followed Celsus more closely than Porphyry, possibly because Celsus was of a more acrid and virulent temperament, while Porphyry was more reasoned and critical. Some questions regarding chronology and the inspiration of Sacred Scripture do not seem to have been touched by Julian, although they were by Porphyry.

The general thesis is that Christianity had no real connection with Judaism. Rather, it was the product of a minute sect of degenerate Hebrews who had no right to represent themselves as the founders of a religion worthy of cultured races such as the Hellenes. The God of the Hebrews deserves respect as a national god (§ 187), even though He is an exclusive and "jealous" God (106e). At any rate one of the many crimes of the Christians was that of having abandoned the God of the Hebrews. God had no need to reveal himself since every man may contemplate Him in the order of nature and in the interior of his own soul. Further, why would He have revealed Himself only to the Hebrews? The prophecies of the Old Testament are on the whole nothing but fables. Jesus was a man without special gifts and prerogatives, who succeeded only in deceiving a few abject individuals, among whom were the ignorant apostles. Of these the most culpable were Paul, who first dared to entice the Hellenes to Christianity, and John, who attributed to Christ divine attributes. The true saviors of humanity, on the other hand, were those worshiped by the Hellenes — Asclepius, Dionysus, and Heracles. Various reflections are also made upon Christian morality to show its inferiority not only to that of the Hellenes, but even to that of the Jews.

In *Against the Galileans* Julian makes a number of acute observations, but he shows an utter lack of any historical sense. His beloved mythology is everywhere mixed in with actual happenings or substituted for them. Unlike Porphyry, he can find nothing good at all in Christianity, which he sees only as a bundle of historical absurdities and moral aberrations. He betrays his own prejudices in his very first line: "It is well, I believe, to reveal to all men the reasons which convinced me that the fabrication ($\sigma\kappa\epsilon\upsilon\omega\rho\iota\alpha$) of the Galileans is a human work wickedly put together" (39a).

195. From transitory evidence we may conclude that Julian expected that this work would have a profound effect on his own generation. It would be like the crash of a battering ram crumbling the tower of Christianity, just as the imminent expedition against the Persians would overthrow the King of Kings.

The immediate effects of the work are not known, but it must have been as widely read by Christians as by pagans. The pagans particularly interested in the work must have been the supporters of Julian's religio-political ideas, the theurgists, and a number of historians such as Libanius. But after Julian's death their interest in the book must have rapidly declined. Educated Christians, on the contrary, may have had a more permanent interest in it since they regularly studied the accusations hurled at them by their adversaries. The library of Mensurius, bishop of Carthage in 303, for example, was well stocked with heretical works (Ricciotti, Martyrs, p. 76). It is rather strange that Gregory Nazianzen does not mention this work in his invective against the dead emperor, nor is it mentioned by Basil of Caesarea, yet both had been Julian's schoolfellows at Athens. Of the refutations written by Theodore of Mopsuestia and Philip Sideta nothing remains. The lengthy refutation composed by Cyril of Alexandria (§ 193) some eighty years after Julian's death seems to have been due to extrinsic reasons — a renewed hostility on the part of the pagans of Alexandria, who, as Cyril observes, extolled Julian's work as the Hellenic refutation of the divinity of Christ. There were no echoes, as far as is known, of this work in the West.

196. Preparations for the campaign against the Persians were completed in the spring of 363. Various offers of auxiliary troops (§ 192), coming especially from the wandering tribes of the Syrian desert, were rejected since these forces were ill-adapted to the discipline and military compactness that Julian sought. Only Arsaces, king of Armenia and friend of the Romans, was invited at this time to hold his troops in

readiness. Later he would learn where he was to march and what he should do (23. 2. 1–2).

The aversion which many in Antioch felt for the war had its repercussions in the army. Libanius (18. 199) mentions a plot on the life of the emperor involving ten soldiers. It was discovered and suppressed when some of the conspirators drank to excess and began to talk freely. Two Christians of the imperial guard, Juventinus and Maximinus, who at a banquet had deplored the apostasy of Julian and his persecution of Christianity, were implicated in this, or possibly another, conspiracy (John Chrysostom, *In Ss. Mm. Juventinum et Maximinum*; Theodoret, 3. 11). The emperor questioned them kindly. They replied that they recognized him as their sovereign but disapproved of him as an adversary of their religion. After confining them for a time in prison, where they were visited by crowds of Christians, Julian had them executed for treason. In this way he sought to save appearances by adhering to a policy of not putting Christians to death merely for their religion.

Immediately before his departure Julian made some changes in the government. These were occasioned by the arrival of an embassy from the senate at Rome (23. 1. 4). The real object of this deputation is not known, but it was made up of outstanding individuals. Julian received them with special deference and conferred high honors upon them. On this occasion Turcius Apronianus was named prefect of Rome, Octavianus became proconsul of Africa, and Rufinus Aradius was raised to the rank of count of the East, thus succeeding to the post of Julian's deceased uncle (§ 179). A certain Alexander of Heliopolis, whom Ammianus describes as "turbulent and cruel," was created prefect of Syria (23. 2. 3). According to Julian, he did not deserve such a position but received it because he was a governor suited for such people as the Antiochians, "greedy and insolent."

Great care was employed to secure the necessary assistance of diviners. In addition to the many prophetic consultations already made (§ 162), a regular bureau of haruspices and augurs was established to assist Julian during his campaign; but since different currents and schools of thought existed about such occult matters, nearly all were represented. It seems that there were two principal groups, the "Etruscan" haruspices, who followed Italic traditions, and the "philosophers," as Ammianus describes them (23. 5. 11), who made use of Chaldaic and theurgic norms. The Etruscan haruspices had at their disposal the *libri exercituales*, which they consulted on every occasion, but they

employed other means of divination also. Frequent disputes seem to
have arisen between the two schools. At such times Julian, convinced
of his own special election by the gods, acted without regard for books
or sacred responses. Just before setting out on his campaign, for
example, he received letters stating that the Sibylline Books at Rome,
which had been consulted at his express command, plainly forbade his
crossing the frontier that year (aperto prohibuisse responso — 23. 1. 7);
but Julian was so hardened in his resolve that he paid no attention to
the response and set out on his way. His uncle Constantine had done
the same in his campaign against Maxentius, conducting it against the
advice of the haruspices (contra haruspicum monita; cf. Ricciotti,
Martyrs, pp. 159–160).

197. The privy council that was destined to accompany him was
composed of especially trusted men, such as Sallustius, praetorian prefect of the East (§ 150); Anatolius, master of the offices; the physician
Oribasius along with Maximus and Priscus, Julian's three beloved masters and secret confreres (§ 180). Libanius, perhaps for reasons of
health, did not take part in the expedition, but immediately after the
emperor's departure there was an exchange of letters between the two.
Julian's letter, which was written from Hierapolis (To Libanius, 399b–
402b), gives a minute description of the road covered during the first
five days. The historian Ammianus Marcellinus, to whom we are
indebted for an expert and detailed description of the whole campaign, took part in it but not apparently from its inception. It seems
rather that he joined the forces at Cercusium (Circesium), since only
after the expedition's departure from this stronghold does he use the
first person plural in his narrative (23. 5. 4, 7). A similar change of
person is noted in the Acts of the Apostles. It is likely that Ammianus
descended with the fleet carrying provisions down the Euphrates,
and then joined the army at Cercusium (§ 200).

The expedition set out from Antioch on March 5, 363. The season
was favorable since the Roman forces had to pass through normally
arid tracts, but which were green with pasturage and irrigated by streams
of water at this time of the year. The road taken passed through
Litarbae, Beroea, and on to Hierapolis, a large and important commercial center of the district of Euphratensis (Commagene) where
other troops that had been stationed on the nearer side of the Euphrates
were being assembled. At his entrance into the city an evil omen
occurred. A colonnade near the gates of the city fell down, crushing

to death fifty soldiers encamped under it and wounding many others. Julian remained for three days in Hierapolis since he had much to do. The new forces had to be incorporated into the army; orders had to be sent to the fleet that had sailed down the Euphrates with an immense amount of material from Samosata; and details of strategy had to be worked out. On March 13, he set out again toward the east, crossing the Euphrates on a pontoon bridge. Under forced marches the army pushed on to Batnae, where another evil omen befell it. A high stack of grain collapsed and buried fifty men who were gathering fodder (23. 2. 6–8). Although he was saddened by the disaster, Julian did not change his plans but hurried on to Carrhae since he was anxious to anticipate any news of his advance reaching the enemy.

Here important decisions had to be made. Julian seems to have had at his disposal about 65,000 combatants (Zosimus, 3. 13), but this figure is questionable since it may or may not include the auxiliary troops. It is certain that Julian departed from his original plan of not accepting such troops (§ 196) and included Scythians, or Goths, among his forces (23. 2. 7) and also Saracens (23. 3. 8; 5. 1; cf. To Libanius, 401d). The fleet on the Euphrates under the command of the tribune Constantius and the count Lucillianus numbered a thousand transports laden with provisions, arms, and war matériel of every sort, besides some fifty ships for fighting and the same number for building bridges. These ships were so numerous that, in the picturesque words of Ammianus, they "crowded the broad Euphrates River" (latissimum flumen Euphraten artabat — 23. 3. 9). Other historians give figures at variance with these, but only slightly.

198. What directions should be given to this great force? The final goal could only be Ctesiphon, the Persian capital, and the heart of the enemy empire. This had been the goal achieved by Trajan in his campaign of the year 116 against the Parthians; but Trajan, whose base of operations was in Armenia, had come down along the more favorable Tigris, leaving his secondary force to advance along the more difficult course of the Euphrates. To deceive the Persians, Julian pretended at first that he was executing a similar pincers' movement, but he soon reversed Trajan's procedure by having his stronger force advance down the Euphrates.

As Ammianus observes (23. 3. 1), two highways left Carrhae for Persia, the one farther north stretched east toward the Tigris, the other to the south descended along the valley of the Euphrates. Julian directed his route along this second road, the same one which Abraham had traversed in the opposite direction so many centuries earlier when, after leaving Ur of the Chaldees to the south of Babylon, he went to Haran, or Carrhae. From very ancient times both places had been centers of worship for the moon god Sin, and during his stay at Carrhae, Julian also performed rites in honor of this god. While going through one of these ceremonies, he entrusted with utmost secrecy the royal purple to Procopius, a cousin on his mother's side, and he bade him take over the supreme command if he heard of his death in Persia.

During these days Julian was troubled with strange forebodings. After one sleepless night he consulted an interpreter and learned that a grave calamity would occur on the following day. And, as a matter of fact, it was learned much later that on the same night the temple of Apollo on the Palatine in Rome had burned, and that the books of the Cumaean Sibyl had been saved with the greatest difficulty.

While Julian was busy arranging his forces and securing supplies, he learned that bands of enemy cavalry had crossed the frontier on a raid and had returned with their plunder. Julian was greatly disturbed by the bad news (atrocitate mali perculsus — 23. 3. 4). This reaction may have been due to his belief that the enemy was much farther off and the necessity now incumbent of making considerable changes in his plan of operation. The pincers' movement was still maintained, but to give effective protection to his left flank much greater importance was given to that arm of the pincers than previously. A strong body of troops was detached and sent from Carrhae in the direction of Nisibis and the Tigris under the command of Procopius, just mentioned, and Sebastian, a former military commander in Egypt. According to Ammianus (23. 3. 5), this armed force was made up of thirty thousand picked men. Other historians, however, give a smaller figure of twenty thousand, or even less.

199. Ammianus describes the sphere of activity for these troops in the following terms: "He ordered them to keep for the present on this side of the Tigris and to be diligently on their guard lest anything unforeseen should rise up on their unguarded flank, as he knew had often occurred in the past. And he ordered them to join King Arsaces (§ 196) if this should prove to be more advantageous, march with him through Corduene and Moxoene, ravage in rapid course Chiliocomum, a rich region of Media, and other places, and meet him while he was still in Assyria, so as to be on hand to help in case of

need" (23. 3. 5). The partial modification of his original plan gave greater prominence to the pincers' movement and a greater resemblance to the strategy that had been employed by Trajan. This prevented the Persian king's seeing as yet whether the main blow would be launched down the Tigris or down the Euphrates, but an observer in the Roman camp could have perceived that Procopius' force was only secondary, and that it did not represent a serious threat unless it was reinforced by the Armenians under the leadership of Arsaces. But Arsaces failed to appear, and Procopius as a consequence seems to have been militarily inactive. He certainly did not take any part in the campaign until after Julian's death.

With his forces thus diminished, Julian renewed his advance toward the south. At the moment of his departure he witnessed a favorable portent. He asked for a horse, but when one named Babylon was brought to him, it was felled by a missile and rolled in pain on the ground scattering its trappings adorned with gems and gold. Julian was overjoyed at the accident and cried out that Babylon had fallen stripped of all its ornaments (23. 3. 6). Such was the importance he gave to events of this kind as signs of the future.

On March 27, Callinicum was reached, a well-fortified city and commercial center. Since at Rome this was the feast of the Mother of the Gods, Julian celebrated the rites of the goddess in the traditional manner. The following day chieftains of nomad Saracens appeared, presented Julian with a golden crown, offered him their homage on bended knees, and hailed him as their master and the lord of the world. Julian received them kindly and accepted the military help they offered since they were excellent at guerilla warfare (ut ad furta bellorum appositi — 23. 3. 8). Soon after this the army was joined by the fleet sailing down the river (§ 197), and from that time on the two forces advanced parallel with each other.

200. Cercusium was reached at the beginning of April. This was a stronghold at the confluence of the Chaboras (Araxes) and Euphrates Rivers which Diocletian had earlier fortified because of its importance for the defense of Syria from the Persian invasions. Julian reinforced the local garrison, detaching four thousand soldiers from his army, and ordered the construction of a pontoon bridge for crossing the tributary. While he was waiting its completion, he received a discouraging letter (tristes litteras) from Sallustius, prefect of Gaul (§ 140), entreating him to put off the expedition. Since Julian had not as yet

offered sufficient prayers for the gods' protection (*nondum pace numinum exorata*), he might be going to his doom. But the letter had no effect. Disregarding his cautious adviser, Julian continued confidently on his course. Immediately after the army had crossed the river, he had the bridge destroyed so that there could be no hope of turning back. To the sane and experienced Ammianus, Julian's stubbornness was simply foreordained (*fatalis ordo* — 23. 5. 5).

Dubious omens began to reappear. The body of a man slain by the hand of an executioner lay stretched out on the ground. Such a sight was always regarded as an evil augury, and in this case was particularly inauspicious since the man had been slain by Sallustius because of an accidental delay in fulfilling a contract for provisions which arrived

Julian's Persian Campaign

JULIAN'S ROUTE
PROCOPIUS' ROUTE

0   100   200   300   400   500

MILES

the day after the execution. Later a group of soldiers presented Julian with the carcass of a huge lion they had slain with arrows when it attacked their line. Its death indicated the demise of a sovereign. But was it to be the king of Persia or the emperor of Rome? A dispute arose between the Etruscan haruspices and the philosophers (§ 196) as to the proper interpretation of the omen. The Etruscans believed that the lion represented the emperor, and they proved it with citations from their books. This interpretation was rejected by the philosophers who maintained that the lion represented the king. According to Ammianus, the philosophers were little acquainted with such matters and were occasionally mistaken, but "at the time their authority was highly respected" (reverenda tunc auctoritas — 23. 5. 11). All this may be easily explained if it is kept in mind that their protectors were Maximus and Priscus (§ 197), stanch advocates of the war (§ 174) and masters of Julian's heart.

Other omens followed: During a storm a stroke of lightning killed a soldier named Jovian, a name derived from Jupiter (genitive case: Jovis — 23. 5. 12); a cyclone tore the soldiers' tents and threw many of the men themselves heavily to the ground; a sudden flood caused a number of the ships to break through the stone dikes along the river and sink (24. 1. 11); and there were other portents of the same nature, but since the favorable interpretations given by the philosophers prevailed, the advance continued.

Ammianus seems to have joined the forces at Cercusium, if not earlier, since he writes, "from there we came to a place called Zaitha, which means, 'Olive Tree'" (23. 5. 7 — § 197). According to this same authority, the soldiers could there contemplate the magnificent tomb of the emperor Gordian. Zosimus (3. 14), however, locates it further south at Dura. Consequently, Ammianus may here be employing a geographical accommodation to give a more dramatic setting to the exhortation Julian was about to deliver to his men.

201. Trying days were obviously ahead, and Julian was anxious to encourage his troops. A summary of his exhortation to the assembled army is preserved in Ammianus (23. 5. 16–23) and has the appearance of being faithful to the original. It is a stirring address, and one admirably adapted to the circumstances. It shows a care not usually found in Julian to highlight the military accomplishments of the Romans, and includes, of course, a special encomium for Gordian. Since there were many Christian soldiers in the army, Julian was circumspect and refers only to "the assistance of the Eternal Deity" (*adiumento numinis sempiterni*). He, their emperor, standard-bearer, and comrade-in-arms, will share all their vicissitudes. The general theme of the harangue is that, like Carthage in the time of Cato, so now Persia must be destroyed.

At the end of the speech the soldiers broke out into the usual manifestations of enthusiasm. Those from Gaul, who had achieved such glorious successes under the guidance of the orator, were particularly aroused.

When they set out again, great pains were taken to prevent any surprise attack of the enemy, especially from the highly maneuverable cavalry. The fleet and the land forces proceeded in close conjunction with each other. The infantry was drawn up in squares. Some fifteen hundred speedy scouts wove back and forth in front and on the sides. The right wing, which was keeping close to the river, was under the command of Nevitta; the left wing, which spread out over the level ground, was made up of cavalry under the command of Arintheus and Prince Ormizda. The latter, a brother of the Persian king, Sapor, had many years before passed over to the Romans. Because of his knowledge of the territory and its languages he was a great asset. The rear guard was commanded by Dagalaif and Victor. The entire column was brought up by Secundinus, duke of Osdroene (24. 1. 2).

Julian, who had placed himself at the center to have closer contact with the entire mass, had the most competent troops under his own immediate command. The baggage had been reduced as far as possible — so much so, in fact, that Julian sent back a caravan of camels loaded with leathern bottles of wine, regarding them as a useless encumbrance. What remained of the baggage and the unarmed attendants were placed between the center and each of the two wings. To give the enemy scouts the impression his force was greater than it actually was, he so extended the ranks of his horses and men that the standard-bearers in front were nearly ten miles ahead of those bringing up the rear (24. 1. 2 ff.; cf. Zosimus, 3. 14).

After two days of marching in this fashion, they arrived at Dura, described by Ammianus as being "deserted" (*desertam* — 24. 1. 5). Though this city was an important center for trade and caravans in the early third century, it had long since been abandoned. Excavations carried out on the site have uncovered a Jewish synagogue with frescoes of the Hebrew patriarchs, a Christian church with its baptistery, and other significant finds. Here Julian's troops encountered many herds of deer. The soldiers killed a great number of them with arrows or with heavy oars as the animals tried to swim to safety, and were thus able to add substance and variety to their meals.

They then drew near Anatha, a small, well-fortified island in the Euphrates. Julian surrounded it with his ships and began an assault with siege artillery. The resistance was brief since Ormizda, with many promises and oaths, induced the habitants to surrender. Among those dwelling at Anatha was an aged Roman. As a young man he had taken part in the campaign of Galerius some seventy years earlier. Left behind because of sickness, he had been given a number of wives in accordance with the custom of the country, and these had borne him many children. He called several to witness that many years before he had foretold that he would be buried on Roman soil when he was nearly a hundred years of age. And as a matter of fact, he was sent by Julian with the other inhabitants of Anatha to Chalcis in Syria. The stronghold was then destroyed.

Descending the river, the troops passed the almost inaccessible fortresses of Thilutha and Achaiachala perched on rocks in the middle of the stream. At Baraxamalcha they crossed to the right bank of the river and moved on to Diacira, a prominent city seven miles further downstream. The city had large stores of grain and fine white salt, but it had been almost completely abandoned by its inhabitants. The few women found there were put to death. Passing a spring bubbling with bitumen, they arrived at Ozogardane, which the inhabitants had likewise deserted. There the army rested for two days.

202. Hitherto there had been military activity, but no real warfare. But now the enemy capital, Ctesiphon, stood at a distance of only a three days' march. A clash between the two forces could not be far off.

After the Romans had set out again on the road from Ozogardane, they saw the helmets and armor of the Persian forces gleaming with the first light of day. It was the army of the *surena*, the official highest in dignity after the king (*post regem apud Persas promeritae dignitatis* — 24. 2. 4). With him was the *malechus* Podosaces, phylarch of the Assanitic Saracens and a notorious raider on Roman territories. The area was laced with canals, and Ormizda, who went up to scout the enemy, would have been captured had he not been rescued by a vigorous counterattack of the Romans.

The advance continued across fields deliberately flooded by the Persians until Macepracta was reached. From here two large canals led off from the Euphrates: one descended south to irrigate the land west of Babylon, the other, bending toward the east, led toward Ctesiphon, emptying into the Tigris some three miles below the capital. This was known as the Naharmalcha, or "River of the Kings."

The approach to Ctesiphon was barred by two fortified cities. The one farther out was Pirisabora; the one behind it, nearer Coche, or Seleucia, was named Maiozamalcha (Maogamalcha). Crossing more marshes and canals Julian's forces reached Pirisabora. The walls of this city were extremely strong, being constructed of baked bricks laid in bitumen. Unsuccessful attempts were made to induce the inhabitants to surrender. When Ormizda came up to speak with the defenders and reminded them that he was a Persian prince, he was greeted with insults and abuse.

The Romans then encircled the city and filled in the ditches in front of the walls as best they could with logs and branches. Catapults and ballistae were brought up and a storm of projectiles hurled at the defenders from dawn until dusk, but they did not surrender. Battering-rams were then thrown against the outer wall. When this was pierced the defenders withdrew into the strongly fortified citadel within the city. Further assaults proved vain, even one directed by Julian himself against the principal gate of the citadel. Recourse was then had to a more effective means of assault. In a very short time a helepolis, an enormous battering-ram protected by high towers, was constructed. At the sight of this monstrous contraption, the besieged were convinced that nothing more could be done and they offered to surrender.

Mamersides, the commander of the citadel, asked for leave to speak with Ormizda. When this was granted, he descended the wall on a rope and was brought to the emperor, who promised to spare the lives of all those in the city. The gates were then opened and the inhabitants came out to greet the victor. In all they numbered only some twenty-five hundred individuals (five thousand, according to Zosimus, 3. 18), since the others had fled across the river on hearing of the Romans' advance. Great quantities of weapons and provisions were found within the citadel. After taking what they could use, the Romans set fire to the rest and to the citadel itself.

203. The splendor of the victory was marred on the following day by a distressing incident. The surena surprised three squadrons of Roman cavalry while they were out scouting. He killed a number of

Romans, including one of the tribunes, and captured a standard. Furious, Julian at once sallied forth in person with an armed force and drove off the marauders. He then cashiered the two surviving tribunes and put to death ten of the soldiers who had fled. In this, according to Ammianus, "he followed the ancient laws" (*secutus veteres leges* — 24. 3. 2), but it could not have been a question of a real decimation.

After sacking and burning Pirisabora, Julian mounted a tribunal, thanked the assembled army, and promised to reward each one of the soldiers with a hundred denarii. The soldiers, who had expected much more, openly showed their resentment. Angered at this, Julian addressed his men in the following terms: The Roman Empire has become bankrupt because men have sought to buy peace from the barbarians. Do you wish to be rich? Seek wealth from those who have it. I am poor. The imperial treasury is exhausted. The cities and provinces are impoverished. Only the Persians abound in wealth of every kind. The treasures of this race can enrich you (*ditare vos poterit opimitas gentis* — 24. 3. 4). If you are victorious you will be rich.

The prospect of great rewards calmed the soldiers; but Ammianus, who knew their mentality, states that they were only "quieted for the time" (*miles pro tempore delenitus*). It was therefore a conditioned calm.

With renewed spirit they set out again. After marching fourteen miles, they arrived at a fertile plain which the Persians had reduced to a swamp by opening up the dikes of the irrigation canals. With considerable danger and hardship the Roman forces crossed the flooded fields and arrived at a wide expanse filled with palm and fruit trees, so that "where formerly there was fear of scarcity there was now a serious danger of being surfeited" (24. 3. 14).

Within this "paradise" was a city with low walls. Zosimus (3. 19) calls it Bithra. Its Jewish inhabitants had fled before the arrival of the Romans. They may have been descendants of Hebrews deported by Nabuchodonosor whose numbers had been augmented by refugees from Palestine at the time of Titus and of Hadrian.

Maiozamalcha was finally reached, "a large city surrounded by strong walls" (*urbem magnam et validis circumdatam moenibus* — 24. 4. 2). During a preliminary inspection of the site, Julian's life was gravely endangered. Ten armed Persians crept out of a secret gate and attacked his small escort. Two of them spotting the emperor's more elegant

attire rushed at him with drawn swords. Julian covered himself with
his shield and then plunged his sword into the side of one of his
assailants. The other was slain by his followers. The remaining Persians
then took to flight.

Many of the inhabitants of Maiozamalcha had already fled toward
Ctesiphon. After a number of skirmishes the city was surrounded by
a triple line of soldiers. In the meantime, Victor set out with a
squadron of cavalry to explore the road to Ctesiphon, only a few
miles distant. Various Roman assaults on Maiozamalcha proved to be
unsuccessful. Nevertheless, while these were in progress, in another less
conspicuous quarter legionary soldiers detailed for mining set about
cutting a tunnel under the wall of the city. Toward the end of the
second day of the siege, a battering-ram was brought up and with a
terrific blow soon caused the highest of the towers to collapse. With
the tower also fell a part of the neighboring wall. During the following night Julian was informed that the sappers had made their way to
the bottom of the wall and were ready to sally forth on the other side
whenever he should give the word. Although the night was already
advanced and the legionaries were taking their rest, the trumpets were
sounded and an attack was made against two sides of the wall to conceal the activity of the soldiers who were about to pass under it. The
Romans occupied the city without encountering serious resistance and
put the inhabitants to the sword. Only Nabdates, the commandant
of the garrison, was spared and eighty of his followers, who were held
as hostages. The booty was distributed to the soldiers according to
their deserts. Julian retained for himself three gold coins and a young
deaf-mute who expressed himself gracefully with his hands. Following the example of Alexander and Scipio Africanus, as Ammianus
observes (24. 4. 27), the pagan ascetic did not even wish to see the
young women who were taken prisoner.

204. There was now no further obstacle on the way to Ctesiphon.
Returning from his exploration of the road to the capital, Victor reported that he had met no resistance but only a Persian division
commanded by a son of the king, which had immediately withdrawn
at the sight of the Romans.

Starting out again, the army came to a fertile area of fields and groves
in which many kinds of plants and trees were flowering. There they
found a palace built in the Roman style which so pleased them that
they left it untouched. In the same region they found an extensive

circular tract enclosed by a fence in which lions, bears, and other wild beasts roamed. It was another "paradise" (§ 203) used as a hunting preserve for the King of Kings. The Roman cavalry burst through the gates of the park and slew the animals with hunting spears and darts. They passed on to Coche, called Seleucia by the Persians, and rested there for two days since they had become somewhat disheartened from fatigue, excessive heat (it was now the latter half of May), and a few unfortunate skirmishes. They then arrived at Naharmalcha, the "River of the Kings" connecting the Tigris and Euphrates (§ 202). The fleet sailed down this artificial canal until it reached a ditch which had originally been dug by Trajan and reopened nearly a century later by Septimus Severus, but which had again been blocked by the Persians. Julian had his soldiers remove the large stones obstructing the channel, and the fleet then was able to continue on their way and arrive opposite, instead of below, Ctesiphon, as would have happened if they had continued down the Naharmalcha.

But even then much remained to be done. Ctesiphon, the final goal of the expedition, lay on the left bank of the Tigris and consequently had to be attacked from that side of the river. The Roman army, hemmed in by the Tigris, the Naharmalcha, and the newly opened canal, was in an awkward position. The coveted left bank of the Tigris, on the other hand, swarmed with Persians supported by cavalry and elephants under the command of the surena. At this juncture Julian made a bold move. To disguise his plans he held a horse race in which prizes were allotted to the victors. While these were being run off, the two armies on either side of the river stood watching. But when darkness had fallen he sent five galleys across the river to land soldiers and establish a bridgehead on the opposite bank. The Persians greeted the galleys with a storm of firebrands. Julian then shouted to the men about him that this was a signal indicating that the landing had been successful and that the bridgehead was established. He gave orders for the rest of the fleet to head toward the ships that had already crossed. Despite the efforts of the Persians, the legions were able to land and draw up their line. On the following day, with Julian himself in the first ranks, they fought from dawn to dusk against the Persian infantry, cavalry, and elephants. The enemy gradually retreated and finally turned in headlong flight toward the city with their leaders, Pigranes, Narseus, and the surena.

With the impetus of their attack the Romans could have occupied the city, entering on the heels of the fugitives; but Victor, though wounded in one shoulder, raised his hand and shouted for them to halt, fearing that they would be trapped if they entered the city (24. 6. 13). Libanius, on the other hand, attributes the failure to seize the city to the avarice of the soldiers who stopped to plunder the enemy camp and the dead. About twenty-five hundred of the enemy were killed, whereas only seventy Romans fell.

After such a glorious victory, Julian distributed honors and awards to his soldiers, but he did not forget the gods. In gratitude he ordered ten magnificent bulls to be sacrificed to Mars the Avenger. But the sacrifice was marred by strange incidents. These are described by Ammianus as follows: "Nine of the ten fine bulls even before they were led up to the altar sank of their own accord in sadness to the ground, but the tenth broke his bonds and escaped, and after he had been brought back with difficulty and sacrificed, he showed ominous signs. Julian, on seeing them, cried out in deep indignation and called Jupiter to witness that he would sacrifice no more to Mars. Nor did he sacrifice to him again since he was carried away by a speedy death" (24. 6. 17).

205. At this point Julian's position was as follows: Ctesiphon the goal of his campaign rose up before his eyes; but, from the information which he already had and from an inspection of the massive fortifications, he knew that it was practically impossible to capture the city. In addition to this, from hour to hour the Roman forces were threatened by the advance of Sapor with his great army. If at the beginning the King of Kings could have been in doubt as to whether Julian would approach along the Tigris or along the Euphrates (§ 199), he had for some time been certain of the route taken by the main body of the Romans, and he was himself advancing toward Julian with all his forces. No news had come to Julian about Procopius and his possible union with Arsaces, whereas Sapor may have learned from his scouts that he had nothing to fear from that quarter.

A council of war held to discuss the siege of Ctesiphon decided that it was impracticable. Provisions were beginning to grow scarce, the heat was becoming ever more suffocating, and the entire area between the rivers and the canals was infested with swarms of flies and mosquitoes which, according to Ammianus, "hid the light of day and the stars that twinkle during the night" (24. 8. 3). These and other difficulties were an increasing source of discouragement not only to the soldiers but also to the officers. There was nothing to do but abandon their prospective goal and move on. But where?

The ancient historians give a somewhat confused and divergent account of the events of these last days. It is possible that Ammianus' text has come down to us with a considerable lacuna at this point (in sections 24. 7. 2–3). Socrates (3. 21) states that Sapor, blockaded by Julian at Ctesiphon, made repeated efforts to come to terms with him, offering to cede a part of his own territory; but Julian rejected the proposals against the better judgment of his own officers. The assertion that Sapor was shut up in Ctesiphon is manifestly absurd, but the same cannot be said about Sapor's attempt to reach an accord, since Libanius also (18. 257–258) mentions an ambassador whom the Persian king sent to Ormizda to ask his intercession with the emperor. Julian refused to hear the envoy and gave orders that he should be sent back without being permitted to speak to anyone.

206. Since the Romans had no choice but to move on, they were compelled to head toward areas where they would find reinforcements of troops or provisions. The troops and a number of the major staff were anxious to retrace their steps along the Euphrates, the route of their advance, but this would have meant traveling through devastated lands without the hope of meeting reinforcements. Julian therefore selected a different route on the far side of the Tigris. He was prompted in this decision by a number of considerations. In the first place, there was the point of honor. Such a route did not imply a retreat but could be considered as a continuance of the expedition. There was, moreover, the possibility of finding provisions without too great a difficulty and of contacting the force under Procopius.

But the choice of this route entailed a fearful sacrifice — that of the fleet. The Tigris had a strong current, making it extremely wearisome to haul a thousand ships and more upstream (§ 197). Ammianus (24. 7. 4) estimated that it would require a force of almost twenty thousand men to tow the ships, and this would have entailed the withdrawal of as many soldiers from the already exhausted army. In such a plight what was to be done with this magnificent fleet, which had proved to be a source of provisions and a place of refuge from the continual assaults of the Persian cavalry? Should they abandon it in enemy territory? The Persians would have been delighted with such an excellent gift left practically at their doorstep, but such a course of action would have been not only a grave humiliation but also an admission of defeat on the part of the Romans. All they could do was to destroy it.

Here the accounts of the ancient historians again become disconnected and even contradictory. According to Ammianus, Julian had all of the ships burned except twelve to be used in the construction of bridges. He then ordered his army to march toward the interior of Persia "with ill-omened guides leading the way" (*infaustis ductoribus praeviis* — 24. 7. 3). The Romans became suspicious, and, "putting the deserters to torture" (*tortique perfugae* — 24. 7. 5), they made the appalling discovery that they had been tricked. The "ill-omened guides" must be the same as the "deserters," that is, Persian agents who had wormed their way into the confidence of the Romans. An order was then given to put out the fires but it was too late and only twelve ships were saved, that is, exactly the same number that Julian had earlier given orders to preserve. It is quite probable that Ammianus' account is here based on two different reports which he placed side by side without making any serious attempt to reconcile them.

According to Sozomen (6. 1), and his account is confirmed by Gregory Nazianzen (5. 11–12), the principal traitor was a prominent Persian of advanced age who let himself be taken prisoner, declaring that he was being persecuted by Sapor and consequently wished to assist the Romans by showing them the shortest and easiest way to return to their own territory. In three or four days he assured them they would arrive at a place well stocked with provisions.

From these ancient sources no exact sequence of events can be reconstructed. The most that can be said is that before making his decision Julian sought the help of the gods. Altars were erected, victims sacrificed, and prayers offered for divine guidance as to "whether they should return through Assyria, or march slowly along the foothills and make an unexpected attack on Chiliocomum, situated near Corduene" (24. 8. 4). When the inspection of the entrails of the victims gave no clear answer to the question, he decided to take a roundabout way back to Roman territory by going up along the Tigris in the hope of meeting up with the army of Procopius.

207. But the Persian reaction had soon to be taken into account, first that of the troops in the vicinity who set about devastating the regions through which the Romans were passing, and then that of the army of Sapor which was coming down along the Tigris in forced marches.

As the Romans drew away from Ctesiphon, they found the harvest

fields on fire and had to halt at times while waiting for the flames to
die out. The Persians not only made sport of them from a safe distance, but every now and then harassed the columns with sudden
attacks. On June 16, after setting out at dawn, the Romans saw afar
off a dark cloud hugging the ground. Some said that it was caused
by herds of wild asses, or onagers, which band together to defend
themselves from the attacks of lions. Others believed that it heralded
the approach of the eagerly sought troops of Arsaces and Procopius.
Still others suspected that it was none other than the army of the
King of Kings advancing like a devastating flood. And this last was
the harsh reality.

Neither Julian nor the legionaries were greatly dismayed by the new
threat. The Romans were eager for a battle that would decide the
whole campaign, but Sapor was of another mind. True to traditional
Persian tactics he set about making small but continuous attacks on
the Romans, particularly with his cavalry. Squadrons of Saracens assisted
the Persians in these harassments. Worn out by fatigue, the heat, and
hunger, the Romans arrived at an estate where, contrary to expectations,
they found an abundance of provisions. This site, where they took
a two days' rest, is called Hucumbra by Ammianus (25. 1. 4) and
Symbra by Zosimus (3. 27). It was located on the Tigris some seventy
miles north of Ctesiphon.

Julian exerted himself prodigiously. He urged his men on with
exortations, threats, practical assistance, and above all by the example
of his own great austerity. He had a large share of the provisions reserved for the officers distributed to the troops, contenting himself
with a scant portion of porridge which even the common soldiers would
have refused (25. 2. 1–2). Despite all this, the strength and spirit
of the legionaries inevitably declined. There were a number of instances
of the soldiers failing in their assigned tasks, but Julian punished the
culprits lightly in view of the general condition of the troops.

Yet shortly afterward, at a place which Ammianus calls Maranga
(25. 1. 11) and Zosimus, Maronsa (3. 28), the Roman army showed
that it still had remarkable reserves of energy. These slumbering
reserves were aroused by the possibility of a pitched battle. According
to Ammianus, "at about daybreak a huge force of Persians appeared
under the command of Merena, a master of their cavalry, two of the
king's sons, and many other nobles. All of the squadrons were clad
in iron, and all the parts of their bodies were covered with thick plates

fitted stiffly together at the junctures of their limbs" (25. 1. 11–12).
Those of the Persians who were armed with pikes stood so still that
they seemed to be held fast by clamps of bronze. Next to them were
archers stretching their bows, and behind these archers could be seen
the awesome figures of elephants. Their trumpeting, odor, and strange
appearance caused even greater fear to the Roman horses than to
the Romans themselves. Julian drew up his soldiers in the form of a
crescent with the two points facing the enemy. To prevent the
Persian arrows from throwing his ranks into confusion, he ordered
his men to advance at a rapid pace. Then the usual signal for battle
was given, and the Roman infantry in close order drove the enemy
before them. But as they retreated, the Persians continued to shoot
their arrows. The plain was strewn with the carnage of battle, the
Persian losses greatly exceeding those of the Romans. The most painful
loss sustained by the latter was the death of Vetranio, who had commanded the legion of the Zianni, an auxiliary force which was probably
of Thracian origin. Though this was certainly a welcome victory for
the Romans, it had little effect on the general outcome of the war.
The Persians even learned from their defeat not to attack again in
large numbers, but rather to adhere to their traditional mode of making
frequent small forays with immediate retreats. A truce of three days
followed the battle so that both sides could take care of the wounded
and recover their strength.

208. Despite his iron will, Julian was weak and drawn from the
physical and mental trials of the past months. His body no longer
responded as before. His mind was in a turmoil with thoughts of the
past and of the future which, like phantoms, flitted incessantly about
preventing his rest. Yet even in such circumstances he did not give
up his beloved reading, which was now his sole comfort and support.

The evening of June 25, after a short sleep, he arose and buried
himself in a philosophical tract. At the depth of night, when his
exhausted soldiers slept about his tent, he suddenly saw, as he later
confided to his friends (*ut confessus est proximis* — 25. 2. 3), somewhat dimly that protecting genius of the state which had already
appeared to him in Gaul on the occasion of his election as Augustus
(§§ 41, 129) pass sorrowfully out through the curtains of his tent
with a veil covering its head and cornucopia. He was stupefied, but
soon recovered himself and, praying to the gods, performed sacred
rites to avert their displeasure. Then he saw a blazing ball of fire plow

through the sky leaving a fiery trail and then disappear. Perhaps it was only a common shooting star, but Julian was seized with terror believing that it might be an omen from angry Mars. Before daybreak the Etruscan haruspices (§ 196) were consulted. They answered that no new undertaking should be essayed at this time, pointing out that the Sibylline Books under the heading De rebus divinis declared that when a meteor was seen in the heavens no battle should be joined or anything similar attempted. But when such answers did not suit his purpose Julian put no stock in them even when they came from the highest authority (§ 196). The haruspices insisted that the march should at least be delayed a few hours, but instead of following their advice Julian gave orders to break camp since the sun had now risen.

The army had hardly set out on its way when the Persians reappeared and began again to accompany the Romans from a distance along the heights, ever ready to attack at a favorable moment. After several hours had thus passed, they fell upon the Roman rear guard and shortly afterward upon the van. They then attacked the companies in the center, routing the left wing with a band of armored cavalrymen and elephants.

At the time Julian was not wearing his breastplate, which he had perhaps removed because of the excessive heat; but at the first alarm, without delaying to put on this highly important piece of armor, he seized a shield and hastened to restore order to the ranks and strengthen their resistance. The Romans charged the Persians with great vigor and put them to flight. Careless of his own safety, Julian cried out that the enemy had fled in disorder. His guards, the candidati, shouted to him to get out of the way of the mass of fugitives, "when suddenly a cavalryman's spear — no one knows whence — grazed the skin of his arm, pierced his ribs, and lodged deep in his liver. As he tried to pull it out with his right hand, he felt the sinews of his fingers cut through on both sides by the sharp steel. He fell from his horse, and all those about him rushed to his side. He was then taken to camp and given medical treatment" (25. 3. 6–7).

The remedy applied by Oribasius somewhat soothed the agony caused by the deep wound, and Julian's ardor for battle was again inflamed. He asked for a horse and weapons so that he might return to the combatants and support them with his presence, but the excitement brought on a further flow of blood and caused a relapse. Then, realizing his condition and the imminent danger that he was in, he remained motionless. He asked the name of the battle's site and learned that it was called "Phrygia." Then Julian remembered that it had been foretold that he would die in Phrygia (25. 3. 9). This prediction had been made to him at Antioch by a redheaded youth who had appeared to him in a dream (Zonaras, 13. 13).

209. The clamor of the battle, which had sprung up again, penetrated into Julian's tent. Infuriated by the disaster that had befallen the emperor, the legionaries hurled themselves desperately into the fray. The Persians, for their part, intensified the launching of their arrows. An immense cloud of dust and a torrid sultriness weighed down upon the plain. Through the center of the cloud, to the terror of the Roman horses and cavalrymen, the elephants slowly advanced. The clash of arms, the cries of the wounded, the neighing of horses created an uproar heard far and wide (procul audiebatur — 25. 3. 12). The sights and sounds of the battle, which lasted until nightfall, filled everyone with terror.

Besides a very large number of common soldiers, fifty Persian satraps or other high dignitaries fell, and among them the commanders in chief Merena and Nohodares. The Romans also sustained heavy losses, particularly on their right wing. Anatolius, chief marshal of the court (§ 197), was among those killed. The prefect Sallustius was at one point in great danger but was saved by his adjutant, though Phosphorious, a councilor who happened to be at his side, was slain. Escaping from the battle, Sallustius ran to Julian's tent and was in time to assist at his death.

Already legends were beginning to rise about the pallet of the dying emperor. They were partly spontaneous and in part deliberately created. According to Ammianus, the dying Julian addressed a long farewell to his friends gathered about him. During the course of this speech he declared that he was ready to abandon his life at the will of the gods; he justified his past rule; and in the end he expressed the hope that a good ruler would be found to succeed him. As his strength failed him (vigore virium labente — 25. 3. 20), he asked for news of Anatolius, whom he did not see among those present. Sallustius, who had just arrived, replied euphemistically, "He is now happy." Julian understood what he said and was troubled, but then seeing that the bystanders were in tears, he chided them, saying that they should not weep for one who was called to union with heaven and the stars (caelo sideribusque conciliatum). After this he engaged Maximus and Priscus in an involved (*perplexius*) discussion on the dignity of the soul (*super animorum sublimitate*). But the wound opened wide again, and his breath failed him. As happens to those who have lost great quantities of blood, he burned with thirst. He asked for a drink of cold water, took it, and in the gloom of midnight (*medio noctis horrore* — 25. 3. 23) quietly passed away. It was June 26, 363. He was at the time in his thirty-second year, and had been Augustus a year and eight months.

This is the account given by Ammianus. It strongly reminds one of the death of Socrates and the dialog preceding it. Is this account of a last discourse pronounced by one exhausted by his exertions and mortally wounded to be taken literally? About all that can be said is that there must have been an exchange of short, philosophical maxims between Julian and his friends, and that Ammianus later used these to reconstruct a scene resembling the last hours of Socrates. Libanius (18. 272) in his usual rhetorical manner insists upon the parallelism between the deaths of Julian and Socrates.

Other legends reflect the environment in which they first arose. Some Christian writers (Theodoret, 3. 20; cf. Sozomen, 6. 2) report a tradition that Julian collected the blood flowing from his wound in the hollow of his hand and tossed it to the sky with the exclamation: "Galilean, thou hast conquered!" A somewhat similar scene, but with an opposite intent, is described by other historians (for example, Philostorgius, 7. 15). According to them Julian directed his reproach not against the God of the Christians, but against his beloved god Helios, accusing him of treachery: "Helios, thou hast ruined me!"

210. Who was the soldier that wounded Julian? A dense cloud blocking a clear view of the events hung over the battlefield, and a cavalryman broke out of this cloud to hurl the murderous lance (Sozomen, 6. 1). It may be said that this cloud of obscurity has continued to hang over the scene, although some historians have believed that they could penetrate it. We have already heard Ammianus confess (§ 208) that he did not know who hurled the weapon, still he subsequently refers to a vague report of deserters that Julian had been struck by a Roman lance (25. 6. 6). Zosimus is noncommittal, but Eutropius (10. 16) and other secondary historians attribute his death to an enemy soldier. Philostorgius (7. 15) says that it was a Saracen. Theodoret mentions a nomad Ismaelite (3. 20), but also reports a rumor according to which it would have been brought about by a soldier unbalanced by hunger and the desert through which they were passing. According to Socrates (3. 21), the commonest report was that it was due to a Roman soldier, but this same author also records the testimony of a certain Callistus who had belonged to Julian's bodyguard and had even composed a hymn in his honor. According to him, the emperor had been laid low by a supernatural being (ὑπὸ δαίμονος), an expression more poetic than historical which can be placed alongside others of a miraculous character coming from Christian writers.

Sozomen (6. 1–2) gives what is perhaps the most interesting account of all. He repeats the various opinions already examined, that Julian had been wounded by a Persian, by a Saracen, by a Roman soldier gone amuck, and finally quotes a passage from Libanius' *Funeral Oration for Julian* (18. 274–275) in which the pagan orator insinuates that the attacker was a Christian. Though he does not know the name of Julian's assailant, he is certain that it was not one of the enemy. If it had been, he would have claimed the reward offered by the Persian king for Julian's slaying. (This argument, however, is refuted by an observation of Philostorgius [7. 15]: Julian's assailant was immediately beheaded by a member of his guard, and he could not as a consequence claim his reward.) Since no reward was claimed, Libanius is convinced that Julian's slayer was a Roman, and goes on to say: "Those who sought his death were men who lived in habitual transgression of laws . . . and who were perhaps indignant at the emperor's attachment to the gods to whom they were themselves opposed." Sozomen concludes from this that Libanius "clearly states that the emperor fell by the hand of a Christian." Though he has no further information on this matter, Sozomen is of the opinion that this is not unlikely. He even has a good word for the Christian, whoever he may have been, "who for the sake of God and of religion performed so bold a deed."

In summing up this evidence it is impossible to come to any certain conclusion. The one who slew Julian could have been a Christian, but this is a simple possibility without real proof. It could have been a Roman legionary, but the proofs for this hypothesis are also very weak. It could have been a Saracen adventurer in the service of the Persians, and this opinion seems more probable than the others. But taken all together, the evidence seems to support the opinion of Ammianus and the other more authoritative historians of the time — the assailant was unknown. This readily agrees with what we know of battles of that era, which were veritable melees of men and beasts madly mingling together, and which often, as in this particular case, were further confused by clouds of dust.

211. With Julian's death the grand tower he was erecting, and which, seemingly, had arrived at such a height that only the pinnacle was lacking, crumbled at a blow. The impression of stability, however, was false: the tower lacked a deep, sound foundation; the emperor had been practically its sole support; and when he fell the tower collapsed.

Dissensions broke out the very day following Julian's death. There was no time, according to Ammianus (25. 5. 1), to weep and lament. It was imperative to find one who would assume the disastrous legacy of the dead Augustus. The high officers separated into two parties. One, headed by Arintheus and Victor, had its roots in the former court of Constantius. The other, centered about Nevitta and Dagalaif, represented Julian's Gallic veterans. Since neither party would yield, a compromise was made and the prefect Sallustius was proposed as emperor. Although he was a man of prudence and esteemed by all, he refused the honor, pleading his advanced age and infirmities. Both parties then settled upon Jovian, the commander of the emperor's household troops and a Christian. He was a soldier without any special distinction, tall, but somewhat stooped. He seems to have been destined to fill the post only temporarily since he lacked the necessary gifts for it. The following February he died in his sleep from asphyxiation, overeating, or poisoning. Various causes are given by the ancient historians, none of which are certain (25. 10. 12–13; Sozomen, 6. 6; Zonaras, 13. 14; John Chrysostom, *In Epist. ad Philipp. Homil.*, 15. 5).

The most urgent task for the new emperor was to extricate his troops and himself from the desperate straits into which they had fallen. Even though the army still preserved a certain measure of efficiency, it was depressed, disheartened, and desperate. Sapor, realizing the Romans' predicament, increased his attacks. Negotiations were opened up for a truce. The conditions imposed by the enemy were accepted almost in their entirety. The Romans had to abandon five provinces beyond the Tigris and fifteen strongholds in Mesopotamia, including Singara and Nisibis. Further, they promised not to intervene in Armenia, where the Persians intended to take vengeance upon King Arsaces, Rome's former ally. Ammianus describes this pact as cowardly (*ignobile decretum* — 23. 13. 1), and from a national viewpoint he may have been right, but from the humane point of view, especially since the war was already lost, there was the question of abandoning to death from hunger and wounds the many thousands of legionaries who had survived the expedition.

The starving Romans finally had news of the forces under Procopius and Sebastian and received from them a convoy of provisions which, however, afforded only a brief respite. Painful days followed as they marched back. The road was strewn with baggage that had to be left behind and with the bodies of soldiers who had died of hunger. When they reached Thilsafata they were kindly received (*benigne suscepti* — 25. 8. 16) by Procopius and Sebastian. Eventually they arrived at longed-for Nisibis (*cupide visa*), where their general condition began to steadily improve.

The new emperor entrusted Julian's body to his cousin Procopius and commissioned him to carry it to Tarsus and bury it there in accordance with his last wishes. The very simple tomb surrounded by an enclosure was located along the road leading from Tarsus to the Taurus Range. Only the width of the road separated Julian's sepulcher from that of his predecessor and exemplar in his struggle with Christianity, Maximinus Daia. Who knows how many times Paul of Tarsus, either as a rabbi or as a Christian apostle, may have passed along that same street centuries before his future adversaries would be there laid to rest!

Some months later Jovian ordered some adornments to be added to the tomb. According to Libanius even the Persians paid homage to the memory of him who had so imperiled their nation: "They are said to have likened him to a thunderbolt, drawing a thunderbolt and writing his name near it; thereby indicating that he had inflicted upon them calamities beyond the power of mere human nature" (18. 305).

*   *   *

As was customary at this time, Julian's friend and admirer, Ammianus, adds to his biography a long list of his qualities both good and bad (25. 4. 1–27). This list is, on the whole, just, and even today an impartial historian can subscribe to it. The most notable of the bad traits listed by Ammianus are a certain fickleness of character (*levioris ingenii*), an intemperance in speech (*linguae fusioris, et admodum raro silentis*), a mentality that was superstitious rather than solidly religious, and an anxious striving for praise and popularity. With respect to his attitude toward Christianity, Ammianus here reproaches him only with his law forbidding Christians to teach. He attributes Julian's final defeat to the hostile policy adopted by Constantine toward the Persians and the decrees of heaven, which "were not in accord with his plans and glorious deeds."

Despite Ammianus' impartiality, we are able today to judge the events connected with Julian's life more objectively than he. Almost sixteen centuries have passed since he wrote. During this time Christianity, which Ammianus tolerated but Julian despised, has spread throughout the world giving a new perspective to the past.

No one today would call Julian into court for his apostasy. This was a matter for his own conscience, and was in large measure provoked by the misfortunes which befell his relatives and by the friendships he formed at Ephesus and Athens. A legitimate charge, however, which can be lodged against Julian purely from a historical point of view is his having been a reactionary, a hankerer for times irrevocably past. Constantine the Great, although he lacked Julian's cultural attainments, was never guilty of such a blunder. To be sure, Julian may be regarded as a knight with an ideal, that of restoring paganism. But unless an ideal has a serious connection with contemporary reality, it is simply an anachronism, and the knight who pursues it will cut the figure of a Don Quixote. This "knight of the sorrowful mien" was also profoundly convinced of his ideals. The only difficulty was that he was some centuries behind the times. Ideally, he belonged in the time of Charlemagne or of the knights-errant, while in reality he was living in the age of Phillip II and the Spanish Inquisition.

Julian's zeal for idolatry was based on purely personal motives. Of a mystic character, he had found complete spiritual satisfaction in the theurgy of Maximus of Ephesus. In that mixture of magic, spiritism, and occultism, he felt at ease. There, too, he found an explanation for all the mysteries of the visible and invisible universe. His fervor as an initiate induced him to become a missionary, and he conscientiously modeled his life as a man and as a ruler to this ideal. In the end he became an intolerant fanatic. Even if he had flourished at the height of paganism, say at the time of Augustus, his projects for pagan reform would have encountered no less hostility than they did under the Christian Constantius. The judicious Horace, *parcus deorum cultor* ("sparing worshiper of the gods" — Carm., 1. 34. 1), would have laughed heartily at the ascetic norms which Julian wished to impose upon the pagan priests. This, of course, would not have checked the pagan reformer in the pursuit of his ideal, just as the canings which Don Quixote received from the farmers did not cause him to give up his knight-errantry.

The outcries of the dying Julian against the god Helios and against the Galilean may be legendary, but they poetically sum up in a telling manner Julian's endeavors. He unexpectedly foundered when he believed that he was already at the entrance of the harbor. Perhaps all this would have ended differently had he avoided the contest with the Galilean. But it was precisely this struggle that had been ordered by Helios, and consequently his cry of despair acquires an even deeper meaning: "Helios, thou hast ruined me!"

BIBLIOGRAPHY

Editions of Julian's Works

BIDEZ, J., *L'empereur Julien: Oeuvres complètes*: 1. 1 *Discours de Julien César* (Budé), Paris, 1932; 1. 2 *Lettres et fragments*, Paris, 1924.

BIDEZ, J., and CUMONT, F., *Juliani imperatoris epistulae leges poemetia fragmenta varia* (Budé), Paris, 1922.

HERTLEIN, F. C., *Juliani imperatoris quae supersunt* (BT), 2 vols., Leipzig, 1875–1876.

SPANHEIM, E., *Juliani imperatoris opera*, Leipzig, 1696.

WRIGHT, W. C., *The Works of the Emperor Julian* (LCL), 3 vols., London and New York, 1913–1923.

Ancient Sources

AMMIANUS MARCELLINUS, *Rerum gestarum libri* (LCL).

CYRIL OF ALEXANDRIA, *Pro Christiana religione adversus Iulianum Imperatorem* (PG 76).

EUNAPIUS, *Lives of the Sophists* (LCL).

EUSEBIUS, *Ecclesiastical History* (LCL).

EUTROPIUS, *Breviarium historiae Romanae* (BT).

GREGORY NAZIANZEN, *Orationes IV et V, contra Iulianum* (PG 35).

JEROME, *Translatio Chronicorum Eusebii* (PL 27).

JOHN CHRYSOSTOM, *In S. Babylam, contra Iulianum et contra Gentiles* (PG 50).

——— *In Ss. Mm. Juventinum et Maximinum* (PG 50).

LIBANIUS, *Orationes XVIII et LX* (BT).

MAMERTINUS, *Gratiarum actio Iuliano Augusto* (PL 18).

OROSIUS, *Historiae adversus paganos* (PL 31).

PHILOSTORGIUS, *Historia ecclesiastica* (PG 65).

RUFINUS, *Historia ecclesiastica* (PL 21).

SOCRATES, *Historia ecclesiastica* (PG 67).

SOZOMEN, *Historia ecclesiastica* (PG 67).

THEODORET, *Historia ecclesiastica* (PG 82).

ZONARAS, *Annales* (PG 134).

ZOSIMUS, *Historia* (Corpus Scriptorum Historiae Byzantinae 30).

More recent editions of a number of these authors may be found in the series: *Corpus Scriptorum Ecclesiasticorum Latinorum, Bibliotheca Teubneriana, Die Griechischen Christlichen Schrifsteller der Ersten Drei Jahrhunderte, Monumenta Germaniae Historica, Biblioteca de Autores Cristianos, Sources Chrétiennes*, or in separately published texts, but the most readily accessible collections, and the most complete, are still the PG and PL.

English translations of many of these works have appeared, or will appear, in the following collections: *Library of the Fathers* (ed. E. B. Pusey, J. Keble, J. H. Newman, 45 vols., Oxford, 1838–1888); *Select Library of Nicene and Post-Nicene Fathers of the Christian Church* (ed. Ph. Schaff and H. Wace, 28 vols., New York, 1886–1900); *Ancient Christian Writers* (ed. J. Quasten and J. C. Plumpe, Westminster, Maryland, 1946 ff.); *The Fathers of the Church* (ed. L. Schopp and R. B. Deferrari, New York, 1947 ff.).

Modern Works

ALLARD, P., *Julien l'Apostat*, 3 vols., Paris, 1906–1910.

ANDREOTTI, R., *Il regno dell'imperatore Giuliano*, Bologna, 1936.

BARTELINK, G. J. M., "L'empereur Julien et le vocabulaire chrétien," *Vigiliae Christianae*, 11 (1957), 37–48.

BAYNES, N. H., "Constantine's Successors to Jovian and the Struggle with Persia," *Cambridge Medieval History*, 1 (New York, 1911), 55–86; 633–635 (bibliography).

BIDEZ, J., *La tradition manuscrite et les éditions des discours de l'empereur Julien*, Gent, 1929.

—— *La vie de l'empereur Julien*, Paris, 1930.

BIHLMEYER, K., *Church History*, revised by H. Tuchle, trans. from the 13th German edition by V. E. Mills, 1 (Westminster, Maryland, 1958).

BORRIES, E. VON, "Flavius Claudius Iulianus," *Paulys Real-Encyclopädie der Classischen Altertumswissenschaft*, 10 (1919), 26–91.

CHINNOCK, E. J., *A Few Notes on Julian and a Translation of his Public Letters*, London, 1901.

FESTUGIÈRE, A. J., "Julien à Macellum," *Journal of Roman Studies*, 47 (1957), 52–58.

GAIFFIER, B. DE, " 'Sub Iuliano Apostata' dans le martyrologe romain," *Analecta Bollandiana*, 74 (1956), 5–49.

GARDNER, A., *Julian, Philosopher and Emperor, and the Last Struggle of Paganism against Christianity*, New York, 1895.

GEFFCKEN, J., *Kaiser Julianus*, Leipzig, 1915.

GILDERSLEEVE, B. L., "The Emperor Julian," in *Essays and Studies: Educational and Literary* (Baltimore, 1890), 355–398, reprinted from the *Southern Review* for January, 1868.

KING, C. W., *Julian the Emperor, Containing Gregory Nazianzen's Two Invectives and Libanius' Monody with Julian's Extant Theosophical Works*, London, 1888.

LABRIOLLE, P. DE, "Julian the Apostate (361–363)," in PALANQUE, BARDY, DE LABRIOLLE, DE PLINVAL, BREHIER, *The Church in the Christian Roman Empire*, 1, trans. by E. C. Messinger (London, 1949), 229–239.

LINDSAY, T. M., "The Triumph of Christianity," *Cambridge Medieval History*, 1 (New York, 1911), 87–117.

NEANDER, A., *The Emperor Julian and his Generation*, trans. by G. V. Cox, London, 1850.

NEGRI, G., *Julian the Apostate*, trans. from the second Italian edition by the Duchess Litta-Visconti-Arese, 2 vols., New York, 1905.

PIGANIOL, A., "Julien l'Apostat (361–363)," *L'empire chrétien: Histoire romaine*, 4. 2, in the *Histoire Générale*, founded by G. Glotz (Paris, 1947), 127–148.

RENDALL, G. H., The Emperor Julian: Paganism and Christianity, London, 1879.

ROSTAGNI, A., Giuliano l'Apostata: Saggio critico con le operette politiche e satiriche tradotte e commentate, Turin, 1920.

SIHLER, E. G., "The Emperor Julian and his Religion," From Augustus to Augustine, Essays and Studies Dealing With the Contact and Conflict of Classic Paganism and Christianity (Cambridge, 1923), 190–217.

SIMPSON, W. D., Julian the Apostate, Aberdeen, 1930.

THOMPSON, E. A., The Historical Work of Ammianus Marcellinus, Cambridge, 1947.

VOGT, J., Kaiser Julian und das Judentum: Studien zum Weltanschauungskampf der Spätantike, Leipzig, 1939.

INDEX

The numbers refer to the various sections in the text (§§).

Abammon, 29
Ablabius, praetorian prefect, 5
Abraham, Hebrew patriarch, 198
Academies, 147
Achaemenids, 119
Achaia, 5
Achaiachala, 201
Achilles, Homeric hero, 51
Acropolis, 41, 61
Adonis, 175, 183
Adonis Tammuz (Tammuz), 175
Aedesius, 31, 35, 59
Aegae, temple of, 154
Aemelian, soldier, 160
Aeruli, 88, 123, 125
Aeschylus, 185 note
Aesop, 45
Aetius of Antioch, 44, 46
Africa, 5, 47, 130, 138, 196
Agenarichus (later called Serapion), 87, 90
Agendicum Senonum (Sens), 79, 80
Agentes in rebus, 173
Agilo, 150
Agnes, martyr, 56
Alemanni, 72, 73, 78, 87, 91, 92, 97, 103, 127, 138
Alexander the Great, 139, 147, 174, 175, 182, 186, 193, 203
Alexander of Heliopolis, 196
Alexandria in Egypt, 15, 26, 35, 122, 157, 158, 166, 185, 186, 195
Alexandria Troas, 50, 51
Aligildus, 149
Alps, 20, 71, 72, 88, 126, 131, 137
Alypius, 188, 189
Ambrose, saint, 110
Amida (Diarbekr), 120, 123, 124, 126, 139
Ammianus Marcellinus, 2, 6, 12, 20–22, 32, 34, 41, 47–50, 53, 55, 56, 59,

62, 64, 67, 68, 70, 71, 73–80, 82–103, 108–110, 113, 115–120, 123–129, 132, 134–141, 143–146, 148–156, 158, 162, 163, 169, 170, 173–175, 177–180, 188, 189, 192, 196–201, 203–211
Ammonius Saccas, 26
Anatha, 201
Anatolius, 136, 180, 185, 197, 209
Ancyra, 160
Andernach (Antemnacum), 103
Anebo, 29
Anomoeans, Arian sect, 44
Antemnacum (Andernach), 103
Anthony, abbot, 186
Antinoë, 186
Antioch, 24, 32, 35, 38, 49, 120, 139, 148, 158, 162–164, 173–180, 188, 192, 196, 197, 208
Antiochians, 13, 24, 32, 135, 162, 163, 176, 177, 180, 181, 192, 196
Antisthenes, 147
Antoninus Pius, emperor, 182
Aphaca (Aphek), temple of, 154
Apis, sacred bull, 177
Apodemius, 151
Apollinaris of Laodicea (father and son), 170
Apollo, 9, 163, 165, 179, 184
Apollo, temple of, at Daphne, 163, 178, 179
Apollo, temple of, on the Palatine in Rome, 198
Apollo of Didyma (Didymus Apollo), 165, 179
Apostles, Church of the, in Constantinople, 23, 150
Apotactistae (or Apotactitae), 185
Aprunculus, 144
Apuleius, 38
Aquileia, 50, 52, 143, 145, 148

Aquitania, 73, 99
Arabia, 160
Aradius (Rufinus Aradius), 196
Araxes (Chaboras), river, 200
Araxius, 43
Arbetio, 148, 150, 152
Archilochus, 18
Archpriest, 165
Ares, 128
Aretas, 193
Arete, 43
Arethusa, 154–159
Argaeus, mountain in Cappadocia, 12
Argentoratum (Strasbourg), 74, 75, 78, 79, 85, 87, 88, 90, 95, 96, 100, 102, 104 note
Arianism, Arians, 2, 3, 46, 47, 84, 121, 122, 156, 171
Arintheus, 201, 211
Aristotle, 13, 14, 29, 112
Arius, 2, 3
Armenia, 5, 119, 139, 196, 198, 211
Armenians, 199
Arsaces, king of Armenia, 139, 196, 199, 205, 207, 211
Arsacius, 165
Artabius, 171
Artemius, 151
Ascalon, 160
Asclepiades, Cynic philosopher, 179
Asclepius, 194
Asia, 5, 8, 141, 165
Asia Minor, 12, 35, 122
Asotia, 183
Asphalt Lake (Dead Sea), 189
Assanitic Saracens, 202
Assyria, 199, 206
Athanasius, saint, 6, 46, 47, 62, 122, 158, 162, 186
Athena, goddess 4, 41, 42, 51, 61, 128
Athenaeum, 167
Athens, 19, 24, 32, 33, 54, 57–59, 61, 63, 66, 170, 195, 211
Attalid dynasty, 35
Atthuarii, a division of the Franks, 73, 78, 137
Attica, 22
Attis, 60, 184
Augst (Augusta Rauracorum), 74, 83, 86, 104, 137
Augusta Nemetum (Spires), 74
Augustabona Tricasium (Troyes), 77, 81
Augusta Rauracorum (Augst), 74, 83, 86, 104
Augustine, saint, 30, 31, 38, 170, 191

Augustodunum (Autun), 20, 73, 77, 81
Aurelian, 17
Aurelius Victor, 145
Aurum coronarium, 173
Autessiodurum (Auxerre), 77, 81
Autun (Augustodunum), 20, 73, 77, 81
Auxerre (Autessiodurum), 77, 81

Baalbek (Heliopolis), 154, 160
Babylas, bishop of Antioch, 178, 179, 190
Babylon, 175, 198, 199, 202
Bagaudae, 72, 73
Bainobaudes, 84, 85, 94
Ballistarii, 77
Baraxamalcha, 201
Barbatio, 83–88
Barnabas, apostle, 176
Basil, priest, 160
Basil of Caesarea, saint, 19, 24, 46, 47, 57, 153, 185, 195
Basilina, mother of Julian the Apostate, 2–4, 8, 9, 46
Basinopolis, city near Nicaea, 4
Batavi, 88, 92, 123, 125
Batnae, 197
Beit Jibrîn (Eleutheropolis), 188
Beirut (Berytus) in Phoenicia, 2
Beleus, 160
Belgica, Secunda, 110
Bellona, goddess, 139, 154
Beroea, 197
Berytus (Beirut) in Phoenicia, 2
Bethlehem, 17
Bezabde, 139
Bingen (Vingo), 103
Birtha (Bithra), 203
Bithynia, 2, 20, 22, 49, 53, 54, 57
Black Forest (Marcianae silvae), 84, 140
Bonn (Bonna), 74, 103
Bononea (Bonmünster?), 142
Borbetomagus Vangionum (Worms), 74
Bosphorus, 136, 150
Bostra in Arabia, 160
Boulogne (Gesoriacum), 136
Bracchiati, auxiliaries, 92
Britain, 5, 69, 73, 99, 103, 123, 125, 126, 127, 136, 151, 188
Brucomagus (Brumath), 74, 79
Brumath (Brucomagus), 74, 79
Bryaxis, 179
Buccellatum, a kind of hardtack, 99
Burgundiones, 104

Caesarea in Cappadocia, 12, 14, 16, 19, 136, 153, 160
Caesarius, brother of St. Gregory Nazianzen, 172
Caligula, 182
Callinicus, 199
Callistus, soldier, 212
Calvary, basilica of, 188
Calypso, 9
Campania, 26
Candidati, members of the imperial bodyguard, 208
Capitatio, 107, 109, 110
Cappadocia, 5, 12, 15, 17, 57
Carausius, 73
Carrhae (Haran), 120, 197, 198
Carterius, 43
Carthage, 195
Casius, mount, 163
Castalia, spring, 178
Castra Herculis, 103
Castra peregrinorum, at Rome, 93
Cataphracti, armored cavalrymen, 77, 89, 90, 94, 208
Cato the Elder, 167, 201
Cebes, 147
Celsus, anti-Christian controversialist, 29, 193, 194
Celsus, friend of Libanius, 58
Celts, 74, 125, 127, 129, 138, 144, 162, 177
Centumcellae (Civitavecchia), 137
Cercusium (Circesium), 197, 200
Cerealis, 2
Chaboras (Araxes), river, 200
Chalcedon, 150, 175, 182
Chalcis in Coelesyria, 29, 201
Chaldean oracles, 29
Chaldees, 198
Chamavi, 73, 78, 100, 101
Charietto, 100, 102
Charisius, gate, 23
Chiliocomum, 199, 206
Chionitae, 118
Chonodomarius, 73, 87, 90, 91, 93, 95, 100
Christ, 22, 42, 51, 122, 161, 167, 170, 171, 176, 179, 183, 186–188, 193–195
Chrysanthius, 31, 35, 36, 153, 164
Chrysostom; see John Chrysostom, saint
Cicero, 167
Cilicia, 49, 144, 148
Circesium (Cercusium), 197
Civitavecchia (Centumcellae), 137
Claudius, emperor, 182

Coblenz (Confluentes), 74, 79
Coche (Seleucia), Persian city, 202, 204
Codex Justinianus, 140, 168, 191
Codex Theodosianus, 48, 77, 110, 140, 168, 191
Coelesyria, 29
Cologne (Colonia Agrippina, or Agrippinensis), 67, 69, 74, 75, 78, 79, 81, 98, 99
Colosseum, 93, 154
Commagene (district of Euphratensis), 171, 197
Commodus, emperor, 59
Como (Comum), 53
Condé, prince of, 142
Confluentes (Coblenz), 74, 79
Constance, lake, 138
Constans, son of Constantine the Great, 5; proclaimed Augustus, 5, 7, 11; on the death of Constantine II is the sole Augustus in the West, 11; dethroned and killed, 20, 82, 154
Constantia, daughter of Constantine the Great; see Constantina
Constantia, widow of the emperor Licinius and sister of Constantine the Great, 2, 3, 5 note
Constantian, tribune, 197
Constantina (Constantia), daughter of Constantine the Great, wife of Hannibalian, 5, 20; later the wife of Gallus, 49, 56
Constantine the Great, 1–6, 17, 20–23, 40, 42, 49, 54–56, 69, 71, 73, 82, 107, 109 note, 132, 145, 148–150, 152–158, 160, 162, 163, 172–174, 179, 182, 183, 188, 196, 211
Constantine II, son of Constantine the Great, 5; proclaimed Augustus, 5, 7, 11
Constantinople, 2, 4, 5, 8, 11, 21–24, 40, 42, 49, 58, 132, 143, 144, 149, 150, 152, 154, 156, 161, 162, 164, 167, 174, 176, 182
Constantinople, council of, 121
Constantius, son of Constantine the Great, 5–9, 11, 12, 14–16, 20–24, 32, 35, 40, 44, 45, 46, 49, 50, 52–56, 58, 59, 61–70, 75, 76, 78, 79, 81–84, 88, 93–95, 98, 99, 101, 104–106, 110, 111, 113, 114, 117–146; his death, 148, 149–160, 173, 174, 176, 179, 182, 186, 190, 192, 211
Constantius Chlorus, father of Constantine the Great, 1, 5, 40, 73

Corduene (Turkestan), 199, 206
Corinth, 2
Cornuti, auxiliaries, 92, 94
Cottian Alps, 138
Crassus, triumvir, 192
Crispus, son of Constantine the Great, 49, 56
Ctesiphon, 198, 202–204, 205, 207
Cumaean Sibyl, 198
Cursus publicus, 174
Cybele (Magna Mater, the Great Mother), 60, 175, 184, 199
Cyril of Alexandria, 193, 195
Cyrinus, 151

Dacia, 144
Dagalaif, 140, 142, 201, 203, 211
Damasus, pope, 48
Danube, river, 20, 84, 118, 123, 140, 141, 143, 145, 149, 174
Daphne, near Antioch, 163, 178, 179, 190
Dardanelles, 50
David, 23
Dead Sea (Asphalt Lake), 189
Decempagi (Dieuze), 78
Decentius, Caesar, brother of Magnentius, 87
Decentius, tribune, 125–129
Decuriones municipales, 107, 173
Delmatius, son of Constantius Chlorus and Theodora, 1, 5
Delmatius, son of Delmatius, half brother of Constantine, 5
Delos, 9, 25
Demeter (Ceves), 59, 177
Demiurge, 27
Demosthenes, 116, 168
Desaix, 141
Dessau, 118
Diacira, 201
Dianaeus, 16
Diarbekr (Amida), 120, 123, 124, 126, 139
Diaspora, 188
Didymus Apollo, 165, 179
Dieuze (Decempagi), 78
Diocaesarea, 49
Diocletian, emperor, 4, 21, 45, 69, 72, 73, 118, 119, 151, 165, 170, 177–179, 182, 200
Diodore, count, 158
Diodore of Tarsus, 193
Diogenes, 185
Dionysus, 18, 147, 160, 194

Dioscori (Castor and Pollux), temple of, 154
Divodurum (Metz), 78, 96
Don Quixote, 211
Dorostorus, in Moesia, 160
Dracontius, 158
Dura (Dura-Europos), 200, 201
Durocortorum Remorum (Reims), 75, 77–79, 81, 89

Ecdicius, prefect of Egypt, 15, 186
Edessa, 19, 120, 148, 171
Edessenes, 171
Edictum de pretiis (Edict on Prices) of Diocletian, 177
Egypt, 5, 15, 22, 29, 150, 151, 177, 182, 198
El elyon (Highest God), 187 note
Eleusis, Eleusinian mysteries, 59, 130
Eleutheropolis (Beit-Jibrîn), 188
Elna, 20
Elpidius, praetorian prefect, 55
Elpidius, treasurer, 179
El-Terib (Litarbae), 197
Emesa (Homs), 160
Enneads of Plotinus, 26, 27
Ephesus, 8, 11, 35, 36, 39, 161, 211
Ephraem Syrus, saint, 19, 171, 188
Epictetus, bishop of Centumcellae, 137
Epictetus, bishop of Gaul, 137
Epicurus, 18
Epiphanius, 187 note
Epiphany, 117, 137
Eretrian school of philosophy, 147
Etruscan haruspices (haruspices), 162, 196, 200, 208
Etruscans, 2
Eucharist, 161
Euhemerus, 66, 130
Eumolpidae, 59
Eunapius, 21, 31, 35, 39, 59, 63, 66, 100, 130, 131, 153
Euphratensis (Commagene), district of, 171, 197
Euphrates, river, 120, 121, 123, 149, 197–201, 204–206
Euripides, 183
Eusebia, empress, 41, 53–56, 61–63, 65, 66, 68, 82, 84, 118
Eusebius, praepositus cubiculi, 50, 52, 112, 113, 124, 149, 151
Eusebius of Caesarea, 2, 6, 38, 154, 187 note
Eusebius of Myndus, 31, 35–37
Eusebius of Nicomedia, 2, 3, 8, 11, 14, 38, 46, 47, 148

Eutherius, eunuch, 81, 82, 134, 153
Eutichian, 209
Eutropius, 6, 149, 172, 210
Euzoius, Arian bishop of Antioch, 148, 179
Evagrius, 151
Evectiones, 174

Fausta, wife of Constantine, 5, 55, 56
Fausta(?), half sister of Julian and wife of Constantius, 5, 21
Faustina, third wife of Constantius, 56, 139
Felix, notary, 136
Felix, superintendent, 179
Firmicus Maternus, 154
Flanona, village, 49
Florentius, condemned by the special tribunal, 151
Florentius, prefect of Gaul, 69, 89, 99, 103, 109–114, 123, 126, 127, 129, 139, 141, 151, 153
Fortune, goddess, 160, 162, 175, 177
Franks, 72, 73, 78, 79, 98

Galatia, in Asia Minor, 165
Galatia (Gaul), 65
Galba, emperor, 182
Galerius, emperor, 42, 123, 192, 201
Galilean (Christ), 209, 211
Galileans (Christians), 15, 18, 22, 47, 58, 114, 117, 135, 161, 162, 164–166, 168, 171, 185, 187, 190, 193
Galla, first wife of Julius Constantius and mother of Gallus, 2
Gallia Belgica, 73, 110
Gallia Lugdunensis, 73
Gallia Narbonensis, 73, 108
Gallia Viennensis, 73
Gallienus, emperor, 26, 72
Gallus, third son of Julius Constantius and of his first wife Galla, half brother of Julian the Apostate, 2, 5 note, 7, 8, 11; banished to Macellum, his boorish nature, 12; inscribed among the Christian clergy, 16, 17, 20; named Caesar, 21, 22, 33, 43, 44, 46; his death, 49, 50, 52, 56, 58, 61, 62, 64, 69, 83, 98, 113, 150, 151, 178
Gaudentius, 70, 113, 124, 138, 148, 151
Gaul, 5, 15, 20, 32, 41, 54, 55, 59, 60, 62–75, 78, 80, 82–85, 87, 94, 98, 99, 102, 104–107, 109–111, 114, 117, 120, 123–125, 127, 129–134,

136–140, 142, 144–146, 150, 151, 157, 176, 194, 201, 208, 211
Gauls, 88, 125, 126, 138
Gaza, 160, 188
Gelani, tribe on the Persian frontier, 118
Genius of the city of Alexandria, temple of, 158
Genius publicus, 41, 129, 139, 208
Gentiles, auxiliary troops, 73, 80, 125, 134
George of Cappadocia, 15, 46, 47, 154, 158, 159, 186
Germani, 90, 92
Germanianus, praetorian prefect, 140
Germany, 67, 73, 74, 98
Gesoriacum (Boulogne), 136
Gintonius, 125
Golgotha, 17
Gomoarius, 136, 148
Gordian, emperor, 200, 201
Goths, 174, 197
Greece, 33, 35, 43, 54, 56, 59, 63, 130, 145
Gregory Nazianzen, 6, 7, 16, 17, 21, 24, 32–34, 39, 44, 46, 57, 58, 110, 158, 161, 163, 172, 174, 180, 188, 192, 193, 195, 206
Gregory of Nyssa, 46

Hadrian, emperor, 59, 167, 178, 182, 203
Hadrianopolis, 121, 143
Haemus, 143
Hannibal, 175, 184
Hannibalian, son of Constantius Chlorus and uncle of Julian the Apostate, 1, 5 note
Hannibalian, son of Delmatius, 5, 20, 56
Haran (Carrhae), 198
Hariobaudes, barbarian king, 104
Hariobaudes, tribune, 103
Haruspices, 162, 196, 200, 208
Hebrew law (Torah), 187
Hebrews, 186, 194; see also Jews
Hecate, 36, 37
Hecebolius, rhetorician, 11, 22, 24, 51
Hector, Homeric hero, 51
Helena, daughter of Constantine the Great and wife of Julian the Apostate, 54–56, 65, 84, 115–118
Helena, empress, mother of Constantine the Great, 1, 17, 174
Heliopolis (Baalbek), 154, 160
Helios, 10, 31, 40–43, 51, 60, 128,

144, 149, 158, 161, 184, 186, 209, 211
Hellenes (idolaters), 16, 22, 47, 159, 166, 178, 187, 194
Heraclea (Perinthus), 150
Heracles, 147, 182, 194
Heraclius, Cynic philosopher, 13, 25, 42, 60, 185
Herculaneum, 26
Hercynian Forest, 88, 97
Hermes, 24, 60, 115, 168, 180, 183
Hermogenes, 150
Herodotus, 111, 168
Hesiod, 3, 10, 13, 14, 165, 166, 168
Hierapolis, 197
Hierophant, 59, 130
Hilary of Poitiers, 76, 122
Himerius, rhetorician, 57, 161, 180
Hipponax, 18
Höhe, 97
Holy Sepulcher, 17, 188
Homer, 3, 9, 10, 13, 14, 50, 64, 165, 166, 168
Homs (Emesa), 160
Horace, 162 note, 167, 211
Hortarius, 87, 102–104
Hucumbra (Symbra), 207
Huns, 19

Iliad, 9, 57, 64, 65
Ilium, 50, 51
Ill, river, 90
Illyricum, 5, 20, 109, 123, 139, 141, 144, 145, 151
Indictio, 107
Indus, river, 174
Innocentius, tribune, 94
Intellect (νοῦς), 27, 30
Ionia, 2, 22, 43, 147
Isocrates, 168

Jerome, saint, 6, 48, 121, 122, 160, 193
Jerusalem, 17, 94, 187–189
Jews, 49, 122, 175, 187–189, 203; see also Hebrews
John Chrysostom, saint, 24, 163, 169, 179, 192, 196, 211
Jovian, emperor, 139, 150, 186, 211
Jovian, soldier, 200
Jovinus, 140, 141, 143, 150
Jovius, 140
Juliacum (Jülich), 98
Julian, count, uncle of Julian the Apostate, 144, 149, 178, 179
Julian, Flavius Claudius, surnamed "the

Apostate," son of Julius Constantius and Basilina, his family and murder of his relatives, 1–8; first teachers, 8–10; banished to Macellum, 11–14; knowledge of Christianity and his baptism, 15–19; departure for Constantinople and Nicomedia, 20–25; his philosophical and moral world, 26–31; character, 32–34; in the school of the theurgists, 35–39; his mysticism, 40–42; gradual withdrawal from Christianity, 43–48; death of his brother Gallus, 49–50; at Milan, Como, Athens, and his initiation into pagan mysteries, 51–60; election as Caesar and marriage to Helena, 61–68; departure for Gaul, 69–71; first undertakings in Gaul, 72–86; battle of Strasbourg and pacification of the areas along the Rhine, 87–98; campaign to the north of Gaul, 99–104; administration of Gaul and attitude toward Christianity, 105–117; revolt at Paris, 118–128; Julian proclaimed Augustus, 129; background for the revolt, 130–131; dealings with Constantius and preparations on both sides for the struggle, 132–140; Julian marches against Constantius, 141–147; death of Constantius: Julian as sole Augustus enters Constantinople and establishes the special tribunal of Chalcedon, 148–151; reforms in the court, 152–153; restoration of idolatry and reform of the pagan priesthoods, 154–165; checks the Christians with his laws on teaching, 166–170; bans Christians from public office, 171–172; reforms and the Persian problem, 173–174; stay at Antioch and increased hostility to Christianity, 175–179; his writings, 180–185; exile of Anthanasius of Alexandria, 186; plan for the reconstruction of the temple of Jerusalem and its failure, 187–189; laws on funerals, 190–191; decides to make a campaign against Persia, 192; his Against the Galileans, 193–195; preparations for and beginning of the expedition, 196–199; advance to Ctesiphon, 200–204; withdrawal from Ctesiphon and retreat, 205–207; death, 208–210, after his death, 211; Julian's works: Encomia in Honor of Constantius and of Eusebia, 82; On

the Heroic Deeds of the Emperor, or On the Kingship, 106; A Consolation to Himself for the Departure of the Excellent Sallustius, 114; To the Senate and People of Athens, 146; Letter to the Philosopher Themistius, 146–147; Hymn to King Helios, 184; To the Mother of the Gods, 184; Against the Ignorant Cynics, 185; Against the Cynic Heraclius, 185
Jülich (Juliacum), 98
Julius Caesar, 97, 132, 139, 182
Julius Constantius, father of Julian the Apostate, 1, 2, 5, 7
Julius Julianus, grandfather of Julian the Apostate, 2, 3
Justin, martyr, 31
Juvenal, 162 note
Juventinus, Christian soldier, 196

Kellen (Tricensima), 103
King of Kings, title of the sovereign of Persia, 119–121, 136, 148, 173, 174, 192, 193, 195, 204, 205, 207
Kore (Persephone), 59

Lactantius, 179
Ladenburg, 197
Laeti, barbarian tribe and auxiliary soldiers, 73, 84, 134, 148
Lagus, father of Ptolemy, 186
Lake Constance, 138
Lancearii, 148
Laodicea, 170
Laumello (Laumellum), 69
Laws of Plato, 26
Leona, quaestor, 121, 136, 137
Lesbos, 35
Libanius, 20, 22–25, 32, 34, 35, 38, 43, 45, 49, 55, 58, 63, 70, 74, 86, 88, 90, 94, 98, 100, 102, 106, 114, 124, 128, 141, 149, 150–152, 156, 160, 162, 166, 167, 172, 174, 175, 179–181, 192–197, 204, 205, 209–211
Liberius, pope, 62
Libino, 138
Libri exercituales, 196
Libya, 66, 130
Libyssa, 175
Licinius, emperor, husband of Constantia, the half sister of Constantine the Great, 2, 5 note, 38, 42, 155, 170
Limes, 72, 73
Litarbae (El-Terib), 197

Logos, 31, 46
Lucian of Samosata, 182
Lucifer of Cagliari, 122
Lucillianus, successor to Sallustius in Gaul, 114; in command in Pannonia, 142; in command of Julian's fleet on the Euphrates, 197
Lucius Verus, emperor, 59, 182
Lugdunum (Lyons), 20, 75, 84
Luke, evangelist, 168
Lupicinus, 103, 123, 125–127, 136
Lutetia Parisiorum (Paris), 41, 75, 98, 99, 102, 108, 113, 115, 128, 129, 131, 133, 134, 136, 137, 139, 143, 146
Lyceum, 147
Lydia, 164
Lydus, 187
Lyons (Lugdunum), 20, 75, 84
Lysias, 168

Macedonia, 5, 119, 145
Macedonius, Christian of Meros, 160
Macellum, 7, 10, 11, 12, 14–17, 19, 21, 22, 52, 164, 194
Macepracta, 202
Macrianus, barbarian king, 104
Magistros studiorum, constitution of Julian the Apostate, 168
Magnentius, Flavius Magnus, 20, 62, 71, 73, 87, 88, 182
Main (Moenus), river, 96, 102
Mainz (Moguntiacum), 74, 75, 79, 96, 97, 103
Maiozamalcha (Maogamalcha), 202, 203
Maiuma, port of Gaza, 160, 176
Malechus, a title of rank among the Persians, 202
Mama (Mamans), martyr, 17
Mambre, 17
Mamersides, 202
Mamertinus, 123, 140, 141, 145, 150, 153
Maogamalcha (Maiozamalcha), 202, 203
Maranga (Maronsa), 207
Marcellinus, 20
Marcellus, 69, 75, 77, 80–82
Marcianae silvae (Black Forest), 84, 140
Marcianus, count, 148
Marcion, 185
Marcus of Arethusa, 7, 154, 159
Marcus Aurelius, emperor, 59, 182
Mardonius, pedagog of Julian the Apos-

tate, 3, 9–11, 13, 14, 23, 76, 114
Marinus, rebel, 54, 62
Maris, bishop of Chalcedon, 162
Marius Victorinus, 31, 170
Marmara, sea of, 11, 143
Maronsa (Maranga), 207
Mars, 208; see also Ares
Mars Avenger, 204
Massa Veternensis (Tuscan Maremma), 2
Mattiarii, soldiers, 148
Maurus, 129
Maxentius, emperor, 196
Maximian, emperor, 1, 72
Maximinus, Christian soldier, 196
Maximinus Daia (Daza), emperor, 38, 122, 164, 170, 211
Maximus, prefect of Rome, 145
Maximus of Ephesus, theurgist, 14, 31, 34–36, 39, 43, 44, 47, 59, 144, 149, 153, 161, 168, 174, 175, 180, 190, 193, 197, 200, 209, 211
Medericus, 87
Media, 199
Megaera (one of the Furies), 49, 56
Megarian school of philosophy, 147
Mensurius, bishop of Carthage, 195
Merena, 207, 209
Meros, in Phrygia, 160
Mesopotamia, 119, 211
Metz (Divodurum, Mettae), 78, 96
Meuse (Mosa), river, 98–101, 104 note
Milan, 49, 50, 52, 58, 61–64, 66, 67, 81, 82
Milan, Edict of, 42, 154
Miletus, 165, 179
Mithra, god, 40, 60, 113, 116, 130, 161, 162, 164, 168, 183, 184
Mithraeum, place of worship of the god Mithra, 158, 161
Mitrovica (Sirmium), 20, 54, 84, 121, 140–144, 145
Moenus (Main), river, 96, 102
Moesi, auxiliaries, 123
Moesia, 143, 160
Moguntiacum (Mainz), 74, 75, 79, 96, 97, 103
Monginevra, 71
Moon (Luna), goddess, 183
Mopsucrene, 148
Mosa (Meuse), river, 98–101
Moselle (Mosella), river, 79
Mount of Olives, 17
Moxoëne, 199
Mundolsheim, 90
Munera civilia, 173

Mursa (Mursia, Osijek), 20
Muses, 25, 43, 115, 168
Musonianus, earlier named Flavius Strategius, 118–120

Nabdates, 203
Nabuchodonosor (Nebuchadnessar), 203
Naharmalcha ("River of the Kings"), 202, 204
Naissus (Nish), 20, 143–145
Napoleon, 96, 139, 141
Narseus, 204
Neapolis, 188
Nebridius, 127, 136, 140
Neckar, river, 97
Nemetae (Spires), 74
Neoplatonism, 15, 26–31, 166; Syrian school of, 29–31
Nepotianus, 20, 21, 62
Nero, emperor, 122, 182
Nerva, emperor, 182
Nestica, tribune, 102
Nevitta, 140–143, 145, 150, 153, 201, 203, 211
Nicaea, 4, 24, 121, 132
Nice (Nicaea), in Thrace, 121
Nicocles, grammarian, 11, 14, 22
Nicomedia, 2, 8, 11, 22–24, 32, 35, 42, 175
Nicopolis, 188
Nigrinus, Avidius, 143
Nish (Naissus), 20, 143–145
Nisibis, 20, 171, 198, 211
Nohodares, 209
Noricum, 49, 140, 142
Novaesium (Neuss, Nys), 103
Novatians, 156
Noviomagus Nemetum (Spires), 74
Numerius, 108

Oberhausbergen, 90
Octavian, proconsul of Africa, 196
Odin, Teutonic god, 87
Odyssey, 9, 41, 128
Olympus, 22, 60, 182
Onias III, Hebrew high priest, 178
Orbilius, 167
Oribasius, 66, 76, 111, 113, 124, 130, 131, 180, 197, 208
Orion, Christian of Bostra, 160
Ormizda, brother of King Sapor, 201, 202, 205
Osdroene, 201
Ostia, on the Tiber, 154
Ozogardane, 201, 202

Palatine, 93
Palatini, 152
Palestine, 17, 49, 122, 154, 176, 188, 194
Palladius, 151
Pamphylia, 173
Panegyrici Latini, 74
Pannonia, 69, 140, 142, 145
Paradise, a Persian park, 203, 204
Paris (Lutetia Parisiorum), 41, 75, 98, 99, 102, 108, 113, 115, 128, 129, 131, 133, 134, 136, 137, 139, 143, 146
Parthians, 198, 207; see also Persians
Parthicus, 174, 193
Paterfamilias, 167
Patris potestas, 167
Paul, apostle, 9, 12, 22, 42, 57, 93, 130, 148, 166, 176, 190, 194, 211
Paul "the Chain," informer, 113, 124, 151
Pavia (Ticinum), 69
Pegasius, bishop of Ilium, 51, 164
Pentadius, 69, 113, 127, 134
Pentadius, accused before the special tribunal, 151
Pergamum, 31, 35, 59, 130
Perinthus (Heraclea), 150
Persephone (Kore), 59
Persia, 118, 193, 198, 200, 206
Persians, 5, 7, 11, 12, 20, 62, 118, 120, 121, 123, 124, 126, 136, 138, 139, 142, 149, 162, 166, 171, 173, 177, 178, 180, 192, 193, 195, 198, 202–204, 206–211
Pessinus, 175
Petulantes, auxiliary troops, 88, 125, 127, 129, 138, 162, 177
Phaedo, 147
Phalerum, bay, 59
Philippopolis, 143
Philip Sideta, 195
Philo of Byblos, 187 note
Philostorgius, 6, 44, 179, 188, 209, 210
Phoenicia (Phoenice), 2, 55, 154, 159, 160
Phosphorius, 209
Photinus, bishop of Sirmium, 193
Phrygia, 43, 116, 147, 160, 184, 208
Picts, 123
Pigranes, 204
Pittacus, 147
Pirisabora, 202
Plato, 13, 14, 26, 28, 29, 31, 57, 75, 112, 147, 184, 185

Platonopolis, 26
Pliny the Elder, 53
Plotinus, 26–31, 60, 170, 184
Podosaces, 202
Poetovio, 49
Pola, 49
Polybius, 167
Polycles, 55
Pompeii, 26
Pontifex maximus, 164, 165
Pontus, 5
Porphyry, 26, 28, 29, 31, 46, 193, 194
Primani, legion of the, 93
Priscus, disciple of Aedesius, 31, 35, 59, 153, 161, 168, 180, 197, 200, 209
Probus, emperor, 72
Procopius, council of Julian the Apostate, 198, 199, 205–207, 211
Prohaeresius, Christian rhetor, 57, 153, 170
Prophets, of the Jews, 189
Propontis (Sea of Marmara), 11, 143
Prusa in Bithynia, 20, 57
Ptolemy, son of Lagus, 186
Pyrenees, 20, 72
Pyrrho, 18
Pythagoras, 31

Quadriburgium, 103
Quintilian, 167, 181
Quixote, Don, 211

Raetia, 78, 83, 104, 138, 140, 142
Regii, auxiliaries, 92
Reims (Durocortorum Remorum), 75, 77–79, 81, 98
Remagen (Rigomagus), 79
Rhine, 72–75, 78, 79, 83–88, 90, 93, 96–100, 102–104, 118, 126, 134, 137, 138, 192
Rhodope, mountain range, 143
Ricciotti, 19, 72, 77, 152, 155, 156, 164, 177, 188, 195, 196
Rigomagus (Remagen), 79
"River of the Kings" (Naharmalcha), 202, 204
Rocroy, 142
Romans, 20, 72, 85, 87–90, 92–94, 96–100, 103, 104, 118, 119, 126, 130, 141, 167, 174, 196, 199, 201–204, 206–209, 211
Rome, 20, 26, 31, 42, 48, 55, 62, 72, 84, 87, 93, 104, 118, 119, 122, 138, 145, 152, 154, 157, 167, 170, 184, 190, 196, 198–200
Romulus, 182

Rufinus, historian, 169, 171, 188
Rufinus Aradius, count, 196

Säckingen (Sanctio), 138
Sagitarii, archers, 89
Salii, Frankish tribe, 100
Saliso (Salisso, Selz), 74
Sallustius, Flavius, prefect of Gaul, 140, 184, 200
Sallustius (Salutius), Secundus Saturninus, 34, 69, 76, 105, 106, 113, 114, 150, 172, 178, 180, 185, 197, 209, 211
Samaria, 188
Samosata, 197
Sanctio (Säckingen), 138
Sapor, king of Persia, 118–121, 201, 205–207, 211
Saracens, 197, 199, 207; Assanatic Saracens, 202
Sardica (Serdica, Sofia), 82
Sarmatians (Sarmatae), 118
Saturn, god, 182
Saturnalia, 182
Saturninus, 151
Saverne (Tabernae), 74, 85, 89, 96
Savus, river, 140
Saxons, 73
Scipio Africanus, 203
Scots, 123
Scutarii, shield-bearers, 80, 102, 125, 134
Scythians, 197
Sebastian, 198, 211
Secundinus, duke of Osdruene, 201
Seine (Sequana), river, 116
Seleucia, council of, 121, 136
Seleucia (Coche), Persian city, 202, 204
Selz (Saliso), 74
Senate of Antioch, 165
Senate of Athens, 5, 7, 8, 11, 12, 32, 41, 52, 61, 74, 83, 93, 94, 99, 104, 125, 127, 128, 129, 136–139, 145, 146
Senate of Constantinople, 62, 120, 153
Senate of Rome, 6, 145, 153, 196
Sens (Agendicum Senonum), 79, 80, 81
Serapion (originally called Agenarichus), 87, 90
Serapis (Sarapis), 159, 186
Severus, 83, 90–92, 98, 102, 103
Sibylline Books, 196, 208
Silenus, 182, 183
Silvanus, 54, 62, 63, 69, 73, 151
Simmias, 147

Sin, moon-god, 198
Singara, 20, 211
Sintula, 125–127, 129, 134
Sirmium (Mitrovica, Mitrovitz), in Pannonia, 20, 54, 84, 121, 140–144, 145
Socrates, historian, 6, 9–11, 22, 23, 43, 44, 88, 148, 152, 158, 160, 162, 168–172, 174, 177, 178, 187, 188, 192, 205, 210
Socrates, philosopher, 13, 14, 63, 113, 147, 209
Sofia (Sardica), 82
Solon, 147
Soucis (Succi, claustra Succorum), mountain pass, 143, 145, 148, 150
Sozomen, historian, 7, 10, 16, 17, 22, 23, 43, 44, 88, 148, 158, 160, 162, 169–171, 178–180, 187, 188, 192, 206, 209–211
Spain, 5, 69, 73, 138, 157
Spires (Augusta Nemetum, Noviomagus), 74
Spoleto, inscription of, 118
Stabula, 174
Stoa, 147
Strasbourg (Argentoratum), 74, 75, 78, 79, 85, 87, 88, 90, 95, 96, 100, 102, 104 note
Stridon, river, 119
Succi, see Soucis
Suetonius, 162 note
Sulpicius Severus, 122
Suomarius, 87, 102, 103
Surena, a Persian title, 202–204
Symbra, 207; see Hucumbra
Symmachus, 145
Synesius, bishops of Cyrene, 10
Syria, 5, 19, 122, 139, 160, 188, 196, 200, 201

Tabernae (Saverne), 74, 85, 89, 96
Tacitus, 87
Tammuz (Adonis Tammuz), 175
Tamsapor, 119, 120
Tarquinian Books, 208
Tarsus, 148, 192, 211
Tatian, Christian of Meros, 160
Taunus, mountain range, 97, 102
Taurobolium, 154, 161
Taurus, mountain range, 148, 211
Taurus, praetorian prefect, 121, 138, 139, 141, 151
Temple of Jerusalem, 187–189
Tenedos, island, 50
Tertullus, 145, 154

Thalassius, 49
Thebaid, 122, 186
Themistius, 52, 106, 120, 146, 147, 181
Theodora, priestess, 165
Theodora, wife of Constantius Chlorus, 1
Theodore, archpriest, 165, 168
Theodore, persecuted Christian, 178
Theodore of Mopsuestia, 193, 195
Theodoret, 7, 16, 17, 39, 43, 169, 171, 178, 179, 188, 192, 196, 209
Theodosius, emperor, 185
Theodulus, Christian of Meros, 160
Theognis, 185 note
Theolaif, 149
Theotecnus, 38, 39
Theurgy, theurgists, 35–39, 57–60, 175, 184, 197, 211
Thilsaphata, 211
Thilutha, 201
Thrace, 5, 59, 121, 123, 143, 145, 148, 150, 207
Thucydides, 168
Tiberias, 49
Tiberius, emperor, 182
Ticinum (Pavia), 69
Tigris, river, 120, 139, 198, 199, 204–207, 211
Titus, emperor, 12, 94, 182, 203
Tolosa (Toulouse), 1
Torah (Hebrew law), 187
Toulouse (Tolosa), 1
Toxiandria (Tessender-Lo), Toxiandri, 100, 105 note
Trajan, emperor, 97, 103, 123, 174, 175, 182, 198, 199, 205
Treves (Treveri, Augusta Treverorum), 72, 73, 79, 122
Tricassae (Troyes), 77, 81
Tricensima (Kellen), 103
Troyes (Augustabona Tricasium, Tricassae), 77, 81
Troy (Ilium), 50–52
Turcius Apronianus, 196
Turin (Augusta Taurinorum), 69
Turkestan (Corduene), 199, 206
Tuscan Maremma (Masa Veternensis), 2

Tuscany, 140
Tyropoeon, valley of, 188

Ur of the Chaldees, 198
Urius, barbarian king, 87, 104
Ursicinus, barbarian king, 87, 104
Ursicinus, Roman general, 69, 75, 77, 83, 150
Ursulus, 70, 102, 151

Vadomarius, 104, 138
Valens, emperor, 186
Valentinian, emperor, 84, 157
Valentinians, 171
Valerian, emperor, 192
Vangiones (Worms), 74
Vercellum (Vercellae), 151
Vespasian, emperor, 12, 94, 167, 182
Vestralpus, barbarian king, 87, 104
Vetranio (Veteranio), 20, 62, 207
Via Nomentana, 56
Victor, 201, 203, 204, 211
Victorinus, Marius, rhetorician, 31, 170
Victory, altar of, 157
Vienne (Vienna), in Gaul, 71, 75, 77, 105, 111, 117, 126, 127, 131, 137
Vindex, emperor, 182
Vingo (Bingen), 103
Vitellius, emperor, 182
Vosges (Vosegus), mountain range, 79, 84, 85

Worms (Borbetomagus Vangionum, Vangiones), 74

Xenophon, 147

Yahweh, 42
Yugoslavia, 140

Zaitha, 197
Zeus, 41, 42, 128, 129, 139, 144, 149, 150, 182, 183, 204; Zeus Casius, temple of, 163; Zeus Philios, 38, 177
Zianni, auxiliaries, 207
Zonaras, 136, 150, 168, 208, 211
Zosimus, 6, 63, 70, 94, 100, 102, 124, 127, 141, 197, 200–203, 207, 208, 210

If you have enjoyed this book, consider making your next selection from among the following . . .

Angels and Devils. *Cruz* 15.00
Creation Rediscovered: Evolution and Origins Debate. *Keane* 21.00
Popes against Modern Errors: 16 Papal Documents 16.50
Ven. Francisco Marto of Fatima. *Cirrincione,* comp. 1.50
Ven. Jacinta Marto of Fatima. *Cirrincione* 2.00
St. Philomena—The Wonder-Worker. *O'Sullivan* 7.00
The Facts About Luther. *Msgr. Patrick O'Hare* 16.50
Little Catechism of the Curé of Ars. *St. John Vianney.* 6.00
The Curé of Ars—Patron Saint of Parish Priests. *Fr. B. O'Brien* 5.50
Saint Teresa of Avila. *William Thomas Walsh* 21.50
Isabella of Spain: The Last Crusader. *William Thomas Walsh* 20.00
Characters of the Inquisition. *William Thomas Walsh* 15.00
Blood-Drenched Altars—Cath. Comment. on Hist. Mexico. *Kelley* 20.00
The Four Last Things—Death, Judgment, Hell, Heaven. *Fr. von Cochem* 7.00
Confession of a Roman Catholic. *Paul Whitcomb* 1.50
The Catholic Church Has the Answer. *Paul Whitcomb* 1.50
The Sinner's Guide. *Ven. Louis of Granada* 12.00
True Devotion to Mary. *St. Louis De Montfort* 8.00
Life of St. Anthony Mary Claret. *Fanchón Royer* 15.00
Autobiography of St. Anthony Mary Claret 13.00
I Wait for You. *Sr. Josefa Menendez* .... .75
Words of Love. *Menendez, Betrone, Mary of the Trinity* 6.00
Little Lives of the Great Saints. *John O'Kane Murray* 18.00
Prayer—The Key to Salvation. *Fr. Michael Müller.* 7.50
Sermons on Prayer. *St. Francis de Sales* 4.00
Sermons on Our Lady. *St. Francis de Sales* 10.00
Passion of Jesus and Its Hidden Meaning. *Fr. Groenings, S.J.* 15.00
The Victories of the Martyrs. *St. Alphonsus Liguori* 10.00
Canons and Decrees of the Council of Trent. *Transl. Schroeder* 15.00
Sermons of St. Alphonsus Liguori for Every Sunday 16.50
A Catechism of Modernism. *Fr. J. B. Lemius* 5.00
Alexandrina—The Agony and the Glory. *Johnston* 6.00
Life of Blessed Margaret of Castello. *Fr. William Bonniwell* 7.50
The Ways of Mental Prayer. *Dom Vitalis Lehodey* 14.00
Catechism of Mental Prayer. *Simler* 2.00
Fr. Paul of Moll. *van Speybrouck* 11.00
St. Francis of Paola. *Simi and Segreti* 8.00
Abortion: Yes or No? *Dr. John L. Grady, M.D.* 2.00
The Story of the Church. *Johnson, Hannan, Dominica* 16.50
Reign of Christ the King. *Davies* 1.25
Hell Quizzes. *Radio Replies Press* 1.50
Indulgence Quizzes. *Radio Replies Press* 1.50
Purgatory Quizzes. *Radio Replies Press* 1.50
Virgin and Statue Worship Quizzes. *Radio Replies Press* 1.50
The Holy Eucharist. *St. Alphonsus* 10.00
Meditation Prayer on Mary Immaculate. *Padre Pio* 1.50
Little Book of the Work of Infinite Love. *de la Touche* 2.00
Textual Concordance of The Holy Scriptures. *Williams* 35.00
Douay-Rheims Bible. *Leatherbound* 35.00
The Way of Divine Love. *Sister Josefa Menendez* 18.50
The Way of Divine Love. (pocket, unabr.). *Menendez* 8.50
Love, Peace and Joy. (St. Gertrude). *Prévot* 7.00

Prices subject to change.

Scripture Alone? 21 Reasons to Reject *Sola Scriptura. Peters* 2.00
Spiritual Exercises. *St. Ignatius Loyola* 12.50
St. Gerard Majella. *Fr. Saint-Omer, C.SS.R.* 8.50
Mystical City of God—Abridged. *Ven. Mary of Agreda* 18.50
Moments Divine—Before the Blessed Sacrament. *Reuter* 8.50
Miraculous Images of Our Lady. *Cruz* 20.00
Miraculous Images of Our Lord. *Cruz* 13.50
Raised from the Dead. *Fr. Hebert* 16.50
Love and Service of God, Infinite Love. *Mother Louise Margaret* 12.50
Life and Work of Mother Louise Margaret. *Fr. O'Connell* 12.50
Autobiography of St. Margaret Mary. 5.00
Thoughts and Sayings of St. Margaret Mary 5.00
The Voice of the Saints. *Comp. by Francis Johnston* 6.00
The 12 Steps to Holiness and Salvation. *St. Alphonsus* 7.50
The Rosary and the Crisis of Faith. *Cirrincione & Nelson* 2.00
Sin and Its Consequences. *Cardinal Manning* 7.00
Fourfold Sovereignty of God. *Cardinal Manning* 5.00
Dialogue of St. Catherine of Siena. *Transl. Algar Thorold* 10.00
Catholic Answer to Jehovah's Witnesses. *D'Angelo* 10.00
Twelve Promises of the Sacred Heart. (100 cards) 5.00
Life of St. Aloysius Gonzaga. *Fr. Meschler* 12.00
The Love of Mary. *D. Roberto* 8.00
Begone Satan. *Fr. Vogl* 3.00
The Prophets and Our Times. *Fr. R. G. Culleton* 13.50
St. Therese, The Little Flower. *John Beevers* 6.00
St. Joseph of Copertino. *Fr. Angelo Pastrovicchi* 6.00
Mary, The Second Eve. *Cardinal Newman* 2.50
Devotion to Infant Jesus of Prague. *Booklet* .... .75
Reign of Christ the King in Public & Private Life. *Davies* 1.25
The Wonder of Guadalupe. *Francis Johnston* 7.50
Apologetics. *Msgr. Paul Glenn* 10.00
Baltimore Catechism No. 1 .... 3.50
Baltimore Catechism No. 2 .... 4.50
Baltimore Catechism No. 3 .... 8.00
An Explanation of the Baltimore Catechism. *Fr. Kinkead* 16.50
Bethlehem. *Fr. Faber* 18.00
Bible History. *Schuster* 10.00
Blessed Eucharist. *Fr. Mueller* 9.00
Catholic Catechism. *Fr. Faerber* 7.00
The Devil. *Fr. Delaporte* 6.00
Dogmatic Theology for the Laity. *Fr. Premm* 20.00
Evidence of Satan in the Modern World. *Cristiani* 10.00
Fifteen Promises of Mary. (100 cards) 5.00
Life of Anne Catherine Emmerich. 2 vols. *Schmoeger* 37.50
Life of the Blessed Virgin Mary. *Emmerich* 16.50
Manual of Practical Devotion to St. Joseph. *Patrignani* 15.00
Prayer to St. Michael. (100 leaflets) 5.00
Prayerbook of Favorite Litanies. *Fr. Hebert* 10.00
Preparation for Death. (Abridged). *St. Alphonsus* 8.00
Purgatory Explained. *Schouppe* 13.50
Purgatory Explained. (pocket, unabr.). *Schouppe* 9.00
Fundamentals of Catholic Dogma. *Ludwig Ott* 21.00
Spiritual Conferences. *Tauler* 13.00
Trustful Surrender to Divine Providence. *Bl. Claude* 5.00
Wife, Mother and Mystic. *Bessieres* 8.00

Prices subject to change.

St. Teresa of Avila. *Forbes* 6.00
St. Ignatius Loyola. *Forbes* 6.00
St. Catherine of Siena. *Forbes* 6.00
The Agony of Jesus. *Padre Pio* 1.50
Sermons of the Curé of Ars. *Vianney* 12.50
St. Antony of the Desert. *St. Athanasius* 5.00
Is It a Saint's Name? *Fr. William Dunne* 2.50
St. Pius V—His Life, Times, Miracles. *Anderson* 4.50
Who Is Therese Neumann? *Fr. Charles Carty.* 2.00
Martyrs of the Coliseum. *Fr. O'Reilly.* 18.50
Way of the Cross. *St. Alphonsus Liguori* 1.00
Way of the Cross. *Franciscan version* 1.00
How Christ Said the First Mass. *Fr. Meagher* 18.50
Too Busy for God? Think Again! *D'Angelo* 5.00
St. Bernadette Soubirous. *Trochu* 18.50
Passion and Death of Jesus Christ. *Liguori* 10.00
Treatise on the Love of God. 1 Vol. *St. Francis de Sales* 24.00
Confession Quizzes. *Radio Replies Press* 1.50
St. Philip Neri. *Fr. V. J. Matthews.* 5.50
St. Louise de Marillac. *Sr. Vincent Regnault* 6.00
The Old World and America. *Rev. Philip Furlong* 18.00
Prophecy for Today. *Edward Connor* 5.50
The Book of Infinite Love. *Mother de la Touche* 5.00
Chats with Converts. *Fr. M. D. Forrest.* 10.00
The Church Teaches. *Church Documents* 16.50
Conversation with Christ. *Peter T. Rohrbach* 10.00
Purgatory and Heaven. *J. P. Arendzen* 5.00
Liberalism Is a Sin. *Sarda y Salvany* 7.50
Spiritual Legacy of Sr. Mary of the Trinity. *van den Broek* 10.00
The Creator and the Creature. *Fr. Frederick Faber* 16.50
Radio Replies. *3* Vols. *Frs. Rumble and Carty* 42.00
Convert's Catechism of Catholic Doctrine. *Fr. Geiermann* 3.00
Incarnation, Birth, Infancy of Jesus Christ. *St. Alphonsus* 10.00
Light and Peace. *Fr. R. P. Quadrupani* 7.00
Dogmatic Canons & Decrees of Trent, Vat. I. *Documents* 9.50
The Evolution Hoax Exposed. *A. N. Field* 6.00
The Primitive Church. *Fr. D. I. Lanslots.* 10.00
The Priest, the Man of God. *St. Joseph Cafasso* 13.50
Blessed Sacrament. *Fr. Frederick Faber* 18.50
Christ Denied. *Fr. Paul Wickens* 2.50
New Regulations on Indulgences. *Fr. Winfrid Herbst* 2.50
A Tour of the Summa. *Msgr. Paul Glenn* 18.00
Spiritual Conferences. *Fr. Frederick Faber* 15.00
Latin Grammar. *Scanlon and Scanlon* 16.50
A Brief Life of Christ. *Fr. Rumble* 2.00
Marriage Quizzes. *Radio Replies Press* 1.50
True Church Quizzes. *Radio Replies Press* 1.50
The Secret of the Rosary. *St. Louis De Montfort* 3.00
Mary, Mother of the Church. *Church Documents* 4.00
The Sacred Heart and the Priesthood. *de la Touche* 9.00
Revelations of St. Bridget. *St. Bridget of Sweden* 3.00
Magnificent Prayers. *St. Bridget of Sweden* 2.00
The Happiness of Heaven. *Fr. J. Boudreau* 8.00
St. Catherine Labouré of the Miraculous Medal. *Dirvin* 13.50
The Glories of Mary. (pocket, unabr.). *St. Alphonsus Liguori* 10.00

Prices subject to change.

St. Athanasius. *Forbes* 6.00
St. Vincent de Paul. *Forbes* 6.00
St. Monica. *Forbes* 6.00
The Three Ways of the Spiritual Life. *Garrigou-Lagrange, O.P.* 6.00
Freemasonry: Mankind's Hidden Enemy. *Bro. C. Madden* 5.00
Fourteen Holy Helpers. *Hammer* 5.00
All About the Angels. *Fr. Paul O'Sullivan* 6.00
AA—1025: Memoirs of an Anti-Apostle. *Marie Carré.* 6.00
All for Jesus. *Fr. Frederick Faber.* 15.00
Growth in Holiness. *Fr. Frederick Faber.* 16.50
Behind the Lodge Door. *Paul Fisher.* 18.00
Chief Truths of the Faith. (Book I). *Fr. John Laux* 10.00
Mass and the Sacraments. (Book II). *Fr. John Laux* 10.00
Catholic Morality. (Book III). *Fr. John Laux.* 10.00
Catholic Apologetics. (Book IV). *Fr. John Laux* 10.00
Introduction to the Bible. *Fr. John Laux* 16.50
Church History. *Fr. John Laux* 24.00
Devotion for the Dying. *Mother Mary Potter* 9.00
Devotion to the Sacred Heart. *Fr. Jean Croiset* 15.00
An Easy Way to Become a Saint. *Fr. Paul O'Sullivan* 5.00
The Golden Arrow. *Sr. Mary of St. Peter.* 12.50
The Holy Man of Tours. *Dorothy Scallan* 10.00
Hell—Plus How to Avoid Hell. *Fr. Schouppe/Nelson* 10.00
History of Protestant Ref. in England & Ireland. *Cobbett* 18.00
Holy Will of God. *Fr. Leo Pyzalski* 6.00
How Christ Changed the World. *Msgr. Luigi Civardi* 7.00
How to Be Happy, How to Be Holy *Fr. Paul O'Sullivan* 8.00
Imitation of Christ. *Thomas à Kempis. (Challoner transl.)* 10.00
Life & Message of Sr. Mary of the Trinity. *Rev. Dubois* 10.00
Life Everlasting. *Fr. Garrigou-Lagrange, O.P.* 13.50
Life of Mary as Seen by the Mystics. *Compiled by Raphael Brown* 12.50
Life of St. Dominic. *Mother Augusta Drane* 12.00
Life of St. Francis of Assisi. *St. Bonaventure* 10.00
Life of St. Ignatius Loyola. *Fr. Genelli* 16.50
Life of St. Margaret Mary Alacoque. *Rt. Rev. Emile Bougaud* 13.50
Mexican Martyrdom. *Fr. Wilfrid Parsons* 10.00
Children of Fatima. *Windeatt.* (Age 10 & up) 8.00
Cure of Ars. *Windeatt.* (Age 10 & up) 12.00
The Little Flower. *Windeatt.* (Age 10 & up) 8.00
Patron of First Communicants. (Bl. Imelda). *Windeatt.* (Age 10 & up) . 6.00
Miraculous Medal. *Windeatt.* (Age 10 & up) 7.00
St. Louis De Montfort. *Windeatt.* (Age 10 & up) 12.00
St. Thomas Aquinas. *Windeatt.* (Age 10 & up) 6.00
St. Catherine of Siena. *Windeatt.* (Age 10 & up) 5.00
St. Rose of Lima. *Windeatt.* (Age 10 & up) 8.00
St. Hyacinth of Poland. *Windeatt.* (Age 10 & up) 11.00
St. Martin de Porres. *Windeatt.* (Age 10 & up) 7.00
Pauline Jaricot. *Windeatt.* (Age 10 & up) 13.00
Douay-Rheims New Testament. *Paperbound* 15.00
Prayers and Heavenly Promises. *Compiled by Joan Carroll Cruz* 5.00
Preparation for Death. (Unabr., pocket). *St. Alphonsus* 10.00
Rebuilding a Lost Faith. *John Stoddard* 15.00
The Spiritual Combat. *Dom Lorenzo Scupoli* 9.00
Retreat Companion for Priests. *Fr. Francis Havey* 7.50
Spiritual Doctrine of St. Cath. of Genoa. *Maribotti/St. Catherine* .. 12.50

Prices subject to change.

Our Saviour and His Love for Us. *Garrigou-Lagrange, O.P.* 18.50
Providence. *Garrigou-Lagrange, O.P.* 15.00
Predestination. *Garrigou-Lagrange, O.P.* 15.00
The Soul of the Apostolate. *Dom Chautard* 10.00
Hail Holy Queen (from *Glories of Mary*). *St. Alphonsus* 8.00
Novena of Holy Communions. *Lovasik* 2.00
Brief Catechism for Adults. *Cogan* 9.00
The Cath. Religion—Illus./Expl. for Child, Adult, Convert. *Burbach* 9.00
Eucharistic Miracles. *Joan Carroll Cruz* 15.00
The Incorruptibles. *Joan Carroll Cruz* 13.50
Pope St. Pius X. *F. A. Forbes* 8.00
St. Alphonsus Liguori. *Frs. Miller and Aubin* 16.50
Self-Abandonment to Divine Providence. *Fr. de Caussade, S.J.* 18.00
The Song of Songs—A Mystical Exposition. *Fr. Arintero, O.P.* 20.00
Prophecy for Today. *Edward Connor* 5.50
Saint Michael and the Angels. *Approved Sources* 7.00
Dolorous Passion of Our Lord. *Anne C. Emmerich* 16.50
Modern Saints—Their Lives & Faces, Book I. *Ann Ball* 18.00
Modern Saints—Their Lives & Faces, Book II. *Ann Ball* 20.00
Our Lady of Fatima's Peace Plan from Heaven. *Booklet* .... .75
Divine Favors Granted to St. Joseph. *Père Binet* 5.00
St. Joseph Cafasso—Priest of the Gallows. *St. John Bosco* 5.00
Catechism of the Council of Trent. *McHugh/Callan* 24.00
The Foot of the Cross. *Fr. Faber.* 16.50
The Rosary in Action. *John Johnson* 9.00
Padre Pio—The Stigmatist. *Fr. Charles Carty* 15.00
Why Squander Illness? *Frs. Rumble & Carty* 2.00
The Sacred Heart and the Priesthood. *de la Touche* 9.00
Fatima—The Great Sign. *Francis Johnston* 8.00
Heliotropium—Conformity of Human Will to Divine. *Drexelius* 13.00
Charity for the Suffering Souls. *Fr. John Nageleisen* 16.50
Devotion to the Sacred Heart of Jesus. *Verheylezoon* 15.00
Who Is Padre Pio? *Radio Replies Press* 2.00
Child's Bible History. *Knecht* 4.00
The Stigmata and Modern Science. *Fr. Charles Carty* 1.50
The Life of Christ. 4 Vols. H.B. *Anne C. Emmerich* 60.00
St. Anthony—The Wonder Worker of Padua. *Stoddard* 5.00
The Precious Blood. *Fr. Faber* 13.50
The Holy Shroud & Four Visions. *Fr. O'Connell* 2.00
Clean Love in Courtship. *Fr. Lawrence Lovasik* 2.50
The Prophecies of St. Malachy. *Peter Bander.* 7.00
St. Martin de Porres. *Giuliana Cavallini* 12.50
The Secret of the Rosary. *St. Louis De Montfort* 3.00
The History of Antichrist. *Rev. P. Huchede* 4.00
St. Catherine of Siena. *Alice Curtayne* 13.50
Where We Got the Bible. *Fr. Henry Graham* 6.00
Hidden Treasure—Holy Mass. *St. Leonard* 5.00
Imitation of the Sacred Heart of Jesus. *Fr. Arnoudt* 15.00
The Life & Glories of St. Joseph. *Edward Thompson* 15.00
Père Lamy. *Biver.* 10.00
Humility of Heart. *Fr. Cajetan da Bergamo* 8.50
The Curé D'Ars. *Abbé Francis Trochu* 21.50

At your Bookdealer or direct from the Publisher.
Call Toll-Free 1-800-437-5876.

Prices subject to change.

.

EDUCATIONAL PROGRAMS AND SPECIAL EDUCATION

ISSUES, CHALLENGES, AND PERSPECTIVES

EDUCATION IN A COMPETITIVE AND GLOBALIZING WORLD

Additional books in this series can be found on Nova's website under the Series tab.

Additional E-books in this series can be found on Nova's website under the E-book tab.

EDUCATION IN A COMPETITIVE AND GLOBALIZING WORLD

EDUCATIONAL PROGRAMS AND SPECIAL EDUCATION

ISSUES, CHALLENGES, AND PERSPECTIVES

SASHA DZIUK
EDITOR

New York

LIBRARY OF CONGRESS CATALOGING-IN-PUBLICATION DATA

ISBN: 978-1-62417-256-4

Published by Nova Science Publishers, Inc. † New York

CONTENTS

Preface   **vii**

Chapter 1   Parental Involvement and Participation of
Monolingual and Bilingual Latino Families
during Individual Education Program Meetings   **1**
Rosalinda Larios and Andrea Zetlin

Chapter 2   Self-concept Enhancement Programs:
Issues, Challenges, and New Perspectives   **29**
*Alexander Seeshing Yeung, Rhonda G. Craven
and A. Katrin Arens*

Chapter 3   Health Training Programmes   **55**
*Caroline Opolski Medeiros,
Terezinha Opolski Medeiros
and Suzi Barletto Cavalli*

Chapter 4   Transforming Teacher Preparation Programs
to Meet the Needs of All Learners   **73**
*Amy Rogers, Rachel Hickoff-Cresko
and Marisa Macy*

Chapter 5   Social-Sexual Education for Mature Students
with Mild Intellectual Disabilities: A Practical
Model for Teachers   **89**
*Iris Manor-Binyamini, Schreiber-Divon Michal
and Stein Racheli*

Index   **105**

PREFACE

In this book, the authors discuss Special Education standards, teaching practices and parent expectations along with Educational Program issues and challenges. Topics discussed in this compilation include transforming teacher preparation programs to meet the needs of all learners; parental involvement and participation of monolingual and bilingual Latino families during individual educational program meetings; self-concept enhancement programs; health training programs; and social-sexual education for mature students with mild intellectual disabilities.

Chapter 1 – Various obstacles and cultural differences hinder the participation levels of Spanish speaking parents during the IEP process. Schools attempt to address the needs of all the students they serve, however parents may not always feel welcomed to openly participate. Factors such as language used during the IEP meeting and the parents' level of acculturation may keep parents from being effective members of the multidisciplinary team. While there are studies that look at parental involvement in other areas of special education or education as a whole, there are limited studies that address these factors within the IEP meeting. Through the analysis of eight case studies, this chapter addresses how parents perceive the IEP meeting and the relationship between acculturation and participation. In addition, differences between levels of participation of monolingual and bilingual Spanish speaking families will be discussed. Finally, recommendations are provided for school personnel to consider when working with culturally and linguistically diverse parents.

Chapter 2 – Educators and researchers attempt to design and implement successful intervention programs to enhance students' academic motivation and self-concept as important non-cognitive determinants of student achievement and long-term gains. Nevertheless, despite the goodwill and effort, such programs are often faced with issues and challenges. In this chapter, we first discuss theories related to such intervention programs. Then we discuss and attempt to address the issues, challenges, and limitations of such programs by illustrating them with examples of evidence-based intervention programs we have conducted in various educational areas including: language, mathematics, cooperative learning, peer support, and anti-bullying. The discussions and illustrations are based on recent advances in self-concept and motivation theory and research. Theory, such as the reciprocal effects model demonstrating the mutually reinforcing relations between academic self-concept and academic achievement, provides the opportunity for designing a dual approach with attention to both self-concept and achievement in the program. The research on internally focused and attributional feedback mechanisms provides the potential of reinforcing self-concept for long-term positive gains. Nevertheless, research findings indicating a general pattern of decrease in self-concept over time constitute a prevalent issue and a challenge to any intervention that attempts to facilitate a significant and noticeable increase. Recent emphasis on the twofold multidimensional structure of academic self-concept implying that intervention programs should target a specific domain and should address both the cognitive and affective components of self-concept further complicates the design and implementation of programs. A further challenge is the occurrence of diffusion effects that might mask the difference between the experimental (target) group and the control group, thus undermining the effectiveness of the intervention. Other issues include: students' cognitive abilities, age, frame of references, and differential gender perceptions. These issues and challenges are illustrated in the light of our previously conducted self-concept enhancement programs in educational settings.

Chapter 3 – This chapter will address the importance and main objectives in the field of health training programs. Initially the methodologies for health educational programs will be discussed. We will also discuss the educational programs with focus on the improvement of the health and the knowledge of the population. The results of training programs will be discussed in this chapter, considering population's behavioral and attitudinal changes. The teaching resources used in training programs may influence the final result of this activity, therefore, recommendations will be presented for the choice of resources to be used in courses. All recommendation and discussion will be made considering the population of programs. Furthermore, the topics discussed will also contribute to improve the health training programs that focus on the population, which constantly needs to learn more about different aspects and concepts in health. Also, the information submitted in the chapter could be used in effective educational programs for health professionals, strengthening its technical capability.

Chapter 4 – Due to national and state policy changes and compliance with No Child Left Behind (NCLB) and Individuals with Disabilities Education Improvement Act (IDEIA), children with special needs are taught in inclusive classrooms. Until recent years, general education teachers were not prepared to instruct students with special needs. Additionally, special education teachers were not fully aware of the general education curriculum. In order to truly meet the diverse needs of all children and prepare teachers to teach all learners, teacher preparation programs need to address thorough and appropriate special education inclusive teaching practices and offer instruction in co-teaching paradigms. This article will discuss current trends in licensing bodies to offer more specified special education teacher preparation and address co-teaching models. Discourse will advance the value of teacher education programs to provide deeper and more relevant instruction and offer field experiences that will prepare teachers who are more skilled and capable of helping all learners reach higher levels of achievement.

Chapter 5 – Children with disabilities are 3.4 times more likely to be sexually abused than their non-disabled peers. Moreover, the abuse will likely be committed by a close figure they know and trust, such as a parent, sibling, teacher, or day-care provider. Despite these alarming data, the issue of social-sexual education for students with intellectual disabilities is very rarely discussed in the literature, and even less is known about practical models for teaching the subject. This chapter explores the reasons which make the teaching of social-sexual education for students with disabilities such a sensitive and complex topic. There is clearly a gap between the importance of the subject and the ability of teachers and other professionals to teach it in class. An innovative practical model focusing on mature students is presented, together with a demo teaching class designed according to the model. This tested model was developed in an Israeli special education school for adolescent and adult students with mild intellectual disabilities. The model was examined using the methodology of collaborative-ethnographic action research by means of conducting interviews, videotaping lessons, and documenting meetings over a five-year period. The model should make a significant contribution to all teachers/professionals who work in special education schools and find themselves struggling with this issue.

In: Educational Programs and Special Education   ISBN: 978-1-62417-256-4
Editor: Sasha Dziuk   © 2013 Nova Science Publishers, Inc.

Chapter 1

PARENTAL INVOLVEMENT AND PARTICIPATION OF MONOLINGUAL AND BILINGUAL LATINO FAMILIES DURING INDIVIDUAL EDUCATION PROGRAM MEETINGS

Rosalinda Larios and Andrea Zetlin

California State University, Los Angeles,
Charter College of Education, Los Angeles, CA, US

ABSTRACT

Various obstacles and cultural differences hinder the participation levels of Spanish speaking parents during the IEP process. Schools attempt to address the needs of all the students they serve, however parents may not always feel welcomed to openly participate. Factors such as language used during the IEP meeting and the parents' level of acculturation may keep parents from being effective members of the multidisciplinary team. While there are studies that look at parental involvement in other areas of special education or education as a whole, there are limited studies that address these factors within the IEP meeting. Through the analysis of eight case studies, this chapter addresses how parents perceive the IEP meeting and the relationship between acculturation and participation. In addition, differences between levels of participation of monolingual and bilingual Spanish speaking families will be discussed. Finally, recommendations are provided for school personnel to consider when working with culturally and linguistically diverse parents.

INTRODUCTION

Public Law 94-142

In 1975, Congress enacted Public Law 94-142, the Education for All Handicapped Children Act (PL 94-142). In 1990, it was amended as the Individuals with Disability Education Act (IDEA). According to the United States Department of Education (1997), PL 94-142 serves four purposes: (a) to assure that all children with disabilities have access to a free appropriate public education (FAPE) in the least restrictive environment (LRE), (b) that the rights of children with disabilities and their parents rights are protected, (c) to aid States and local agencies in providing education to all children with disabilities, (d) to assess and assure the effectiveness of efforts to educate all children with disabilities. IDEA has since been amended in 1997 and 2004.

Individual Education Program

The Individual Education Program (IEP) is the primary component of Part B of IDEA. The IEP is a written academic plan that establishes annual goals and benchmarks based on the child's academic and prevocational needs. The IEP is prepared by the IEP team which is comprised of a multidisciplinary group of individuals who work directly with the student that is receiving services. The multidisciplinary team typically consists of the child's parent or legal guardian, a general education teacher, a special education teacher, a school psychologist, an administrator, a specialist of any educational related service, and anyone who the family feels should be there. In an initial or triennial evaluation, the child's skills are assessed using a battery of assessments and rating scales administered by members of the team prior to the IEP meeting. The team does this to gain a better insight into the current levels of performance of the child and determine their areas of need. The team also determines the least restrictive environment (LRE) appropriate for the student. The LRE is a requirement of IDEA which ensures that the child receives his or her education, to the fullest extent possible, and with non-disabled peers. Under IDEA, the IEP team must meet periodically to review the child's progress. The law requires the team to meet at least once a year to determine whether the annual goals are being achieved and revise the IEP as appropriate.

Parental Involvement and Individual Education Program Meetings

Part B of IDEA mandates that parents should be active in all aspects of educational programming for students who receive special education services (Garriott, Wandry, and Snyder, 2000; Pruitt, Wandry, and Hollums, 1998). In 2008, Fish conducted a study to investigate how 51 parents of children who receive special education services perceive the IEP meeting as well as their perceptions of how much educators value their opinions and input. Fish found that of the parents surveyed, most either agreed or strongly agreed that their involvement enhanced the IEP meetings, and that their input influenced the outcome of the meeting (Fish, 2008). His findings supported previous research on parents' views of the IEP meeting experience, perceptions of their knowledge level, as well as the educators' knowledge of the IEP process (see Gariott et al., 2000; Salembier and Furney, 1997; Vaughn et al., 1988; and Spann, Kohler, and Soenksen, 2003). Fish concluded that it is important for educators to build positive relationships with parents during IEP meetings. By creating a positive relationship, educators prevent adversarial and intimidating experiences for the families of children who are receiving special education services. Interestingly, Fish noted that the parents in his study, 80% of whom were white, had a good grasp of the IEP process and sufficient knowledge of the special education law because they were actively involved with community organizations and supported by a family service agency (p. 13).

Culturally Linguistic Diverse (CLD) Parental Perceptions of Special Education

The significance of the participation and input of all parents –mainstream and CLD - cannot be understated (Salas, 2004). Awareness and understanding of the role of participants' cultural background can influence the effectiveness of the IEP team (Dabkowski, 2006). The attitude and beliefs of the school personnel can determine how a parent is accepted as a member of the team

(Briggs, 1997; Dabkowski, 2006). While schools generally attempt to address the needs of all the students they serve, parents may not always feel welcomed or comfortable to openly participate in the IEP process. Factors such as language used during the IEP process, the scheduling of the meetings, and the various levels of acculturation expected, keep parents from being effective members of the multidisciplinary team. Parents may remain silent when they attend the IEP meeting as an act of deference to authority, compliance, or disapproval (Kalyanpur and Harry, 1999; Harry, 1992; Harry, Allen, and McLaughlin, 1995). In some instances, low participation levels and other issues of culture and language differences may be perceived by IEP team members as hindrances in the flow of communication during the IEP meeting.

Harry (1992) reviewed studies pertaining to parental involvement of culturally and linguistically diverse families in special education programs and reported that CLD parents are being less involved and informed than mainstream parents (Bennett, 1988; Chan, 1986; Connery, 1987; Figler, 1981; Leung, 1988; Lowry, 1983; Lynch and Stein, 1987; Marion, 1979, 1980a; Sharp, 1983; Smith and Ryan, 1982; Tran, 1982). She identified eight factors that contribute to less involvement and participation in special education by CLD families. These include:

(1) Lower levels of involvement than White counterparts,
(2) Less awareness of special education procedures, rights, and available services,
(3) An expressed sense of isolation and helplessness,
(4) Low self- confidence in interaction with professionals,
(5) Stressful life circumstances that overwhelm parents,
(6) Need for logistical supports such as transportation, childcare, and respite,
(7) Culturally based assumptions of noninterference on the part of parents in school matters, and
(8) Professionals' implicit or explicit discouragement of parents' participation in the special education process (p. 100).

A deficit is formed when parents, whether monolingual Spanish or bilingual, may not be able to communicate thoughts, ideas, or concerns as articulately as the professionals involved. Genuine participation includes *all* members of the IEP team. "The IDEA is very specific on the role of the parent participation in special education and it does not omit parents who are culturally and linguistically diverse" (Salas, 2004, p. 191). In other words, although "Parent participation in IEP meetings is mandated by law" (Lo, 2008, p. 25), this is not always the case and so, some parents feel disconnected from this formal process.

Intimidation can also be created through this legal process--the gaps where CLD parents feel they cannot compete with the level of knowledge of the IEP process that the professionals bring to the meeting. When some parents feel that the playing field is not level, they naturally begin to feel excluded from the IEP process. The language used in IEP meetings is filled with legal jargon and appears "designed to exclude and not include" those who do not naturally speak nor utilize such vocabulary on a daily bases (Salas, 2004, p. 185). Hardin, Mereoiu, Hung, and Roach-Scott's (2009) study confirms that parents are intimidated and feel confused at IEP meetings. All their participants expressed anxiety about "the context of language barriers and shortage of interpreters" (p 99). Professionals also expressed concern about the verbiage used at such meetings. Not only are there language barriers but level of vocabulary acquisition that challenge parents and " ...they [parents] know a little amount of English but when you get into an IEP, the language is very specific and technical..." which lead to meetings that can be very emotional and overwhelming to parents (Hardin, et al, 2009).

Instead, IEP members should use a user-friendly dialog that consists of less technical jargon, and/or an explanation of what such words mean. By doing so, parents can share(take) a more intimate (active) role in the process and contribute a deeper understanding of their child's strengths and needs. Parents have many areas of strength that can contribute to a deeper awareness into their children's lives that can help schools and educators have a better insight to the child's needs (Kalyanpur and Harry, 1999; Lo, 2008; Orozco, 2008).

Acculturation and Parental Participation

When parents feel a separation between their role in their child's academic life and their role as an advocate in their child's IEP meeting, they continue to work through the process disenfranchised. Many parents are unaware that they have legal rights that are equal to that of administrators and educational professionals (Martin, Marshall, and Sale, 2004). These rights have nothing to do with a person's gender, language, or "immutable characteristics" that some professionals may perceive as factors related to who are entitled to certain rights (Kalyanpur and Harry, 1999; Friedman, 1996). However, a parent's level of acculturation comes into play when participating in the IEP.

The few studies that have researched parental participation report that it is parents' disenchantment, negative experiences, and direct disrespect from the school and professionals that cause the disconnect between school and home (e.g., Hughes, Valle-Riestra, and Arguellas, 2002; Salas, 2004; Fish; 2006; Lo, 2008). According to Salas (2004), there was very high dissatisfaction of IEP meetings from Mexican American parents' which easily lends itself to the continuous decrease in parent participation. In Lo's (2008) study, a Chinese parent shared that she found meetings were anxiety filled and overwhelming, because "that there was often too much information to digest" (p. 24).

When parents choose to exclude themselves from the IEP process or involvement with their child's school, the perception is that minority parents place little to no value on their child's academics and success when in fact it may be due to a growing mistrust. Parents feel lost in the bureaucracy, overwhelmed with expectations of them in their new country, and have negative perceptions of administrators as a whole that fuels their apprehension to continue trying to connect with their child's school (De Gaetano, Williams, and Volk, 1998; Inger, 1992; Nicolau and Ramos, 1990; De Gaetano, 2007). It can also be that CLD parents give such high regard to schools and teachers that they would not dare challenge, nor question the authority of those who they feel may be the best decision makers in their child's academic life (Lo, 2008). In other words, parents may feel muted if they are unfamiliar with the system of education in their new country or in a country they still do not feel a sense of acculturation.

Community Cultural Wealth in the IEP Process

Harry (1999) argues that because parents are cast in the role of "temporary members," during IEP meetings, the cultural capital that would enable them to negotiate participation in this pattern of discourse is not apparent. By cultural capital, she is referring to the social and cultural resources of families as members of society (Lareau, 1987). Therefore, the formal meeting becomes yet another forum for compliance with the law rather than "communication" in the full meaning of the term, and the absence of meaning in parent participation is startling (p. 72). Kozoleski et. al (2008) suggests that families' judgments, observations, and perspectives are subordinated to professional knowledge building and judgment. Families, in particular CLD families, are at a disadvantage by those perspectives. First, professionals' values are majority-based. Secondly, families are led to believe and made to feel that the professionals' judgment is better and more accurate during IEP's because the professionals' values may differ from the families' views on the communal family lifestyle (Kalyanpur andHarry, 2004). Many special education programs reflect the notion that beneficial family environments are the ones that adopt mainstream American values and norms (Laosa, 1983; Ramirez and Cox, 1980; Harry, 1992).

Yosso's (2006) model of Community Cultural Wealth (CCW) is a response to French social theorist Pierre Bourdieu's notion of cultural capital. Bourdieu argues that schools attempt to reproduce the current social class system by valuing the dominant culture as better than the culture and values of CLD families. Cultural capital does not demonstrate all of the values, attributes, and efforts that CLD families bring into the IEP process. CCW is an asset for working to lower class families and CLD families to help them navigate a school system that was not designed to meet their needs. Through CCW which focuses more specifically on six tenets of cultural capital (i.e., aspirational, linguistic, navigational, social, familial, and resistance capital), many functions and needs for succeeding in the school system are met, keeping the community alive and striving for equality and social justice. Therefore, CLD families can be recognized for their efforts which may not otherwise be taken into account.

In sum, multidisciplinary teams may unintentionally fall into deficit thinking when interacting with Spanish speaking families. Whether the outcome of such thinking is that (a) families with higher levels of acculturation and cultural capital are more able to provide input or be seen as equal team members during the IEP meeting or (b) families without cultural capital and less acculturation are more likely to be unintentionally excluded from the IEP process even though they are physically present needs to be investigated. Spanish speaking parents may perceive the IEP process as not being a vital part of their ability to move through social institutions that were not created with them in mind and therefore render them unequipped to be active participants in the IEP process. Other bilingual families may feel that the process is part of their ability to navigate the social institution, and will therefore utilize resistance to challenge the IEP process. Specifically this study was designed to examine: (1) How do monolingual (Spanish) and bilingual families who attend the IEP meeting perceive the process and the actual meeting?; (2) Is their level of inclusion or exclusion during the meeting a result of their level of acculturation?; and (3) How can cultural wealth empower CLD families to plan for and navigate an IEP meeting? The study was intended to describe the gaps and or misunderstandings that may currently exist when including CLD families in the IEP process and provide school personnel ways to better communicate with Latino families to serve the students' needs.

METHODOLOGY

This comparative qualitative study was conducted at two school sites in a small Southern California school district comprised of mostly Latino students. At the first school site, there were 561 students during the 2009-10 school year. Sixty five percent of the student population was socioeconomically disadvantaged, 22% were English learners, 12% were students with disabilities, and 77% were Latino. The special education program consisted of two full time education specialists, and a speech language pathologist and school psychologist on site part time. One education specialist worked with special day class (SDC) and resource students in kindergarten thru third grade and had 21 students on her caseload. The second education specialist worked with nine resource students providing push-in and pull-out services collaboratively with general education teachers in fourth grade and fifth grade.

There were 405 students at the second site during the 2009-10 school year. Seventy four percent of the student population was socioeconomically disadvantaged, 28% were English learners, 10% were students with disabilities, and 82% were Hispanic or Latino. The special education program consisted of two education specialists and one part time speech language pathologist and one part time school psychologist. One education specialist worked with SDC and resource students in kindergarten thru third grade and had 12 students on her caseload. The second education specialist was on site part time and had 16 students on her caseload. The students worked in the general education class and were pulled out to work on individual skills three days per week when the education specialist was on site.

Participants Characteristics

The study sample included two participants from each linguistic group from each school: four monolingual (Spanish speaking) and four bilingual (Spanish/English speaking) families who had a child receiving services from the special education department. The eight participants were parents of students. (See Table 1).

Although all the families who participated in the study were Spanish speaking, their level of acculturation varied. Acculturation as defined by Salvia, Ysseldyke, and Bolt (2007) is a matter of experiential background rather than of gender, skin color, race, or ethnic background. Kalyapur and Harry (1992) explained the process of acculturation as being introduced to a new system and gradually accommodating to it. They found that at any given time one's acculturation might be on any point on a spectrum. Harry (1992) described that the process of acculturation as "the intermingling of cultures in response to contact - a process of modifying one's original 'belief, styles of being and adapting' to those of another culture (p. 13)." In this study, the level of acculturation was measured through language preference and the amount of schooling in the United States. Table 2 provides descriptions of the participants' language preferences and educational levels. This was important for this study because although all of the participants are Latinos, they vary in their experiences with the schooling system and familiarity with the mainstream social structure of the United States.

PROCEDURE

With the support of the site administrator, school psychologist and speech and language pathologist, eight families were identified whose child was scheduled for an upcoming IEP meeting for initial or annual evaluation. Each family was interviewed by the first author before the IEP meeting. Participants were recorded using an audio recorder during the interviews to ensure accuracy. Participants were asked a series of semi-structured and unstructured questions to gain insight into each of the participant's backgrounds, thoughts, and perceptions of the IEP process.

At the actual IEP meeting, the first author attended as a nonparticipant observer. She did not speak nor participate in the meeting other than as a researcher. During the IEP, she completed an observation checklist, which assessed the roles that the parents played, any team rituals (i.e. who spoke when, how members were addressed, and what the seating arrangements were), how the meeting environment influenced the parents' comfort level, and if the language spoken during the meeting resulted in a mutual understanding for the entire team. In addition, she took detailed notes of questions, concerns, or opinions voiced by the families. (See Appendix A).

Table 1. Participant Characteristics

Child's Name	Gender of Participant(s)/ relationship to child	Language Preference	Age/Grade of child	Years in Special Education
Jorge Lara-Garcia	Female, mother	Spanish	10 years old, 5th grade	Two years
Marisol Solis	Female, mother	Spanish	8 years old, 3rd grade	Initial
Andrew Acosta-Hernandez	Female, mother	Spanish, limited English	8 years old, 3rd grade	Initial
Bertha Almanza	Female, mother	English	8 years old, 3rd grade	One
Alfonso Panduro-Mendez	Female, mother	Spanish	5 years old, Kindergarten	Initial
Isabel Acosta	Female, mother	English	8 years old, 3rd grade	One
Manuel "Manny" Andrade	Female, mother Male, father	Spanish English	7 years old, 3rd grade	Four
Tonantzin Rodriguez	Female, mother	English	8 years old, 3rd grade	One

Following the IEP meeting, the first author conducted a post-interview with the family approximately one day after the meeting. Parents were asked another series of semi-structured and unstructured questions. The purpose of the pre and post interviews was to obtain a vivid description of the families' perception for the IEP process.

DATA ANALYSIS

Data from all sources formed the basis for the development of eight descriptive individual case studies. Responses to questions asked during the pre and post meeting interviews, meeting notes, and student reports for each of the eight families were included in the case study descriptions. All the audio recordings from the interviews were transcribed verbatim and relevant information was included in each case study. The eight case studies were initially compared to identify variations based on two organizing variables: (a) family familiarity with the IEP and (b) parents input during the IEP and post-meeting interview. Miles and Huberman (1994) suggested, "cross-case construct tables are an excellent way to understand a core concept because the way the variable plays out in different contexts illuminates its essential nature" (p. 184).

Table 2. Level of Acculturation

Most Unacculturated / Spanish Only / No Formal US education	Acculturated / Bilingual / High School or College	Assimilated / Primarily English / High School or College
Jorge: Mrs. Garcia only speaks Spanish, multiple family home, the family has lived in Mexico within the last four years. She completed secondary school in Mexico (the equivalent of ninth grade in the United States).	Andrew: Ms. Hernandez speaks English and Spanish, although she prefers Spanish. Ms. Hernandez graduated from U.S. high school and has a high school diploma.	Bertha: Ms. Almanza provided conflicting information regarding the languages spoken at home. In the pre-meeting interview she shared that the family only spoke English at home. Although according to Ms. Almanza she does not speak Spanish at home Ms. Almanza has only completed up to the 11th grade.
Alfonso: Mrs. Mendez only speaks Spanish, she reported that she is trying to make sense of the "American" culture, and that her husband would like to visit Mexico this summer.	Manny: per Mr. Andrade, the family speaks English and Spanish at home. However, Mrs. Andrade only speaks Spanish. Mr. and Mrs. Andrade are U.S. high school graduates.	Isabel: Mrs. Lopez reported that the family only speaks English at her ex-husband's house and both Spanish and English at her mother's house. She has taken some classes at a community college and her brother has taken classes at the university.
Marisol: Mrs. Solis reported that the family only speaks Spanish at home. Mrs. Solis finished secondary school in Mexico (the equivalent of ninth grade in the United States).		Tonantzin: Mrs. Rodriguez reported that the family speaks English at home and Spanish with her mother. Both of Tonantzin's parents have some college, but have not completed their AA.

Table 3. Families Familiarity with the IEP

Misinformed	No Knowledge	Limited Knowledge	Knowledgeable
Jorge: Mrs. Garcia believes that an IEP helps with homework and pronunciation.	Alfonso: Mrs. Mendez did not know what an IEP was, but thought it's a time to talk about her son's inability to speak and understand the material in his class.	Andrew: Ms. Hernandez reported more or less what an IEP was. She feels that in an IEP the district should explain themselves and try to help people.	Manny: Mr. Andrade feels, they should explain how Manny has shown growth or regression and how his behavior is. Then discuss what they will do the following year to improve or review what will benefit him. Mrs. Andrade agreed.
Bertha: Ms. Almanza feels that an IEP is a "follow up" about her semester progress.	Isabel: Mrs. Lopez reported that she did not know what an IEP was.	Tonantzin: Mrs. Rodriguez did not know what an IEP was, but asked what it was and that it be explained. She was asked if she knew what the process was and she replied, "they explained it at the last meeting (the first one)".	Bertha: Ms. Almanza feels that an IEP is a follow up about her whole semester.
	Marisol: Mrs. Solis did not know what an IEP was and had no idea what should happen at the IEP meeting.		

Two cross case tables were developed to contrast each family's level of awareness with the IEP and experiences with and perception of the IEP meeting (see tables 3 and 4). Miles and Huberman (1994) refer to this process as meta-matrices analysis, which involves the assembling of master charts with descriptive data from each of several cases in a standard format. These tables served as the conceptual framework to discuss the variations and emerging themes.

FINDINGS

The findings of this study are discussed in three themes. The first theme is an analysis of how familiar the families were with the IEP process and what they knew before the actual meeting. The second theme examines the parents' level of participation in relation to their level of satisfaction. The third theme connects how their level of acculturation impacted their familiarity with the process as well as their overall participation at the meeting.

Familiarity/Knowledge of an IEP

The families in this study expressed various levels of understanding the IEP process. All of the participants were asked if they knew what an IEP was and if they knew what services were available through special education. Through their responses, the participants were categorized into four groups (a) misinformed, (b) no knowledge, (c) limited knowledge, and (d) knowledgeable. The four groups were determined by the type of responses given during the pre meeting interview as well as their response to knowing what an IEP is.

Of the eight families none of their responses were the same. Each participant had their own idea of what happens in the IEP and two of the three families who were going to participate in initial meetings did not even attempt to answer the question. Harry (1992) proposed two levels that could explain parent's lack of awareness and information. The first level is that parents had not participated in placement meetings. The second was the lack of understanding that the parents had about how special education works (p. 174).

All the families in this study were physically present at the meetings. Regardless of whether the meeting was for initial or annual evaluation, they were all offered a copy of their parent rights at the start of the meeting. Records indicated that those parents attending their child's annual evaluation had been present at the initial placement meeting for their son or daughter. It does not appear that the first level that Harry (1992) presented was the case for these parents. The second level described by Harry as "an absence of meaning" (p. 177) was more apparent within this study.

Misinformed. Two parents, Mrs. Garcia and Ms. Almanza, were misinformed about the purpose of an IEP meeting. Mrs. Garcia felt that it was about having her son receive assistance with homework and pronunciation.

Table 4. Parents Input during the IEP and Post Meeting Interview

Child's Name	Asked for Clarification/ Expressed Concern	Influenced Decisions or Goals	Parent(s) were satisfied with outcome	Questions and Concerns answered
Jorge	Mrs. Garcia told the team that Jorge's father was upset with Jorge's grades. Mrs. Garcia brought up Jorge's handwriting and that Jorge is very distracted in the back of the room.	The outcome was that the classroom teacher would only send home good grades from quizzes and tests. Jorge will not be required to write in cursive and he would be moved to the front of the room.	Yes	Yes
Marisol	Mrs. Solis told the team that she feels Marisol was inadequately prepared in preschool. She asked if her learning two languages might be slowing her down.	The principal and classroom teacher told her preschool is not required. The school psychologist reported scores from assessments administered in both languages.	Yes, if it helps her daughter	Yes
Andrew	Ms. Hernandez asked what phonemic awareness is. She asked what was wrong with his writing sample and if asking him comprehension questions in Spanish might be slowing him down. She asked what a specific learning disability was.	The team explained what phonemic awareness was. They said they would give her a writing rubric to help him with writing. The school psychologist answered her question about language showing the assessment scores from both languages.	Yes, with hesitation. She said that she will also monitor his progress at home and ask the school how he is doing. She agreed to the placement after a site visit.	Yes
Bertha	Ms. Almanza asked if language concerns were related to her speaking Spanish.	The speech and language pathologist told her that she did not feel it was and that is why they wanted to further assess Bertha.	Yes, now she knew her weaknesses and strengths.	Yes

Child's Name	Asked for Clarification/ Expressed Concern	Influenced Decisions or Goals	Parent(s) were satisfied with outcome	Questions and Concerns answered
Manny	Mr. Andrade asked if teeth had to do with Manny's speech concerns.	The speech pathologist answered his question, saying they did not.	Yes	Yes, both parents were very happy with the meeting and felt better about this team than the previous one.

Ms. Almanza felt noted during the pre-meeting interview, that the meeting was a follow-up to review her daughter's semester progress. Both were misinformed about what special education is and what services are provided. While special education can include speech and language services, Jorge was not receiving services from the speech and language pathologist for articulation. In addition, Mrs. Garcia believed that he was getting support with his homework. What Mrs. Garcia did not understand was that Jorge was receiving specialized instruction for 90 minutes outside of his regular classroom three times per week.

No Knowledge. Alfonso and Marisol's mothers were new to the IEP process and this was the initial meeting for their child. Neither of these mothers knew what an IEP was, however, based on their child's needs at home they had an idea of how they wanted their child to be supported by the school. They both stated they wanted the best for their child. Mrs. Mendez had a sense of understanding why her son was being referred to special education and knew that they were going to discuss his lack of progress as well as how they could all help him. Mrs. Solis on the other hand, was far more hesitant to meet with the school and felt that it would be better to retain Marisol than to put her in special education.

Limited Knowledge. Mrs. Lopez, Isabel's mother also said that she did not know what an IEP was both on the phone during the initial contact and during the pre meeting interview. Nonetheless, she appeared very comfortable going into the meeting. After the annual meeting Mrs. Lopez still said that she did know what an IEP was but she saw how special education was benefiting her daughter. Even though she was not clear about the process she did not think it was anything for her to worry about.

Ms. Hernandez and Mrs. Rodriguez both had a limited sense of what an IEP was during the pre meeting. Ms. Hernandez said she was familiar with the process from family members. Mrs. Rodriguez said she did not know what an IEP was initially, but without hesitation asked the interviewer what it was. After the interviewer told her what it was she agreed and said that was what she had been told the previous year. Mrs. Rodriguez was the only participant that asked for an explanation. Ms. Hernandez was very vague in her explanation, but knew that an IEP should help.

Knowledgeable. Manny's parents were able to provide the most accurate description of what an IEP is. They were very clear in their explanation and provided an example of how the IEP team can determine the parent's comfort level during a meeting. After the interview, Mrs. Andrade shared that she has taken classes offered in the community and has learned how to make sense of an IEP.

Level of Participation in Relation to Parent Satisfaction

All of the families in the study participated in the IEP process for their child by their mere attendance. The literature has found that although parents are at the IEP meeting they are not necessarily active participants, sitting in silence or not fully understanding what is happening. For this study the level of participation was examined through the questions and concerns initiated by the parents as well as any clarification they may have asked for during the meeting. Table 4 summarizes parents' input during their meeting as well as their responses during the post meeting interview.

Parental Concerns Related to Determining Eligibility. Salvia, Ysseldyke, and Bolt (2007) reported that in many states with substantial Spanish-speaking populations, students are tested in English, even if it is not their primary language. Diana v. State Board of Education (1970) ruled that intelligence testing of students needed to be in their primary language. Harry, Klingner, and Cramer (2007) argue that although intelligent tests include a verbal and visual/performance components, some cross-cultural research has found that there is a discrepancy between peoples' ways of thinking and mannerisms depending on their cultural background, which can alter the validity of the assessment (p. 10).

During three of the eight meetings the parents expressed concerns about the role that language may have played in the team's decision to assess or determine goals. Ms. Almanza asked the team whether the fact that her daughter was learning two languages – Spanish at home and English at school - might be slowing down her progress in the classroom. Ms. Hernandez told the team that she and her son would often read in English and answer the questions in Spanish. She wanted to know if that was the reason he was struggling and asked if his areas of concern were not related to his bilingualism. Ms. Solis asked if her daughter's language and learning needs were possibly related to her trying to make sense of what was being said in Spanish.

Two of the three parents who asked if language was considered, were attending initial IEP meetings to determine eligibility. The school had asked the third parent if they could re-evaluate her daughter completing a full psycho-educational evaluation. The questions raised by these parents were very appropriate, considering that the team was determining if the children qualified for services. Prior to this school year, the school district used non-verbal assessments to evaluate children who were Spanish speakers. This particular school psychologist assessed children in both English and Spanish. At all three initial meetings that the first author observed, the school psychologist included an assessment that looked at the child's ability to respond first in English then in Spanish if the response was incorrect. The school psychologist described the procedures and assured that her findings were valid. Her explanation was very thorough and parents did not express concerns with language again.

Parents Response to Interventions. Beekman (2005, as cited in Hoover et. al. 2008) discussed the significance of IDEA (2004) which emphasized early intervention services. IDEA allows school districts to allocate up to 15 percent of special education funds to provide early intervention services to students at risk academically or behaviorally (p.115). The school district where the study was conducted implements Student Study Team (SST) reviews and Response to Intervention (RTI) district wide. Marisol, Andrew, and Alfonso had all been reviewed at an SST meeting prior to being referred for a full psycho-educational evaluation. As a result of being part of the SST process, these parents had more background information about their child's academic performance and therefore were able to contribute to the IEP meeting.

Mrs. Solis, Mrs. Mendez, and Ms. Hernandez were aware of their child's academic present levels of performance. In their attempt to keep their child from having to receive special education services, Mrs. Solis and Ms. Hernandez brought up, more than once during the meeting, what they had done at home to help their child academically. Mrs. Mendez, on the other hand, was not trying to make a case why her son would not benefit from special education.

At Isabel's annual meeting, the IEP team discussed the pull out services she was receiving in addition to the interventions she was participating in at school. The team created a warm environment by providing refreshments during the IEP. Although, Mrs. Lopez did not verbally participate in the conversation, she nodded her head in agreement with the conversation between the principal, school psychologist, classroom teacher, and education specialist. Interventions were noted and documented because Isabel had still not demonstrated growth and was falling further behind in her regular education classroom. The team informed Mrs. Lopez that they recommended a change of placement to a more restrictive placement, a special day class. Mrs. Lopez appeared to be in agreement with what was being said and did not question what the team proposed. After the meeting, Mrs. Lopez said that she was satisfied with the meeting.

RTI provided the parents with background into the discussion as it pertained to their child's academic progress. Therefore, during the IEP meeting, when the education specialist reported on the academic findings, the parents were most actively involved. They closely looked at work samples, provided observations of their child at home, and raised questions or concerns. However, when the school psychologist gave her report, the parents were very quiet and passive. None of parents asked questions until the recommendations were given. The recommendations were the most dramatic part of the process in all three initial placement meetings.

Parent Satisfaction. All three mothers who had initial meetings were concerned about what would happen to their child and where they would go to school. During the pre meeting interviews with the mothers, it was clear that they were not sure of what to expect in the IEP meeting. Therefore, although they knew their child's current levels of performance, they were not clear on how special education would help the child. In fact, Ms. Hernandez had been under the impression that they wanted to move Andrew to another school. All three mothers agreed to the placement and said they were satisfied with the outcome of the meeting because they hoped it was in the best interest of their child.

All of the participants expressed that they were satisfied with the IEP meeting and team's decisions. Mr. and Mrs. Andrade did not raise any concerns during the meeting. After the meeting Mrs. Rodriguez reported that even though the meeting was very brief she felt that her questions were answered and she has been able to see growth with her daughter's speech. She said that she is very happy with the district and knows that everyone is doing everything they can for Tonantzin. As the notes were reviewed, there was one comment made by Mrs. Rodriguez that was overlooked by the team. She told the team that Tonantzin shows signs of anxiety, depression, and shared that she had lit a trashcan on fire. The speech and language pathologist, who was conducting the meeting responded by acknowledging that Tonantzin is honest. Here, the district could have offered alternative interventions, including a social skills group or counseling (related services), referral to community based counseling services, or considered a behavior support plan. At the very least there could have been a conversation regarding Mrs. Rodriguez's observations.

Mr. and Mrs. Andrade expressed complete satisfaction with the team and the meeting. They have been a part of other IEP teams within the same district. However, this was their first annual meeting with this particular team other than the transition meeting which had taken place earlier in the school year. Mr. Andrade felt that he was part of the team and made comparisons to the previous IEP team. Mrs. Andrade was very happy with the level of communication that she has with Manny's current teacher. After meeting with Mr. and Mrs. Andrade, Manny's teacher informally shared that she regularly talks with Mrs. Andrade, which shortened the discussion during the IEP.

The only parent who had multiple concerns addressed and ultimately impacted change for her son was Mrs. Garcia. Mrs. Garcia raised questions that should have been addressed by the education specialist and the classroom teacher prior to the meeting. The IEP, which took place after the first grading period, was the first time that the subject of grading and penmanship were discussed. After the meeting, Mrs. Garcia was happy with the outcome and felt that the meeting was a success.

The Level of Inclusion versus Exclusion

None of the families were overtly excluded from the IEP process. However, the teams did not all demonstrate the same level of professionalism when interacting with the families.

During Manny's IEP, the team joked with the parents and everyone appeared relaxed. Mr. Andrade understood what was being said and he was on one side of Mrs. Andrade with the district interpreter sitting on the other side. At Isabel's annual meeting the team shared refreshments with Mrs. Lopez and had a conversation about Isabel's needs while periodically filling in Mrs. Lopez regarding the interventions being implemented. Tonantzin's meeting lasted only 15 minutes and Mrs. Rodriguez herself acknowledged that it was the last day before spring break and everyone probably wanted to get home. At Bertha's meeting everyone shared observations and information with Ms. Almanza, again her meeting was relaxed and less formal. At Andrew's meeting there were moments where the meeting was relaxed and both the classroom teacher and educational specialist had a conversation with Ms. Hernandez. However, when Ms. Hernandez heard the recommendation of the team, she began to cry. The principal called her by her first name and asked her what she was upset about. The room became very quiet and the home school liaison became more of a support for Ms. Hernandez than an interpreter. Ms. Hernandez agreed to the IEP proposed days later.

At Jorge's IEP meeting Mrs. Garcia spoke in a very low tone and depended on the interpreter to relay information to the rest of the team. Mrs. Garcia watched the conversations taking place, but only summaries of the conversations were explained to her by the interpreter. At Marisol's meeting the home school liaison also served as the interpreter, although she and the education specialist both interpreted at different times in the meeting. The classroom teacher barely spoke throughout the meeting, and only shared the work samples with the researcher while the interpreter explained to Mrs. Solis that Marisol had a learning disability. Alfonso's meeting was the same day as Manny's meeting and the district interpreter was at both meetings. The meeting went much faster than when the home school liaison interpreted because the district interpreter interprets simultaneously. However, that created an issue for Mrs. Mendez who reported that the interpreter was speaking too fast and she did not understand some of the big words. At another point in the meeting the team made a light hearted joke and Mrs. Mendez had a very confused look on her face.

The families that only spoke Spanish depended on the interpreter to keep them up to speed with what was being said at the meeting. The school staff appeared to be more comfortable and at ease with the families that spoke both languages than the families that were monolingual. However, all of the families replied yes when asked if they were satisfied with the meeting.

CONCLUSION

The IEP process which is very legal in its design mandates that the parent must be included in the decision making process. However, like any other legal process, it generally benefits those who know how to navigate the system and have a clear understanding of its implications.

All the parents of this study did not demonstrate the same level of understanding regarding the IEP process. The primary purpose for looking at two groups within the same culture was to determine if their participation varied as a result of their language, or if there was an underlying form of institutional racism taking place throughout the process. What was found was that the school personnel whether intentionally or not were more at ease with the bilingual participants than with the monolingual Spanish-speaking participants.

The teams followed the district practices, such as using multiple measures to determine eligibility, implementing the response to intervention model, and meeting with the parents during a student study team meeting before referring a child for evaluation for special education. A shortcoming that was apparent was consideration for the parent's language needs, which resulted in an absence of meaning for four out of the eight families. The families that relied on the interpreter appeared to be a burden to the school personnel: the district had to get an interpreter, the staff had to wait for the interpreter, and the school had to provide forms in both languages. The district employs only one Interpreter to serve the whole district. Therefore, schools often have to rely on the home school liaison who has other responsibilities. The home school liaison was called out of the meeting in one IEP, and had to leave before another IEP ended. The district interpreter on the other hand, worked out well for the mother who has taken classes about the IEP process and was versed in the terminology. However, for the mother who had never previously participated in an IEP the interpreter spoke too fast and used terminology that was inaccessible.

The home school liaison became a support person in two of the meetings. Harry (1992) interviewed two district liaisons who saw their role as advocates, but added that parents should be encouraged to provide their own interpreter or support person apart from the school's interpreter. During the post-meeting interview the families were asked if they were encouraged to bring a support person. Only Mrs. Rodriguez answered yes, her husband, who was unable to attend due to work.

Rhodes (1996) developed twelve strategies as recommendations when working with Spanish-dominant migrant parents in rural/agriculturally-based settings. Since the setting this study took place in was urban, not all of the recommendations are applicable in this community. Incorporating at least some of Rhodes' recommendations would promote community cultural wealth. Based on Rhodes' twelve recommendations, six suggestions were developed for school personnel to consider when working with CLD families.

These suggestions also take into account the suggestions from the parent participants of this study. These six suggestions incorporate cultural wealth by promoting a more welcoming discussion about the children and developing the multiple strengths of CLD families.

1. Provide Background

Giving families an overview of what to expect during an IEP before the IEP takes place. The overview can be a brief checklist of what will be discussed. It could consist of a booklet or flyer with some of the various services available as well as the various models of instruction offered through the school district. The parents in this study were unclear of services that can be provided, terminology, location of services, and the implications that the label of special education would have on their child. If the school offered some information aside from the parents' rights in the parents' preferred language, the parents would attend the meeting with less resistance and reluctance to make decisions that are in their child's best interest.

2. Encourage a Support Person

Parents should be encouraged to bring a family member or family advocate to help them process all of the information as well as give them personal support. The district should inform the parent in advance that the team will be talking about their child's overall ability and also encourage them to bring someone who knows both languages.

3. Provide a Consistent Interpreter

Maintain the same interpreter throughout the duration of the meeting. The district has the opportunity to not only demonstrate empathy for the family, but to also promote linguistic capital. Lo (2008) suggested that the case carrier meet with the interpreter before the meeting to make sure that the interpreter knows the terminology or what is trying to be conveyed to the parent. An interpreter should be available even if the family brings their own interpreter. Having an interpreter from the district would mitigate any potential miscommunication. It would also show the family the level of commitment on behalf of the district to ensure a clear understanding of the meeting.

4. Report Regularly on Student Progress

Maintain ongoing communication regarding assessments and progress. To send home regular updates or communicate on the child's progress gives a message to the family that the school is also part of their community. The school and family are not separate entities. Again, the parents in this study wanted to know how their child was doing. Ms. Hernandez said that she had not heard from the school since her son's transition to special education pull out services and that she would go to the school if they did not get in touch with her soon. Mrs. Andrade shared that she was really happy with the school and the team because her son has improved and there is good communication. If the family only speaks Spanish the team should utilize the home school liaison to check in with the family.

5. Include the Parent in Pre-Meeting Planning

Include the parents in the planning phase on a more personal level. Parents are sometimes given questionnaires to fill out and send in prior to the meeting, but a personal call prior to the meeting could assure that their concerns and questions are met with minimal awkwardness. Someone from the school should call the parent one week before the meeting, and again one day before the meeting.

6. Parent Education

If parents learn how the process works and know what resources are available they will become better advocates for their children. If feasible the school should offer parent education on various topics within special education. If there are limited resources through the school to fund a workshop, the school could provide the families with a list of local agencies that provide such trainings and parent education classes.

REFERENCES

Briggs, M.H. (1997). *Building early intervention teams: Working together for children and families*. Gaithersburg, MD: Aspen.

Dabkowski, D.M. (2004). Encouraging active parent participation in IEP team meetings *Teaching Exceptional Children, 36*(3), 34-39.

De Gaetano, Y. (2007). The role of culture in engaging Latino parents' involvement in school. *Urban Education, 42*:145-162.

De Gaetano, Y., Williams, L. R., and Volk, D. (1998). *Kaleidoscope: A multicultural approach to the early elementary classroom.* Cleveland, OH: Prentice Hall.

Fish, W.W. (2006). Perceptions of parents of students with aurism towards the IEP meeting: A case study of one family support group chapter. *Education, 127*(1), 56-68.

Fish, W.W. (2008). The IEP Meeting: Perceptions of parents of students who receive special education services. *Preventing School Failure, 53*(1), 8-14.

Garriot, P.P., Wandry, D., and Snyder, L. (2000). Teachers as parents, parents as children: What's wrong with this picture? *Preventing School Failure, 45*(1), 37-43.

Hardin, B.J., Mereoiu, M., Hung, H.F., and Roach-Scott, M. (2009). Investigating parent and professional perspectives concerning special education services for preschool Latino parents. *Early Childhood Education Journal. 37*(93), 102.

Harry, B. (1992). *Cultural diversity, families, and the special education system: Communication and Empowerment*. New York: Teachers College Press.

Harry, B., Allen, N., and McLauglin, M. (1995). Communication versus compliance: African American parents' involvement in special education. *Exceptional Children, 61*, 354-377.

Harry, B., Klingner, J.K., and Cramer, E. (2007). *Case studies of minority student placement in special education*. New York: Teachers College Press.

Hoover, J.J., Klingner, J.K., Baca, L.M., and Patton, J.M. (2008). *Methods for teaching culturally and linguistically diverse exceptional learners*. Colombus, Ohio: Pearson Merrill Prentice Hall.

Hughs, M.T., Valle-Riestra, D.M., and Arguelles, M.E. (2002). Experiences of Latino families with their child's special education program. *Multicultural Perspectives, 4(1)*, 11-17.

Individuals with Disabilities Education Act Amendments of 1997, PL 105-17, 20 U.S.C § § 1400 *et seq.*

Kalyanpur, M. and Harry, B. (1999). *Culture in special education: Building reciprocal family professional relationships.* Baltimore, MD: Paul Brookes.

Kozleski, E.B., Engelbrecht, P., Hess, R., Swart, E., Eloff, I., Oswald, M., Jain, S. (2008). Where differences matter: A cross-cultural analysis of family voice in special education. *Journal Special Education, 42*(26), 26-35.

Laosa, L.M. (1983). Parent education, culture and education, cultural pluralism, and public policy: The uncertain connection. In R. Haskins and D. Adams (Eds.), *Parent education and public policy* (pp. 331-345). Norwood, NJ: Ablex.

Lareau, A. (1987). Social class differences in family school relationships: The importance of cultural capital. *Sociology of Education, 60*(2), 73-85.

Lo, L. (2008). Chinese families level of participation and experiences in IEP meetings. *Preventing School Failure, 53*(1), 21-27.

Martin, J. E., Marshall, L. H., and Sale, P. (2004). A three-year study of middle, junior high, and high school IEP meetings. *Exceptional Children, 70,* 285-297.

Miles, M.B. and Huberman, A.M. (1994). *Qualitative data analysis* (2nd ed.). Thousand Oaks, CA: Sage.

Orozco, G.L. (2008). Understanding the culture of low-income immigrant Latino parents: Key to involvement. *The School Community Journal, 18*(1), 21-37.

Pruitt, P., Wandry, D., and Hollums, D. (1998). Listen to us! Parents speak out about their interaction with special educators. *Preventing School Failure, 42,* 161-166.

Ramirez III, M. and Cox, B.G. (1980). Parenting for multiculturalism: A Mexican American model. In M.D. Fantini and R. Cardenas (Eds.), *Parenting in a multicultural society* (pp. 54-62). New York: Longman.

Rhodes,R.L. (1996). Beyond our borders: Spanish-dominant migrant parents and the IEP process. *Rural Special Education Quarterly 15*(2), 19-22.

Salas, L. (2004). Individualized Educational Plan (IEP) meetings and Mexican American parents: Let's talk about It. *Journal of Latinos and Education, 3*(3), 181-192.

Salembier, G., and Furney, K.S. (1997). Facilitating participation: Parents' perceptions of their involvement in the IEP/transition planning process. *Career Development for Exceptional Individuals,* 20(1), 29-42.

Salvia, J., Ysseldyke, J.E. and Bolt, S. (2007). Assessment in special and inclusive education. (10th ed.). Boston: Houghton Mifflin.

Spann, S. J., Kohler, F. W., and Soenksen, D. (2003). Examining parent's involvement in and perceptions of special education services: An interview with families in a parent support group. *Focus on Autism and other Developmental Disabilities*, *18*, 228-237.

U.S. Department of Education. (2007). *Individuals with Disabilities Education Improvement Act of 2004.* Retrieved from http://www.ed.gov/policy/speced/gui/idea/idea2004.html.

Vaughn, S., Bos, C.S., Harrell, J.E., and Lasky, B.A. (1988). Parent participation in the initial placement/IEP conference ten years after mandated involvement. *Journal of Learning Disabilities, 21*(2), 82-89.

Yosso, T.J. (2006). *Critical race counterstories along the Chicana/Chicano educational pipeline.* New York: Routledge.

APPENDIX A

Team Meeting Observation and Analysis of Practices*

1. What professional disciplines are represented at the meeting? What role does each play?

Discipline_____ Role_____
Discipline_____ Role_____
Discipline_____ Role_____

2. What roles do the parents play?

_____ Observer   _____ Provider of information
_____ Decision maker   _____ None or very little
_____ Moderate provider   _____ actively involved in providing info

3. What team rituals are observed (e.g., who speaks when, how members are addressed, seating arrangement)?

_____

4. What effects does the meeting environment have on parental comfort level and establishing equity among team members?

5. What is the evidence that professionals have an awareness of the parent's cultural beliefs about disability?

6. What kind of information is shared and who presents it?

* adapted from Dabkowski, 2004.

In: Educational Programs and Special Education   ISBN: 978-1-62417-256-4
Editor: Sasha Dziuk   © 2013 Nova Science Publishers, Inc.

Chapter 2

SELF-CONCEPT ENHANCEMENT PROGRAMS: ISSUES, CHALLENGES, AND NEW PERSPECTIVES

Alexander Seeshing Yeung[1,*], Rhonda G. Craven[1] and A. Katrin Arens[2]

[1]University of Western Sydney, Australia
[2]German Institute for International Educational Research, Germany

ABSTRACT

Educators and researchers attempt to design and implement successful intervention programs to enhance students' academic motivation and self-concept as important non-cognitive determinants of student achievement and long-term gains. Nevertheless, despite the goodwill and effort, such programs are often faced with issues and challenges. In this chapter, we first discuss theories related to such intervention programs. Then we discuss and attempt to address the issues, challenges, and limitations of such programs by illustrating them with examples of evidence-based intervention programs we have conducted in various educational areas including: language, mathematics, cooperative

* The research was supported by the Australian Research Council. Address for correspondence: Alexander S. Yeung, Centre for Positive Psychology and Education, University of Western Sydney, Locked Bag 1797, Penrith, NSW 2751, Australia; phone: +61(2) 97726264, fax: +61(2) 97726432, email: a.yeung@uws.edu.au.

learning, peer support, and anti-bullying. The discussions and illustrations are based on recent advances in self-concept and motivation theory and research. Theory, such as the reciprocal effects model demonstrating the mutually reinforcing relations between academic self-concept and academic achievement, provides the opportunity for designing a dual approach with attention to both self-concept and achievement in the program. The research on internally focused and attributional feedback mechanisms provides the potential of reinforcing self-concept for long-term positive gains. Nevertheless, research findings indicating a general pattern of decrease in self-concept over time constitute a prevalent issue and a challenge to any intervention that attempts to facilitate a significant and noticeable increase. Recent emphasis on the twofold multidimensional structure of academic self-concept implying that intervention programs should target a specific domain and should address both the cognitive and affective components of self-concept further complicates the design and implementation of programs. A further challenge is the occurrence of diffusion effects that might mask the difference between the experimental (target) group and the control group, thus undermining the effectiveness of the intervention. Other issues include: students' cognitive abilities, age, frame of references, and differential gender perceptions. These issues and challenges are illustrated in the light of our previously conducted self-concept enhancement programs in educational settings.

Feeling positively about oneself and one's abilities is a desirable goal in of itself. Positive self-concept has been found to facilitate a broad range of desirable outcomes (academic, physical, art) including sharing a reciprocal and causal relation with academic achievement (Craven & Marsh, 2008; Marsh & O'Mara, 2008). Hence, interventions that aim to enhance students' self-concept are likely to facilitate desirable educational outcomes and psycho-social adaptive functioning. The purpose of this chapter is to discuss the rationale for self-concept intervention research; the issues, challenges, and limitations of self-concept enhancement research; and provide an overview of some examples of evidence-based self-concept enhancement interventions. This chapter begins by giving an overview about the important contribution of self-concept to desirable outcomes. Next, the issues, challenges, and limitations of self-concept enhancement research are discussed. Finally, we provide an overview of some examples of evidence-based intervention programs we have conducted in various educational areas including: language, mathematics, cooperative learning, peer support, and anti-bullying.

THE CONSTRUCT AND IMPORTANCE OF SELF-CONCEPT

In general terms, self-concept can be defined as an individual's self-perceptions. The multidimensional and hierarchical model of Shavelson, Hubner, and Stanton (1976) constitutes the first theoretical account for the structure of self-concept.

In the Shavelson et al. model, global self-concept (often referred to as self-esteem) was assumed to be located at the apex of a multidimensional and hierarchical self-concept structure. Global self-concept was assumed to be separable into global academic and nonacademic self-concept facets that were both assumed to be further differentiable into domain-specific self-concept facets. For the academic dimension, academic self-concept was conceptualized to encompass students' self-perceptions related to specific academic domains (i.e., math, verbal). For the nonacademic dimension, physical, social, and emotional self-concepts were each proposed to be further differentiable into more specific self-concepts in nonacademic domains (e.g., physical self-concept including physical ability and physical appearance self-concepts).

The Shavelson et al. (1976) self-concept model has been of great heuristic value in providing a blueprint and a basis for subsequent self-concept research and measurement for the last three decades.

CONCEPTUALIZATION AND MEASUREMENT

The suite of Self Description Questionnaire (SDQ) instruments (Marsh, 1986, 1990b, c, d; Marsh & O'Neill, 1984) are amongst the most widely used self-concept measurement instruments and have been rigorously evaluated cross-culturally. They were designed on the basis of the Shavelson et al. (1976) model for measuring the multidimensional self-concepts of students from different age groups: the SDQ I for preadolescents (Marsh, 1990c), the SDQ II for adolescents (Marsh, 1990d), and the SDQ III for late adolescents and young adults (Marsh & O'Neill, 1984).

The availability of these multidimensional instruments has facilitated the voluminous research findings in support of the conceptualization of the multidimensional nature of self-concept.

STRONG DOMAIN SPECIFICITY

The strong multidimensional nature was probably best illustrated in recent research demonstrating that self-concept measurement, research, and theory are inextricably intertwined within a multidimensional conceptual framework (Marsh, 1990b). For academic self-concept, the demonstrably low correlation (often zero) between math and verbal self-concepts, which is not commensurate with the mostly positive correlation between math and verbal achievement (Marsh, 1986, 1990a) has challenged the Shavelson et al. conceptualization of a global academic self-concept construct. Evidence has shown that math and verbal self-concepts should be treated as separate self-concept facets and should not be put together to infer a global academic self-concept (Marsh, 1990e). The very strong domain specificity was also supported by research on nonacademic self-concepts. For example, physical appearance and physical ability self-concepts were found to constitute distinct self-concept facets that could not be combined to form a higher-order physical self-concept (Marsh, Relich, & Smith, 1983). These findings have led to the conclusion that intervention programs that are designed for self-enhancement need to account for the multidimensionality of the self-concept construct (Craven & Yeung, 2008).

DOMAIN SPECIFIC RELATIONS BETWEEN SELF-CONCEPT AND OUTCOMES

The enhancement of self-concept is important in any program that targets achievement and performance in specific domains (Craven & Yeung, 2008). The tenet is that although we may enhance achievement in a specific domain (e.g., math) by improving skills (e.g., computation), the positive effects gained from the intervention will be sustainable only if the learner has also built positive self-beliefs of competence. Hence, researchers have emphasized a dual approach of simultaneously improving both skills and self-concept within a targeted domain in designing intervention programs. This argument is supported by research evidence showing that improved self-concept brings better performance, which further enhances self-concept (Craven & Yeung, 2008). The mutually reinforcing effects between self-concept and outcomes within the domain-specific framework have provided a very useful direction for effective intervention designs. Outcomes that were found to be substantially related to self-concept include academic achievement (Marsh & Craven, 2005, 2006; Marsh & Yeung, 1997a, 1998), intrinsic motivation (Skaalvik & Rankin, 1995), attribution of success and failure (Marsh, 1984), interest (Marsh, Trautwein, Lüdtke, Köller, & Baumert, 2005), and coursework selection (Marsh & Yeung, 1997b). In practical terms, within a specific domain, attempts to improve verbal abilities should go together with attempts to improve verbal self-concept; whereas designs for improving math performance should also include math self-concept enhancement elements. Because of the strong domain specificity of the different domains, positive effects found in a verbal enhancement program are unlikely to be transferable to an unrelated domain such as math (Marsh & Craven, 1997). Evidence of the domain-specific reciprocal effects between self-concept and outcomes has significant implications for the design of programs to make a difference (Marsh & Craven, 2005, 2006). In essence, skill enhancement attempts are unlikely to have sustainable positive effects unless the program includes respective self-concept enhancement initiatives. That is why self-concept is so important in any intervention program that works.

SELF-CONCEPT INTERVENTIONS: ISSUES AND CHALLENGES

A fundamental question we need to ask is: "Are self-concept enhancement interventions effective?" A useful starting point is to review some of the relevant meta-analytic studies. Meta-analyses provide an adequate tool in order to estimate the effectiveness of self-concept enhancement intervention as they aggregate the effects of all available primary studies in the field over a period and serve to integrate and explicate empirically the effective features of self-concept interventions.

A seminal meta-analysis conducted by Hattie (1992) integrated 89 self-concept intervention studies conducted prior to 1983 providing 458 effect sizes. Hattie found that the mean effect size of the integrated self-concept interventions was 0.37. Subsequently, Haney and Durlak (1998) analyzed 102 self-concept intervention studies with children and adolescents that were conducted prior to 1992. Direct self-concept enhancement intervention programs were found to be effective with a mean effect size of 0.57. More recently, O'Mara, Marsh, Craven, and Debus (2006) found an overall effect size of 0.51 for self-concept interventions based on 501 effect sizes resulting from 145 studies conducted with students younger than 18 years. O'Mara, Green, and Marsh (2006) constrained their meta-analyses to self-concept enhancement interventions conducted in the school setting. This meta-analysis based on 105 studies evaluating 152 self-concept enhancement programs administered between 1960 and 2000 revealed an overall mean effect size of 0.51. Hence, in sum, the results of meta-analyses imply that self-concept enhancement intervention programs are effective and thus illustrate the potential capability of self-concept interventions. However, in order to make self-concept interventions effective, researchers and practitioners are faced with various challenges some of which are discussed in the next sections.

(1) Domain Specificity

Although self-concept interventions are found to be generally effective given the moderate overall effect sizes revealed in meta-analyses, the highest effect sizes were found for interventions that considered the domain specificity of self-concept. In their meta-analysis, O'Mara, Marsh et al., (2006) found the highest effect sizes for intervention programs that targeted a specific self-concept domain and measured this specific self-concept domain subsequently (1.16). Hence, the effectiveness of self-concept enhancement interventions is likely to be optimal when targeting a specific domain of self-concept to account for the construct's multidimensionality. In contrast, interventions that targeted the self-concept of a mismatched domain were found to result in lower effect sizes (0.41). These results attest to the issue of domain specificity in program designs.

From a multidimensional perspective, self-concept enhancement programs need to be designed to ensure that the aims of the program, measurement tools, and statistical analyses employed are aligned and clearly focus on a specific domain of self-concept most relevant to the goals of the intervention. For example, a self-concept intervention program focusing on the math domain is expected to increase students' math self-concept but will be totally inefficient in influencing nonacademic self-concept facets (Craven, Marsh, & Burnett, 2003; Craven & Yeung, 2008; O'Mara, Marsh et al., 2006). A clear pattern of differential effectiveness of self-concept enhancement interventions relative to the degree of domain specificity (i.e., the highest effects on target-domains, medium effects on target-related domains, but no effects on nontarget domains) has been demonstrated in various studies evaluating the effectiveness of self-concept enhancement programs. For example, the

Outward Bound Bridging Program was designed to enhance academic achievement and academic self-concept of low-achieving students. Corresponding to this academic orientation, participants of this program were found to display an increase in math, reading, and general school self-concepts upon completion of the program while their nonacademic self-concepts facets remained unaffected (Marsh & Richards, 1988). In contrast to the academic orientation of the bridging program, the Outward Bound Program comprises physically challenging activities in order to strengthen students' physical fitness and awareness of their own strength and difficulties in coping with challenges. With the strong emphasis on the physical domain and the physical activities involved, the Outward Bound Program was found to foster participants' physical ability self-concept (Marsh, Richards, & Barnes, 1986a, 1986b). These studies clearly demonstrate the significance of considering the domain specific nature of self-concept enhancement processes.

In the academic domains, Craven, Marsh, and Debus (1991) conducted a self-concept enhancement program that aimed to enhance primary school students' reading and math self-concepts by employing internally focused and attributional feedback in response to students' math and verbal accomplishments. As expected based on the multidimensional structure of self-concept and based on the differentiation between target, target-related, and nontarget domains, students' math and verbal self-concepts (target domains) were found to increase respectively subsequent to this intervention. Transfer effects could be observed for school and general self-concepts (target-related domains), but students' nonacademic self-concept facets were not affected (nontarget domains). Leung, Marsh, Craven, Yeung, & Abduljabbar (2012) examined the effectiveness of two types of peer support programs. One peer support program was academically oriented. Students from 11th grade served as tutors who mentored tutees from 7th grade in their English school work. Compared to a control group, the 7th graders' English self-concept (target domain) was found to increase after this academically focused peer support program. All other facets of the students' multidimensional self-concept (academic or nonacademic) were found to remain stable for both students of the control and the experimental (intervention) groups. The other peer support program evaluated by Leung et al. (2012) was socially-orientated in nature. It was geared towards enhancing 7th grade students' social and interpersonal relationship skills. The participants of this peer support program, but not control students, were found to show an increase in their self-concepts for same-sex peer relations. Both students of the experimental (intervention) group and the control group did not change in any other self-concept facets subsequent to the intervention. In sum, evidence shows that domain specificity is a critical consideration in the design and implementation of self-concept enhancement programs.

(2) Measurement Issues

The critical issue of domain specificity also leads to another related issue – measurement. As intervention effects would be expected to vary relative to the relevance of the program to certain domains of interest, researchers need also to consider the appropriate measurement of effects for such domains. Hence, the measurement of effects of a program targeting math should clearly include a domain-specific scale measuring math self-concept and the extent of change as a function of the intervention (Craven, Marsh, & Burnett, 2003; Craven & Yeung, 2008; O'Mara, Marsh et al., 2006). For example, Craven and Yeung (2008) have demonstrated the importance of using a peer relations measure to assess the effectiveness of a peer support program, a math self-concept measure to assess the effectiveness of a math-focused intervention, and a range of reading-related measures to assess the effectiveness of a literacy intervention program. Using a scale that measures a nontarget domain (e.g., English) will not be useful in detecting intervention effects when the program targets a different specific domain (e.g., math). However, including nontarget domains of self-concept is useful to employ a construct validity approach (Craven et al., 2003) to the study of intervention effects in order to test the saliency of the intervention in enhancing only the target and associated domains of self-concept. Measures of associated domains (e.g., school self-concept) are useful to include because they enable an examination of whether gains in a specific self-concept domain (e.g., reading self-concept) generalize to an associated domain (e.g., school self-concept) and transfer to a wider context (e.g., general self-concept). Similarly, using a measure at a higher level within the hierarchical self-concept structure (e.g., school self-concept) to scrutinize intervention effects at a lower level (e.g., math self-concept) or at a subdomain level (e.g., algebra self-concept) is inappropriate and violates the multidimensional and hierarchical conceptualization of the self-concept construct (Yeung, 2005) and the specificity matching principle (Swann, Chang-Schneider, & Larsen McClarty, 2007). This can result in flawed interpretations of domain-specific effects based on domain-unspecific measurement, or making target-related claims based on target-unrelated data.

(3) The Chicken and Egg Issue

A consideration in self-enhancement programs is whether to attempt to enhance self-concept by improving skills (the skill enhancement model) or directly enhancing self-concept (the self-concept enhancement model) – a chicken and egg issue. Our argument is that for an intervention to work, we need to do both simultaneously. Numerous studies on the relations between self-concept and achievement have found support for the reciprocal effects model (REM) showing reciprocal, mutually reinforcing relations between self-concept and achievement. The REM has been found to be generalizable across academic (Marsh & Craven, 2005, 2006; Marsh & Yeung, 1997a, 1998) and nonacademic (e.g., physical ability; Marsh, Gerlach, Trautwein, Lüdtke, & Brettschneider, 2007; Marsh & Perry, 2005) domains and across students of different age groups (Guay, Marsh, & Boivin, 2003). Therefore, employing the REM to strengthen the design of self-concept enhancement interventions implies that self-concept and achievement should be enhanced simultaneously in order to achieve long-lasting and mutually reinforcing positive effects. Only focusing on students' academic achievement through skill development without facilitating their competence beliefs is unlikely to yield sustainable gains. Even with enhanced skills, students who lack a positive self-concept in the relevant domain are likely to suffer from underachievement in the long term. Similarly, approaches that only focus on students' self-concept without enhancing students' skills are limited because students will miss experiences of success that reinforce their self-concept. Hence, self-concept interventions should combine skill development and self-concept enhancement approaches in order to promote students' self-concept and achievement in a long-lasting way (Craven & Yeung, 2008). Again, the domain specificity issue comes into play because the skill and self-concept elements of interest need to be parallel and be within the same domain and at the same level on the self-concept hierarchy for the REM to operate. Testing the mutual relations between a domain-specific self-concept and a domain-unspecific skill is likely to lead to misinterpretations of intervention effects.

(4) Detection of Intervention Effects

There is a low representation of experimental studies in the self-concept literature. It is not surprising for two reasons: (1) experimental designs, however sophisticated, may not result in what the researcher expects, and (2) self-concept enhancement interventions, however well designed and implemented, may not improve self-concept to a sizeable increase. The first issue is associated with classroom environments. In experimental studies examining the effectiveness of self-concept interventions, students are often assigned to experimental and control groups within a class setting. Those students assigned to the experimental group would receive a well defined treatment and those assigned to the control group would not be targeted for the treatment but may attend the same class as students in the experimental group. In this situation, diffusion effects are likely to occur (Craven, Marsh, Debus, & Jayasinghe, 2001). Teachers who were supposed to administer self-concept enhancement strategies only to the target students (i.e., the experimental group) may unconsciously apply these strategies also to the nontarget students as well. Even if the teacher is careful in directing the treatment to the target students only, the students of the within-class control group witness the self-concept intervention procedures which may influence their own self-perceptions. These processes may result in positive changes in the self-concept of both the experimental and the control students. Craven et al. (2001) therefore recommend that in order to test and control for potential diffusion effects, self-concept intervention studies should include within-class (internal) control groups and between-class (external) control groups. This enables researchers to test for diffusion effects in the internal, within-class control condition, which would result in the within-class control group displaying higher self-concept than the students in the external, between-class control group.

The issue of weak detectable intervention effects often found in experimental studies is a difficult issue to address because research has shown that self-beliefs of competence tend to decline over time. As students grow older, their sense of competence goes down (Yeung, 2011; Yeung, Lau, & Nie, 2011). These patterns seem to be generalizable across different cultures. For example, Yeung (2011) using an Australian sample and Yeung et al. (2011), using a sample of Singapore students, came to similar conclusions. Gender differences may further complicate the developmental patterns because a program that works for boys within a specific domain (e.g., physical) may not work as well for girls, and vice versa. Hence the interplay between design, measurement, and analysis is a complicated issue that researchers often find challenging in experimental studies, and the most disheartening is that despite strong interventions, positive effects may at best result in maintaining self-concept at a reasonable level instead of allowing it to decline.

(5) Agent of Change

Researchers and practitioners are also faced with the issue of the practical aspects of self-concept intervention procedures. This issue is sometimes related to the person who administers the intervention and sometimes to the specific procedures used to enhance students' self-concept. In examining the agent of interventions, Hattie's (1992) meta-analysis led to pessimism regarding the effectiveness of teachers as administrators of self-concept enhancement programs, based on the finding showing a considerably lower than average effect size when the programs were administered by teachers. For example, Craven et al. (1991) could only demonstrate positive effects of feedback strategies on students' academic self-concepts when the feedback was delivered by research assistants, not by teachers. In contrast, however, some other meta-analyses (O'Mara et al., 2006) found no difference in program effectiveness for different administrator types. Hence, self-concept interventions conducted by teachers were found to be equally effective as those administered by other agents including researchers, mental health professionals, professional trainers, or school counselors. These inconclusive results imply the need for further research to understand the differential effectiveness of self-concept interventions conducted by different agents. The effectiveness of teacher-conducted self-concept enhancement programs may depend upon students' age, how long the teacher has taught the students, the subject domain targeted by the intervention, and other variables that may not have been controlled. However, the issue remains as how to build teacher capacity to deliver effective self-concept interventions along with skill development to benefit learning.

(6) Strategies of Self-concept Enhancement

With regard to the specific mechanisms involved in self-concept interventions, feedback and praise have been found to be the most effective ways for enhancing students' self-concept (O'Mara, Green et al., 2006; O'Mara, Marsh et al., 2006). Craven et al. (1991) have demonstrated positive effects of internally focused feedback (i.e., feedback on students' strengths in specific tasks generalized to the subject area), and attributional feedback (attributing success to students' ability or effort while attributing failure to lack of effort) on students' academic self-concepts. When differentiating between different types of feedback and praise, attributional feedback was found to yield the highest positive effect on self-concept followed by contingent praise, goal feedback, and noncontingent praise (O'Mara, Marsh et al., 2006). This finding qualifies the overall positive effect of feedback and praise on students' self-concept illustrating that some forms of feedback and praise are more beneficial for students' self-concept than others. However, there does not seem to be sufficient evidence to show that these differential effects can be generalized to different sample characteristics (e.g., culture, gender). Hence the choice of self-concept enhancement strategies is primarily an unresolved issue.

(7) Student Characteristics

Meta-analyses have consistently demonstrated higher effect sizes for self-concept enhancement programs conducted with students with previously diagnosed problems. Hence, treatment studies were found to be more effective than prevention studies (Haney & Durlak, 1998; Hattie, 1992; O'Mara, Marsh et al., 2006). Children at risk who seem to particularly benefit from self-concept enhancement programs include students with: low self-concept, behavioral problems, and learning disorders (LD). The studies of Elbaum and Vaughn (2001, 2003) particularly examined the effectiveness of self-concept enhancement programs with LD students. In their meta-analysis, Elbaum and Vaughn (2001) reported a weighted mean effect size of 0.19 resulting from 82 analyzed school-based self-concept enhancement interventions. Hence, the self-concept of LD students participating in enhancement programs seemed to modestly, but significantly increase compared to those LD students who did not participate the programs. Several variables were found to moderate the effectiveness of self-concept interventions for LD students. One variable was age. Preadolescents seemed to benefit more from self-concept interventions than younger children or adolescents but the gain for a specific age group seemed to depend upon the specific intervention type used. For elementary LD students, only academic interventions aiming at academic skill development were found to significantly enhance self-concept. In middle and high school years, only counseling interventions with a focus on changing students' self-perceptions based on therapeutic models were demonstrated to substantially foster self-concept.

For LD samples, the type of intervention and the target self-concept facet influence effectiveness. When aggregating across different types of self-concept intervention methods, academic self-concept was found to be the most malleable, followed by social and general self-concept domains, while physical and personal self-concept domains were unaffected by self-concept interventions. However, when differentiating between different types of self-concept interventions, physically-oriented interventions (fitness programs, physical recreation, motor skills programs, etc.) were found to be the only type of self-concept interventions that significantly enhances students' physical self-concept. For promoting general self-concept, counseling and involving students' significant others to change their behavior were found to be most effective strategies. To foster students' academic self-concept, academic and counseling interventions were found to be the most effective. These results were consistent with: (1) the domain specificity of self-concept, and (2) the REM. That is, specific types of self-concept interventions were found to yield the greatest effect on the self-concept domains that are matched logically to the content of the intervention (e.g., physical intervention improves physical self-concept), and simultaneous skill development and self-concept enhancement interventions were most effective for LD samples.

(8) Purpose of Intervention

Given the higher effectiveness of treatment studies compared to prevention studies, researchers and practitioners may question whether to advocate treatment or prevention. Students with LD, for example, are often found to be targets of self-concept interventions given the implicit assumption that they are suffering from poor self-concept together with their low performance. However, recent research on the self-concept of LD students implies a more differentiated view. The meta-analysis conducted by Bear, Minke, and Manning (2002) demonstrated that LD students may indeed display lower levels of academic self-concept compared to non-LD students, but they do not differ in other facets of self-concept (e.g., social, behavioral, and general self-concept). Hence, LD students may benefit from intervention programs targeting academic self-concept, but it does not seem to be justifiable to engage LD students in intervention programs involving a wide range of self-concept facets (e.g., social and physical self-concept in which they are not deprived of). Among LD students, however, those with a low initial self-concept prior to self-concept interventions were found to benefit over three times as much from interventions than students with average or high initial self-concept. The mean weighted effect sizes for students with low, average, and high self-concept prior to intervention were 1.22, 0.29, and 0.23, respectively, illustrating a clear advantage of self-concept interventions for students of low initial self-concept. Hence, the selection of students as targets for self-concept enhancement programs and the purpose of the program itself would both influence the evidence of program effectiveness. As such, the selection of target students for interventions should include an assessment of their initial self-concept together with a diagnosis leading to the identification of LD students. In essence, as Bear et al. (2002) noted: "For some students with LD, school psychologists are likely to observe lower academic self-perceptions, but deficits should be assessed, not assumed, prior to intervention" (p. 419).

(9) Visibility and Sustainability of Effects

Given the REM demonstrating mutually reinforcing relations between self-concept and performance, self-concept interventions together with skill development are likely to yield sustainable, long-lasting positive effects. However, given the limited time for most intervention programs in real-life settings, there is the risk of obtaining short-term positive effects that fades quickly upon completion. Hence the duration of interventions is often a critical issue. There is also a lack of follow-up posttests to examine the potential of delayed gains or maintenance of gains observed during the program implementation. Recent research has conveyed some optimism regarding the long-term effects of self-concept interventions. The effect sizes of self-concept intervention programs were not found to significantly drop during follow-up periods (O'Mara, Marsh et al., 2006). For example, in the study of Ellis, Marsh, and Craven (2005), an Australian peer support program that was widely used to facilitate 7th graders' transition into adolescence and secondary school, both short-term and long-term effects were observed. Results for the experimental group were compared to results for the control group prior to the intervention, at the end of the intervention, and three months after the conclusion of the intervention (i.e., a pretest-posttest-follow-up design). The experimental group displayed a significant increase in verbal and general school self-concepts between pretest and posttest. They also displayed superior levels of verbal and general self-concepts at the follow-up, indicating maintenance of the positive effects. The experimental group also demonstrated higher levels of self-concept in honesty, trustworthiness, and opposite-sex relations subsequent to the intervention, and the effect was also found to be retained over a three month period when the follow-up test was conducted.

The issue is that intervention programs usually have a short duration and need to be completed within a limited number of sessions in a few months. As such, the effects may not be readily detectable and the gains may not last after the completion the program.

Another issue is potential sleeper effects, that is, the effects may not be detectable at the posttest but may grow after the conclusion of the program. Ellis et al. (2005), for example, in evaluating a peer support program for easing students' transition to secondary school, provided a good example of the occurrence of sleeper effects in self-concept enhancement programs. Neither the experimental nor control group showed any increase in cooperative teamwork subsequent to the conclusion of the program. However, at follow-up, the experimental participants reported higher levels of cooperative teamwork than non-participants indicating a sleeper effect for cooperative teamwork. Similar results were also observed for the students' self-efficacy. Hence, immediately after the conclusion of the peer support program, participants and non-participants did not differ in their self-efficacy scores, but the experimental students outperformed control students in their level of self-efficacy at the follow-up test. Sleeper effects in self-concept enhancement programs are quite possible as self-concept needs time to build up and students may need some time to apply their newly acquired skills so as to reinforce their self-concept. Experiences of success in applying those skills may be subsequently internalized into the students' self-perceptions resulting in delayed observable gains.

The possible occurrence of sleeper effects pose a challenge to researchers and practitioners as follow-up assessments need to be integrated in the evaluation of self-concept enhancement interventions. Measuring students' self-concept only immediately after the intervention may result in an underestimation of the effectiveness of the intervention, as this may mask potential sleeper effects. Hence, multiple measurement points after the completion of an intervention are needed to explicate both the short-term and long-term effectiveness of an intervention program.

(10) Paradoxical Issues

In their classical self-concept definition, Shavelson et al. (1976) noted that self-concept is formed through the individual's experiences with and within the environment and through the individual's interpretation of these experiences. In a school environment, for example, when academic performance is concerned, social comparison processes are experienced by every student. Social and internal comparison processes have been found to jointly contribute to self-concept formation. Marsh (1986, 1990a; also see Möller, Pohlmann, Köller, & Marsh, 2009) proposed an internal/external frame of reference (I/E) model to illustrate the effects of internal and external comparisons on students' academic self-concept. In social (external) comparison processes, students contrast their own performance with the performance of other students in the same domain. In internal comparison processes, students compare their own accomplishments in one domain (e.g., math) with those in another domain (e.g., English). The issue for self-concept interventions is that a self-enhancement program targeting a specific domain (e.g., math) would benefit the participants by having a superior self-concept in the targeted domain relative to others (math in this case), but would also lead to an inferior self-concept in a nontarget domain (such as English). These paradoxical relations between comparison processes and various domains may be a concern to educators and practitioners. Fortunately, Möller, Retelsdorf, Köller, and Marsh (2011) could find only weak evidence of negative effects of prior academic self-concept in a certain domain (e.g., math self-concept) on subsequent achievement in a nonmatching academic domains (e.g., verbal achievement). Hence, while the enhancement of students' math self-concept will benefit math achievement, the enhancement of math self-concept may not weaken performance in any nonmatching domains (such as English).

The I/E model is but one of the examples of paradoxical concern. Next to the I/E model which involves dimensional comparisons (i.e., contrasting one's achievement in one domain to that in another domain), other types of internal comparisons (i.e., temporal comparisons, comparisons of achievements with pretentions) may also influence self-concept formation (Skaalvik & Skaalvik, 2002). Hence, the effectiveness of self-concept interventions may vary depending on the frame of reference which the students are directed to use for self-concept formation. Marsh and Peart (1988) illustrated an example of how standards of comparison may influence the effectiveness of self-concept interventions. Australian high school students were assigned to a control condition or to one of two different types of fitness programs. One of these fitness programs was competitively-oriented emphasizing individual accomplishments and individual superiority relative to others, while the other program was cooperatively-oriented, requiring team-work to achieve success. Both the competitive and the cooperative fitness programs were found to significantly enhance physical fitness compared to the control group. However, only the cooperative intervention enhanced students' physical ability self-concept. In contrast, students' physical ability self-concept was found to decrease from pretest to posttest in the competitive program. Using social comparison processes, students in the competitive program had weakened physical ability self-concept. This finding illustrates the differential effectiveness of interventions contingent upon the frame of reference the students use for self-concept formation. Designers of self-concept interventions should therefore consider the paradoxical concerns related to the participants' interpretations of the social environment.

SELF-CONCEPT INTERVENTION RESEARCH: FUTURE PERSPECTIVES

In the above, we have explained the importance of self-concept enhancement and the need for effective self-concept interventions. We have also discussed and illustrated the potential and challenges of conducting self-concept enhancement programs. The message from the discussion above can be summarized in a simple statement: true effectiveness can only be achieved if the intervention program has a strong theoretical underpinning. Concretely, the focus, content, procedure, and evaluation should be well defined in terms of theory, and researchers and educators should be aware of the paradoxical concerns that have not been resolved. In essence, self-concept research has given us a lot of insight into designing and conducting effective self-concept intervention programs, but at the same time, there remain a number of issues that require further research.

(1) Intervention from a Twofold Multidimensional Perspective

The domain specificity of academic self-concept separating distinct facets such as math and verbal self-concepts is a widely accepted conceptualization of the academic self-concept structure (Marsh & Craven, 1997). Recent research has further extended the domain-specific academic self-concept structure to the differentiation between competence and affect components (Arens, Yeung, Craven, & Hasselhorn, 2011; Marsh, Craven, & Debus, 1999). Accordingly, within each domain-specific facet of academic self-concept (e.g., math, verbal) a competence component depicting students' self-perceptions of competence in that domain can be separated from an affect component referring to students' affective and motivational responses. This twofold multidimensional structure of academic self-concept (i.e., its domain specificity and competence-affect separation) should be seriously considered in the design and implementation of academic self-concept interventions. Future intervention studies should explore whether differential designs and procedures are necessary in order to effectively and sustainably foster the competence component and affect component of academic self-concept. For example, effective feedback strategies designed to enhance students' sense of competence in math may be different from effective feedback strategies for motivating students to be interested in math learning. The competence and affect components might further differ in their malleability and stability and thus in their responsiveness to self-concept interventions and sustainability of effects. The twofold multidimensional conceptualization of academic self-concept has the potential of opening up new directions for self-concept intervention research.

(2) Formative Evaluation of Self-concept Interventions

In previous research, the effectiveness of self-concept intervention approaches has been mainly tested by posttests conducted upon the conclusion of the intervention. Thus, a summative evaluation approach has been predominantly applied to self-concept intervention research focusing on the final outcome of interventions. In future research, it would be useful to employ a formative evaluation approach in addition to the summative approach. In this regard, students' self-concept would be measured regularly throughout the ongoing implementation of the intervention. This would allow testing the trajectory of students' self-concept throughout the intervention and may provide insight into which stages students' self-concept might benefit most, or least, from the intervention. Such information would aid the modification of self-concept interventions to gain optimal results by adjusting the duration of intervention to obtain the best overall effectiveness and efficiency. However, this also raises the issue of measurement which will not be practical when the participants are asked to complete lengthy instruments at multiple time points. Hence for this to be feasible, well validated short forms of instruments should be made available for this purpose (Arens, Yeung, Craven, & Hasselhorn, 2012).

(3) Developmental Concerns

The enhancement of self-concept through intervention at critical stages of development has not been thoroughly explicated in research. In particular, primary students' transition to secondary school has been found to be a critical period for self-concept development as studies have shown that students' self-concepts in math, verbal, social, and general domains decrease across transition (e.g., Anderman & Midgley, 1997; Eccles, Wigfield, Flanagan, Miller, Reuman, & Yee, 1989; Wigfield, Eccles, MacIver, Reuman, & Midgley, 1991). During the developmental stage when students progress from primary to secondary school, self-concept enhancement interventions may be of particular importance. The stage-environment fit model offers a theoretical account for the decrease of students' self-concept across transition (Eccles et al., 1993; Eccles & Midgley, 1989). According to this model, students' self-concept weakens as a result of a mismatch between their psychological needs and what the environment offers at secondary school. Students' need for autonomy and responsibility is undermined by the increasing degree of teacher control found in the secondary school context. Superficial relations between students and teachers, and among students themselves, do not parallel their increasing need for close social relationships. Whereas the stage-environment fit model has been predominantly used for explaining the decrease of students' self-concept and motivation across transition, it could also serve as a guideline for designing intervention programs to foster students' self-concept at this critical development stage. The model would imply the need for environmental-based interventions. In concrete terms, modifying the secondary school context in ways such that it corresponds to students' psychological needs would be expected to have a positive impact on students' self-concept trajectory across transition. Correspondingly, Anderman, Maehr, and Midgley (1999) found that students' motivational trajectory after entering middle school depended upon the learning environment. The decline in task goal orientation and increase in performance goal orientation across transition was less marked when students moved to a middle school that used task-focused instructional practices which de-emphasize competitive grading and ability grouping and increase the meaningfulness of tasks. Hence, future research on self-concept interventions should particularly consider critical developmental stages and students' needs at those stages. As such, the period of students' transition to secondary school would be an important focus in future intervention research.

CONCLUSION

In this chapter, we have examined the issues related to self-concept intervention programs and suggested some new perspectives for researchers and practitioners to consider. We argue that the major factor for success in intervention is a strong theoretical basis established on the basis of empirical evidence. New self-concept interventions will further benefit from new advances in self-concept research that will guide the design, practice, and evaluation of programs to maximize the potentials of students at various developmental stages.

REFERENCES

Anderman, E. M., Maehr, M. L., & Midgley, C. (1999). Declining motivation after the transition to middle school: Schools can make a difference. *Journal of Research and Development in Education. 32*, 131-147.

Anderman, E. M., & Midgley, C. (1997). Changes in achievement goal orientations, perceived academic competence, and grades across the transition to middle-level schools. *Contemporary Educational Psychology, 22*, 269-298.

Arens, A. K., Yeung, A. S., Craven, R. G., & Hasselhorn, M. (2011). The twofold multidimensionality of academic self-concept: Domain specificity and separation between competence and affect components. *Journal of Educational Psychology, 103*, 970-981.

Arens, A. K., Yeung, A. S., Craven, R. G., & Hasselhorn, M. (2012). A short German version of the Self Description Questionnaire I: Theoretical and empirical comparability. *International Journal of Research and Method in Education.* DOI:10.1080/1743727X.2012.710503

Bear, G. G., Minke, K. M., & Manning, M. A. (2002). Self-concept of students with learning disabilities: A meta-analysis. School Psychology Review, 31, 405-427.

Craven, R. G., & Marsh, H. W. (2008). The centrality of self-concept construct for psychological wellbeing and unlocking human potential: Implications for child and educational psychologists. *Educational and Child Psychology, 25*, 104-118.

Craven, R. G., Marsh, H. W., & Burnett, P. (2003). Cracking the self-concept enhancement conundrum. A call and blueprint for the next generation of self-concept enhancement research. In H. W. Marsh, R. G. Craven & D. M. McInerney (Eds.), *International advances in self research: Speaking to the future* (pp. 91-126). Grennwich, CT: Information Age.

Craven, R. G., Marsh, H. W., & Debus, R. L. (1991). Effects of internally focused feedback and attributional feedback on the enhancement of academic self-concept. *Journal of Educational Psychology, 83*, 17-27.

Craven, R. G., Marsh, H. W., Debus, R. L., & Jayasinghe, U. (2001). Diffusion effects: Control Group Contamination Threats to the Validity of Teacher-Administered Interventions. *Journal of Educational Psychology, 93*, 639-645.

Craven, R. G., & Yeung, A. S. (2008). International best practice in effective educational interventions: Why self-concept matters and examples from bullying, peer support, reading, and mathematics research. In D. M. McInerney, A. Darmanegara Liem & S. Van Etten (Eds.) *Teaching and learning: International best practice.* Charlotte, NC: Information Age Publishing.

Eccles, J. S., & Midgley, C. (1989). Stage/environment fit: Developmentally appropriate classrooms for early adolescents. In R. Ames & C. Ames (Eds.), *Research on motivation in education* (Vol. 3, pp. 139-181). New York: Academic Press.

Eccles, J. S., Midgley, C., Wigfield, A., Buchanan, C. M., Reuman, D., Flanagan, C., & MacIver, D. (1993). Development during adolescence. The impact of stage-environment fit on young adolescents' experiences in schools and families. *American Psychologist, 48*, 90-101.

Eccles, J. S., Wigfield, A., Flanagan, C. A., Miller, C., Reuman, D. A.,, & Yee, D. (1989). Self-concepts, domain values, and self-esteem: Relations and changes at early adolescence. *Journal of Personality, 57*, 283-310.

Elbaum, B., & Vaughn, S. (2001). School-based interventions to enhance the self-concept of students with learning disabilities: A meta-analysis. *The Elementary School Journal, 101,* 303-329.

Elbaum, B., & Vaughn, S. (2003). For which students with learning disabilities are self-concept interventions effective? *Journal of Learning Disabilities, 36,* 101-108.

Ellis, L. A., Marsh, H. W., & Craven, R. G. (2005). Navigating the transition to adolescence and secondary school: A critical evaluation of the impact of peer support. In H. W. Marsh, R. G. Craven & D. M. McInerney (Eds.), *International advances in self research: New frontiers in self research* (pp. 329-355). Greenwich, CT: Information Age Publishing.

Guay, F., Marsh, H. W., & Boivin, M. (2003). Academic self-concept and academic achievement: A developmental perspective on their causal ordering. *Journal of Educational Psychology, 95*, 124-136.

Haney, P., & Durlak, J. A. (1998). Changing self-esteem in children and adolescents. A meta-analytic review. *Journal of Clinical Child Psychology, 27*, 423-433.

Hattie, J. (1992). *Self-concept.* Hillsdale, NJ: Lawrence Erlbaum.

Leung, K. C., Marsh, H. W., Craven, R. G., Yeung, A. S., & Abduljabbar, A. S. (2012, online fist). Domain specificity between peer support and self-concept. *The Journal of Early Adolescence.* online first published on March 4, 2012, DOI:10.1177/0272431611436130.

Marsh, H. W. (1984). Relations among dimensions of self-attribution, dimensions of self-concept, and academic achievements. *Journal of Educational Psychology, 76*, 1291-1308.

Marsh, H. W. (1986). Verbal and math self-concepts: An internal/external frame of reference model. *American Educational Research Journal, 23*, 129-149.

Marsh, H. W. (1990a). Influences of internal and external frames of reference on the formation of math and English self-concepts. *Journal of Educational Psychology, 82*, 107-116.

Marsh, H. W. (1990b). A multidimensional, hierarchical self-concept: Theoretical and empirical justification. *Educational Psychology Review, 2*, 77-172.

Marsh, H. W. (1990c). *Self Description Questionnaire-I (SDQ I). Manual.* Macarthur, N.S.W. Australia: University of Western Sydney.

Marsh, H. W. (1990d). *Self Description Questionnaire-II (SDQ II). Manual.* Macarthur, N.S.W. Australia: University of Western Sydney.

Marsh, H. W. (1990e). The structure of academic self-concept: The Marsh/Shavelson model. *Journal of Educational Psychology, 82*, 623-636.

Marsh, H. W., & Craven, R. (1997). Academic self-concept: Beyond the dustbowl. In G. Phye (Ed.), *Handbook of classroom assessment: Learning, achievement, and adjustment* (pp. 131-198). Orlando, FL: Academic Press.

Marsh, H. W., & Craven, R. G. (2005). A reciprocal effects model of the causal ordering of self-concept and achievement. New support for the benefits of enhancing self-concept. In H. W. Marsh, R. G. Craven, & D. M. McInerney (Eds.), *International advances in self research: New frontiers for self-research* (pp. 17-51). Greenwich, CT: Information Age.

Marsh, H. W., & Craven, R. G. (2006). Reciprocal effects of self-concept and performance from a multidimensional perspective. Beyond seductive pleasure and unidimensional perspectives. *Perspectives on Psychological Science, 1,* 133-163.

Marsh, H. W., Craven, R. G., & Debus, R. (1999). Separation of competency and affect components of multiple dimensions of academic self-concept: A developmental perspective. *Merrill-Palmer Quarterly, 45,* 567-601.

Marsh, H., Gerlach, E., Trautwein, U., Lüdtke, O., & Brettschneider, W.-D. (2007). Longitudinal study of preadolescent sport self-concept and performance: Reciprocal effects and causal ordering. *Child Development, 78,* 1640-1656.

Marsh, H. W., & O'Mara, A. J. (2008). Self-Concept is as multidisciplinary as it is multidimensional. In H. W. Marsh, R. G. Craven, & D. M. McInerney (Eds.), *Self-processes, learning, and enabling human potential. Dynamic new approaches* (pp. 87-115). Charlotte, NC: Information Age.

Marsh, H. W., & O'Neill, R. (1984). Self-Description Questionnaire III: The construct validity of multidimensional self-concept ratings by late adolescents. *Journal of Educational Measurement, 21,* 153-174.

Marsh, H. W., & Peart, N. D. (1988). Competitive and cooperative physical fitness training programs for girls: Effects on physical fitness and multidimensional self-concepts. *Journal of Sport and Exercise Psychology, 10,* 390-407.

Marsh, H. W., & Perry, C. (2005). Does a positive self-concept contribute to winning gold medals in elite swimming? The causal ordering of elite athlete self-concept and championship performance. *Journal of Sport and Exercise Psychology, 27,* 71-91.

Marsh, H. W., & Richards, G. E. (1988). The Outward Bound Bridging Course for low-achieving males: Effects on academic achievement and multidimensional self-concepts. *Australian Journal of Psychology, 40,* 281-298.

Marsh, H. W., Richards, G. E., & Barnes, J. (1986a). Multidimensional self-concepts: A long term follow-up of the effect of participation in an Outward Bound program. *Personality and Social Psychology Bulletin, 12,* 475-492.

Marsh, H. W., Richards, G. E., & Barnes, J. (1986b). Multidimensional self-concepts: The effect of participation in an Outward Bound Program. *Journal of Personality and Social Psychology, 50*, 195-204.

Marsh, H. W., Relich, J. D., & Smith, I. D. (1983). Self-concept: The construct validity of interpretations based upon the SDQ. *Journal of Personality and Social Psychology, 45,* 173-187.

Marsh, H. W., Trautwein, U., Lüdtke, O., Köller, O., & Baumert, J. (2005). Academic self-concept, interest, grades and standardized test scores: Reciprocal effects model of causal ordering. *Child Development, 76,* 397-416.

Marsh, H. W., & Yeung, A. S. (1997a). Causal effects of academic self-concept on academic achievement: Structural equation models of longitudinal data. *Journal of Educational Psychology, 89*, 41-54.

Marsh, H. W., & Yeung, A. S. (1997b). Coursework selection: The effects of academic self-concept and achievement. *American Educational Research Journal, 34*, 691-720.

Marsh, H. W. & Yeung, A. S. (1998). Longitudinal structural equation models of academic self-concept and achievement: Gender differences in the development of math and English constructs. *American Educational Research Journal, 35*, 705-738.

Möller, J., Pohlmann, B., Köller, O., & Marsh, H. W. (2009). A meta-analytic path analysis of the internal/external frame of reference model of academic achievement and academic self-concept. *Review of Educational Research, 79,* 1129-1167.

Möller, J., Retelsdorf, J., Köller, O., & Marsh, H. W. (2011). The reciprocal internal/external frame of reference model: An integration of models of relations between academic achievement and self-concept. *American Educational Research Journal, 48,* 1315-1346.

O'Mara, A. J., Green, J., & Marsh, H. W. (2006). Administering self-concept interventions in schools: No training necessary? A meta-analysis. *International Education Journal, 7,* 524-533.

O'Mara, A. J., Marsh, H. W., Craven, R. G., & Debus, R. L. (2006). Do self-concept interventions make a difference? A synergistic blend of construct validation and meta-analysis. *Educational Psychologist, 41,* 181-206.

Shavelson, R. J., Hubner, J. J., & Stanton, G. C. (1976). Self-concept: Validation of construct interpretations. *Journal of Educational Research, 46*, 407-441.

Skaalvik, E. M., & Rankin, R. J. (1995). A test of the internal/external frame of reference model at different levels of math and verbal self-perception. *American Educational Research Journal , 32,* 161-184.

Skaalvik, E. M., & Skaalvik, S. (2002). Internal and external frames of reference for academic self-concept. *Educational Psychologist, 37,* 233-244.

Swann, W. B., Jr., Chang-Schneider, C., & Larsen McClarty, K. (2007). Do people's self-views matter? Self-concept and self-esteem in everyday life. *American Psychologist, 62,* 84-94.

Wigfield, A., Eccles, J., MacIver, D., Reuman, D. A., & Midgley, C. (1991). Transitions during early adolescence: Changes in children's domain-specific self-perceptions and general self-esteem across the transition to junior high school. *Developmental Psychology, 27,* 552-565.

Yeung, A. S. (2005). Reconsidering the measurement of student self-concept: Use and misuse in a Chinese context. In H. W. Marsh, R. G. Craven, & D. M. McInerney (Eds.), *International advances in self-concept research: Theory, measurement, research and application* (pp. 233-257). Sydney: Information Age.

Yeung, A. S. (2011). Student self-concept and effort: Gender and grade differences. *Educational Psychology, 31,* 749-772.

Yeung, A. S., Lau, S., & Nie, Y. (2011). Primary and secondary students' motivation in learning English: Grade and gender differences. *Contemporary Educational Psychology, 36,* 246-256.

In: Educational Programs and Special Education   ISBN: 978-1-62417-256-4
Editor: Sasha Dziuk   © 2013 Nova Science Publishers, Inc.

Chapter 3

HEALTH TRAINING PROGRAMMES

Caroline Opolski Medeiros[*1],
Terezinha Opolski Medeiros[#2] *and Suzi Barletto Cavalli*[†3]

[1]Nutrition Department and Nutrition in Foodservice Research Nucleus
(NUPPRE) of Federal University at Santa Catarina, Florianópolis, Brazil
[2]Integrated Health Center (CESIN), Paranaguá, Paraná, Brazil
[3]Nutrition Department and Nutrition in Foodservice Research Nucleus
(NUPPRE) of Federal University at Santa Catarina, Florianópolis, Brazil

ABSTRACT

This chapter will address the importance and main objectives in the
field of health training programs. Initially the methodologies for health
educational programs will be discussed. We will also discuss the
educational programs with focus on the improvement of the health and
the knowledge of the population. The results of training programs will be
discussed in this chapter, considering population's behavioral and
attitudinal changes. The teaching resources used in training programs
may influence the final result of this activity, therefore, recommendations
will be presented for the choice of resources to be used in courses. All

* Correspondent: Caroline Opolski Medeiros – Present Address: Street Dr. Antonio Augusto de
  Almeida, number 694. Cidade Universitária, Campinas, São Paulo, Brazil. Zip code 13083-
  755. Email: caroline.opolski@gmail.com.
Email: tereopol@hotmail.com.
† Email: suzi@ccs.ufsc.br.

recommendation and discussion will be made considering the population of programs. Furthermore, the topics discussed will also contribute to improve the health training programs that focus on the population, which constantly needs to learn more about different aspects and concepts in health. Also, the information submitted in the chapter could be used in effective educational programs for health professionals, strengthening its technical capability.

INTRODUCTION

The concept of health involves a state of physical development, social and mental well-being. Then, the concept is not only related to an absence of disease or infirmity [1].

To World Health Organization the health is fundamental human rights, then everybody must have access to basic health care [2]. Also, "a comprehensive understanding of health implies that all systems and structures which govern social and economic conditions and the physical environment should take account of the implications of their activities in relation to their impact on individual and collective health and well-being" [2, p.1].

The health can be seen as a positive concept that emphasizes the social and personal resources and the physical capacity. The people must be able to identify and to do the aspirations, satisfy their needs and change or adapt to the environment. So the health is not only a responsibility of the health sector, and it is important that people acquire a healthy life styles to their well-being [3].

Health promotion is a process of enabling people to increase control over their health, as well as to improve their health [2-4]. The health promotion is a wide social and political process, which includes the improving of the skills and capabilities of individuals, and actions focused on social, environmental and economical changes, in order to lessen their impact on public health and on the individual level [2,4].

In 1986, in Ottawa city, it was the first International Conference on Health Promotion. In this meeting it was written the charter for action to achieve health. The Ottawa Charter identified three basic strategies for health promotion: *advocacy* that focus on the essential conditions for health (social resource, economic and personal development); *enabling* to people do healthy choices; and *mediating* by all those concerned about contributing to health promotion (governments, health sectors, social and economic sectors, non-governmental organizations, local authorities, industry and the media) [2,4]. In this chapter we will focus on the process of enabling people.

In this chapter, education and training for specific diseases will not be discussed, since it would require a greater depth for each pathology. The intent of this material is to expose some important concepts in relation to health education for the population, in general, to contribute with the improvement of the educational programs.

HEALTH EDUCATION

The education is a development action about people into society. The objective is to enable people in a consciously and efficiently way, permitting that people create a value of the acquired content and use this day by day. In general the definitions of education put the individual as a subject in the center of the activities, and characterize the education as a process that influences the people to do changes, enabling the interaction with the environment [5].

According to World Health Organization a health-related education and information is a right of population, a right to health [6]. The health education involves some form of communication to increase the health knowledge, as well as the development of skills to improve the health of people and community [2]. The education program should not focus only on the transmission and communication of information. It is important that the program encourages and motivates people, contributing to the improvement of skills, and to increase self-confidence of the public. These factors are important to promotion of health [2]. The people must receive the information in a health education program, understand these information and be able to use them to make healthy decisions (eg.: choosing food to eat after having participated of a nutrition education).

In the health education the health professionals have an important role in the health promotion. These professionals should contribute in the development and offering of health education [3].

THE IMPORTANCE OF HEALTH EDUCATION FOR THE POPULATION

The health education contributes to people to have the opportunity to achieve their potential of health. This is possible because the access to information could enable healthy choices [4].

The preoccupation with the health of the population is continuing. With greater access to information by individuals, health education becomes an essential action. According to the Ottawa Charter, it is essential to teach people in all stages of their life, and enabling to act in the stages of the chronic diseases and injuries [4]. This action should be done in every place – in the work, at the school, at home – by health professionals and educators, for example.

It is possible to see the importance of this topic in the scientific publications. A simple research was carried out in May 2012, in Scopus and Scielo digital databases (Jan. 2007 until May 2012) to identify the studies published about this topic. The search was made with the following descriptors: [{training} or {education} or {teach}] and [{health}] and [{population}]. Considering the electronic databases investigated, 10,577 articles were found. Considering the year of publication of the articles it is possible to observe the current importance of this subject, since there is a continuous growth in the number of publications (figure 1).

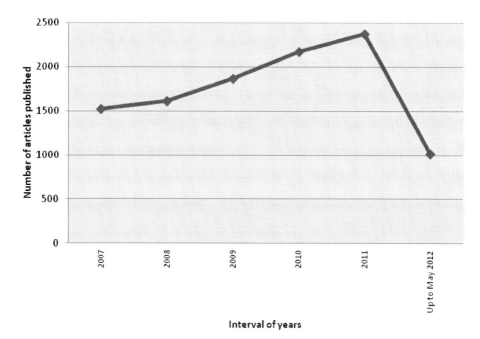

Figure 1. Number of published articles related to health training programs to population, according to the period of publication.

Table 1. Some studies about health education published in the last 3 years

Studies (authors and year of publication)	Topic of health training	Population (n)	Control group	Information about the methodology of training	Training results
Martínez et al, 2009	Nutrition education	Student (adolescent) (372)	No	One class (seminar) per month on nutrition education (for 6 months) and dietary prescription	Increase in intake of fruit and vegetables, decrease of the body mass index, increased breakfast consumption
Hsieh et al, 2009	Family-based nutrition health education and risk factors of stroke	Hypertensive patients and pre-hypertensive subjects and family members (all adults) (390)	Yes	Communication; website of program[1]; availability of consultation by telephone	In the intervention group: significant reduction in SBP and the blood pressure, improvement of total cholesterol and LDL cholesterol, increase in intake of fruit and vegetables and decrease of the body mass index
Calderon et al, 2009	Sex educative and/or HIV prevention	Adults (128)	Yes	Fifteen-minute of a HIV prevention video and in-person counseling	Mean scores of knowledge about HIV prevention was higher in the intervention group
Malow et al, 2009	Sex educative and/or HIV prevention	Adolescents (246)	Yes	Group sessions composed of 4–8 participants; 90-minute sessions during 8 weeks. Used an adaption of BART[2] (Becoming a Responsible Teen)	In the intervention group: greater knowledge about HIV prevention, more intention to use condoms, improved attitude about condom use, and higher safer sex self-efficacy
Yera-Casas et al, 2009	Cardiovascular diseases education	Elderly (100)	No	5 sessions by 60 days (from 15 to 15 days) to do an educational care plan individualized	Increase of knowledge about the disease (signs, symptoms, complications, etc.)
Landaeta-Jimenez et al, 2010	Nutrition education	Adults (1000)	No	Television campaign and printed education material	Increase in intake of fruit, vegetable and breakfast
Purcell et al, 2010	Cancer-related fatigue	Radiotherapy patients (9)	No	Two fatigue education and support sessions using *Power Point* presentation for 60 to 45 minutes; follow-up phone calls; a goal sheet and a strategy table	All patients rated as very good and excellent the new skill and information that they received in program; and they feel confident to manage fatigue

Table 1. (Continued)

Studies (authors and year of publication)	Topic of health training	Population (n)	Control group	Information about the methodology of training	Training results
Wu et al, 2010	Colorectal cancer education	Adults (304)	NO	Educational seminar using *Power Point* presentation on early detection of CRC; Educational brochures about CRC; health exam	Increase of knowledge about CRC and an improvement in attitude about importance to do screening
Barysch et al, 2010	Skin cancer education	General population (>12000)[3]	No	Use of internet; a website developed: Skincheck® website	Approximately 85% of women and 82% of men who visited the site, followed the recommendations about visiting a health professional. Eight participants had malignant lesions detected
Malekafzali et al, 2010	Nutrition, mental health, and physical activity	Elderly (100)	No	Home visits and face to face elderly education and referral to physicians	Increased the aerobic exercises in women; the life satisfaction among women; feeling happy most of the time in women and in men respectively
Comellas et al, 2010	Type 2 diabetes and heart disease	Adults with diabetes (6)	No	10-hour education class, 2-hours per week for 5 consecutive weeks	Significant improvements in several physical activity and nutrition activities
Philis-Tsimikas et al, 2011	Diabetes education	Adults (207)	Yes	8 week, 2-hours diabetes self-management classes and monthly support groups	In the intervention group: significant improvements absolute levels of HbA1c and HDL cholesterol, absolute levels of HbA1c, total cholesterol, HDL cholesterol, and LDL cholesterol
Surjadi et al, 2011	Hepatitis C education	Adults (201)	No	2-hours of education, using *Power Point* presentation	Significant improvement in the overall test scores by 14%, specifically about HCV transmission, general knowledge, and health care maintenance

Studies (authors and year of publication)	Topic of health training	Population (n)	Control group	Information about the methodology of training	Training results
Allaire et al, 2011	Education Program on Patient Blood Pressure	Adults (8183)	Yes	Lectures	In the intervention group: Decrease of SBP and DBP
Thakur et al, 2012	Nutrition education and breastfeeding	Newborns and their mothers (184)	Yes	Nutrition education twice a week for 2 months	In the intervention group: The rate of early initiation of breastfeeding and the exclusive breastfeeding was higher; lower respiratory illness

SBP: systolic blood pressure; DBP:dyastolic blood pressure; CRC: colorectal cancer; HCV: Hepatitis C.

[1]Website developed by researchers, which had all materials of health education programme.

[2]Becoming a Responsible Teen (BART) was development by St. Lawrence et al [40]. It is a cognitive-behavioral intervention based on information-motivation-behavior model (IMB model).

[3]More than 12,000 visitors visited the webpage.

In the table 1 it is possible to see some studies published in the last 3 years, in which a specific public received health education. Although the topics of the education programs have been different, it is possible to see that all programs have had success. The health education program enables increasing the knowledge of the people, and can contributes to behavioral change and the attitude that will be good for life, welfare and health of people.

TRAINING TOPICS

There are a lot of health education programs in the world. Among the topics of Health dealt with in the training courses there are: eating health and nutrition education [7-10], sex educative and HIV prevention [11,12], cardiovascular diseases education [8,13,14], public health [15], cancer education [16-18], diabetes education [19-21], rabies prevention [22], hepatitis C [23], hypertension prevention and control [24] and others (table 1).

Some times there are two or more topics included in the same education program. For example in a nutrition education it is possible that the educator speaks about the importance of physical activity; or in a program about hypertension control is also common and necessary to include information about nutrition.

When the focus is on health education, it is possible to link together a lot of topics in the same training. It is important that the topics of the education program are well-crafted. As well as, one must be careful not to put too much information in education program to be passed for the target audience. If necessary, it is recommended that more sessions about health education be conducted for the population, so that they can assimilate better the information, as in the study of Yera-Casas *et al*, Malow *et al* and Comellas *et al* [12,14,20] (table 1). Also, in order to make an effective action of health promotion it is necessary to include together to formal evidence, external information, practical experience and individual [25].

In health education it is important to include information related to social, economical and environmental conditions of the people, because it can have impacts on their health. Moreover it must be discussed the individual and behavioral risk factors, and the use of health systems in this process [2]. Buta *et al* did a formative research to identify some health problems in the population, and discussed the materials that would be used in the health education program [26]. A participative method and the importance of the "listening to each other" were discussed by Levesque *et al* in the development of a original video to be used in dental education [27]. Katz *et al* also verified the value to listen the target public, when the participants of the study provided important information in the development of an educational video to colorectal cancer screening and to improve patient knowledge about this disease. Through focal group participation, patients contributed with the production of this video, identifying colorectal cancer screening barriers and making suggestion about the information that the researchers could include in the video [28].

TRAINING METHODS AND STRATEGIES

Knowing the methods and strategies that are being used in health programs is important, because the teaching resources used in training programs can influence the final result of this activity. Medeiros *et al* evaluated methodological strategies adopted by food safety training for food service workers. In this review the authors found evidence that the methodology of training can influence the final results of behavior of the food handlers. The interactive media was the most widely accepted resource by food handlers – particularly audiovisuals, videos and lectures – in addition to recreational activities involving hands-on courses, all of which brought more benefits to the trainees [29].

Others researchers also evaluated the training methods and strategies in health program, as Randolph, Whitaker and Arellano, that researched the health promotion intervention strategies. The authors classified some strategies to use in programs. Among the strategies identified there are the entertainment education, internet-based education and mass media advertising, which are also discussed below [30].

Entertainment-Education Communication Strategy

In the entertainment education, the educators use these resources to teach people about health aspects [30]. There is the intentional incorporation of educational messages into of the entertainment with objective of the behavioral change of the audience public [31]. This entertainment medium can be film, radio, talk show, soap opera, and others. The advantage of using entertainment education in health promotion is the possibility of involving the target population in the stories, such that members can self-identify [30]. Another advantage is the fact that these programs can be entertaining and educational at the same time, different from the boredom-education in some types of programs [32].

Rogers *et al* investigated the effect of radio soap opera on family planning behavior in Tanzania, in 1993 to 1997 [31]. The authors observed a significant increase in the knowledge about the contraceptive methods and in the use of the contraceptives in the intervention site. Similar results were found by Vaughan, Regis and Catherine after analyzing an entertainment-education radio soap opera that focused on the promotion of family planning, HIV prevention and other social development topics [33]. The authors observed an increase of awareness of the use of contraceptives.

Internet-Based Education

The internet is a good opportunity to promote health education. The computer and others telecommunication technologies have been used to educate people by health professionals [30]. The education can be done to specific website on the promotion of health or between an online communication between doctor and patient (online patient-provider communication). Moreover, a lot of materials as booklets, folders and important documents about promotion of health are available in official websites. These materials can also be used in education programs of the population. We emphasize that it is important that the materials posted on the website, which are intended to health education of the population, have a scientific basis, so that the population can be educated properly.

Among the available websites, that one from the World Health Organization is one of the best known (http://www.who.int/en/). The documents have a scientific basis, and many papers are published in more than one language (eg. English and Spanish), which enable the access of a lot of people. A material of World Health Organization, which can be used, is Health Promotion Glossary [2]. In this material there are important definitions, and is revised and supplemented from time to time. Moreover, World Health Organization has several educational materials on healthy eating, food security and nutrition, prevention of chronic non-communicable diseases, among others. Furthermore it is recommended to use materials prepared by health organization of the country, where the health education will be made.

Another example of internet use for education of the population is the project "Food Care" developed by Waissmann and collaborators, in Brazil. The authors developed a website and three educational videos to alert the public about foodborne illness at home. There was a concern to develop differentiated information for children and others to adults, as well as describing specifications for special groups (pregnant women, elderly and immunocompromised) [34]. Another initiative had Barysch *et al* to make available a website for education of skin cancer [16]. In the latter work the authors contributed to diagnosis of eight detections of malignant tumors (table 1). Hsieh *et al* chose to develop a site and provide educational information in the same time, as an additional education program to hypertensive patients [8].

Mass Media

Mass media strategies have been used extensively in health promotion campaigns [30], for example, in prevention message to use drug [35], the message to change HIV-AIDS-related behaviors [36,37], support to alcohol consumption prevention [38,39], and nutrition education [9].

The use of these methods in health education can be done in televisions, radios and newspaper, for example. These strategies can be used during a short or a long time periods. Frequently this technique is used when the professionals want to focus on a large number of people [30].

For example, the use of television in this strategy of mass media. Today a lot of people have a television in their houses. This mass media is a good option to health promotion in federal, state and municipal level. The television is a medium of communication that besides carrying out an awareness in the population about something related to health (eg. a campaign about the importance of self-breast examination) could also educate the population, teaching how to make (eg. teach how to make the self-breast examination).

Communication in the Classroom

In this strategy the health information is taught in a lecture. This communication is very frequently in the health promotion program [eg.7,8,10,12,14,17,18]. The educator speaks to people in a place that can be in a school, hospital or in a place on the community [eg. church]. The duration of the lecture topics change in different programs, but we observed that oftentimes each session last no more than one hour [eg.17,26]. In educative program about HIV prevention done by Malow *et al* the duration of each session was of 90 minutes (table 1) [12].

The communication in the classroom can be used together with other strategies.

Audiovisual Resources

Audiovisual resources are frequently used in education programs, principally there is the inclusion of this means in the communication in the classroom.

Among the audiovisual resources we can cite the multimedia and videos. The presentation of a lecture using the multimedia may be more effective in education when compared to only a "class with speech." When videos are used, can be used a film to portray the topic of educational program [eg.26], a documentary with the same focus [eg.26], or an own material, designed to be used in the program or done in other similiar program [eg.27]. In the use of multimedia, the material could be presented using the *Power Point* [eg.17,18,23].

The audiovisual resources are being used by many researchers in the health education programs [eg.11,13,17,18] and the results are satisfactory. Aldana *et al* conducted 28 video classes in worksite about coronary risk reduction. The topics of the videos were: modern medicine and medical myths, nutritional status, healthy diet, physical activity, self-worth, atherosclerosis, coronary risk factors, diabetes, hypertension, cholesterol, osteoporosis, cancer, lifestyle and health. Among participants of educational program it was observed a decrease of the body mass index, weight, systolic blood pressure, dyastolic blood pressure, resting heart rate, total cholesterol, HDL cholesterol, LDL cholesterol, triglycerides and glucose [13]. Purcell *et al* and Wu *et al* also found satisfactory results using the *Power Point* in their health education program (table 1) [17,18].

Printed Material

The production of printed material is a good option to health education. The flyers and handbook informative can be used alone, or together with other resources to educate. Purcell *et al* designed a handbook about cancer-related fatigue for participants accompanied by a verbal presentation (lecture) and a *Power Point* presentation [17]. In education program developed by Aldana *et al* the participants received materials (textbook and workbooks) to follow the video topics about colorectal cancer [13]. Landaeta-Jimenez, Patiño and Galicia used printed material, with information about nutrition, at the same time that had an education program on the television [9].

Note also the Ministry of Health of the countries publishes flyers, manuals, guide pockets, and other printed materials for education to population. There are different health topics, as well as the materials are focused on the age group (eg children, adults, elderly) and on characteristics of the population (eg pregnant women and immunocompromised). These materials are often available on the internet for the community in general. The use of these materials for educational programs in health is also important.

CONCLUSION

Health approaches of population-based to promote healthy behaviors may change according population group: students, teenagers, adults, seniors, pregnant women, low-income people among others. Thus, it is necessary to consider the characteristics of the target population since the elaboration phase of the educational program. Whenever it is necessary, the program should also be adapted to the local needs.

Different topics are focused on health education programs: public health, diabetes education, eating health and nutrition education, educative sex and HIV prevention, cardiovascular diseases education, cancer education, rabies prevention, and others. Sometimes there is more than one topic in the health education program.

The language must be appropriate for the target population. When the intention is to conduct a training in a community which has individuals with different characteristics, it is recommended to perform different groups, separated by age for example, focusing on the content and on the understanding of each person.

It is recommended that the material to be used in courses and training is specific for each population. It is important to the realization of previous studies to identify the gaps of knowledge of the population, and thus a suitable training material can be prepared. But if it is not possible to develop a specific material for education, pre-existing materials can be used, such as those published by World Health Organization and by the governments of each country by its health agencies.

If in the education program there is a lot of information, it is recommended to divide the topic of the education program to teach in different days. Thus, the information will be better used by the target population.

Different types of methodologies and strategies for health education are being successfully used in educational programs: entertainment-education communication strategy, internet-based education, mass media, communication in the classroom, audiovisual resources and printed material. The communication in the classroom is frequently used in the education programs, as well as, audiovisual resources and printed material. Oftentimes, audiovisual resources and printed material are used together with other strategies, for example, the communication in the classroom. The delivery of printed materials for participants accompanied of lectures or videos is a good option, because even after the "course", participants will have the health information. It can be seen in researches that the use of the internet to improve health education is increasing. The studies have demonstrated good acceptance and participation of the population in these types of education. Also, most of researches also developed a new material to health information, according to the characteristics of the target public of the program.

Regardless of the type of strategy and methodology to be used in educational programs, it is important to make a discussion with the participants so that the doubts are solved. Furthermore it is recommended to do the evaluation of the program to verify if the objectives are being achieved.

The development and provision of training courses are crucial to achieve behavioral changes and improve skills and knowledge. Additional studies are recommended to verify if the health behavior changes achieved after the trainings are kept during the time. If necessary, new educational programs should be conducted.

ACKNOWLEGMENTS

Reviewed by Mariana Schievano Danelon - State University of Campinas (UNICAMP), Campinas, São Paulo, Brazil.

Reviewed by Gabriela Datsch Bennemann - State University of MidWest (UNICENTRO), Guarapuava, Paraná, Brazil.

REFERENCES

[1]   World Health Organization – WHO. WHO Definition of Health. 1948 [cited 2012-08-20]. Available from: *http://www.who.int/en/*

[2]   World Health Organization – WHO. Health promotion glossary. 1998 [cited 2012-06-15]. Available from: *http://www.who.int/en/*

[3]   [3] World Health Organization – WHO. Milestones in Health Promotion Statements from Global Conferences. 2009 [cited 2012-06-15]. Available from: *http://www.who.int/en/*

[4]   World Health Organization – WHO. *Ottawa charter for health promotion.* 1986 [cited 2012-06-15]. Available from: *http://www.euro.who.int/en/*

[5]   Calleja, J.M.R. (2008). Os professores desde século. Algumas reflexões. *Revista institucional Universidad Tecnológica del Chocó: Investigación, Biodiversidad y Desarrollo*, 27 (1), 109-117.

[6]   World Health Organization – WHO. Governance for health in the 21st century. 2012 [cited 2012-08-20]. Available from: *http://www.euro.who.int/en/*

[7] Martínez, Ma.I., Hernández, M.D., Ojeda, M., Mena, R., Alegre, A., & Alfonso, J.L. (2009). Desarrollo de un programa de educación nutricional y valoración del cambio de hábitos alimentarios saludables en una población de estudiantes de Enseñanza Secundaria Obligatoria. *Nutricion Hospitalaria*, 24 (4), 504-510.

[8] Hsieh, Y.-C., Hung, C.-T., Lien, L.-M., Bai, C.-H., Chen, W.-H., Yeh, C.-Y., Chen, Y.-H., Hsieh, F.-I., Chiu, H.-C., Chiou, H.-Y., & Hsu, C.Y. (2009). A significant decrease in blood pressure through a family-based nutrition health education programme among community residents in Taiwan. *Public Health Nutrition*, 12 (4), 570-577.

[9] Landaeta-Jimenez, M., Patiño, E., & Galicia, N. (2010). Campaña de educación nutricional contra la malnutrición por medios de comunicación masivos en Venezuela. *Anales Venezolanos de Nutricion*, 23 (1), 26-33.

[10] Thakur, S.K., Roy, S.K., Paul, K., Khanam, M., Khatun, W., & Sarker, D. (2012). Effect of nutrition education on exclusive breastfeeding for nutritional outcome of low birth weight babies. *European Journal of Clinical Nutrition*, 66 (3), 376-381.

[11] Calderon, Y., Leider, J., Hailpern, S., Haughey, M., Ghosh, R., Lombardi, P., Bijur, P., & Bauman, L. (2009). A randomized control trial evaluating the educational effectiveness of a rapid hiv posttest counseling. *Sexually Transmitted Diseases*, 36 (4), 207-210.

[12] Malow, R.M., Stein, J.A., McMahon, R.C., Dévieux, J.G., Rosenberg, R., & Jean-Gilles, M. (2009). Effects of a Culturally Adapted HIV Prevention Intervention in Haitian Youth. *Journal of the Association of Nurses in AIDS Care*, 20 (2), 110-121.

[13] Aldana, S.G., Greenlaw, R.L., Diehl, H.A., Merrill, R.M., Salberg, A., & Englert, H. (2008). A video-based lifestyle intervention and changes in coronary risk cardio material. *Health Education Research*, 23 (1), 115-124.

[14] Yera-Casas, A.M., Mateos-Higuera del Olmo, S., Ferrero-Lobo, J., & Páez-Gutiérrez, T.D. (2009). Evaluación de la intervención educativa al paciente anciano con insuficiencia cardíaca, realizada por enfermería a través de un plan de cuidados estandarizado. *Enfermeria Clinica*, 19 (4), 191-198.

[15] Malekafzali, H., Eftekhari, M.B., Hejazi, F., Khojasteh, T., Noot, R.H., Falahat, K., & Faridi, T. (2010). The effectiveness of educational intervention in the health promotion in elderly people. *Iranian Journal of Public Health*, 39 (2), 18-23.

[16] Barysch, M.-J., Cozzio, A., Kolm, I., Hrdlicka, S.R., Brand, C., Hunger, R., Kreyden, O., Schaffner, R., Zaugg, T., & Dummer, R. (2010). Internet based health promotion campaign against skin cancer – Results of www.skincheck.ch in Switzerland. *European Journal of Dermatology*, 20 (1), 109-114.

[17] Purcell, A., Fleming, J., Bennett, S., & Haines, T. (2010). Development of an educational intervention for cancer-related fatigue. *British Journal of Occupational Therapy*, 73 (7), 327-333.

[18] Wu, T.-Y., Kao, J.Y., Hsieh, H.-F., Tang, Y.-Y., Chen, J., Lee, J., & Oakley, D. (2010). Effective colorectal cancer education for Asian Americans: A Michigan program. *Journal of Cancer Education*, 25 (2), 146-152.

[19] Lalonde, J., Jeambey, Z., & Starkey, L.J. (2007). Media training for diabetes prevention: A participatory evaluation material. *Canadian Journal of Dietetic Practice and Research*, 68 (3), 132-136.

[20] Comellas, M., Walker, E.A., Movsas, S., Merkin, S., Zonszein, J., & Strelnick, H. (2010). Training community health promoters to implement diabetes self-management support programs for urban minority adults. *Diabetes Educator*, 36 (1), 141-151.

[21] Philis-Tsimikas, A., Fortmann, A., Lleva-Ocana, L., Walker, C., & Gallo, L.C. (2011). Peer-led diabetes education programs in high-risk Mexican Americans improve glycemic control compared with standard approaches: a Project Dulce promotora randomized trial. *Diabetes care*, 34 (9), 1926-1931.

[22] Kikuti, M., Paploski, I.A.D., Silva, M.D.C.P., de Oliveira, E.A., da Silva, A.W.C., & Biondo, A.W. (2011). Prevention educational program of human rabies transmitted by bats in rain forest preserved area of southern Brazilian coast. *Zoonoses and Public Health*, 58 (8), 529-532.

[23] Surjadi, M., Torruellas, C., Ayala, C., Yee Jr., H.F., & Khalili, M. (2011). Formal patient education improves patient knowledge of hepatitis C in vulnerable populations. *Digestive Diseases and Sciences*, 56 (1), 213-219.

[24] Allaire, B.T., Trogdon, J.G., Egan, B.M., Lackland, D.T., & Masters, D. (2011). Measuring the impact of a continuing medical education program on patient blood pressure. *Journal of Clinical Hypertension*, 13 (7), 517-522.

[25] Tang, K.C., Ehsani, J., & McQueen, D. (2003). Evidence based health promotion: recollections, reflections and reconsiderations. *Journal of Epidemiology and Community Health*, 57 (11), 841–843.

[26] Buta, B., Brewer, L., Hamlin, D.L., Palmer, M.W., Bowie, J., & Gielen, A. (2011). An innovative faith-based healthy eating program: from class assignment to real-world application of PRECEDE/PROCEED. *Health promotion practice*, 12 (6), 867-875.

[27] Lévesque, M.C., Dupéré, S., Loignon, C., Levine, A., Laurin, I., Charbonneau, A., & Bedos, C. (2009). Bridging the poverty gap in dental education: how can people living in poverty help us? *Journal of Dental Education*, 73 (9), 1043-1054.

[28] Katz, M.L., Heaner, S., Reiter, P., van Putten, J., Murray, L., McDougle, L., Cegala, D.J., Post, D., David, P., Slater, M., & Paskett, E.D. (2009). Development of an educational video to improve patient knowledge and communication with their healthcare providers about colorectal cancer screening. *American Journal of Health Education*, 40 (4), 220–228.

[29] Medeiros, C.O., Cavalli, S.B., Salay, E., & Proença, R.P.C. (2011). Assessment of the methodological strategies adopted by food safety training programmes for food service workers: A systematic review. *Food Control*, 22 (8), 1136-1144.

[30] Randolph, K.A., Whitaker, P., & Arellano, A. (2012). The effects of environmental strategies in health promotion campaigns: A review. *Evaluation and Program Planning*, 35 (3), 344-353.

[31] Rogers, E.M., Vaughan, P.W., Swalehe, M.A., Rao, N., Svenkerud, P., & Sood, S. (1999). Effects of an entertainment–education radio soap opera on family planning behavior in Tanzania. *Studies in Family Planning*, 30 (3), 193–211.

[32] Brown, W.J., & Singhal, A. (1999). Entertainment-Education Media Strategies for Social Change: Promises and Problems. In D. Demen II. K. VIIInnmath (Ed.L), *Mass Media. Social Control and Social* (pp. 263-280). Amea, Iowa: Iowa State Univenity Press.

[33] Vaughan, P.W., Regis, A., & St. Catherine, E. (2000). Effects of an Entertainment-Education Radio Soap Opera on Family Planning And HIV Prevention in St. Lucia. *International Family Planning Perspectives*, 26(4), 148–157.

[34] Fiocruz. Website Cuidar dos alimentos. 2012 [cited 2012-07-01]. Available from: *http://www.cuidardosalimentos.fiocruz.br/*.

[35] Crano, W.D, & Burgoon, M. (2002). *Mass Media and Drug Prevention: Classic and Contemporary Theories and Research*. Mahwah, NJ: Lawrence Erlbaum Associates.

[36] Bertrand, J., O'Reilly, K., Denison, J., Anhang, R., & Sweat, M. (2006). Systematic review of the effectiveness of mass media communication programs to change HIV/AIDSrelated behaviors in developing countries. *Health Education Research*, 21 (4), 567–597.

[37] Babalola, S., & Vonrasek, C. (2005). Communication, ideation and contraceptive use in Burkina Faso: An application of the propensity score matching method. *Journal of Family Planning and Reproductive Health Care*, 31 (3), 207–212.

[38] Casswell, S., & Gilmore, L. (1989). An evaluated community action project on alcohol. *Journal of Studies on Alcohol*, 50 (4), 339–346.

[39] Mattern, J.L., & Neighbors, C. (2004). Social Norms Campaign: Examining the relationship between changes in perceived norm and changes in drinking levels. *Journal of Studies on Alcohol*, 65 (4), 89–93.

[40] St. Lawrence, J.S., Brasfield, T.L., Jefferson, K.W., Alleyne, E., O'Bannon, R.E., & Shirley, A. (1995). Cognitive-behavioral intervention to reduce African-American adolescents' risk for HIV infection. *Journal of Consulting and Clinical Psychology*, 63 (2), 221–237.

In: Educational Programs and Special Education   ISBN: 978-1-62417-256-4
Editor: Sasha Dziuk   © 2013 Nova Science Publishers, Inc.

Chapter 4

TRANSFORMING TEACHER PREPARATION PROGRAMS TO MEET THE NEEDS OF ALL LEARNERS

*Amy Rogers, Rachel Hickoff-Cresko
and Marisa Macy*
Lycoming College, Williamsport, Pennsylvania, US

ABSTRACT

Due to national and state policy changes and compliance with No Child Left Behind (NCLB) and Individuals with Disabilities Education Improvement Act (IDEIA), children with special needs are taught in inclusive classrooms. Until recent years, general education teachers were not prepared to instruct students with special needs. Additionally, special education teachers were not fully aware of the general education curriculum. In order to truly meet the diverse needs of all children and prepare teachers to teach all learners, teacher preparation programs need to address thorough and appropriate special education inclusive teaching practices and offer instruction in co-teaching paradigms. This article will discuss current trends in licensing bodies to offer more specified special education teacher preparation and address co-teaching models. Discourse will advance the value of teacher education programs to provide deeper and more relevant instruction and offer field experiences that will prepare teachers who are more skilled and capable of helping all learners reach higher levels of achievement.

INTRODUCTION

Both general education and special education teacher preparation programs are changing across the nation. According to a summary report from the Center on Personnel Studies in Special Education (2003), general education teachers are being better prepared to deliver inclusive services to students with disabilities (Geiger, Crutchfield, and Mainzer, p. 4). Changes in law and policy emphasizing student access to, and achievement in, the general education curriculum have led to changes in teacher preparation programs. Teacher education programs are in a position to ensure that preservice teachers acquire the knowledge, dispositions, and performances required to succeed in educating students with disabilities before they get to the classroom (Turner, 2003).

The National Comprehensive Center for Teacher Quality's (NCCTQ) Issue Paper on Improving Student Outcomes in General and Special Education (2008) presents a brief review of the legal and policy foundations and best professional practices for inclusive services.

According to this report, there are key components that should be incorporated into teacher preparation programs. These services include effective inclusion of students with disabilities, including general and special education teachers' and teacher candidates' knowledge of inclusion and diverse instructional strategies, collaborative skills and experience for general and special education teachers and teacher candidates, competencies with promoting student and family involvement, and leadership skills required to implement and sustain inclusive efforts (Holdheide and Reschly, p. 14).

In the last twenty years there have been a variety of studies and literature reviews on the requirements for special education licensure and general education teacher preparation. This commentary is not intended to be a literature review, but rather a glimpse into why teacher preparation programs nationwide have changed their licensing bodies to ensure quality teacher preparation for 21st Century learners by exploring legal and policy foundations that have set the stage for changes.

It also provides a discussion on how teacher education programs have incorporated changes in policy by embracing the value of co-teaching and field experiences. Teacher preparation programs are equipping preservice teachers with more specialized knowledge and skills by better preparing teachers to help all students meet the changing academic needs set forth by national and state governing boards.

POLICY CHANGES

We are living in a time of constant educational change, a time where social and political transformation has affected our schools and children. To keep up to par with these trends, teacher preparation programs must make changes in the way that they prepare teachers to meet the needs of all level learners.

This being said, preparing general education teachers to work effectively with all students is critical. The number of states requiring general education teachers to take coursework in special education has risen over the past 30 years (Geiger, 2006; Geiger, Crutchfield, and Mainzer, 2003) from 10 in 1979 to 37 in 1990 (Geiger, 2006). A nationally representative survey of teacher preparation programs found that most (95 percent of those surveyed) require at least some training in serving students with disabilities and that more than half require field experience (US Government Accountability Office, 2009).

The following legal and policy changes have prompt edinstitutions that offer teacher preparation programs to provide more in-depth training for teachers working with all children who will be in their future classrooms.

Least Restrictive Environment (LRE)

Federal policies contributed to the need to better train general education teachers to work with students with disabilities. The principle of least restrictive environment (LRE) was foundational in the landmark Education of All Handicapped Children Act (1975), which was reauthorized as the Individuals with Disabilities Education Act (IDEA) in 1991 and 1997, and then reauthorized as the Individuals with Disabilities Education Improvement Act (IDEIA) in 2004 (Holdheide andReschly, 2008). Researchers Bocala, Morgan, Mundry, and Mello (2010) at the Regional Education Laboratory Northeast and Islands recent study on certification requirements for preparing general education teachers to teach students with disabilities confirmed that more than half of children with disabilities are being educated in general education classrooms. As cited in Bocala et al. (2010), IDEIA 2004 seeks to ensure that both general and special education teachers understand how to work effectively with students with disabilities (Arthaud, Aram, Breck, Doelling, and Bushrow, 2007). IDEIA 2004 recommends that students with disabilities be placed "in the regular classroom, to the maximum extent possible" while also recognizing the need for "a continuum of alternative placements" (Individuals with Disabilities Education Act of 2004, Sections 682c and 300.115).

Recent IDEIA Reauthorizations

IDEIA requires that state education agencies provide guidance on licensure and certification requirements to ensure that general education teachers receive training in the subject matter and pedagogy that will enable them to effectively serve students with disabilities. Research by Bocala et al. (2010) reported that reforms to special education and general education programs were supported by federal laws allowing states to allocate funds to prepare general education teachers to teach students with disabilities (p. 1). These changes were brought about to ensure that:

- Special education and general education teachers have the training and information to address the full range of needs of children with disabilities across disability categories and have the subject matter knowledge and teaching skills, including technology literacy, to help students with disabilities meet challenging state student academic achievement and functional standards (Bocala et al., p. 3).
- Special and general education teacher certification or licensing requirements are aligned with challenging state academic content standards (Bocala, et al., p. 3).

No Child Left Behind

IDEIA and the No Child Left Behind (NCLB) Act (2002) advanced results for students with disabilities by holding them to high standards and improved results on state standardized assessments. Research demonstrates the clear correlation between student academic achievement and teacher quality. Mandates by NCLB require also that all teachers with primary responsibility for direct instruction in one or more of NCLB's core academic content areas are required to demonstrate that they satisfy the definition of a "Highly Qualified Teacher" (HQT). According to the NCLB Act (2002), a highly qualified teacher must have: (a) a bachelor's degree; (b) full state certification, as defined by the state; and (c) demonstrated competency, as defined by the state, in each core academic subject he or she teaches. Local education agencies resumed the responsibility of providing technical assistance and close monitoring to ensure that students are taught by highly qualified teachers (Harvey, Yssel, Bauserman, and Merbler, 2010). This requirement added an increased attention to teacher education programs to prepare talented and adept teachers.

NEW DIRECTIONS

As a consequence of policy changes, education leaders and practitioners have been charged with changing licensing requirements for special education teachers and general education teachers for teaching students with disabilities. As more students with identified disabilities participate in general education classrooms, their teachers need to know how to serve them well (Daane, Beirne-Smith, and Latham, 2000). Furthermore, the inclusive education movement emphasizes collaboration between special and general education programs, again requiring that all teachers know how to effectively teach students with disabilities (Jenkins, Pateman, and Black, 2002; McKenzie, 2009).

The Interstate New Teacher Assessment and Support Consortium 2001 document entitled "Model Standards for Licensing General and Special Education Teachers of Students with Disabilities" addresses the collaborative relationship between the general and special education teacher. This document was intended as a guide for states, professional organizations, and teacher preparation programs as they altered their programs to meet the growing changes in teacher preparation. The document states:

> The INTASC Special Education Committee endorsed a collaborative framework for the teaching of students with disabilities, one in which general and special education teachers work together as members of a team who bring their respective strengths to the task at hand. While general education and special education teachers possess much knowledge and skills in common, they also have differing areas of expertise. One of the purposes of these standards is to articulate similarities and differences in roles, knowledge and skill (Interstate New Teacher Assessment and Support Consortium, 2001, p. 54).

After an extensive literature review addressing the integration of students with disabilities in the general education classroom, NCCTQ outlined nine essential components for including inclusive services in regular education classrooms (Holdheide and Reschly, 2008). These services, outlined in NCCTQ's report, recommends training in the legal foundations of inclusion, models of effective inclusive service integration, collaboration with other educators, access for all students to the general education curriculum, pedagogical strategies, family involvement, and student self-determination and advocacy (Holdheide and Reschly, 2008).

Future studies will show the effects of even more changes to licensing bodies and teacher preparation programs as states and Institutions of Higher Education (IHE) align their programs to common core standards. The Common Core State Standards Initiative is a state-led effort coordinated by the National Governors Association Center for Best Practices (NGA Center) and the Council of Chief State School Officers (CCSSO). The standards were developed in collaboration with teachers, school administrators, and experts to provide a clear and consistent framework to prepare our children for college and the workforce (Common Core Standards Initiative, 2012). These new "common core standards" for grades K-12 go into effect in fall 2014 for English Language Arts and math. Revisions to the curriculum and assessments for other subjects, such as science and history, will follow in later years.

CASE STUDY: PENNSYLVANIA CALLS FOR CHANGES

Pennsylvania's commitment to the goals advanced by the NCLB is evidenced by the changes in the certification requirements for state teacher certification programs. Likewise, Pennsylvania recognizes that teacher quality has a major impact on student achievement and remains committed to the goal of ensuring that every child in Pennsylvania be taught by a high quality teacher who is equipped to teach in a way that enables every student to experience academic success. (Pennsylvania Department of Education, 2007) After careful research and consideration to the needs of children and teachers, Pennsylvania recently mandated that institutions of higher education make major revisions to their teacher education preparation programs. These changes are part of PDE's strategy to boost student achievement by enhancing teacher quality through:

- Changing the scope of the certificate to better tailor teacher preparation to stages of child learning and development.
- Requiring all teachers have better preparation in teaching children with disabilities and English language learners.

- Ensuring that special education teacher are dually certified in both special education and the appropriate content area (Brumbaugh, 2007).

Changes in teacher preparation programs in Pennsylvania were meant to ensure opportunities for all teachers to be able to effectively teach all learners – including students with disabilities and English language learners. The increased focus on educating all students in a least restrictive environment meant that student success required changes in the way teachers were prepared and licensed. Sharon Brumbaugh, Special Assistant to the Secretary of Education, shared with the Pennsylvania Senate Education Committee in February 2007 that "by narrowing the scope of the teaching certificate, teacher preparation programs will be able to adapt their programs to provide deeper and more relevant instruction and practice in these areas as well as age-appropriate academic content" (p. 3).

Since this time, teacher preparation programs in Pennsylvania have risen to the challenge and changed their certification programs. Pennsylvania IHEs have made the commitment to improving teacher education programs by recognizing that quality teaching leads to improved student achievement. Research indicates that teacher effectiveness relates strongly to teacher preparation and certification (Darling-Hammond, Holtzman, Gatlin, Heilig, 2005). All teacher candidates in Pennsylvania are required to take nine credits or 270 hours, or an equivalent combination thereof, on accommodations and adaptations for students with disabilities in an inclusive setting. Within the content of those credit or hours, instruction in literacy skills development and cognitive skill development must be included. At least three credits or 90 additional hours or an equivalent combination, shall address the instructional needs of English language learners (Pennsylvania Department of Education, 2007).

This included adapting the special education certification model to increase training in collaboration between special and general education teachers and revising the requirements for content that all teachers must know in order to work with students with disabilities. With a growing number of students with disabilities served in a general education classroom, it is necessary for special and general education teachers to learn to work together to ensure the needs of all students are being met. Likewise, it is the goal of teacher education programs to prepare teachers who will in turn guide their students to learn how to compete and succeed in the global economy of the 21st Century.

CO-TEACHING

Co-teaching is an approach where two professionals share instructional duties. The instructional approach is gaining popularity in elementary and secondary classrooms across the country. As a result of the growing demand for co-teaching approaches, IHEs are infusing the model in their curricula. Although there are various arrangements, typically a general education professional is paired with a special education professional IHEs are introducing co-teaching by having pre-service teacher candidates practice co-teaching in college courses by writing lesson plans with a fellow student and teaching the lesson in their methods course(s).

Another strategy IHEs are using to prepare teacher candidates is implementing co-teaching within the field work environment. Preservice teachers co-teach with their cooperating professional(s), supervisor(s), and sometimes paraprofessional(s). A university supervisor often provides feedback to the pre-service student on their use of co-teaching, as well as their co-teacher.

Advantages of co-teaching include collaborative partnerships between general and special educators (Solis, Vaughn, Swanson, and Mcculley, 2012). Students benefit in co-taught classrooms because their teachers are combining their diverse backgrounds and training. For example, in an inclusive high school biology class, the general education teacher has advanced training in content, whereas the special educator has specialized training to address the learning and developmental needs of students. Having two instead of one teacher can also be beneficial to students when increasing the teacher to student ratio. Another advantage is that educators can share the workload and utilize resources more efficiently.

There are potential drawbacks to the co-teaching approach. Co-teachers may not get along with one another. Faculty and staff may not have adequate support to implement and sustain a co-teaching arrangement. Training and professional development may not exist or be enough to fully prepare the co-teaching dyad. Teachers may feel an imbalance in workload. Role confusion or oppression can also take place in co-taught classrooms. A risk is that the special educator takes on a role as an aid rather than an equal with the general education teacher.

If a school decides to implement the approach, at least three aspects of co-teaching should be considered. First, co-teachers should be matched appropriately. Matching can be done by providing teachers an opportunity to select the co-teacher. Alternatively, administrators can approach teachers they think would work well together. Second, professional development on co-teaching should occur to insure that the approach is implemented with fidelity and rigor (Nevin, Thousand, and Villa, 2009). Teacher preparation programs are increasingly including co-teaching in methods courses. Training pre-service and in-service teachers is necessary.

Finally, a program evaluation plan should be created and used to monitor the progress of the co-teaching approach. The co-teaching program will need to examined on an ongoing basis to enhance effectiveness. With planning and special considerations, co-teaching can be a viable option in inclusive classrooms.

The Value of Field Experience

A substantial number of newly graduated teachers report dissatisfaction with their teacher preparation program, with one reason being they feel they lack the essential training competencies needed to solve the various challenges they experience in the classroom setting (Forlin, Loreman, Sharma, and Earle, 2009). Forlin, Keen, and Barrett (2008) state the lack of pre-service teacher training for inclusive settings is an important concern for teacher educators. These authors examined the concerns of teachers regarding the inclusion of students with intellectual disabilities in regular settings and found that 93% of the 228 respondents felt they had received insufficient training to support those students. Teacher candidates today must be prepared to teach in inclusive settings as they will experiences progressively more diverse student populations once they enter the field (Forlin et al., 2009).

Teacher preparation programs that have a focus on inclusive education tend to positively impact the teacher candidates' attitudes towards inclusion and people with disabilities. These programs are more apt to produce graduates that not only have the necessary knowledge and skills, but the confidence to be more proactive in furthering inclusive practices (Forlin et al., 2009). With the perspective of teachers towards inclusion creating a strong impact on the practice, pre-service teacher education is often viewed as a crucial vehicle to ensuring teachers acquire the appropriate attitudes and skills to enable inclusion to be successful (Forlin et al., 2009).

A fundamental element in the success or otherwise of inclusive education is the role of the generalist teacher (Forlin and Chambers, 2011). Their knowledge, skills, and beliefs about people with disabilities need to be developed and supported in their teacher preparation program in order to have all stakeholders value and successfully implement inclusion.

Forlin, Loreman, Sharma, and Earle (2009) found that including curriculum in teacher preparation programs that specifically focuses on providing for diversity can make a significant difference in beginning to prepare teachers for inclusive classrooms. Teacher preparation programs that prepare candidates to teach in inclusive settings "should undeniably focus on improving the self-efficacy of pre-service teachers, developing more positive attitudes and reducing their concerns by increasing their understanding and confidence in meeting the needs of diverse learners" (Forlin et al., 2009, p. 205).

Forlin and Chambers (2011) found that although teacher preparation programs may increase their students' knowledge about legislation and policy related to inclusion, they do not address those student's concerns or perceived challenges regarding having students with disabilities in their classes.

Teacher preparation programs that focus on knowledge and skills, as well as positive attitudes towards inclusive education, graduate teacher candidates who are more supportive of students with special needs (Lancaster and Bain, 2010). Furthermore, course experiences that encourage greater contact with people with disabilities result in more positive attitudes and support for inclusion (Lancaster and Bain, 2010). Forlin and Chambers (2011) discuss field experiences where interactions with students with special needs who are included in regular settings as one way of ensuring pre-service teachers have inclusive experiences.

The National Research Council (2010) and the National Council for Accreditation of Teacher Education (2010) have both reported on the value of field experience in teacher preparation.

According to the National Research Council (2010), one of three critical aspects of effective teacher preparation involves structured and systematic field experience throughout the teacher preparation program. Furthermore, the National Council for Accreditation of Teacher Education (2010) discusses it as essential to improvement in teacher preparation.

Eisenhardt, Besnoy, and Steele (2012) state that teacher candidates have preconceived notions about what it means to be a teacher and notions about students' abilities when they enter teacher preparation programs. Structured field experiences that immerse teacher candidates in real classroom settings and systematically confront their beliefs about diverse students will provide graduates with greater readiness skills (Eisenhardt, Besnoy, and Steele, 2012). Many beginning teachers will design their classroom environment around their own personal educational experiences, even when the knowledge acquired from university course work opposes such design (Eisenhardt, Besnoy, and Steele, 2012). Structured field experience allows teacher candidates hands-on practice to develop their own repertoire of skills which will be readily available when they become full time teachers and encourage them to utilize the knowledge and skills acquired from university coursework.

Furthermore, such experiences encourage crucial professional skills such as collaboration, leadership, teamwork, reflection, critical thinking, and the ability to communicate effectively (Meyers, 2011).

According to Capraro, Capraro, and Helfeldt (2010), field experiences for teacher candidates involve a variety of systematic P-12 classroom-based opportunities in which teacher candidates may observe, tutor, teach, and/or conduct research, all beginning early on their teacher preparation program.

For several decades, many individual researchers and professional groups have advocated the essential role of field experience in the preparing of teachers (Capraro, Capraro, and Helfeldt, 2010).

Interestingly, field experiences have been recognized traditions in teacher training programs dating back to the American Normal School. However, not all field experiences support the connection between theory and practice. More so, it should not be assumed that increasing the amount of field experience is necessarily better (Allsopp, DeMarie, Alvarez-McHatton, and Doone, 2006).

It is essential for colleges and universities to align field assignments and activities with the theoretical and evidence-based instructional procedures taught in the methods courses (Allsopp et al., 2006). Capraro, Capraro, and Helfeldt (2010) examined three types of field-based experiences: a more traditional school-based experience that involved basic coordination between the cooperating teachers/school and the university professors, a Professional Development School (PDS) model that involved in-depth communication and collaboration between all stakeholders, and a third experience that involved the same in-depth collaboration and experiences as the second type but included an additional action research component. They found the third type, which they refer to as an Inquiry model, to be the most effective on the teacher candidates learning and self-perception of their instructional competence. This finding supports the concept that it is not the amount of time but how the time is structured that has the most impact on teacher candidates' learning. Additional components to successful field experiences include dialogue and reflection about practice and shared responsibility for learning, mentoring, and organizational structures, policies, and procedures (Graham, 2006).

Challenges for Field Experience

With field experience being a crucial element to preparing competent and knowledgeable teacher candidates, it must be noted that the practice does not come without some specific challenges. First, there are of course certain components of the inclusion process that may be difficult for teacher preparation programs to ensure their teacher candidates experience. One reason is that students with disabilities and their parents have the right of confidentiality, as protected by IDEIA. There is no question that this affords a reasonable right, but it does pose some challenges for the training of teachers (Burden, Tinnerman, Lunce, and Runshe, 2010). One particular challenge revolves around training teacher candidates in the individual education program (IEP) process. Burden, Tinnerman, Lunce, and Runshe (2010) report that case study and role-play have proven to be effective in preparing teacher candidates. These researchers found that developing a video simulation of an IEP review allowed pre-service teachers to have an understanding of the inner workings of the IEP process, yet still maintained the right of confidentiality afforded by IDEIA.

Another challenge associated with field experience being such a crucial component to teacher preparation programs, is it forces the programs to rely heavily on practicing teachers to be agents of learning. One particular difficulty of this reliance involves the task of recruiting large numbers of teachers every semester to serve as cooperating or mentor teachers. Not only is the number of teachers required at times difficult to obtain, but the need to recruit teachers that are effective not only in increasing their own students' achievement, but effective in mentoring pre-service teachers can also be challenging (Sykes, Bird, and Kennedy, 2010). Furthermore, field experiences need to support the bridging of theory and practice. Settings that conflict with the pedagogy taught in the university coursework may cause novice teachers to adopt the practices and values of the P-12 classroom and dismiss the knowledge and skills they were taught in their preparation program (Capraro, Capraro, and Helfeldt, 2010; Sykes, Bird, and Kennedy, 2010). As Sykes, Bird, and Kennedy (2010) discuss, if "secret suspicions and antagonisms infect" (p. 474) the relationship between universities and schools, the teacher candidates will be the ones who feel the effects. Universities must do more to reach out to cooperating teachers and find placements where their teacher candidates will be successful. One way to do this is for university faculty to get to know the schools, teachers, curriculum, and instructional practices and embrace those as a place to begin working with, not against, the practitioners (Sykes, Bird, and Kennedy, 2010).

CONCLUSION

An evident challenge to teacher preparation is the immenseness of the occupation. In recent years, it has grown from roughly 2 million to 3.2 million practitioners and to further complicate matters, it is largely differentiated by grade levels, content areas, and specializations (Sykes, Bird, and Kennedy, 2010). Allowing pre-service teachers the variety and number of opportunities needed to gain the knowledge, skills, and beliefs that will allow them to be competent in effectively tackling the various challenges in supporting all of the students in their classrooms are critical goals for preparation programs. As classrooms change, IHEs need to be dynamic and ready to change along with the evolving classroom demographics. In keeping with federal and state mandates, teacher preparation programs are addressing thorough and appropriate special education inclusive teaching practices to all teacher candidates.

REFERENCES

Allsopp, D. H., DeMarie, D., Alvarez-McHatton, P., and Doone, E. (2006). Bridging the gap between theory and practice: Connecting courses with field experiences. *Teacher Education Quarterly*, *33*(1), 19-35.

Arthaud, T. J., Aram, R. J., Breck, S. E., Doelling, J. E., and Bushrow, K. M. (2007). Developing collaboration skills in pre-service teachers: a partnership between general and special education. *Teacher Education and Special Education*, 30(1), 1–12.

Bocala, C., Morgan, C., Mundry, S., and Mello, D. (2010). *Do states have certification requirements for preparing general education teachers to teach students with disabilities? Experience in the Northeast and Islands Region* (Issues and Answers Report, REL 2010–No. 090). Washington, DC: US Department of Education, Institute of Education Sciences, National Center for Education Evaluation and Regional Assistance, Regional Educational Laboratory Northeast and Islands. Retrieved from http://ies.ed.gov/ncee/edlabs.

Brumbaugh, S. (2007, February). Remarks to the Pennsylvania Senate Education Committee. Symposium conducted Special Assistant to the Pennsylvania Secretary of Education. Harrisburg, PA.

Burden, R., Tinnerman, L., Lunce, L., and Runshe, D. (2010). Video case studies: Preparing teachers for inclusion. *TEACHING Exceptional Children Plus,* 6(4), 2-9.

Capraro, M., Capraro, R. and Helfeldt, J. (2010). Do differing types of field experiences make a difference in teacher candidates' perceived level of competence? *Teacher Education Quarterly,* 37(1), 131-154.

Common Core Standards Initiative. Preparing America's Students for College and Career. (2012). *About the Standards.* Retrieved from http://www. corestandards.org/

Daane, C., Beirne-Smith, D. and Latham, D. (2000). Administrators' and teachers' Perceptions of the collaborative efforts of inclusion in the elementary grades. *Education,* 121(2), 331-39.

Darling-Hammond, L., Holtzman, D., Gatlin, S., and Heilig, J., (2005) Does Teacher Preparation Matter? Evidence about teacher certification, Teach for America, and teacher effectiveness. *Education Policy Analysis Archives,* 13 (42). Retrieved from http://epaa.asu.edu/ epaa/v13n42/.

Eisenhardt, S., Besnoy, K. and Steele, E. (2012). Creating dissonance in pre-service teachers' field experiences. *Southeastern Regional Association of Teacher Educators Journal,* 21(1), 1-10.

Forlin, C., Keen, M. and Barrett, E. (2008). The Concerns of Mainstream Teachers: Coping with inclusivity in an Australian context. *International Journal Of Disability, Development and Education*, 55(3), 251-264. doi:10.1080/10349120802268396

Forlin, C., Loreman, T., Sharma, U., and Earle, C. (2009). Demographic differences in changing pre-service teachers' attitudes, sentiments and concerns about inclusive education. *International Journal of Inclusive Education,* 13(2), 195-209.

Forlin, C. and Chambers, D. (2011). Teacher preparation for inclusive education: Increasing knowledge but raising concerns. *Asisa-Pacific Journal of Teacher Education,* 39(1), 17-32.

Geiger, W. L. (2006). A compilation of research on states' licensure models for special education teachers and special education requirements for licensing general education teachers. Online submission. (ERIC Document Reproduction Service No. ED491706).

Geiger, W. L., Crutchfield, M. D. and Mainzer, R. (2003). *The status of licensure of special education teachers in the 21st century* (COPSSE Document No. RS-7E). Gainesville, F. L.: Universityof Florida, Center on Personnel Studies in Special Education.

Government Accountability Office. (2009). *Teacher preparation* (GAO-09-573). Washington, DC: US Government Accountability Office.

Graham, B. (2006). Conditions for successful field experiences: Perceptions of cooperating teachers. *Teaching and Teacher Education: An International Journal Of Research And Studies*, 22(8), 1118-1129.

Harvey, M.W., Yssel, N., Bauserman, A. D., Merbler, J. B. (2010). Preservice teacher preparation for inclusion: an exploration of higher education teacher-training institutions. *Remedial and Special Education,* 31(1), 24–33.

Holdheide, L. R. and Reschly, D. J. (2008).*Teacher preparation to deliver inclusive services tostudents with disabilities.* Washington, DC: National Comprehensive Center for TeacherQuality (NCCTQ). Retrieved from www.tqsource.org/publications/.

Holland, D., Detgen, A. and Gutekunst, L. (2008). *Preparing elementary school teachers in the Southeast Region to work with students with disabilities* (Issues and Answers Report, REL 2008–No. 065). Washington, DC: US Department of Education, Institute of Education Sciences, National Center for Education Evaluation and Regional Assistance, Regional Educational Laboratory Southeast. Retrieved from http://ies.ed.gov/ ncee/edlabs.

Individuals with Disabilities Education Act of 2004. (2004). Pub. L. No. 108-446, Section 118Stat. Retrieved from http://idea.ed.gov/explore/view/ p/%2Croot%2Cstatute% 2CI%2CD%2C654%2C.

Interstate New Teacher Assessment and Support Consortium. (2001, May). Model standards for licensing general and special education teachers of students with disabilities: a resource for state dialogue. Washington, DC: Council of Chief State School Officers.

Jenkins, A. A., Pateman, B. and Black, R. S. (2002). Partnerships for dual preparation in elementary, secondary, and special education programs. *Remedial and Special Education,* 23(6), 359–71.

Lancaster, J. and Bain, A. (2010). The design of pre-service inclusive education courses and their effects on self-efficacy: a comparative study. *Asia-Pacific Journal Of Teacher Education*, 38(2), 117-128. doi:10.1080/13598661003678950

McKenzie, R. G. (2009). A national survey of pre-service preparation for collaboration. *Teacher Education and Special Education,* 32(4), 379–393.

Meyers, S. (2011). Life skills training through situated learning experiences: An alternative instructional model. *International Journal of Special Education,* 26(3), 142-149.

National Council for Accreditation of Teacher Education. (2010). Report of the blue ribbon panel on clinical preparation and partnerships for improved student learning. Retrieved from http://www.ncate.org/ LinkClick.aspx?fileticket=zzeiB1OoqPk%3dandtabid=715

National Research Council (2010). Preparing teachers: Building evidence for sound policy. Retrieved from http://www.nap.edu/catalog.php? record_id=12882.

Nevin, A. I., Thousand, J. S. and Villa, R. A. (2009). Collaborative teaching for teacher educators—What does the research say?. *Teaching And Teacher Education,* 25(4), 569-574.

No Child Left Behind Act. (2002). Pub. L. No. 107-110, §115, 1425 Stat.

Pennsylvania Department of Education.(2007,January).*Pennsylvania Department of Education: Background paper*. Harrisburg, PA.

Solis, M., Vaughn, S., Swanson, E., and Mcculley, L. (2012). Collaborative models of instruction: The empirical foundations of inclusion and co-teaching. *Psychology In The Schools*, 49(5), 498-510.

Sykes, G., Bird, T. and Kennedy, M. (2010). Teacher education: Its problems and some prospects. *Journal of Teacher Education,* 61(5), 464-476.

Turner, N. D. (2003). Preparing preservice teachers for inclusion in secondary classrooms. *Education,* 123, pp. 491-495.

Whitehurst, G. (2002). *Research on Teacher Preparation and Professional Development*.Washington, D.C.: White House Conference on Preparing Tomorrow's Teachers, 2001.

In: Educational Programs and Special Education   ISBN: 978-1-62417-256-4
Editor: Sasha Dziuk   © 2013 Nova Science Publishers, Inc.

Chapter 5

SOCIAL-SEXUAL EDUCATION FOR MATURE STUDENTS WITH MILD INTELLECTUAL DISABILITIES: A PRACTICAL MODEL FOR TEACHERS[*]

Iris Manor-Binyamini[1], Schreiber-Divon Michal[2] and Stein Racheli[3]

[1]University of Haifa, Haifa, Israel
[2]Talpiot Collage, Holon, Israel; Hativat Shalom School, Petah-Tikva, Israel
[3]Hativat Shalom School, Petah-Tikva, Israel

ABSTRACT

Children with disabilities are 3.4 times more likely to be sexually abused than their non-disabled peers. Moreover, the abuse will likely be committed by a close figure they know and trust, such as a parent, sibling, teacher, or day-care provider. Despite these alarming data, the issue of social-sexual education for students with intellectual disabilities is very rarely discussed in the literature, and even less is known about practical models for teaching the subject. This chapter explores the reasons which make the teaching of social-sexual education for students with disabilities

---

[*] The proposed research was made through the support and assistance of The Division for Experiments and Entrepreneurship of the Ministry of Education in Israel.

such a sensitive and complex topic. There is clearly a gap between the importance of the subject and the ability of teachers and other professionals to teach it in class.

An innovative practical model focusing on mature students is presented, together with a demo teaching class designed according to the model. This tested model was developed in an Israeli special education school for adolescent and adult students with mild intellectual disabilities.

The model was examined using the methodology of collaborative-ethnographic action research by means of conducting interviews, videotaping lessons, and documenting meetings over a five-year period. The model should make a significant contribution to all teachers/professionals who work in special education schools and find themselves struggling with this issue

INTRODUCTION

Children with disabilities are 3.4 times more likely to be sexually abused than their non-disabled peers (Skarbek et al., 2009: Sullivan and Knuston, 2000).

Moreover, the abuse will likely be committed by a close figure they know and trust, such as a parent, sibling, teacher, or day-care provider. Individuals with intellectual disabilities may lack the needed experience and skills to build relationships, including healthy sexual relationships, making them particularly vulnerable to sexual abuse and exploitation.

Despite this alarming situation, social-sexual education for mature students with intellectual disabilities is very rarely discussed in the literature. Even less is known about practical models for teaching the subject due to its complex and sensitive nature.

Although there has been much progress in the last two decades on integrating mature individuals with intellectual disabilities into the general community, the aspect of their social-sexual behavior remains largely neglected (Brown, 1994; Young et al, 2001).

This attitude is manifested both by the lack of literature on the subject (Howard-Barr et al., 2005; Zambonu, 2009) and by the complete absence of a well-prepared curriculum of sex education for this population (Remigiusz, 2011). Without any educational mediation, the already difficult challenge of how to deal with the growing awareness of physical maturation is complicated even further.

In the absence of a well-constructed teaching program around the theme of social-sexual behavior, we can see a variety of unacceptable behaviors on the part of students at school, including sexually charged language, masturbation in public, and abusive physical contact between the students and staff and among the students themselves. Due to the embarrassment raised when these behaviors are made the topic of public discussion, there is little specialized treatment being offered for students with intellectual disabilities in the area of sex education.

Many publications addressing the attitudes of professionals (e.g., special educators, psychologists, social workers, and physicians) towards the sexuality of people with disabilities stress the critical role that these specialists play in shaping the development of their sexual identity and sexual expression (Swango-Wilson, 2008).

In addition, it is important that professionals offer these individuals general support in the process of adapting to their given disability and dealing with its accompanying personal and social limitations, particularly with a view towards building a healthy self-image and developing life competencies, such as the skills required to meet their psychosexual needs. However, many professionals do not have adequate abilities to effectively implement these objectives.

They may be limited by a lack of knowledge and skills, by the formal constraints of their organizational structure, or by their own personal attitudes (Fairbairn and Rowley, 2005). As a result of these factors, people with disabilities are deprived of the support they need in the development of their sexuality (Ostrowska, 2005).

Hence, the role of the education system is to provide students with the appropriate tools to live the fullest and highest quality life possible as adults and to integrate into the general community to the greatest extent possible, taking their skills and limitations into account. By cultivating the students' competence and autonomy, the school is able to better prepare them for adult life in the community.

Based on this goal, a project was conducted in an Israeli school for adolescent and adult students with mild intellectual disabilities on the subject of social-sexual education. The practical model presented in this chapter builds on the work of the multidisciplinary team in this project. It is important to remember that for special populations, the school constitutes a social environment that is in many ways more important than either the home or the neighborhood.

At any rate, the school provides ample opportunities for social interactions and the evolution of intimate relationships. In light of the importance of the school environment, the team developed a new approach to the field of social-sexual education for individuals with intellectual disabilities. Following are the main assumptions and goals of this social-sexual education program:

The premises behind the practice of social-sexual education:

1) All individuals are social-sexual beings and are therefore entitled to express and realize their social and sexual needs.
2) The ability to create a significant system of relationships will contribute to the quality of life of these students as adults.
3) Students with intellectual disabilities are exposed to risks of harm and exploitation to a far greater extent than their normal peers and therefore need social-sexual education to protect them.
4) It is important to see these students through a holistic prism, that is, in relationship to the environment and to the totality of the elements of their own personalities.

The goals of social-sexual education:

• Promote and strengthen the ability of students to build meaningful social and intimate relationships, both at the present time and in the future.
• Promote and strengthen the ability of students to realize their sexuality in line with their age and the degree of their development as well as the environment in which they live.
• Develop the ability of students to protect themselves from exploitation and harm.

In order to implement the program at school, a spiral curriculum was designed with specific subjects to be taught in each grade. The program is based on the assumptions and objectives presented above. Figure 1 shows the main topics taught in each grade.

The topics were selected according to the chronological age of the students, but also with consideration of their actual level of maturity. Major issues are repeated by way of delving deeper into their meaning at each level. For example, the issue of sexual harassment was studied in each age group in different degrees of depth and from different angles.

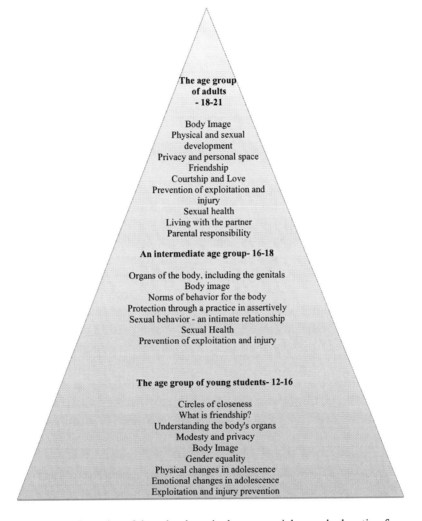

The age group
of adults
- 18-21

Body Image
Physical and sexual
development
Privacy and personal space
Friendship
Courtship and Love
Prevention of exploitation and
injury
Sexual health
Living with the partner
Parental responsibility

An intermediate age group- 16-18

Organs of the body, including the genitals
Body image
Norms of behavior for the body
Protection through a practice in assertively
Sexual behavior - an intimate relationship
Sexual Health
Prevention of exploitation and injury

The age group of young students- 12-16

Circles of closeness
What is friendship?
Understanding the body's organs
Modesty and privacy
Body Image
Gender equality
Physical changes in adolescence
Emotional changes in adolescence
Exploitation and injury prevention

Figure 1. The main topics of the school curriculum on social-sexual education for adolescent and adult students with mild intellectual disabilities.

METHODOLOGY

Background of the Study Population

The Israeli education system in 2011 consisted of 1,557,000 students, of whom 146,000 students with special needs were enrolled in special education schools. Of these students with special needs, 27,000 (18%) had various intellectual disabilities (Fnsirr, 2011). By Israeli law, children aged 3 through 21 who have intellectual disabilities are eligible for special education in the school system. The school year for these students runs for 11 months, and they are entitled by the compulsory education law to receive state education even during vacations and holidays. The school day begins at 8:00 in the morning and ends at 4:00 in the afternoon. The focus of this chapter is on the special education population described here, and the study was conducted in one of the special education schools for children with mild intellectual disabilities.

Background of the School Used in This Study

The junior high school Shalom is a school for adolescent and adult students, aged 12-21, with mild intellectual disabilities. In 2011, the population of the school included 87 students, who were studying in 10 classes. The diverse professional team of the school includes teachers, a treatment team, and a paramedical team. In educational practice, the school is involved in the long process of preparing the students for adult life in the community, specifically by cultivating their independence and autonomy.

The Benefits of Collaborative-Ethnographic Action Research in Constructing an Applied Model for a Social-Sexual Education Program

The model presented in this chapter was examined using the methodology of collaborative-ethnographic action research conducted over a five-year period in the school. Through this process, each side is allowed to bring unique skills to the study. In this case, the research was conducted in partnership between an academic researcher and two teachers in the field of special education. Their systematic and documented observations included 92 written records of lessons in social-sexual education; 39 records of meetings of the multidisciplinary team on this subject; 29 interviews with teachers; and 22 photographs and videotapes of social-sexual education classes. This process of collaborative-ethnographic action research enabled an interaction of the researchers' methodological and theoretical knowledge in social science with the teachers' practical experience from the field itself. In this kind of collaboration, the information is built on a shared understanding between the practitioners and the scholars, and the data are collected and coordinated through a long-term, systematic process of observation (Oja, 2001). A long-term study such as this one is significant because of its contribution to narrowing the existing gap between theory and practice, as well as its contribution to the personal and professional development of practitioners in the field (Alpert, 2006).

A synthesis of two research methods, performed on such a complex reality as the one in this study, demands that both sides, namely the researcher and the teachers, deconstruct the overall image into its details in an attempt to understand the mutual assemblage of influences and interactions within the familiar structure and to identify the components of power and centers of influence. Such an investigation allows the different partners to take a step back and to challenge, from a distance, the reality which they experience and to deal with their feelings by way of critical rationality.

For example, the team argued that there was no meaning or rationality in teaching students the subject of marriage, as it would be nearly impossible for them to satisfy the required commitment and remain faithful to one person. However, this claim was contradicted by the theoretical knowledge that even adults with intellectual disabilities can sustain an intimate relationship over a long period of time. Indeed, the experiences with the students and the work carried out according to our model demonstrated that many students were looking for a meaningful relationship and were quite capable of commitment and fidelity. As a result of the learning process, "a couples group" was developed at the school to help its members raise different relationship issues and solve problems.

Stages of Analysis and Interpretation

The research was advanced in two parallel axes. The first is the axis of the process, by which we learned about the dispositions and perceptions of the team regarding different aspects of social-sexual education at school (see Manor-Binyamini et al., in press). The second is the axis of the contents, through which we fused the working model that was developed during the five years of exploration at the school. The analysis and interpretation of the collected data were done by combining the external researcher's observations from a distance with the expert opinions of the teachers from the field on what constituted the essence of the collected data. This working method entailed constant deliberations within the team.

THE LEARNING MODEL FOR THE DEVELOPMENT OF SOCIAL-SEXUAL CAPACITIES IN ADOLESCENT AND ADULT STUDENTS WITH MILD INTELLECTUAL DISABILITIES

The model presented in this chapter is based on the simple premise that a person, any person – including an adult with an intellectual disability – is a competent learner. This means that everyone has the ability to reach an understanding of the environment in which they live, to control their own behavior, to set goals and plan their implementation, and to work towards their actualization. Individuals with intellectual disabilities need mediation in order to develop and refine the ability to exert control over their lives. The diagnosis of events is a means by which students can change their behavior in accordance with established norms. The purpose of events' analysis is to illuminate and bring to a state of awareness the experiences of the students, which will in turn, would afford them the opportunity to build effective coping strategies for their integration into the community. Figure 2 displays the learning model for the development of social-sexual capacities in adolescent and adult students with mild intellectual disabilities.

The entire model is based on learning by raising and processing events, with the learning taking place in the peer group. The events are derived from two sources: either they are presented by the teacher according to the topics in the school curriculum, or they are actual events and situations encountered by the students as individuals or as a group. These actual events are viewed firsthand by the teacher or reported by the student/ parent/ team). During the raising of the event, all the students sit in a circle to facilitate dialogue and interpersonal interaction between them. The teacher presents the event in an experiential way, causing the students to relate to the characters in the event. The presentation of the event is done via video, image, simulation, puppetry, song or story, among others. After presentation of the event, the learning process takes place. The model is processed according to three main aspects: the emotional aspect, the educational-academic aspect, and the behavioral aspect. The emotional aspect: Students raise the emotions of each character in the event and explain why they think the character has certain kinds of feelings. They also share with the rest of the group if a similar event happened to them and how they felt while experiencing it. In this way, the students can relate to the event. The teacher also teaches other emotional concepts that are related to the event in question.

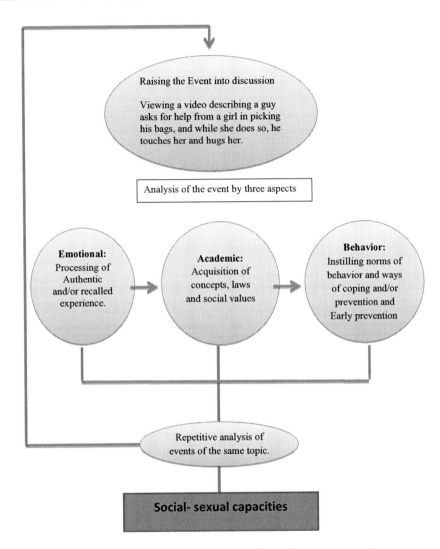

Figure 2. The learning model for the development of social-sexual capacities in adolescent and adult students with mild intellectual disabilities.

The educational-academic aspect: The teacher guides a discussion among the students about the event, while checking that they students comprehend what happened at the event and how each character acted in it. A discussion ensues regarding the question of whether each character's behavior is normative and whether it would have been preferable if the character had behaved differently. In this part, the teacher provides the concepts and develops the students' ability to think through the processes of problem-solving and reasoning. The teacher uses the opportunity to lead the discussion in the direction of learning concepts, laws, and social values.

The behavioral aspect: In the discussion about the normative behavior required in any given situation, students who have experienced such situations can learn how to deal with them in a better way. Students who have not experienced these situations can benefit from a kind of early prevention, so that if they were to come across such a situation in the future, they would know how to function in it normatively and effectively. The group helps the students to identify the factors leading to tensions, frustrations, anxieties, and concerns. With the aid of the group, the students discover the resources that can be helpful in coping with the given events. The peer group reflects to its individual members their inherent capabilities to follow the right path.

For example, the teacher brings up an event that deals with "courtship," and the class conducts a discussion about the issue. One student claims that he has no problem in approaching a girl directly and divulging his feelings for her face to face. Another student shares that this approach is quite difficult for him and that he prefers courting a girl through writing letters. The group members discuss the advantages and disadvantages of each solution, with one's preferred solution varying in accordance with personal coping skills, abilities, and self-knowledge.

The analysis of the event is based on a combination of circuit internalization (Reiter et al., 1999) and the coping model of Zeitlin and Williamson (Zeitlin and Williamson, 1994), with the students developing their social-sexual abilities by processing their own direct and indirect experiences. The analysis of events also allows the teacher to develop the students' personal and interpersonal coping skills in the process of constructing a personal identity of the student as an adult. After the processing of the event and the insights following it, the teacher presents other events on the same issue so that the students can internalize what they have learned. Figure 3 presents a learning model for the development of social-sexual capacities regarding sexual harassment.

Raising the event: The teacher shows a video that describes the event: "Anat is walking on the sidewalk on her way home from school. Suddenly, she sees a guy carrying heavy bags. The guy asks for her help, and she responds quite willingly and happily. They start talking as they walk together, and then the guy puts his hand on Anat's shoulder, stroking her hair.

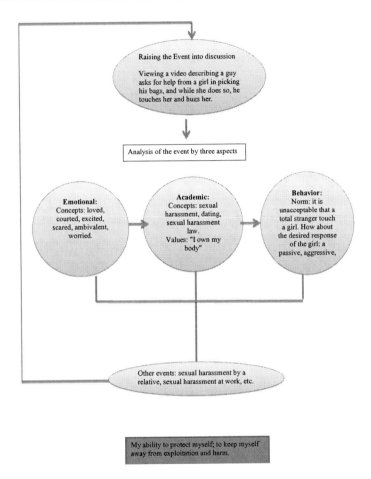

Figure 3. A learning model for the development of social-sexual capacities regarding sexual harassment.

He compliments her on her beautiful name and on her overall beauty and character. They rest on the bench, and the guy asks Anat to rub his sore shoulders a little. Then he puts his hand on Anat's knee. They continue to walk again, and the guy asks Anat to come up to his house."

PROCESSING THE EVENT FROM THREE ANGLES

Emotional aspect: With mediation by the teacher, the students raise the possible feelings of Anat following the situation. Her feelings are ambivalent.;

On the one hand, she is flattered and she seems to like the guy. She feels loved, courted, and has a good sense of a promising meeting that could lead to a successful relationship. On the other hand, she feels a little scared and hesitant because the guy does not know her and yet touched her shoulder and hair. She does not know whether his intentions are pure, and she feels exposed and vulnerable.

Educational-academic aspect: The event which was presented sparked a discussion about whether the event portrays sexual harassment or legitimate and normative courtship. This discussion raised a series of questions as well: What is courtship? What is sexual harassment? The students learned about sexual harassment laws and discussed ethical issues, such as the right to make decisions about one's own body.

Behavioral aspect: Many questions were raised about Anat's behavior: Is her behavior normative? Is the guy she just met authorized to touch her? To stroke her hair? To put his hand on her shoulder? On her knee? Should Anat tolerate this behavior? Does the case call for passivity and the exercise of restraint? Or rather, should she resist assertively or even aggressively? Is it possible that the guy's intentions are pure after all and that he really likes her? And if so, aren't his actions a threat to the possibility of a genuine relationship between them? Is there a chance for love and not necessarily a risk? How should she act in a situation like this? Should she go to his house as he asks?

The simultaneous dwelling upon the cognitive and emotional aspects leads to behavioral change among the students. At the end of the processing, the teacher presents additional events which reflect the reality of sexual harassment: sexual harassment on the Internet, by a relative, neighbor, or employer. The learning in this subject matter will come to an end when the teacher reckons that it was covered in depth and that the students are capable of identifying such events and know how to behave optimally in a way that will allow them to avoid situations of exploitation and harm. At this point, the teacher will move on to a different subject.

CONCLUSION

Sexuality is considered an important attribute of human individuality and a multidimensional component of human functioning. The lack of attention to the development of healthy sexual relationships in individuals with intellectual disabilities increases the risk of harm for this vulnerable population. A proper education has been recognized as a mechanism to reduce susceptibility to sexual abuse and encourage positive sexuality, as well as to improve decision-making abilities and promote empowerment. The analysis of events is recognized as a tool that empowers individuals with intellectual disabilities to act on their own in a conscious and normative way and to make choices that are based on knowledge.

The collaborative-ethnographic research used in this research allowed the development of a curriculum and application of a theory into a practical model that was put into action in classes of adolescents and adults with mild intellectual disabilities. The study showed that it is very important for students with intellectual disabilities to master this subject – a process that requires professional knowledge in the area of sexual development in general and among mature students with intellectual disabilities in particular. In order to facilitate this process, the education system should earmark time and financial means for the instructional activities of the team. Regular hours should be allocated for study of the subject, and it is highly recommended that the majority of topics be taught in gender-mixed groups so as to increase contact between the members.

The learning process of teachers and other specialists requires a focus on the team. Getting to know the attitudes and experiences of the professionals is one of the key conditions that can lead to the favorable organization of a supportive environment for people with disabilities. The learning in the classroom should include practical knowledge, as well as a close examination of the students' current attitudes and feelings on social-sexual issues. Towards this end, the use of cases involving a change in attitudes and feelings is crucial for properly advancing the ability of the students to cope with these issues. It is essential that all the teachers speak the same language and transmit the identical message to their students. For that purpose, clear "do and don't do" procedures must be spelled out at school, including common principles to be observed in the social-sexual context. For example, educational messages must be consistent regarding what constitutes permissible and forbidden or unacceptable touching between the students themselves. Moreover, there should be a uniform code of conduct in regard to public masturbation and the like.

Finally, the effective application of the method described in this chapter requires that the subject be presented in a way which personally speaks to the lives of the students. At the same time, it should be clarified that the purpose of the learning process is to help them minimize the risks to themselves while they are developing their intimate relationships. The premise behind the model is that the lack of emotional involvement of the students is contrary to internalization of the learning process. In this context, the role of the teachers is to allow the students to experience the personal and practical relationship between the events analyzed in the classroom and the real-life events occurring outside the classroom. In order for such educational interventions to be successful, it is essential that sex educators working with adolescents and adults analyze events with their peer group according to three aspects: emotional, educational-academic, and behavioral. As such, it is imperative that the teachers and other professionals working in this area receive the proper knowledge and training to implement this type of social-sexual education program.

ACKNOWLEDGMENTS

This five-year study was funded by the Department of Experimental Schools in the Ministry of Education, Israel.

REFERENCES

Alpert, B. (2001). Writing qualitative research. In: Ben-Yehoshua, Z., (Ed.), *Traditions and Currents Qualitative Research* (403-369), Lod. Dvir.

Alpert, B. (2006). Two modes of participation in research quality in schools: the researcher ethnographer and researcher in action research team. In Levi, D. (Ed.) *Action Research: Theory and Practice* .Mofet Publishing.

Brown, H. (1994). "An ordinary sexual life?": A review of the normalization principle as it applies to sexual options of people with learning disabilities. *Disability and Society*, 9, 123-145.

Fairbairn, G., and Rowley, D. (2005) Ethical aspects of sexuality of people with intellectual disabilities. In: Glodkowska, J., Girynski, A. (Eds.) Sexuality of people with intellectual disabilities, 9-23. APS, Warszawa.

Fals-Borda, O. (, 2002). Participatory (action) research in social theory: Origins and challenges. In P. Reason and Bradbury (Eds.), *Handbook of Action Research* (27-37). CA, Thousand Oaks: Sage.

Fly, M., Vinz, R., Downing, M. and Anzul, M. (, 1997*). On Writing Qualitative Research: Living By Words*. London: Falmer.

Howard-Barr, M. Rienzo, B., Pigg, M. and Delores, j. (2005). Teacher beliefs, professional preparation and practices regarding exceptional student and sexuality education. *Journal of School Health*. 75 (3). 99-105.

Manor- Binyamini, I, Schreiber Divon M. Sternlict T. and Amihod A. (*In Press, 2011*). Chapter in the book: Alpert, B. and Slaski,. Ethnography in School . Chapter title; *Change in the Perception of the Multidisciplinary Team Regarding the Sex Education for Students with Intellectual Disabilities in Religious Schools*. Mofet Publications.

Oja, SN (2001). *Collaborative Action Research and Social Role Taking*. Paper presented at the European Association for Research on Lesrning and Instructin (EARLI), Switzeland: University of Fribourg.

Ostrowska, A. (2005). *Sexuality of the disabled*. In: Ostrowaks, A. (Ed.) The sexuality of people with disabilities, pp.8-21. IRSS, Warszawa.

Reiter, S., Shlomi, D., and Sadr, H. (1999). *Into maturity "Heart 21" - program for adolescents and adults aged 16-21*, Unit A social education. Jerusalem: Ministry of Education, Culture and Sport, Department of Curriculum and Special Education Division.

Remigiusz, J.K,. (2011). A Desire for Love: Considerations on Sexuality and Sexual Education of People with Intellectual Disability in Poland. *Sexuality and Disability*. 29. 65-74.

Skarbek, S. Hahn, K., and Parrish, P. (2009). Stop Sexual Abuse in Special Education; An Ecological Model of Prevention and Intervention Strategies for Sexual Abuse in Special Education. *Sexuality and Disability*.27. 155-164.

Special education law. (1988). Rule book in 1256, (114-118). Jerusalem.

Sullivan, P.M,. and Knuston, J.F., (2000). Maltreatment and disabilities: a population-based epidemiological study. *Child Abuse and Neglect*. 24 (10), 1257-1273.

Swango-Wilson, A. (2008) Caregiver Perceptions and Implications for Sex Education for Individuals with Intellectual and Developmental Disabilities. *Sex Disabilities*. 26. 167-174.

Young, L., Ashman, A.F,. Sigafoos, J., and Grevell, P. (2001). Closure of the Challinor Centre: II. An extended report on 95 individuals after 12 monthe of community living. An extended report on 95 individuals after 12 monthe of community living. An extended report on 95 individuals after 12 monthe of community living. *Journal of Intellectual and Developmental Disability*, 26, 51-66.

Zambonu, B. (, 2009). Identity, Training, and Expertise among Sexual Health Professionals. *International Journal of Sexual Health*, 21, 132-144.

Zeitlin, S., and Williamson, G.G., (1994). *Coping in young children: Early intervention practices to enhance adaptive behavior and resilience.* Baltimore: Paul h. Brookes.

INDEX

#

21st century, 68, 87

A

abuse, ix, 89, 90, 101
academic motivation, vii, 29
academic performance, 17, 44
academic progress, 18
academic success, 78
access, 2, 56, 57, 58, 64, 74, 78
accommodations, 79
acculturation, vii, 1, 4, 6, 7, 9, 13
action research, ix, 83, 90, 94, 102
adaptations, 79
adaptive functioning, 30
adjustment, 50
administrators, 5, 6, 39, 78, 80
adolescents, 31, 33, 40, 49, 50, 51, 72, 101, 102, 103
adults, 59, 64, 66, 70, 91, 92, 95, 101, 102, 103
advocacy, 56, 78
aerobic exercise, 60
African-American, 72
age, viii, 30, 31, 37, 39, 40, 66, 67, 79, 92
agencies, 2, 23, 67, 76, 77
AIDS, 64, 69
alcohol consumption, 64

anxiety, 5, 6, 19
apex, 31
articulation, 15
Asia, 87
Asian Americans, 70
assessment, 14, 16, 17, 42, 50
atherosclerosis, 66
attitudes, 81, 82, 86, 91, 101
attribution, 33, 50
authority, 4, 6
autonomy, 47, 91, 94
awareness, 4, 5, 12, 13, 14, 27, 35, 63, 65, 90, 96

B

background information, 17
barriers, 5, 62
beginning teachers, 82
behavioral change, 61, 63, 68, 100
behavioral problems, 40
behaviors, 64, 66, 72, 91
benchmarks, 2
benefits, 20, 50, 63
bilingual Spanish speaking families, vii, 1
bilingualism, 17
birth weight, 69
blood, 59, 61, 66, 69, 70
blood pressure, 59, 61, 66, 69, 70
blueprint, 31, 48

body mass index, 59, 66
boredom, 63
Brazil, 55, 64, 68
breastfeeding, 61, 69
bullying, viii, 30, 49
bureaucracy, 6
Burkina Faso, 72

C

campaigns, 64, 71
cancer, 60, 61, 62, 66, 67, 70
cancer screening, 62
Cancer-related fatigue, 59
candidates, 74, 79, 80, 81, 82, 83, 84, 85, 86
cardiovascular disease(s), 61, 67
case study(s), vii, 1, 10, 24, 84, 86
certificate, 78, 79
certification, 75, 76, 78, 79, 85, 86
challenges, vii, viii, 29, 30, 34, 35, 45, 81,
    82, 84, 85, 102
chicken, 37
childcare, 4
children, ix, 2, 3, 5, 17, 22, 23, 24, 33, 40,
    50, 53, 64, 66, 73, 75, 76, 78, 94, 104
cholesterol, 59, 60, 66
chronic diseases, 58
classes, 11, 16, 21, 23, 60, 66, 82, 94, 101
classroom, 14, 15, 16, 18, 19, 20, 24, 38, 50,
    65, 67, 74, 75, 77, 79, 81, 82, 83, 84, 85,
    101, 102
classroom environment, 38, 82
classroom settings, 82
classroom teacher, 14, 18, 19, 20
cognitive abilities, viii, 30
collaboration, 77, 78, 79, 83, 85, 88, 94
Collage, 89
colleges, 83
color, 9
colorectal cancer, 61, 62, 66, 70, 71
communication, 4, 6, 19, 23, 57, 64, 65, 67,
    71, 72, 83
community, 3, 7, 11, 16, 19, 21, 23, 57, 65,
    66, 67, 69, 70, 72, 90, 91, 94, 96, 103
compilation, vii, 86

compliance, ix, 4, 6, 24, 73
complications, 59
comprehension, 14
compulsory education, 94
computation, 32
computer, 63
conceptualization, 31, 32, 36, 45
conference, 26
confidentiality, 84
conflict, 84
Congress, 2
construct validity, 36, 51, 52
consumption, 59
contraceptives, 63
control condition, 38, 44
control group, viii, 30, 35, 38, 42, 43, 44
conversations, 20
cooperative learning, viii, 30
coordination, 83
coping strategies, 96
correlation, 32, 76
counseling, 19, 40, 41, 59, 69
course work, 83
courtship, 98, 100
critical period, 47
critical thinking, 83
CT, 49, 50
cultural beliefs, 27
cultural differences, vii, 1
culture, 4, 7, 9, 11, 21, 24, 25, 40
curricula, 80
curriculum, ix, 73, 74, 78, 82, 84, 90, 92,
    93, 96, 101
CV, 61

D

data analysis, 25
DBP, 61
DEA, 75
decision makers, 6
deficit, 4, 7
Department of Education, 2, 26, 78, 79, 85,
    87, 88
depression, 19

depth, 57, 75, 83, 92, 100
detectable, 38, 43
detection, 60
developing countries, 72
diabetes, 60, 61, 66, 67, 70
diet, 66
diffusion, viii, 30, 38
disability, 14, 20, 27, 76, 91, 96
diseases, 57, 59, 64
dissatisfaction, 6, 81
dissonance, 86
diversity, 24, 82
DOI, 48, 50

E

educational experience, 83
educational materials, 64
educational programs, viii, 55, 57, 66, 67, 68
educational psychologists, 48
educational settings, viii, 30
educators, 3, 5, 25, 44, 45, 58, 63, 78, 80, 81, 88, 91, 102
egg, 37
elaboration, 67
elementary school, 87
empathy, 22
empowerment, 101
English Language, 78
environment, 2, 9, 18, 26, 43, 47, 49, 56, 57, 75, 79, 92, 96, 101
environmental conditions, 62
equality, 7
equity, 26
ethical issues, 100
ethnic background, 9
everyday life, 53
evidence, viii, 27, 29, 30, 32, 36, 40, 42, 44, 48, 62, 83, 88
evolution, 92
exclusion, 7
exercise, 100
experimental design, 37
expertise, 77

exploitation, 90, 92, 100

F

faith, 71
families, vii, 1, 3, 4, 6, 7, 8, 9, 10, 13, 16, 19, 20, 21, 22, 23, 24, 25, 26, 49
family environment, 7
family life, 7
family members, 16, 59
family planning, 63, 71
family support, 24
federal law, 76
feelings, 95, 96, 98, 99, 101
fidelity, 81, 95
financial, 101
fitness, 41, 44, 51
food, 57, 62, 64, 71
food safety, 62, 71
food security, 64
foodborne illness, 64
formation, 44, 50
foundations, 74, 78, 88
funds, 17, 76

G

GAO, 87
gender differences, 53
general education, ix, 2, 8, 73, 74, 75, 76, 77, 79, 80, 85, 86
general knowledge, 60
Germany, 29
global economy, 79
glucose, 66
governments, 56, 67
grades, 14, 48, 52, 78, 86
grading, 19, 47
grouping, 47
growth, 12, 18, 58
guardian, 2
guidance, 76

H

hair, 98, 100
handwriting, 14
harassment, 100
health, vii, viii, 55, 56, 57, 58, 59, 60, 61,
    62, 63, 64, 65, 66, 67, 68, 69, 70, 71
health care, 56, 60
health education, viii, 55, 57, 58, 59, 61, 62,
    63, 64, 66, 67, 69
health information, 65, 67
health problems, 62
health promotion, 56, 57, 62-65, 68- 71
health training programs, vii, viii, 55, 58
heart disease, 60
heart rate, 66
helplessness, 4
hepatitis, 61, 70
high school, 11, 25, 40, 44, 80
high school diploma, 11
higher education, 78, 87
history, 78
HIV, 59, 61, 63, 64, 65, 67, 69, 71, 72
HIV/AIDS, 72
homework, 12, 13, 15
honesty, 42
human, 48, 51, 56, 70, 100
human right(s), 56
husband, 11, 21
hypertension, 61, 62, 66

I

identification, 42
IEP meeting, vii, 1, 2, 3, 4, 5, 6, 7, 9, 10, 12,
    13, 16, 17, 18, 20, 24, 25
image, 95, 96
immunocompromised, 64, 66
improvements, 60
income, 25, 66
independence, 94
individuality, 100
individuals, 2, 56, 58, 67, 90, 91, 92, 96,
    100, 103

Individuals with Disabilities Education Act,
    25, 75, 87
Individuals with Disabilities Education
    Improvement Act, ix, 26, 73, 75
industry, 56
infection, 72
initiation, 61
injuries, 58
institutions, 78, 87
instructional activities, 101
instructional practice, 47, 84
instructional procedures, 83
integration, 52, 77, 96
intellectual disability(s), vii, ix, 81, 89, 90,
    91, 92, 93, 94, 95, 96, 97, 100, 101, 102,
    103
intelligence, 16
internalization, 98, 102
interpersonal relations, 35
intervention, vii, 17, 21, 24, 29, 30, 32, 33,
    34, 35, 36, 37, 38, 39, 40, 41, 42, 43, 44,
    45, 46, 47, 48, 59, 60, 61, 63, 69, 70, 72,
    104
intervention strategies, 63
intrinsic motivation, 33
Iowa, 71
isolation, 4
Israel, 89, 102
issues, vii, viii, 4, 29, 30, 45, 48, 92, 95, 101

J

junior high school, 53, 94
justification, 50

K

kindergarten, 8

L

language barrier, 5
languages, 11, 14, 16, 20, 21, 22
Latinos, 9, 25

laws, 98, 100
LDL, 59, 60, 66
lead, 5, 37, 44, 98, 100, 101
leadership, 74, 83
learners, vii, ix, 8, 24, 73, 74, 75, 78, 79, 82
learning, 14, 16, 20, 30, 39, 40, 46, 47, 48,
    49, 51, 53, 78, 80, 83, 84, 88, 95, 96, 97,
    98, 99, 100, 101, 102
learning disabilities, 48, 49, 102
learning environment, 47
learning process, 95, 96, 101
legislation, 82
lesions, 60
lesson plan, 80
life satisfaction, 60
light, viii, 20, 30, 92
literacy, 36, 76, 79
local authorities, 56
long-term positive gains, viii, 30
love, 100

M

majority, 7, 101
malignant tumors, 64
management, 60, 70
marriage, 95
mass, 59, 63, 65, 66, 67, 71
mass media, 63, 65, 67, 71
materials, 61, 62, 64, 66, 67
mathematics, viii, 29, 30, 49
matter, 9, 25, 53, 76, 100
measurement, 31, 32, 34, 36, 38, 43, 46, 53
media, 56, 62, 64, 65
mediation, 90, 96, 99
medical, 66, 70
medicine, 66
mental health, 39, 60
mental health professionals, 39
mentor, 84
mentoring, 83, 84
messages, 63, 101
meta-analysis, 33, 34, 39, 40, 41, 48, 49, 52
methodology, ix, 59, 60, 61, 62, 68, 90, 94
Mexico, 11

mild intellectual disabilities, vii, ix, 90, 91,
    93, 94, 96, 97, 101
Ministry of Education, 89, 102, 103
miscommunication, 23
misuse, 53
models, ix, 22, 40, 52, 73, 78, 86, 88, 89, 90
motivation, viii, 30, 47, 48, 49, 53, 61
motor skills, 41
multiculturalism, 25
multidimensional, viii, 30, 31, 32, 34, 35,
    36, 46, 50, 51, 100
multidisciplinary team., vii, 1, 4
multimedia, 65

N

National Research Council, 82, 88
negative effects, 44
negative experiences, 6
next generation, 48
No Child Left Behind, ix, 73, 76, 88
normative behavior, 98
nutrition, 57, 59, 60, 61, 64, 66, 67, 69
nutritional status, 66

O

obstacles, vii, 1
OH, 24
opportunities, 79, 83, 85, 92
oppression, 80
optimism, 42
osteoporosis, 66

P

Pacific, 86, 87
parallel, 37, 47, 95
parental involvement, vii, 1, 4
parental participation, 6
parents, vii, 1, 2, 3, 4, 5, 6, 7, 9, 10, 11, 13,
    15, 16, 17, 18, 19, 21, 22, 23, 24, 25, 26,
    84

participants, 3, 5, 7, 8, 9, 13, 16, 18, 21, 22, 35, 43, 44, 45, 46, 59, 60, 62, 66, 67, 68
path analysis, 52
pathologist, 8, 9, 14, 15, 19
pathology, 57
pedagogy, 76, 84
peer group, 96, 98, 102
peer support, viii, 30, 35, 36, 42, 43, 49, 50
personal development, 56
personal identity, 98
pessimism, 39
photographs, 94
physical activity, 60, 61, 66
physical environment, 56
physical fitness, 35, 44, 51
physicians, 60, 91
pipeline, 26
playing, 5
pleasure, 51
pluralism, 25
Poland, 103
policy, ix, 25, 26, 73, 74, 75, 77, 82, 88
population, viii, 8, 55, 57, 58, 60, 62, 64, 65, 66, 67, 90, 94, 100, 103
population group, 66
positive attitudes, 82
positive correlation, 32
positive relationship, 3
poverty, 71
practical knowledge, 101
preadolescents, 31
preparation, ix, 73, 74, 77, 78, 79, 81, 82, 84, 85, 86, 87, 88, 103
preschool, 14, 24
preservice teachers, 74, 88
prevention, 40, 41, 59, 61, 63, 64, 65, 67, 70, 98
primary school, 35
principles, 101
problem-solving, 98
professional development, 80, 81, 95
professionalism, 19
professionals, ix, 4, 5, 6, 7, 27, 56, 57, 58, 63, 65, 80, 90, 91, 101, 102
programming, 3

project, 64, 72, 91
pronunciation, 12, 13
psychologist, 2, 8, 9, 14, 17, 18
public education, 2
public health, 56, 61, 67
public policy, 25

Q

qualitative research, 102
quality of life, 92
quizzes, 14

R

race, 9, 26
racism, 21
radio, 63, 71
rain forest, 70
rating scale, 2
rationality, 95
reading, 35, 36, 49
reality, 95, 100
reasoning, 98
recommendations, vii, viii, 2, 18, 21, 55, 60
recreation, 41
recreational, 63
recruiting, 84
reforms, 76
regression, 12
relevance, 36
REM, 37, 41, 42
requirements, 74, 75, 76, 77, 78, 79, 85, 86
researchers, vii, 29, 32, 34, 36, 38, 39, 41, 43, 45, 48, 61, 62, 63, 66, 83, 84, 94
resilience, 104
resistance, 7, 22
resources, viii, 6, 23, 55, 56, 62, 63, 65, 66, 67, 80, 98
response, 7, 9, 13, 17, 21, 35
responsibility for learning, 83
responsiveness, 46
rights, 2, 4, 5, 13, 22

risk(s), 17, 40, 42, 59, 62, 66, 69, 70, 72, 80, 92, 100, 101
risk factors, 59, 62, 66

S

school, vii, ix, 2, 3, 4, 5, 6, 7, 8, 9, 11, 14, 15, 16, 17, 18, 19, 20, 21, 22, 23, 24, 25, 34, 35, 36, 39, 40, 42, 43, 47, 48, 49, 52, 58, 65, 75, 78, 80, 83, 84, 90, 91, 92, 93, 94, 95, 96, 98, 101, 102
school work, 35
schooling, 9
science, 78, 94
scientific publications, 58
scope, 78, 79
secondary students, 53
self-concept, vii, 29, 30, 31, 32, 33, 34, 35, 36, 37, 38, 39, 40, 41, 42, 43, 44, 45, 46, 47, 48, 49, 50, 51, 52, 53
self-confidence, 57
self-efficacy, 43, 59, 82, 87
self-enhancement, 32, 37, 44
self-esteem, 31, 49, 50, 53
self-image, 91
self-knowledge, 98
self-perceptions, 31, 38, 40, 42, 43, 45, 53
self-view, 53
self-worth, 66
Senate, 79, 86
services, 2, 3, 4, 8, 13, 15, 17, 18, 19, 22, 23, 24, 26, 74, 77, 87
sex, 35, 42, 59, 61, 67, 90, 91, 102
sexual abuse, 90, 101
sexual behavior, 90, 91
sexual development, 101
sexual harassment, 92, 98, 99, 100
sexual identity, 91
sexuality, 91, 92, 101, 102, 103
shortage, 5
showing, 14, 32, 37, 39
sibling, ix, 89, 90
signs, 19, 59
simulation, 84, 96
Singapore, 38

skills training, 88
skin, 9, 64, 70
skin cancer, 64, 70
social class, 7
social comparison, 44, 45
social development, 63
social environment, 45, 91
social institutions, 7
social interactions, 92
social justice, 7
social relations, 47
social relationships, 47
social skills, 19
social structure, 9
social theory, 102
social workers, 91
social-sexual education, vii, ix, 89, 90, 92, 93, 94, 95, 102
society, 6, 25, 57
solution, 98
special education, vii, ix, 1, 2, 3, 4, 7, 8, 9, 13, 15, 17, 18, 21, 22, 23, 24, 25, 26, 73, 74, 75, 76, 77, 79, 80, 85, 86, 87, 90, 93, 94
specialists, 8, 91, 101
specifications, 64
speech, 8, 9, 14, 15, 18, 65
stability, 46
stakeholders, 82, 83
state(s), ix, 16, 56, 65, 73, 74, 75, 76, 77, 78, 81, 82, 85, 86, 87, 94, 96
stress, 91
stroke, 59, 100
structure, viii, 30, 31, 35, 36, 45, 50, 91, 95
student achievement, viii, 29, 78, 79
student populations, 81
style, 7
supervisor, 80
susceptibility, 100
sustainability, 46
Switzerland, 70
symptoms, 59
synthesis, 95
systolic blood pressure, 61, 66

T

Taiwan, 69
Tanzania, 63, 71
target, viii, 30, 34, 35, 36, 38, 40, 42, 62, 63, 67
target population, 63, 67
teacher effectiveness, 79, 86
teacher preparation, vii, ix, 73, 74, 75, 77, 78, 79, 81, 82, 83, 84, 85, 87
teacher training, 81, 83
teachers, ix, 6, 8, 39, 47, 73, 74, 75, 76, 77, 78, 79, 80, 81, 82, 83, 84, 85, 86, 87, 88, 90, 94, 95, 101, 102
team members, 4, 7, 26
teams, 7, 19, 21, 24
technical assistance, 77
technology(s), 63, 76
teeth, 15
telephone, 59
tensions, 98
test scores, 52, 60
testing, 16, 46
textbook, 66
thoughts, 4, 9
time periods, 65
total cholesterol, 59, 60, 66
traditions, 83
trainees, 63
training, vii, viii, 51, 52, 55, 57, 58, 59, 60, 61, 62, 63, 67, 68, 70, 71, 75, 76, 78, 79, 80, 81, 84, 87, 102
training programs, vii, viii, 51, 55, 58, 62
trajectory, 46, 47
transformation, 75
transmission, 57, 60
transportation, 4
treatment, 38, 40, 41, 91, 94
trial, 69, 70
triglycerides, 66
trustworthiness, 42

U

uniform, 101
United, 2, 9, 11
United States, 2, 9, 11
universities, 83, 84
urban, 21, 70

V

validation, 52
variables, 10, 39, 40
variations, 10, 12
vegetables, 59
Venezuela, 69
videos, 63, 64, 65, 66, 67
vocabulary, 5

W

walking, 98
Washington, 85, 87, 88
wealth, 7, 21
websites, 64
welfare, 61
well-being, 56
White House, 88
WHO, 68
work environment, 80
workers, 62, 71
workforce, 78
workload, 80
World Health Organization, 56, 57, 64, 67, 68
worry, 15

Y

yield, 37, 40, 41, 42
young adults, 31